The gardener plucks fruits and flowers, but does not harm the trees; the bee sucks the honey but does not damage the flowers. In the same way the king should collect his taxes but should not cause any suffering to his subjects. One who kills the goat at best gets one meal; one who feeds it well can get milk for several years. **Kautilya in *Arthashastra***

Tax System in India

Evolution and Present Structure

Tax System in India

Evolution and Present Structure

By

M.M. Sury

New Century Publications
New Delhi, India

NEW CENTURY PUBLICATIONS
4800/24, Bharat Ram Road,
Ansari Road, Daryaganj,
New Delhi - 110 002 (India)

Tel.: 011 - 2324 7798, 4358 7398, 6539 6605
Fax: 011 - 4101 7798
E-mail: indiatax@vsnl.com • info@newcenturypublications.com
www.newcenturypublications.com

Editorial office:
LG–7, Aakarshan Bhawan
4754-57/23, Ansari Road, Daryaganj,
New Delhi - 110 002

Tel.: 011 - 4356 0919

First Published: **July 2015**

ISBN: **978-81-7708-410-8**

Published by New Century Publications and printed at Salasar Imaging Systems, New Delhi

Designs: Patch Creative Unit, New Delhi

PRINTED IN INDIA

To My Wife

Shashi

About the Book

Taxes are as old as civilizations. Taxes are imposed so that a government may perform its traditional functions (defence, and maintenance of law and order), undertake welfare and developmental activities, and make provision for public goods to satisfy collective needs of the people. It has also to pay for its own administration. It needs financial resources for these purposes and taxation is one method of transferring money from private to public hands. Taxation is necessary because what the government gives it must first take away.

The Indian tax system has undergone major structural changes since Independence in 1947. It has become comprehensive and complicated over the years. It has successfully mobilised resources to finance developmental, welfare and administrative activities of public authorities. Besides being the main source of revenue, both for the Central and State Governments, it is an effective instrument to realise various socio-economic objectives of national policies. However, the tax system has been relying heavily on indirect taxes and suffering extensively from fiscal malady called tax evasion.

Restructuring of the tax system has constituted a major component of fiscal reforms initiated since 1991. The main focus of the tax reforms has been on simplification and rationalisation of both direct and indirect taxes with the objective of augmenting revenues and removing anomalies in the tax structure. Tax reforms in recent years have brought the tax system much closer to international tax practices.

The post-1991 period has witnessed a sharp decline in the rates of income tax, excise duty and customs tariff. The theory that high rates of duty lead to higher revenue collection has been discarded in favour of lower rates with fewer exemptions and concessions.

The strategy in respect of direct taxation is to minimise distortions in tax structure by expanding the tax base, moderating tax rates, improving efficiency of tax administration and increasing the deterrence level. The strategy in respect of indirect taxes is to move towards a fully integrated national level goods and services tax (GST).

This book provides an exhaustive and analytical account of tax structure developments in India since Independence in 1947 with focus on post-1991 reforms. It places current developments in the field of taxation in perspective. Containing 25 chapters (divided into 7 theme parts), it explains and examines almost every aspect of the Indian tax system. Besides, it provides detailed time-series tax statistics of India for the period 1950-51 to 2013-14/2015-16. The overall approach to the subject is descriptive, and at places analytical.

The book is designed to interest a cross-section of readers, viz. teachers and students of economics, commerce, law, public administration, business management, chartered accountancy and company secretaryship. It will also serve the needs of legislators, business executives, entrepreneurs and investors, and others interested in tax structure developments in India.

Author's Profile

M.M. Sury received his B.A. (Hons.), M.A., and Ph.D. degrees in economics from the University of Delhi. He taught economics in the same university for 42 years. Specialising in fiscal economics, he has published extensively on Indian fiscal system in recognised national and international journals, including *Small Industry Bulletin for Asia and the Pacific* (United Nations, Bangkok), *Bulletin for International Fiscal Documentation* (International Fiscal Association, Amsterdam), *Asian-Pacific Tax and Investment Bulletin* (Singapore), *Journal of the Indian School of Political Economy* (Pune), *Indian Economic Journal* (Bombay), and *Margin* (New Delhi). He was a Visiting Fellow at the International Bureau of Fiscal Documentation, Amsterdam (May 1989), a Fellow at the Indian Institute of Advanced Study, Shimla (1991-92) and a Visiting Fellow in the Department of Law and Management, University of Mauritius, Mauritius (September-October, 2000). He was Economic Adviser, First Delhi State Finance Commission (1996-97).

Contents in Brief

Contents in Detail

Part I: Pre-Independence Tax System

Part II: Post-Independence Tax Policy

Part III: Combined (Centre and States) Tax Revenue

Part V: Structure of State Taxes

Part VIII: Time Series Tax Statistics of India: 1950-51 to 2013-14/2015-16

Preface

Taxes are imposed so that a government may perform its traditional functions (defence, and maintenance of law and order), undertake welfare and developmental activities, and make provision for public goods to satisfy collective needs of the people. It has also to pay for its own administration. It needs financial resources for these purposes and taxation is one method of transferring money from private to public hands. Taxation is necessary because what the government gives it must first take away. In his work *Raghuvansa*, Kalidasa, the greatest Sanskrit scholar of ancient India, observed, "Just as the sun extracts water from the reservoirs and gives it back in the form of showers, so does the ruler extract tax from his subjects and gives it back to them in the form of prosperity".

Tax System in Ancient India and During Mughal Period

References to taxes in ancient India are found in *Arthashastra* the famous work of Kautilya (also known as Chanakya and Vishnugupta). He wrote, "The gardener plucks fruits and flowers, but does not harm the trees, the bee sucks the honey but does not damage the flowers. In the same way the king should collect his taxes but should not cause any suffering to his subjects. One who kills the goat at best gets one meal; one who feeds it well can get milk for several years".

Arthashastra embodies values, norms, and beliefs pertaining to public administration, economics, ethics and diplomacy. Taxes in ancient India were levied both in cash and in kind and were collected by local officers. Major sources of revenue for the king included land tax, octroi, taxes on liquor shops, gambling houses and on professionals like dancing girls.

Vivid accounts of tax system during Mughal rule are found in contemporary court chronicles, particularly *Ain-i-Akbari* (the official chronicler of the reign of Emperor Akbar) compiled by Abul Fazl, one of Akbar's courtiers. The work describes, *inter alia*, matters pertaining to taxes, other revenues, expenditure, salaries of public officers etc. Travel accounts of visitors, especially those who came from the West, also throw light on the Mughal system of revenue administration.

Land revenue by far was the most important source of income for the Mughal rulers. Other means of lining the emperor's treasury were gifts, import and export duties and *jizya* (or *zazia*). There were monopolies on some goods, for instance on salt and saltpetre. The monopoly on indigo yielded a few million rupees to the Treasury. *Jizya*, the tax on non-Muslims, abolished by Akbar, was reintroduced by Aurangzeb in 1679 in the form of a degressive income tax.

Tax System during British Rule

The tax system of British India reflected characteristics of a traditional agricultural economy. Revenues of the Central Government were dominated by customs duties as domestic requirements for manufactured goods were met mostly by imports, chiefly from Britain and other Commonwealth countries. Import duties were levied on almost all items of imports whereas major items subject to export duties were jute and tea in which India enjoyed near-monopoly in the world market. Before 1857, the regulation of customs duties in India was haphazard and lacked all-India uniformity due to unstable political and economic conditions. Rates of import duty, though not uniform, were relatively low, ranging from 3 to 5 percent *ad valorem* on raw materials and manufactured articles. These rates were doubled in the case of goods imported from countries other than Britain. Having consolidated political power after the disturbances of 1857, the British Indian Government introduced in 1859 a uniform all-India customs tariff which replaced separate provincial rates of duty.

During British rule, excise taxation in India was selective in terms of commodity coverage and modest from revenue angle. Excise duties were not important as a source of revenue due to the narrow production base of the Indian economy. The selected commodities on which excise duties were imposed included cotton textiles, salt, motor spirit, and kerosene. A commodity-wise history of excise taxation is as follows.

Among the direct taxes, the only important source of revenue was the income tax introduced in India by the British in 1860 to overcome the financial difficulties created by the events of 1857. However, the imposition of income tax remained irregular till the year 1886 when a systematic legislation was enacted for its operation on a permanent basis. A tax on capital gains was in operation in India for a short period in respect of capital gains which arose during the period April 1, 1946 to March 31, 1948. The tax was revived in 1956 and made applicable on capital gains arising on or after April 1, 1956. It is levied within the framework of Indian Income Tax Act, 1961.

As for the British Indian Provinces, the chief source of income was land revenue followed by Provincial excises, mainly on liquor. Although under the Government of India Act, 1935, Provincial Governments had been authorised to levy sales tax, it formed a very low component of their revenue till Independence. The Province of Bombay levied a tax on the sale of tobacco in 1938. A retail sales tax on motor spirit and lubricants was imposed by Central Provinces (now Madhya Pradesh) in the same year. A multi-point general sales tax was levied in Madras Province at the rate of half percent in 1939 under the Madras General Sales Tax Act.

The Princely States did not form part of the structure of public finance of British

India. They had separate budgets and separate sources of revenue. The maritime States imposed their own customs duties.

Constitutional Provisions Pertaining to Taxes

The Constitution of India adopted on November 26, 1949, became operative on January 26, 1950. It provides for two layers of Government, one at the Central level, and the other at the level of the States. A federal polity of this kind requires division of powers and responsibilities between the Centre and the States. The Constitution describes in detail the legislative powers and functions of the two tiers of Government. Under Article 246 read with Seventh Schedule of the Constitution, these powers have been defined through precise entries in the three lists in the Schedule. Thus, the Centre has exclusive powers to legislate in respect of matters contained in List I (Union List). Entries 82 to 92C of this list pertain to taxation powers. Similarly, the States enjoy the power to legislate on matters mentioned in List II (State List). Entries 45 to 63 of this list relate to taxation powers of the States. The Parliament and the State Legislatures have concurrent powers to make laws on any matters in List III (Concurrent List). However, this list does not contain any head of taxation which means the Centre and the States have no concurrent powers of taxation. Residuary powers of legislation including taxation belong to the Centre as per Entry 97 of List I.

Commissions/Committees for Tax Reforms

The Indian tax system has undergone major structural changes since Independence in 1947. It has become comprehensive and complicated over the years. It has successfully mobilised resources to finance developmental, welfare and administrative activities of public authorities. Besides being the main source of revenue, both for the Central and State Governments, it is an effective instrument to realise various socio-economic objectives of national policies. However, the tax system has been relying heavily on indirect taxes and suffering extensively from fiscal malady called tax evasion.

After Independence, various committees have been appointed, from time to time, to review the tax system to make it more relevant to the needs of a developing economy.

On April 1, 1953, the Government of India appointed the Taxation Enquiry Commission under the chairmanship of John Matthai. The Commission presented its landmark report in three volumes in the following year. The Commission was the first to undertake a systematic and comprehensive study of the incidence of Central and State indirect taxes on rural and urban households in different expenditure groups.

The Commission dealt at length with the administration of income tax and found staggering levels of tax evasion. The Commission maintained that improvement and strengthening of the enforcement machinery was the only way to tackle evasion effectively. The Commission, after having studied the then existing excise system, made important recommendations in terms of commodity coverage.

In mid-1950s, British economist Nicholas Kaldor carried out, at the request of the Government of India, a review of the Indian tax system particularly with reference to personal and business taxation. Kaldor made the first systematic estimates of income tax evasion in India. He estimated income tax loss through tax evasion at ₹ 200 to ₹ 300 crore for the year 1953-54. Following the recommendations of Kaldor, an *integrated direct tax system* was introduced in India. In 1957 and 1958, three new taxes were introduced, viz. wealth tax, expenditure tax, and gift tax. Estate duty was already in operation since 1953. The basic philosophy underlying the introduction of the system of integrated direct taxes was to prevent evasion and avoidance of direct taxes and thereby to reduce inequalities of income and wealth.

On March 2, 1970, Government of India constituted the Direct Taxes Enquiry Committee under the chairmanship of K.N. Wanchoo to recommend, *inter alia*, concrete and effective measures to unearth black money and prevent its proliferation through tax evasion. The Committee established the income on which tax was evaded for 1968-69 at a figure of ₹ 1,400 crore. The amount of tax evasion for the same year was put at ₹ 470 crore. The Committee suggested various measures to fight the evil of tax evasion.

The Indirect Taxation Enquiry Committee was set up by the Government of India on July 19, 1976, under the chairmanship of L.K. Jha, to review the existing structure of indirect tax system. Computations of the Committee revealed poor elasticity of the indirect tax system, except import duties. The Committee undertook a comprehensive study of the incidence of indirect taxes for the year 1973-74. The Committee, which made an in-depth study of the cascading effect of input excises, recommended the introduction of value added tax (VAT) at the manufacturing stage, called MANVAT, to tackle the problem of cascading effect of excise taxation.

In August 1991, the Government of India constituted a Tax Reforms Committee under the chairmanship of Raja Chelliah to recommend a comprehensive reform of both direct and indirect tax laws. The Committee submitted its report in three instalments.

- An Interim Report in December 1991.
- Final Report Part-I in August 1992.
- Final Report Part-II in January 1993.

These Reports contained recommendations for restructuring and rationalisation of personal income tax, corporate income tax, wealth tax, excise duties, import tariff, tax administration and enforcement machinery.

In September 2002, Government of India set up two task forces to recommend measures for simplification and rationalization of direct and indirect taxes. The two task forces were set up under the chairmanship of Vijay Kelkar.

The Task Force on Direct Taxes presented its consultation paper to the Government on November 2, 2002. The discussion paper on indirect taxes was presented on November 25, 2002. These consultation papers were made public to facilitate an informed discussion on tax policy.

After taking into account the response on the discussion papers, the Task Forces submitted their final reports to the Government in December 2002. These Task Forces made important recommendations on toning up tax administration to put in place a system that is simple, effective and at par with international standards. The main recommendations on direct taxes related to raising of exemption limit of personal income tax, rationalization of exemptions, abolition of concessional treatment to long-term capital gains, and abolition of wealth tax. In respect of indirect taxes, the main recommendations related to widening of the tax base, removal of exemptions, expansion in the coverage of service tax etc.

Other committees/working groups which have reported on tax matters include, *inter alia*, the following:

- Income Tax Investigation Commission (Chairman: Srinivasa Varadachariar), 1948.
- Customs Reorganisation Committee, (Chairman: F.C. Budhwar), 1957-58.
- Direct Taxes Administration Enquiry Committee (Chairman: Mahavir Tyagi), 1958-59.
- Central Excise Reorganisation Committee (Chairman: A.K. Chanda), 1963.
- Committee on Sales Tax (Chairman: R.G. Saraiya), 1964.
- Report on Rationalisation and Simplification of Tax Structure (Chairman: S. Bhoothalingam), 1968.
- Committee on Taxation of Agricultural Wealth and Income (Chairman: K.N. Raj), 1972.
- Central Excise (Self-Removal Procedure) Review Committee (Chairman: B. Venkatappiah), 1973.
- Report of Direct Tax Laws Committee (Chairman: C.C. Chokshi), 1978.
- Expert Committee on Tax Measures to Promote Employment (Chairman: V.M. Dandekar), 1980.
- Report on Tax Administrations, Economic Administrative Reforms Commission,

1981-83.

- Expert Committee on Replacement of Sales Tax by Additional Excise Duty (Chairman: Kamlapati Tripathi), 1983.
- Long Term Fiscal Policy, December 1985.
- Technical Study Group on Central Excise Tariff (Chairman: J. Datta), 1985.
- Study Group on Taxation of Expenditure, 1987.
- Commission on Centre-State Relations (Chairman: R.S. Sarkaria), 1988.
- Advisory Group on Tax Policy and Tax Administration for the Tenth Plan (Chairman: Parthasarathi Shome), 2001.
- Inter-ministerial Working Group on Customs Tariff (Chairman: Arvind Virmani), 2002.
- White Paper on State-Level Value Added Tax (Chairman: Asim Kumar Dasgupta), 2005.
- Rationalisation of Customs and Excise Duties on Edible Oils and Oilseeds (Chairman: Ashok Lahiri), 2006.
- White Paper on Black Money, May 2012.

Recommendations of various commissions/committees/working groups on taxation have constituted the core of tax policies followed in India during the post-Independence period.

Tax Reforms since 1991

Restructuring of the tax system has constituted a major component of fiscal reforms initiated since 1991. The main focus of the tax reforms has been on simplification and rationalisation of both direct and indirect taxes with the objective of augmenting revenues and removing anomalies in the tax structure. Tax reforms in recent years have brought the tax system much closer to international tax practices.

In fact, tax reforms are a part of the package to liberalise and globalise the Indian economy. The post-1991 period has witnessed a sharp decline in the rates of income tax, excise duty and customs tariff. The theory that high rates of duty lead to higher revenue collection has been discarded in favour of lower rates with fewer exemptions and concessions. These measures have rationalized and simplified the tax system considerably. The rates have been moderated and many exemptions and concessions have been weeded out.

The strategy in respect of direct taxation is to minimise distortions in tax structure by expanding the tax base and moderating tax rates on the one hand and improving the efficiency of tax administration and increasing the deterrence level on the other, so as to encourage voluntary compliance.

The strategy in respect of indirect taxes is to continue the tariff reform process towards mean ASEAN levels of customs tariff, convergence towards CENVAT rate for excise duty, widening of service tax base and phased move towards a fully integrated goods and services tax (GST).

The cascading effect of indirect taxes has been reduced by the adoption of State VAT by almost all the States and Union Territories. However, the rates of indirect taxes in India remain among the highest in the world. Most industrial products are subject to CENVAT on the manufactured value, at an average of 16 percent and a State VAT at a modal rate of 12.5 percent of retail value. Broadly speaking, the incidence of CENVAT and State VAT together is about 23 percent. In addition, States and local levels of government levy such taxes as octroi or entry tax etc. The overall rate of indirect taxes compare unfavourably with those prevailing in ASEAN countries, which are closer to 10-12 percent.

In the Central Government Budget for 2009-10, the importance of continuing the process of structural changes in direct taxes was reiterated and a comprehensive code to this effect was envisaged. The Government signalled its intention to consolidate and comprehensively amend the existing Income Tax Act, 1961 and Wealth Tax Act 1957 through a single legislation, by releasing a draft Direct Taxes Code (DTC) and a Discussion Paper for public comments in August 2009. Based on analysis of the numerous inputs received from stakeholders, a Revised Discussion Paper was released in June 2010 followed by the introduction of the Direct Taxes Code Bill, 2010 in Parliament in August 2010. It was proposed to make it effective from April 1, 2012.

However, the Union Finance Minister informed the Parliament in his budget speech for 2012-13 that the Government received the Report of the Parliamentary Standing Committee on March 9, 2012. Enactment of DTC would take place after the report is examined.

DTC seeks to consolidate and amend the law relating to all direct taxes, namely income tax, dividend distribution tax and wealth tax so as to establish an economically efficient, effective and equitable direct tax system which will facilitate voluntary compliance and help increase the tax-GDP ratio.

All the direct taxes have been brought under a single code and compliance procedures unified, which will eventually pave the way for a single unified taxpayer reporting system. The need for DTC arose from concerns about the complex structure of half a century old Income Tax Act, 1961, which has been amended a large number of times, making it incomprehensible to the average taxpayer. In his Budget Speech to the Parliament on February 28, 2015, the Finance Minister saw 'no great merit in going ahead with the Direct Tax Code as it exists today'.

National level goods and services tax (GST) is a part of the proposed tax reforms to evolve an efficient and harmonized consumption tax system in the country.

Presently, there are parallel systems of indirect taxation at the Central and State levels. Each of the systems needs to be reformed to eventually harmonize them.

GST is proposed to be a comprehensive indirect tax levy on manufacture, sale and consumption of goods as well as services at the national level. GST would give India a world class tax system and improve tax collections. It would end the long standing distortions of differential treatment of manufacturing and service sector. The introduction of GST will lead to the abolition of various Central and State indirect taxes and eliminate the cascading effects of multiple layers of taxation. It is claimed that GST will facilitate seamless credit across the entire supply chain and across all states under a common tax base.

The changeover to GST will be a game-changing tax reform measure which will significantly contribute to the buoyancy of tax revenues, acceleration of growth, and generation of many positive externalities.

Once the integrated GST across the country is introduced, it will simplify tax administration and eliminate cascading of taxes. It will lead to reduction in the distortions in the structure of production, consumption and exports and further to a more efficient allocation of resources. The demand for manufactured goods can be expected to grow significantly.

The country is keenly awaiting implementation of GST. It is India's most ambitious indirect tax reform. Its objective is to levy a single national uniform tax across India on all goods and services.

In his Budget Speech to the Parliament on February 28, 2015, the Finance Minister resolved to implement GST from April 1, 2016.

The Lok Sabha passed the 122nd Constitutional Amendment—Goods and Services Tax Bill on May 6, 2015.

In short, tax reforms are geared to build a structure which is simple, relies on moderate tax rates but with a wider base and better enforcement. Despite wide-ranging tax reforms since 1991, the Indian tax system still suffers from various drawbacks. A case in point is the intermingling and overlapping of Central excise duty (now CENVAT) and States' sales tax (now VAT) over a wide range of Commodities. This overlapping has hindered rationalisation and simplification of commodity taxation in order to determine judiciously the impact of these levies on investment, production, and burden on the consumers. The varying VAT practices in different States have impeded free flow of trade and industrialisation.

Scheme of the Book

This book provides an exhaustive and analytical account of tax structure developments in India since Independence in 1947 with focus on post-1991 reforms. It places current developments in the field of taxation in perspective.

The book is divided into 8 Parts.

Part I, consisting of 2 chapters, describes pre-Independence tax system. Chapter 1 gives a brief account of tax system in ancient India and during the Mughal period. Chapter 2 explains at some length the tax system during British rule, providing the necessary backdrop to the post-Independence evolution of the present structure of taxation in India.

Part II, comprising 3 chapters, explains the post-Independence tax policy. Chapter 3 focuses on constitutional provisions pertaining to taxes. Socio-economic objectives of tax policy are set forth in Chapter 4. Chapter 5 traces tax reforms, as apart of economic reforms, since 1991.

Part III, containing 5 chapters, analyses trends in combined (Centre and State) tax revenues. Chapter 6 describes trends in tax-GDP ratio. Chapter 7 records trends in the relative revenue significance of direct and indirect taxes. Chapter 8 presents estimates of buoyancy and elasticity of tax revenue for different periods by various studies. Chapter 9 provides estimates of tax incidence for different periods by various studies. Chapter 10 focuses on causes of tax evasion and measures/policies adopted by the Government to deal with it.

Part IV, consisting of 8 chapters, examines the structure of Central taxes. Chapter 11 records trends in the level and composition of Central taxes. Chapters 12, 13, 14, 15 and 16 discuss income tax, wealth tax, Union excise duties, taxation of services, and customs duties respectively. Chapter 17 explains the proposed Direct Taxes Code (DTC) while chapter 18 focuses on the proposed Goods and Services Tax (GST).

Part V, comprising 3 chapters, is devoted to the structure of State taxes. Chapter 19 records trends in the level and composition of State taxes. Chapters 20 and 21 discuss taxation of agricultural income, and sales tax/VAT respectively.

Part VI, consisting of 2 chapters, is devoted to federal aspects of Indian taxation. Chapter 22 discusses Centre-State financial relations while chapter 23 examines the nature of State-Local financial relations.

Part VII, consisting of 2 chapters, relates to international aspects of Indian taxation. Chapter 24 deals with international double taxation while chapter 25 explains Indian law on double tax relief.

Part VIII presents time-series tax statistics of India for the period 1950-51 to 2013-14/2015-16.

The overall approach to the subject is descriptive, and at places analytical.

New Delhi **M.M. Sury**
June 2015

Unit and Currency Conversion Table

Unit Conversion

1 lakh = 0.1 million
10 lakh = 1.0 million
1 crore = 10.0 million
100 crore = 1.0 billion

Currency Conversion

The unit of currency in India is Indian Rupee, symbolized as ₹. As per reference rate of Reserve Bank of India (RBI) for May 19, 2015,

US$ 1 = 63.68
UK£ 1 = 99.72
Euro (€) 1 = 71.90
Japanese Yen (¥) 100 = 53.09

Fiscal Year

Fiscal year in India runs from April 1 to March 31 of the following year

Pre- and Post-metric Systems of Currency and Measures in India

Metric system of currency in India was introduced from April l, 1957
In the Pre-metric system, one Rupee was = 16 annas and one anna was = 4 paise
In the Post-metric system,
One Rupee = 100 paise
One mile = 1.6 kilometres
One yard = 0.9144 metre
One acre = 0.4046 hectare

Part I: Pre-Independence Tax System

1

Taxes in Ancient India and during Mughal Period

Taxes are as old as civilizations. Taxes are imposed so that a government may perform its traditional functions (defence, and maintenance of law and order), undertake welfare and developmental activities, and make provision for public goods to satisfy collective needs of the people. It has also to pay for its own administration. It needs financial resources for these purposes and taxation is one method of transferring money from private to public hands. Taxation is necessary because what the government gives it must first take away.

1.1 Taxes in Ancient India

References to taxes in ancient India are found in *Arthashatra* the famous work of Kautilya (also known as Chanakya and Vishnugupta). He wrote, "The gardener plucks fruits and flowers, but does not harm the trees, the bee sucks the honey but does not damage the flowers. In the same way the king should collect his taxes but should not cause any suffering to his subjects. One who kills the goat at best gets one meal; one who feeds it well can get milk for several years".

Arthashatra embodies values, norms, and beliefs pertaining to public administration, economics, ethics and diplomacy. Taxes in ancient India were levied both in cash and in kind and were collected by local officers. Major sources of revenue for the king included land tax, octroi, taxes on liquor shops, gambling houses and on professionals like dancing girls.

In his work *Raghuvansa*, Kalidasa, the greatest Sanskrit scholar of ancient India, observed, "Just as the sun extracts water from the reservoirs and gives it back in the form of showers, so does the ruler extract tax from his subjects and gives it back to them in the form of prosperity".

In India, the system of direct taxation as it is known today has been in force in one form or another even from ancient times. There are references both in *Manu Smriti* and *Arthasastra* to a variety of tax measures. Manu, the ancient sage and law-giver stated that the king could levy taxes, according to *Sastras*. He advised that taxes should be related to the income and expenditure of the subject. He, however, cautioned the king against excessive taxation and stated that both extremes should be avoided namely either complete absence of taxes or exorbitant taxation. According to him, the king should arrange the collection of taxes in such a manner that the subjects did not feel the pinch of paying taxes. He laid down that traders and artisans should pay one-fifth of their profits in silver and gold, while the agriculturists were to pay one-sixth, one-eighth and one-tenth of their produce depending upon their circumstances. The detailed analysis given by Manu on the subject clearly shows the existence of a well-planned taxation system, even in ancient times. Not only this, taxes were also levied on various classes of people like actors, dancers, singers and even dancing girls. Taxes were paid in the shape of gold coins, cattle, grains, raw materials and also by rendering personal services.

However, it is Kautilya's *Arthasastra*, which deals with the system of taxation in an elaborate and planned manner. This well-known treatise on statecraft—written sometime in 300 B.C., when the Mauryan Empire was at its glorious upwards move—is truly amazing for its deep study of the civilisation of that time and the suggestions which should guide a king in running the State. A major portion of *Arthasastra* is devoted by Kautilya to financial matters including financial administration. The Mauryan system, so far as it applied to agriculture, was a sort of state landlordism and the collection of land revenue formed an important source of revenue to the State. The State not only collected a part of the agricultural produce which was normally one-sixth but also levied water rates, octroi duties, tolls and customs duties. Taxes were also collected on forest produce as well as from mining of metals. Salt tax was an important source of revenue and it was collected at the place of its extraction.

Kautilya describes in detail the trade and commerce carried on with foreign countries and the active interest of the Mauryan Empire to promote such trade. Goods were imported from China, Ceylon and other countries and a levy known as *vartanam* was collected on all foreign commodities imported into the country. There was another levy called *dvarodaya* which was paid by the concerned businessman for the import of foreign goods. In addition, ferry fees of all kinds were levied to augment the tax collection.

Collection of income tax was well-organised and it constituted a major part of the revenue of the state. A big portion was collected in the form of income tax from dancers, musicians, actors and dancing girls. This taxation was not progressive but proportional to the fluctuating income. An excess profits tax was also collected. General sales tax was also levied on sales. Even gambling operations were centralised and tax was collected on these operations. A tax called *yatravetana* was levied on pilgrims. Though revenues were collected from all possible sources, the underlying philosophy was not to exploit or over-tax the people. The revenues collected in this manner were spent on social services such as laying of roads, setting up of educational institutions, setting up of new villages and such other activities beneficial to the community.

The reason why Kautilya gave so much importance to public finance and the taxation system in the *Arthasastra* is not far to seek. According to him, the power of the government depends upon the strength of its treasury. However, he regarded revenue and taxes as the earning of the sovereign for the services which were to be rendered by him to the people and to afford them protection and to maintain law and order. Kautilya emphasised that the King was only a trustee of the land and his duty was to protect it and to make it more and more productive so that land revenue could be collected as a principal source of income for the state. According to him, tax was not a compulsory contribution to be made by the subject to the state but the relationship was based on Dharma and it was the King's sacred duty to protect its citizens in view of the tax collected and if the King failed in his duty, the subject had a right to stop paying taxes, and even to demand refund of the taxes paid.

Kautilya has also described in great detail the system of tax administration in the Mauryan Empire. It is remarkable that the present day tax system is in many ways similar to the system of taxation in vogue about 2,300 years ago. According to the *Arthasastra*, each tax was specific and there was no scope for arbitrariness. Precision determined the schedule of each payment, and its time, manner and quantity being all pre-determined. The land revenue was fixed at one-sixth share of the produce and import and export duties were determined on *ad valorem* basis. The import duties on foreign goods were roughly 20 percent of their value. Similarly, tolls, road cess, ferry charges and other levies were all fixed. Kautilya's concept of taxation is more or less akin to the modern system of taxation. His overall emphasis was on equity and justice in taxation. The affluent had to pay higher taxes as compared to the not so fortunate. People who suffered from diseases were exempted from tax or given suitable remissions. The revenue collectors maintained up-to-date records of collection and exemptions. The total revenue of the state was collected from a large number of sources as enumerated above.

Kautilya also laid down that during war or emergencies like famine or floods, etc. the taxation system should be made more stringent and the king could also raise war loans. The land revenue could be raised from one-sixth to one-fourth during the emergencies. The people engaged in commerce were to pay big donations to war efforts.

In short, Kautilya's *Arthasastra* was the first authoritative text on public finance, administration and the fiscal laws in India. His concept of tax revenue was a unique contribution in the field of tax administration.

1.2 Taxes during Mughal Period

Vivid accounts of tax system during Mughal rule are found in contemporary court chronicles, particularly *Ain-i-Akbari* (the official chronicler of the reign of Emperor Akbar) compiled by Abul Fazl, one of Akbar's courtiers. The work describes, *inter alia*, matters pertaining to taxes, other revenues, expenditure, salaries of public officers etc. Travel accounts of visitors, especially those who came from the West, also throw light on the Mughal system of revenue administration.

In fact, Babur, founder of the Mughal rule in India, had no tax policy as such. To quote, "Babur did not even have an orderly tax system. Plundering was his main source of state income, and he wrote very frankly in his diary that he had decided to advance on an area to the west of Agra at a time when he needed money, because there were some pickings left for him there. In October 1528, he had to levy a tax on his amirs of 30 percent of their salaries, since he had given away everything in India and did not have enough funds at his disposal for war equipment, gunpowder and the operation of cannons". [1]

Land revenue by far was the most important source of income for the Mughal rulers. Other means of lining the emperor's treasury were gifts, import and export duties and *jizya* (or *zazia*). [2] That the tax policy of the Mughals was guided by religious considerations also is clear from the following account, "In the large market cities, in the sea harbours and at the borders of the Empire, import and export duties of 2.5 percent ad valorem were levied; later on Aurangzeb doubled this percentage for Hindus who had to make use of Muslim friends to evade this taxation. There were monopolies on some goods, for instance on salt and saltpetre. The monopoly on indigo yielded a few million rupees to the Treasury.

Jizya, the tax on non-Muslims, abolished by Akbar, was reintroduced by Aurangzeb in 1679 in the form of a degressive income tax. Those who had more than 2,500 rupees per year paid 48 dirhams (tax sums were expressed in dirhams in accordance with the words of the shariah; 48 dirhams was about 13 rupees), those with an income between 250 and 2,500 rupees paid 24 dirhams (about 6.5 rupees), those of limited means, who had an income of at least 52 rupees and could support a wife and children, paid 12 dirhams (about 3.25 rupees) and the real minimum wage earners paid nothing at all (Table 1.1). For the levying of the *jizya* a special service with new collectors of taxes was created. This service was led by a high official who had to control whether the colleting was taking place and whether it was done in a regular way. It is not known how much the new tax yielded, but that was not very important either, for the religious motive—encouraging Hindus to convert to Islam—prevailed over the financial objective". [3] The discriminatory tax policy based on religion adopted by some of the

Mughal rulers was a contributory factor to the decline of Mughal Empire after the death of Aurangzeb in 1707.

Table 1.1: Rate of Zazia during the Rule of Aurangzeb

Income Level Per Year	**Rate of Zazia**
More than 2,500 rupees	48 dirhams (or 13 rupees)
Between 250 and 2,500 rupees	24 dirhams (or 6.5 rupees)
Between 52 and 250 rupees	12 dirhams (or 3.25 rupees)
Less than 52 rupees	Exempted

Ferdinand H.M. Grapperhaus has noted, "According to *The Cambridge Economic History of India, Volume I*, the value of the rupee in 1600 should be equated with twelve rupees in 1970. Considering the inflation since then, which made the price index for commodities rise by a factor of six, we may equate a rupee in 1600 to seventy rupees in 1995". (Ferdinand H.M. Grapperhaus, *Tax Tales from the Second Millennium* (International Bureau of Fiscal Documentation (Amsterdam), 1998, p. 110.

Source: Ferdinand H.M. Grapperhaus, *Tax Tales from the Second Millennium* (International Bureau of Fiscal Documentation (Amsterdam), 1998, pp. 143-144.

Endnotes

1. Ferdinand H.M. Grapperhaus, *Tax Tales from the Second Millennium* (International Bureau of Fiscal Documentation (Amsterdam), 1998, pp. 113-114.
2. It is an Islamic direct tax of the nature of a poll tax. In India, under some Mughal emperors, *zazia* or capitation tax was levied on all non-Muslims in lieu of military service which was required of all Mohammedans.
3. Ferdinand H.M. Grapperhaus, *Tax Tales from the Second Millennium,* op. cit., pp. 143-144.

2

Taxes during British Rule

Prior to 1947, India was a dependency of the United Kingdom and encompassed the entire area which now forms the three countries of India, Pakistan, and Bangladesh. It consisted of the British Indian Provinces, and the Indian Princely States. The political and economic scene changed greatly after 1947 when India emerged as an independent country merging with itself the former Princely States (called Part B States), but excluding areas of the other two countries mentioned above.

The tax system of British India reflected characteristics of a traditional agricultural economy. Revenues of the Central Government were dominated by customs duties as domestic requirements for manufactured goods were met mostly by imports, chiefly from Britain and other Commonwealth countries. Import duties were levied on almost all items of imports whereas major items subject to export duties were jute and tea in which India enjoyed near-monopoly in the world market.

The Princely States did not form part of the structure of public finance of British India. They had separate budgets and separate sources of revenue. The maritime States imposed their own customs duties.

2.1 Financial Administration

Till 1857, when India was under the rule of the East India Company, there was hardly any centralized or systematic financial administration in the country. After the events of 1857, the administration of India was taken over directly by the British Government in 1858. It established a highly centralized system of financial and administrative control with the purpose of consolidating its hold on the vast territory of India. The system of centralized financial control was exercised through the establishment of Finance Department which functioned rather well till the late 1930s. A Comptroller and Auditor-General was appointed in 1860 by amalgamating audit and accounts functions. However, in the absence of a Government responsible to the legislature, he submitted his Annual Reports to the secretary of State for India in Britain.

In matters of rules, regulations, procedures, compilation of annual budgets, audit and accounts etc., the Indian system of financial administration was based on the pattern of treasury control prevalent in Britain. All revenues were required to be credited to a Public Account. Similarly, annual budgets included demands for grants and appropriation accounts as also taxation proposals. They were, however, passed with the Governor-General's approval instead of that of the legislature as was the practice in Britain.

The Government of India was also responsible for the financial administration of Provincial Governments till the introduction of Provincial Autonomy in 1937 when popularly elected Provincial governments responsible to legislatures were established. From 1921 onwards, the Central Legislative Assembly, with a non-official majority, was for the first time given the right to discuss and pass the Annual Budget of the Government of India in respect of *non-reserved* subjects, as also to pass the Finance Bill containing taxation proposals. A committee on Public Accounts, with 8 non-official members of the Central Legislative Assembly and 4 official members (including the Finance Member as chairman) was also constituted to receive and examine Annual Reports of the Auditor-General.

The system of financial control in accordance with the rules and orders in force prior to Independence was continued after August 15, 1947, pending the framing of the new constitution of India. When the new constitution was promulgated on January 26, 1950, the then prevailing system of financial control was permitted to continue, with necessary changes.

2.2 Income Tax

Consequent upon the financial difficulties created by the events of 1857, income tax was introduced in India for the first time by the British in the year 1860. [1] However, the imposition of income tax remained irregular till the year 1886 when a systematic legislation was enacted for its operation on a permanent basis. Since then the form of income tax has undergone a series of changes to meet the changing requirements of Government finances and economic policy.

2.2.1 Income Tax Act, 1860: The Act of 1860 was passed only for five years and therefore it lapsed in 1865. It was replaced in 1867 by a licence tax on professions and trades and the latter was converted into a certificate tax in the following year. The certificate tax was replaced in 1869 by a general income tax which after remaining in force for four years was abolished in 1873. In 1876, the Government imposed a licence tax on traders to create a famine fund to deal with the famine of 1876-78. This licence tax on traders remained in operation till 1886 when it was merged in the Income Tax Act of that year. Noting the haphazard nature of enactments, the Indian Taxation Enquiry Committee, 1924-25, remarked, "...the whole period (1860-1886) was one of continuous trial and error with different schemes of direct taxation, no less than 24 Acts being passed in 26 years". [2]

2.2.2 Income Tax Act, 1886: The Act of 1886 levied a tax on the income of residents as well as non-residents in India. The Act defined agricultural income and exempted it from tax liability in view of the already existing land revenue, a kind of direct tax. (In the 1860 legislation, agricultural income was also subject to taxation). The absolute exclusion of agricultural income from the purview of income tax law continued till the Government of India Act, 1935 made it a provincial (State) subject. This provision was retained in the Constitution of independent India.

The Act of 1886 exempted life insurance premiums paid by an assessee on policies on his own life or on that of his wife, a provision that has continued till now. Under another provision of the Act, a Hindu undivided family was treated as a distinct taxable entity, a position maintained by all subsequent Income Tax Acts.

The assessment and collection procedures of income tax in the early days of its operation were simple and somewhat arbitrary. As the Taxation Enquiry Commission, 1953-54 noted, "The Income Tax Act of 1886 laid an obligation only on companies to file every year statements of their net income and it was entirely within the discretion of the Collector to devise means for finding out other persons likely to have taxable income and to adopt the appropriate method of determining their income ... the procedure for assessment was summary, and the Collector could intimate the amount of income and tax determined by him to the assessee either through a list published in his office or through an individual notice". [3] In 1886-87, the total income assessed was ₹ 33 crore and the net collection from income tax was ₹ 1.37 crore. The Act of 1886 remained in force for 32 years, i.e. until 1918 and during this period a number of amendments were made in it including the introduction of the principle of graduation in income tax in 1916 and of super tax in 1917.

2.2.3 Income Tax Act, 1918: The Act of 1918 brought under charge also receipts of casual or non-recurring nature pertaining to business or profession. This was contrary to the generally accepted meaning of income that it should, *inter alia*, be received with some degree of regularity. The Act granted exemption to contributions to provident funds governed by the Provident Funds Act.

Although income tax in India has been a charge on net income since inception, it was in the Act of 1918 that specific provisions were inserted for the first time pertaining to business deductions for the purpose of computing net income. Prior to that, deductions were granted on the basis of executive orders. For example, there was no specific provision for depreciation allowance in the

Act of 1886 but the Act of 1918 inserted in the statute itself the provision for depreciation allowance on the straight-line method.

The Act of 1918 remained in force for a short period and was replaced by a new Act (Act XI of 1922) in view of the reforms introduced by the Government of India Act, 1919.

2.2.4 Income Tax Act, 1922: The Act of 1922 provided for the first time the set off of loss from one source against income from other sources in the same year. An amendment of the Act in 1939 permitted carry forward of unabsorbed business losses for a period of six years with the restriction that carried forward loss could be set off only against the profits of the same business. Pursuant to a recommendation of the Income Tax Investigation Commission (1948), the income tax law was appropriately amended in 1953 to provide for the set off of speculative losses, even during the same year, only against speculative gains.

Under the Act of 1886, the paying officers had the obligation to deduct tax at source from the salaries of Government servants and employees of local bodies. However, the Act of 1922 extended to all employers the responsibility to deduct tax at source on salaries. Prior to 1922, there was no separate department for income tax administration. The assessment and collection of income tax was done by the land revenue officers as a subsidiary duty. It was only in 1922 that a separate Central Department was created to deal with income tax administration.

2.2.5 Recommendations of the Indian Taxation Enquiry Committee (Chairman: Charles Todhunter), 1924-25: The Government of India appointed this Committee under the chairmanship of Sir Charles Todhunter to examine in detail the entire field of taxation in India. Chapter IX of its report contained recommendations pertaining to income tax. The Committee rejected the idea of differentiation between earned and unearned income for income tax purpose.

A major recommendation of the Committee pertained to the distribution of income tax revenue between the Centre and the Provinces. Prior to 1919, income tax was a 'divided head' of revenue. However, the Montague-Chelmsford Reforms resulted in a complete separation of Central and Provincial finances, and income tax became a part of the Central revenues. The Todhunter Committee opined that in the event of any division of taxes between the Centre and the Provinces, the choice of income tax as the main balancing factor was inevitable. The Government of India Act, 1935, did assign to the Provinces a part of the net proceeds of income tax levied by the Centre.

2.2.6 Recommendations of the Income Tax Enquiry Committee, 1935: This Committee was appointed by the Government of India "to make an investigation of the Indian income tax system in all its aspects and to report upon both the incidence of the tax and the efficiency of its administration". Many amendments based on its recommendations became law in 1939. According to one such amendment, the then prevailing *step* rates system of income tax was changed to a *slab* rates system in 1939. Under the step system of rates, all persons in a particular income bracket bear the same effective rate on every rupee of their income. Under a slab system of rates, tax on each slab of income is calculated separately and then added up. Under another amendment, closely-held companies were required to distribute 60 percent of their net of tax profits as dividend. The Income Tax (Amendment) Act, 1939, provided also for the taxation of profits of the business of mutual life insurance which had remained exempt from tax prior to 1939.

2.2.7 Excess Profit Tax: Another notable development in the evolution of income tax was the imposition of excess profit tax in 1940. It was levied on profits earned by businesses and professions between September 1, 1939 and March 31, 1946. A 'standard profit' was calculated for each accounting year falling within the above years. Standard profit was approximately equated with the profits earned in normal times, i.e. in the pre-War years. Companies started before 1936 had the following five options to choose from for determining standard profit: profits during 1935-36 or 1936-37 or average of the profits during 1935-36 and 1936-37 or 1936-37 and 1937-38 or 1937-38 and 1938-39. In the case of companies started after 1936, the 'capital standard' was used. Thus, a statutory 8 percent of the capital invested was considered the standard rate of profit. Excess profit tax was levied at the rate of 50 percent on the excess over the standard profits earned between September 1, 1939 and March 31, 1941. For the period between April 1, 1941 and March 31, 1946, the rate of excess profit tax was 66.66 percent.

2.2.8 Income Tax Investigation Commission, 1947: Shortly after Independence, the Government appointed the Income Tax Investigation Commission (Chairman: Srinivas Varadachariar) 1947 to: (a) investigate and report on all matters relating to taxation of income, with particular reference to preventing evasion and avoidance, and (b) to investigate specific cases referred to the Commission by the Government. The Commission submitted its report in 1948 and recommended several changes in the law to plug loopholes in the income tax system. For example, it recommended that the law should be amended so as to allow speculative losses to be set off only against speculative gains. A number of Commission's recommendations were incorporated in the law by the Income Tax (Amendment) Act, 1953.

During the pre-Independence period, revenue-raising was the main purpose of income tax system. There were hardly any concessions/exemptions for savings, investments, industrial growth, and other desirable socio-economic objectives.

Incentives for such activities started building up in the system soon after Independence. Thus, a provision introduced in 1949 exempted from tax new industrial undertakings for the first five years of their manufacturing operations.

2.3 Excise Duties

In India, the history of excise taxation in its modern form can be traced back to the year 1894 when excise duty at the rate of 5 percent was imposed on yarn above twenty counts. Since then, the Indian excise system has undergone various changes. Excise at the rate of 6 *annas* [5] per Imperial Gallon was imposed on motor spirit in 1917 and on kerosene at the rate of one *anna* per Imperial Gallon in 1922. Another landmark in the history of excise taxation was the year 1934 when excise duties were imposed on sugar, matches, and steel ingots. Duties were imposed on tyres in 1941 and on vegetable products and tobacco in 1943, mainly to meet the exigencies of war finances. The year 1944 saw excise duties being imposed on coffee, tea and betel nut. Cigarettes came within the excise net in 1948 and mill-made cotton cloth in 1949. Before 1944, excise duties were levied under separate enactments for different goods, e.g. tobacco levies were imposed under the Tobacco (Excise Duty) Act, 1943. About 16 such separate laws were in force till 1944. However, in that year the various enactments were consolidated into the Central Excises and Salt Act and the Central Excise Rules, 1944.

Prior to Independence in 1947, excise taxation in India was selective in terms of commodity coverage and modest from revenue angle. Excise duties were not important as a source of revenue due to the narrow production base of the Indian economy.

The relative share of Central excises in total tax revenue of the Government was 4.7 percent and 4.4 percent in 1920-21 and 1925-26 respectively. The policy of *discriminating protection* followed from the mid-1920s did give some impetus to domestic industry and the share of excise revenue increased to 8.8 percent in 1931-32. At the start of the Second World War, the contribution of excise revenue was 10.7 percent (Table 2.1).

The selected commodities on which excise duties were imposed included cotton textiles, salt, motor spirit, and kerosene. A commodity-wise history of excise taxation is as follows.

2.3.1 Cotton Textiles: Cotton textile mills were first built in India in the 1850s. By 1896 their number had risen to 167 and by 1923 to 323. Following pressure from Britain, an excise duty of 5 percent, corresponding to the duty imposed on imported goods, was imposed in 1894 on Indian yarn above twenty counts. It was in the nature of a countervailing duty on domestic yarn and hence on cloth which competed with imported goods from Lancashire. In 1896, excise duty on yarn was changed to duty on cloth at a reduced rate of 3.5 percent. Simultaneously, import duty was reduced to the same level as the excise duty. The policy of equal duties on imported and domestically produced goods continued till 1917. It was from this year that the period of differential duties started with the raising of the import duty on cloth to 7.5 percent. It was further raised to 11 percent in 1921. The domestic producers thus enjoyed protection to the extent of 7.5 percent on cloth. The Indian Fiscal Commission 1921-22, examined in detail the question of protection to domestic industries and recommended that the Tariff Board should consider the rate of import duty necessary for the protection of the domestic industry. When duty is imposed on local production, the import duty should be enhanced by a like amount. Following its recommendations, the Government adopted what came to be called the policy of 'discriminating protection' under which tariff protection was granted to selected industries against foreign competition. The industries which benefited from the policy of discriminating protection included, *inter alia*, iron and steel, cement, textiles, sugar, paper, matches, and jute.

Table 2.1: Pre-Independence Trends in the Relative Share of Excise Duties in Total Tax Revenue of the Central Government: Selected Years

(₹ crore)

Year	Total Tax Revenue	Central Excise Revenue	Col. 3 as percent of Col. 2
1	2	3	4
1920-21	60.85	2.85	4.7
1925-26	72.86	3.21	4.4
1931-32	75.62	6.19	8.2
1938-39	81.37	8.72	10.7

Source: Government of India, Ministry of Finance, *Report of the Taxation Enquiry Commission* 1953-54, Volume II, p. 258, Table 3 (excerpted).

2.3.2 Salt: Excise on salt was another important source of revenue for the Government during pre-Independence days. The commodity was preferred for taxation because of its inelastic demand and also because it is used in small quantity by all strata of society. Even a low rate of duty on this essential commodity yields some revenue for the exchequer without anybody feeling the pinch. However, the duty was opposed on the ground that it falls on an absolute necessity of life. Since salt is necessary for human existence, duty on it is in the nature of a poll tax. Even the poorest of the poor are made to contribute to state exchequer.

The Indian Taxation Enquiry Committee, 1924-25, examined in detail the pros and cons of salt duty. It opined, "It may be concluded that, if it is desirable to impose any tax on the mass of the community at all, there is much to be said for the continuance of the salt tax. The present rate of duty is appropriate and causes no serious hardship". [4] Excise duty on salt remained a major source of revenue till Independence. Abolition of salt duty was chosen by Mahatma Gandhi to spearhead his non-co-operation movement against the British rulers. The duty on salt was abolished with the achievement of Independence in 1947.

2.3.3 Petroleum Products: Excise duty at the rate of 6 *annas* (₹ 0.37) per Imperial Gallon (4.55 litres) was imposed on motor spirit in 1917. The purpose of this levy was to restrict consumption of petrol to conserve supplies for war needs. Kerosene was another petroleum item placed on the tariff list in 1922. The rate of duty was one *anna* (₹ 0.06) per Imperial Gallon. The duty on motor spirit was mainly a tax on transport while the burden of kerosene duty fell chiefly on almost all classes of the population. For the next 34 years (i.e. until 1956) there was no addition to the list of petroleum products subject to excise tariff. It may be mentioned here that before Independence, the Indian oil industry was characterised by small-scale, localised operations under foreign firms. The Assam Oil Company (a subsidiary of Burmah Oil Company) produced about half a million tonnes of crude oil in Assam. A small refinery of the company at Digboi processed this crude. With the Digboi refinery producing about 7 percent of the total consumption of petroleum products in India, the remainder was imported and marketed by various foreign oil companies operating in India, the chief among them being Burmah Oil, and Stanvac.

2.3.4 Tobacco: Taxation of tobacco and tobacco products in India was suggested, for the first time, by the Indian Taxation Enquiry Committee, 1924-25. It observed, "The absence of any internal taxation on tobacco is a feature which distinguishes the fiscal system of India from that of almost every other civilised country in the world. The considerations which have led in other countries to the selection of tobacco as one of the principal subjects for consumption taxation apply with equal force to India. It is a typical instance of a conventional luxury whose use goes down to the poorest classes, and it is an article the consumption of which can be varied greatly both in quality and quantity according to the means of the consumer". [6] Following the recommendations of the Committee, the taxation of tobacco was examined on various occasions, but the administrative difficulties involved in implementing such a levy prevented its imposition. Moreover, taxation of tobacco was a State subject before the enactment of the Government of India Act, 1935. After this enactment, the power to impose tobacco excise was vested in the Central Government.

Excise on unmanufactured tobacco was levied for the first time with effect from April 1, 1943 with a view to mobilising additional resources to meet the requirements of the Second World War. The levy was imposed under the Tobacco (Excise Duty) Act, 1943 which was subsequently merged with the consolidated Central Excises and Salt Act, 1944. The revenue realised from tobacco in the first year of the excise, viz. 1943-44 was ₹ 9.65 crore.

The rates of duty levied on unmanufactured tobacco in 1943 were designed on a progressive scale depending upon the intended use of the commodity. In addition to this, a graduated duty on the basis of value slabs was imposed on the higher grades of the manufactured cigars and cheroots. The tobacco tariff was extended in 1948 when an excise duty was imposed on cigarettes on the same pattern as the tariff for cigars and cheroots, namely value slabs for fixation of rates. Duty on unmanufactured tobacco brought the excise machinery into contact with a large number of growers and licensees and thus led to tariff complexities and administrative difficulties.

2.3.5 Other Products: Excise duty on silver was imposed in 1930. To quote, "It was in 1934 that the first step in the rationalisation of excise levies was made and their coverage extended. Excise duties were imposed mainly as a revenue measure on sugar, matches, steel ingots and mechanical lighters. Sugar and matches production had made rapid strides under heavy protection in the years following the First World War and the stage had been reached when they could be taxed". [7] Duties were imposed on tyres in 1941 and on vegetable products and tobacco in 1943, mainly to meet the exigencies of war finances. The year 1944 saw excise duties being imposed on coffee, tea, and betel nut. Cigarettes came within the excise net in 1948. Prior to 1944, excise duties were levied under separate enactments for different goods. For example, tobacco levies were imposed under the Tobacco (Excise Duty) Act, 1943. About 16 such separate laws were in force till 1944. However, in that year the various enactments were consolidated into the Central Excises and Salt Act and the Central Excise Rules, 1944.

According to Lakdawala and Nambiar, "In the early stages of its evolution, the Indian excise system has had a basic purpose and philosophy behind its development. The main objective was either to restrict internal consumption of such commodities whose supply was scarce or to make good the loss of revenue resulting from the shrinkage of revenue from protective customs duties on imports of parallel commodities. The initial imposition of duties on items such as motor spirit and kerosene belonged to the first category while the subsequent levies on items such as tyres, textiles and cigarettes belonged to the second category". [8]

2.3.6 Rules of Excise Taxation: The Indian Fiscal Commission, 1921-22 enunciated the following five golden rules of excise taxation which, with necessary modifications, seem to be relevant to this day.

1. "Excise duties should ordinarily be confined to industries which are concentrated in large factories or small areas.
2. They may properly be imposed for the purpose of checking the consumption of injurious articles and especially on luxuries coming under this category.
3. Otherwise they should be imposed for revenue purpose only.
4. While permissible on commodities of general consumption, they should not press too heavily on poorer classes.
5. When an industry requires protection, any further necessary taxation on its products may, if the other conditions are fulfilled, take the form of excise duty *plus* an additional import duty. The latter should fully countervail the former and may be pitched at a higher price". [9]

2.4 Customs Duties

Prior to 1857, the regulation of customs duties in India was haphazard and lacked all-India uniformity due to unstable political and economic conditions. Rates of import duty, though not uniform, were relatively low, ranging from 3 to 5 percent *ad valorem* on raw materials and manufactured articles. These rates were doubled in the case of goods imported from countries other than Britain.

Having consolidated political power after the disturbances of 1857, the British Indian Government introduced in 1859 a uniform all-India customs tariff which replaced separate provincial rates of duty. Various customs and tariff enactments were passed from time to time but the following two were the main: (a) The Sea Customs Act, 1878, and (b) The Tariff Act, 1934.

After Independence, the Sea Customs Act and other allied enactments were repealed by a consolidating and amending legislation entitled the Customs Act, 1962. Similarly, the Tariff Act of 1934 was repealed by the Customs Tariff Act, 1975. Customs tariff, has been subjected to a series of changes to act as a policy instrument to generate revenue, protect the domestic industry, conserve and ration foreign exchange and frame general international trade policy.

2.4.1 Period 1859 to 1894: Under the uniform all-India tariff, introduced by the British in 1859, almost everything imported into India was assessed at 10 percent of its value for purposes of customs duty. Some important articles, viz. tobacco, beer, wines, and spirits were taxed at 20 percent. Likewise, nearly all exports from India paid 3 percent rate of duty. High rates of customs duty soon proved counter-productive and by mid-1860s a process of lowering import tariff had started. Moreover, the country was also showing signs of recovery from the trauma of 1857. Import duties were reduced to 7.5 percent in 1864 and further down to 5 percent in 1875. Import duties were abolished in 1882, except those on arms and liquors. For all practical purposes, the import of goods into India was free until 1894. According to K.T. Shah, "...from 1875 to 1900, the Indian customs policy became the subject of a violent controversy between doctrinaire free traders and passionate protectionists; and in consequence there were frequent changes. The ruling caste, taking their cue from the prominent British statesmen, adopted an attitude of uncompromising freedom in trade, irrespective of India's economic or financial interests. The Indian public opinion of the day, such as it was, was gradually driven by the sheer intolerance of the rulers in their second-hand exposition of the free trade principles, to an attitude of equally unyielding protectionism". [10]

Broadly speaking, from mid-1870s the Government of India was well on the path of establishing freedom of trade. Even in the case of exports, exemptions from duty were granted freely and in 1875 the only commodities which were still subject to export duties were rice, indigo, and lac.

2.4.2 Period 1894 to 1919: The euphoria for free trade which dominated Government's policy between 1875 and 1890 gave way to economic realism with the beginning of 1890s. The loss of revenue from the abolition of import duties was felt to be adversely affecting Central finances. Hence, in a reversal of tariff policy, a general import duty of 5 percent was re-imposed in 1894. A notable exception to this rate was the duty free import of railway materials and machinery. Similarly, a low duty of 1 percent was imposed on iron and steel. There were a few commodities, viz. arms, liquors, and tobacco which were subject to a comparatively high rate of duty. This arrangement continued till the outbreak of the First World War.

The outbreak of the War led to an urgent need for additional revenues and customs duties came in handy for the Government. The general rate of import duty was raised from 5 percent to 7.5 percent in 1916. In the same year, an export duty was imposed on jute. A duty on raw hides and skins at 5 percent *ad valorem* was imposed in 1919.

Export duties formed an important part of the customs tariff soon after the events of 1857. They were gradually abolished and between 1880 and 1916, rice was the only item subject to export duty. The financial difficulties created by the First World War led to their revival. Jute and tea were brought under the export duty net in 1916, and hides and skins in 1919. Justifying the export duty on rice, the Indian Taxation Enquiry Committee, 1924-25, observed, "Though rice is not a monopoly of India, the export duty has been in operation for many years without any bad effects. Its justification lies in special circumstances. The only countries which export appreciable quantities of rice are India, Siam (now Thailand), and Indo-China. The Indian share of the trade varies between one-third and one-half. As each of these countries levies an export duty, the Indian duty does not handicap the producer and its remission would in fact put an equivalent amount of money into the hands of the producers and the middlemen". [11] Export duty on tea was justified on similar grounds because India's principal competitor Ceylon (now Sri Lanka) also imposed export duty on tea.

2.4.3 Inter-War Period: The general rate of import duty was raised from 7.5 percent to 11 percent in 1921, and further up to 15 percent in 1922. A new category of *luxury goods* (such as motor cars, silk goods, and watches) was introduced in 1921 for which a 20 percent rate was prescribed and the same was increased to 30 percent in the following year. Although, the successive upward revisions in import tariff were made for additional revenue, they did provide the much-needed protection to the domestic industry.

In 1921, the Indian Fiscal Commission was appointed to examine the tariff policy of the Government of India. It submitted its report in 1922 with the following main recommendations:

1. That the Government of India should adopt a policy of protection to be applied with discrimination along the lines indicated in this report.
2. That discrimination be exercised in the selection of industries for protection, and in the degree of protection afforded, so as to make the inevitable burden on the community as light as is consistent with the due development of industries.
3. That the Tariff Board in dealing with claims for protection should satisfy itself: (a) that the industry possesses natural advantages, (b) that without the help of protection it is not likely to develop at all, or not so rapidly as is desirable, and (c) that it will eventually be able to face world competition without protection.
4. That raw materials and machinery be ordinarily admitted free of duty and that semi-manufactured goods used in Indian industries be taxed as lightly as possible.
5. That industries essential for purposes of national defence and for the development of which conditions in India are not unfavourable be adequately protected, if necessary.
6. That no export duties be ordinarily imposed except for purely revenue purposes and then only at very low rates; but that when it is considered necessary to restrict the export of foodgrains, the restriction be effected by temporary export duties and not by prohibition. [12]

The recommendations of the Fiscal Commission were debated in the

Legislative Assembly in February 1923 and a resolution was passed accepting in principle the need to tailor India's tariff policy for encouraging Indian industries. As suggested by the Fiscal Commission, a Tariff Board was set up which investigated the claims of a number of industries for protective duties. Following the recommendations of the Tariff Board, the Government adopted what came to be called the policy of *discriminatory protection* under which tariff protection was granted to select industries against foreign competition. The industries which benefited from the policy of discriminating protection included, *inter alia,* iron and steel, cement, textiles, sugar, paper, matches, and jute.

An adverse consequence of the high rates of customs duty during and after the First World War was the encouragement to smuggling. The Indian Taxation Enquiry Committee, 1924-25, examined the smuggling problem at length and observed, "...while the present high tariff offers great temptations to the smuggler, there is a lack of cohesion in the preventive arrangements, which certainly offer many facilities for his operations. It is not desirable to recite instances of the way in which advantage has been taken of these facilities, but it may be said that, though there is no evidence that any considerable percentage of the customs revenue is lost through smuggling, it is clear that there is a loss amounting at least to several lakhs a year". [13]

The economic depression of early 1930s resulted in heavy deficits in the finances of the Central Government. The general rate of import tariff was raised to 25 percent as a part of additional taxation efforts introduced under the Indian Finance Act, 1931.

During the inter-War period, customs duties remained the single largest source of Central revenues. In 1921-22, they accounted for 39.5 percent or two-fifths of the Central revenues. By 1938-39, their share had gone up to almost one-half, 48.9 percent to be exact. At the end of the Second World War, i.e. in 1944-45, their contribution was as low as 11.9 percent: ₹ 39.77 crore out of total revenue of ₹ 334.40 crore (Table 2.2).

2.4.4 Second World War: In the Finance Act of 1942, an overall surcharge of one-fifth on all duties was imposed. It continued from year to year till 1951 when it was increased to one-fourth in the wake of Korean boom. In 1944, the rate of surcharge on certain items, viz. potable spirits, cigars, cigarettes, and tobacco was increased from one-fifth to one-half. During the War, an export duty at 3 percent was imposed on cotton cloth and yarn but the same was converted into an export cess in 1945.

Another important wartime development was the introduction of import control (quotas) to ensure that available foreign exchange and shipping space were utilised for essential imports. The policy of import control continued during the post-War period to meet conditions created by the partition of the country, particularly the import of massive quantities of foodgrains.

Table 2.2: Pre-Independence Trends in the Relative Share of Customs Duties in Total Revenues of the Central Government

(₹ crore)

Year	Total Central Revenues	Customs	Col. 3 as percent of Col. 2
1	2	3	4
1921-22	80.00	31.61	39.5
1936-37	81.45	38.11	46.8
1938-39	82.90	40.51	48.9
1944-45	334.40	39.77	11.9

Figures for 1921-22 and 1936-37 are inclusive of those for Burma. Figures for 1938-38 and 1944-45 relate to undivided India.

Source: Government of India, Ministry of Finance, *Report of the Taxation Enquiry Commission,* 1953-54, Volume I, p. 23, Table 5 (excerpted).

It is pertinent to note that during the pre-Independence period, maritime Princely States enjoyed the right to levy and retain sea customs duties at their own ports. However, the States were not allowed, through conventions with the British Indian Government, to levy such duties at rates lower than those charged at entry into British Indian ports. This arrangement ensured that there was no undue diversion of trade from British Indian ports to ports developed and maintained by the States. The maritime Princely States of British India with their major ports mentioned in parentheses were the following: Travancore State (Trivandrum, Quilon, Alleppey), Cochin State (Cochin), Bhavnagar State (Bhavnagar), Junagadh State (Verawal, Mangrol), Porbandar State (Porbandar), Baroda State (Okha), Nawanagar State (Bedi, Rozi), Morvi State (Navlakhi), and Cutch State (Mandvi, Kandla).

The authority of the Princely States in terms of sea customs and ports was well-recorded in the Report of the Indian States Enquiry Committee (Financial), 1932. It observed, "...the revenue they (Princely States) derive from these customs duties is substantial, elastic, and an important part of their total revenues, from which their State expenditure (including that on nation building activities) has to be met; that the appointment of staff by which they collect, and the manner in which they disburse, the revenue so realised from customs duties are entirely matters for their own decision; and, in particular, that they cannot be debarred from utilising that revenue in the maintenance and development of the ports at which the customs duties are levied". [14]

2.5 Sales Tax

The Government of the Central Provinces (now Madhya Pradesh) was the first to take advantage of this provision when it levied a retail sales tax on motor spirit and lubricants in 1938. This so-called 'petrol tax' was a selective sales tax imposed through the Central Provinces and Berar Sales of Motor Spirit and Lubrication Taxation Act, 1938.

In 1939, Madras levied a general multi-point sales tax through the Madras General Sales Tax Act, 1939. The tax levied at the rate of half percent was ostensibly meant to compensate the loss of revenue resulting from the policy of prohibition.

Entry 48 of List II in the Seventh Schedule of the Government of India Act, 1935, vested in the Provinces the power to levy 'taxes on the sale of goods and on advertisements'.

The Government of the Central Provinces (now Madhya Pradesh) was the first to take advantage of this provision when it levied a retail sales tax on motor spirit and lubricants in 1938. This so-called 'petrol tax' was a selective sales tax imposed through the Central Provinces and Berar Sales of Motor Spirit and Lubrication Taxation Act, 1938.

In 1939, Madras levied a general multi-point sales tax through the Madras General Sales Tax Act, 1939. The tax levied at the rate of half percent was ostensibly meant to compensate the loss of revenue resulting from the policy of prohibition.

2.5.1 Initial Legal Hurdles: Since its very inception, sales tax has been a controversial levy embroiled in legal wranglings. Thus, soon after its enactment, the Central Provinces Act referred above was challenged by the Central Government as unconstitutional. It may be recalled that Entry 45 of List II in Seventh Schedule of the Government of India Act, 1935 had given the Central Government the power to levy excise on tobacco and other goods manufactured or produced in India. Hence, the Central Government maintained that sales tax on motor spirit and lubricants by Central Provinces was *ultra vires* because the power to levy excise on such products belonged to it (Central Government). Deciding in favour of the Provincial Government, the Federal Court observed that such taxes were in no way connected with the production or manufacture of goods, but were imposed on their sale.

In another legal battle, the Central Government contested the Madras General Sales Tax Act, 1939 referred to above. Being a multi-point sales tax, it covered sales by manufacturers also which was challenged by the Central Government. Once again, the Federal Court decided in favour of the Provincial Government and held that it had the power to tax sales of every kind, including sales by a manufacturer or producer.

The above two judicial pronouncements made it clear that the Provinces were competent to tax sales of any commodity and at any stage. In other words, a clear-cut distinction was drawn between the two, excise to be a tax on the act of production or manufacture, and the sales tax to be a levy on the act of sale.

Initial legal squabblings over, sales tax gained rapid popularity among the Provinces with the beginning of 1940s. Bengal adopted a single-point general sales tax levied at retail level in 1941. In the same year, Punjab introduced a general sales tax broadly based on the multi-point model of Madras. A general sales tax on the lines of single-point system of Bengal was introduced by Bihar in 1944 and by Bombay in 1946. Other Provinces followed suit and by 1948, all of them were operating sales tax in one form or the other with the notable exception of Jammu and Kashmir. This State was the last to introduce sales tax in 1962.

2.5.2 Beggar-my-neighbour Policies: There was no provision in the Government of India Act, 1935, to restrict or prohibit the Provinces from levying sales tax on inter-State transactions. In other words, the Act did not require the Provinces to levy sales tax only on those transactions which exclusively took place in their respective territories.

Taking advantage of this loophole in the Act, almost all the Provincial legislatures enacted sales tax laws which enabled them to tax goods exported from one State to another. These practices led to multiple taxation of the same transaction by different Provinces. As one scholar remarked, "Perhaps, the most important problem relating to sales taxation in the pre-Constitution period was the taxation of inter-State sales. All the Provinces, with the exception of West Bengal, were collecting sales tax on goods being sent to other Provinces and were, in effect, indulging in 'beggar-my-neighbour policies". [15]

In order to sort out these problems and to ensure all-India co-ordination, the Government of India convened a conference of the Finance Ministers of States in October, 1948. At this conference, attempts were made to achieve some degree of uniformity in the taxation of inter-State sales. However, these attempts failed in view of the widespread disagreement among the States. In particular, States which produced important raw materials/manufactured goods were opposed to changes that would result in the exclusion of inter-State trade from the purview of their sales tax laws. In short, the system of sales tax during the pre-Constitution period was arbitrary and bereft of national considerations.

2.6 Structure of Government Tax Revenue

Out of a Central tax revenue of ₹ 73.90 crore in 1938-39, customs accounted for ₹ 40.51 crore, Central excises ₹ 8.66 crore, and income tax ₹ 13.74 crore (Table 2.3).

Table 2.3: Structure of Central and Provincial Tax Revenues: 1938-39

(₹ crore)

Central Tax Revenue		**Provincial Tax Revenue***	
Total taxes	73.90	Total taxes	56.07
of which		*of which*	
Customs	40.51	Land revenue	25.40
Taxes on income	13.74	State excises	13.08
Corporation tax	2.04	Stamps	9.53
Central excise duties	8.66	Registration	1.09
Salt duty	8.12	Devolution of taxes from the Centre	3.98

Note: Figures relate to undivided India.

* Data refer to nine Provinces including Sind and N.W.F.P. (now in Pakistan).

Source: Government of India, Ministry of Finance, *Report of the Taxation Enquiry Commission,* 1953-54, Volume I, Tables 4 (p. 20), 5 (p. 23), and 7 (p. 25).

As for the British Indian Provinces, the chief source of income was land revenue followed by Provincial excises, mainly on liquor (Table 2.3). Although under the Government of India Act, 1935, Provincial Governments had been authorised to levy sales tax, it formed a very low component of their revenue till Independence. The Province of Bombay levied a tax on the sale of tobacco in 1938. A retail sales tax on motor spirit and lubricants was imposed by Central Provinces (now Madhya Pradesh) in the same year. A multi-point general sales tax was levied in Madras Province at the rate of half percent in 1939 under the Madras General Sales Tax Act.

2.7 Centre-State Financial Relations

The present fiscal structure of India is the result of a gradual evolution over the last 144 years. The pre-1947 arrangements for intergovernmental financial transfers had a strong bearing on the framing of Indian constitution, operative since 1950.

2.7.1 Mayo Scheme, 1870: After the events of 1857, the British Crown assumed sovereignty over India from East India Company in 1858. The British had realised that governance of so vast and diverse a country of sub-continental size through centralisation of all power was difficult and some degree of decentralisation of authority to Provinces (or States) was necessary. [16] Prior to 1871, the administration of the country was rigidly centralised, characterised by absolute imperial control over Provincial revenues and expenditures. Provinces were entirely dependent on annual cash assignments from the Centre for the maintenance of their administration.

The first beginning towards decentralisation of finances was made when the resolution of Lord Mayo was issued on December 14, 1870. The Mayo resolution explained the scheme by which the Government of India envisaged enlargement of the powers and responsibilities of the Provinces. Thus, services like jails, police, education, medical, roads and civil works were transferred to the administrative control of the Provinces and to meet their costs, the departmental receipts under these heads were also assigned to them. This was done to encourage their interest in collections as well as to induce economy in expenditure. This arrangement came to be known as *Provincial Financial Settlements*. However, due to the inadequacy of these new heads of revenue, the existing system of fixed grants from Central revenues also continued. To quote, "The system of decentralisation was welcomed by the Provinces, because friction with the Central Government was thereby obviated and much useless correspondence avoided. But it did not give adequate resources to the Provinces nor provide conditions for the progressive administration of the services transferred to them. The only consideration which really weighed with the Government of India was that of administrative convenience". [17]

Satisfied with the Mayo scheme, the Government decided to carry it further and the next step towards decentralisation was taken in 1877 when subjects like land revenue, and general administration were transferred to the Provinces. The Mayo settlements were subject to revision annually but from 1882, they were made on quinquennial basis. Over the period 1882 to 1904, these settlements gave rise to the system of *divided heads of revenue.* Under the system, the Centre retained the entire profits of the commercial departments and the proceeds of revenue whose locale was no guide to its true incidence, such as the net receipts from customs, salt and opium. As the income derived from these sources was not sufficient to cover the central expenditure, other sources of revenue including income-tax were divided between the Central and Provincial Governments. The Central Government retained a proportion—fixed in the case of each Province, but not uniform as between the Provinces—of the proceeds of the main heads of revenue collected in the Provinces, based on an assessment of the respective needs of the Provinces. In practice, since no definite standards of needs had been evolved, allocations to the Provinces were largely a result of history. The revenue from *divided heads*, being insufficient to meet the needs of the Provincial Governments, was supplemented by means of fixed cash assignments, recurring as well as non-recurring, which continued to remain an important feature of the system.

In 1904, the settlements were made quasi-permanent and in 1911 began the period of permanent settlements. As the Indian Taxation Enquiry Committee (1924-25) observed, "The intention of the Government in adopting this change was on the one hand to give more elasticity to the settlements and more freedom to Local Governments in working them, and, on the other hand, to protect the general taxpayer of India against possible mismanagement in any particular province, and to put an end to the frequent and undesirable controversies over the adequacy of the existing settlements". [18]

2.7.2 Government of India Act, 1919: The next landmark in the history of Centre-State financial relations was the Montague-Chelmsford Report on Constitutional Reforms which led to the passing of the Government of India Act, 1919. The Act sought to secure for the Provinces a greater degree of financial independence by abolishing the *divided heads* and effecting a complete separation between the Central and Provincial heads of revenue. Thus, revenue heads like income tax, non-alcoholic excises including salt, customs, currency and mint, and contributions from railways, and post and telegraph came to the share of Central Government while relatively inelastic sources of revenue like land revenue, alcoholic excises, irrigation charges, judicial stamps, forest receipts, and registration fee were assigned to the Provinces. These arrangements enabled the Provinces to run their administration with the help of revenue raised by themselves. The Provincial budgets were separated from that of the Government of India and each Province presented its own budget and levied taxes assigned to it. With revenue heads distributed on these lines, it was estimated in the Report that there would remain a large deficit in the Government of India budget. It was, therefore, proposed in the Report that the Provinces should make contributions to the Central budget.

2.7.3 Meston Settlement, 1920: The Financial Relations Committee presided over by Lord Meston was appointed to advise on the amounts of provincial contributions, and also on the claims of Bombay to a share of the proceeds of income tax. The Meston Committee reported in March 1920.

While recognising that it would not be possible permanently to exclude Provincial Governments from some form of direct taxation upon the industrial and commercial earnings of their people, the Committee advised against the division of income tax with the Provinces. They recommended that general stamps be made provincial for financial and administrative reasons.

The Committee proposed a scheme of initial contributions and of standard contributions to be attained over a period of 7 years. The standard contributions, which were based on the relative taxable capacity of the Provinces and other economic factors, never came into operation. The initial contributions were computed on the increased spending power of each Province resulting from the new scheme of distribution, i.e. the additional income which each Province would acquire on the separation of the sources of revenue. The scheme of contributions was subjected to criticism from various quarters. Some Provinces disliked the initial contributions, others the standard contributions, and industrial Provinces like Bombay were opposed to the whole basis of the revised scheme.

The Joint Select Committee of Parliament on Draft Rules made under the Government of India Act, 1919, suggested a gradual reduction of the aggregate contribution of all Provinces and underlined the idea that contributions should cease at the earliest possible moment.

The Committee was opposed to provincialising income tax but recommended that some share in the growth of revenue from taxation of income should be granted to all Provinces in so far as that growth was attributable to an increase in the amount of incomes assessed in each Province. The scheme of financial arrangements contained in the Report on Indian Constitutional Reforms, as modified on the recommendations of the Joint Select Committee on Draft Rules, was incorporated in the Devolution Rules under the Government of India Act, 1919, which were promulgated in December 1920.

The recommendations of the Joint Select Committee relating to income tax provided that a Province should receive 3 pies in each rupee of the amount by which the assessed income of any year exceeded that of the year 1920-21. Inasmuch as collection might not accurately reflect the income tax revenue due to the economic activity of a Province, some ad hoc adjustments were made on account of industrial units located in a Province different from the Province in which they were assessed to income tax. The operation of the rule gave unequal results as between Provinces. It did not lead, on the whole, to any significant accretion to provincial revenues and, in particular, virtually failed to secure for the larger industrial Provinces a share in the yield of income tax. The rule, however, represented a slight departure in principle from the scheme of complete division of sources originally proposed, and thus marked the beginning of the use of income tax as a balancing factor.

From the very beginning, the scheme of *provincial contributions* came in for sharp criticism from various quarters, particularly from the Provinces themselves. The trends in the Central and Provincial budgets in the early 1920s vindicated the stand of critics and the demand for abolition of contributions grew still more persistent with the result that contributions were abolished from 1928-29. Provincial contributions under the Meston Settlement during the 1920s provide, perhaps, the only example of transfer of funds from the Provinces to the Centre in the long history of fiscal federalism in India.

There were some important lessons to be learnt from the Reforms of 1919. According to the Fourth Finance Commission, "The failure of the system of a rigid division between the Central and Provincial heads of revenue introduced by the Government of India Act of 1919 could not be prevented by the Meston award and the ultimate result was unsatisfactory both to the Centre and to the units. The experience of the nineteen-twenties led, however, to the emergence of the idea that the authority most suited for discharging a particular governmental function need not necessarily be the authority most suited to raise the financial resources required to discharge the function. The taxes on income had already been recognized before 1919 as a balancing factor and it continued to be recognized as such after 1935. But it also came to be recognized that other taxes could appropriately be levied and collected by the Central Government and distributed, wholly or partly, to the Provinces or States. The Government of India Act of 1935 recognised this principle and the Constitution adopted in 1950 made clear provision for (i) the assignment of the taxes raised by the Union Government under article 269 wholly to the States, (ii) for the obligatory division of the income-tax proceeds between the Union and the States, and (iii) for the division, with the approval of Parliament, of the proceeds of the Union excise duties". [19]

However, the framework of fiscal federalism set up in 1919 remained unaltered, by and large, till the Government of India Act, 1935 came into operation. The period covered by the Government of India Act, 1919, was marked by frequent discussions on the structure of financial relations between the Centre and the units. A principal objective of these discussions was to equip the Provincial Governments with greater financial resources. The inadequacy of the existing resources, both of the Centre and the units, and a search for fresh avenues of taxation, also represented a thread running through the discussions.

2.7.4 Indian Taxation Enquiry Committee, 1924-25: In the meantime, the Indian Taxation Enquiry Committee (President: Sir Charles Todhunter), 1924-25 examined, *inter alia,* the division of sources of revenue between the Centre and the Provinces. It recommended that the excise duty on country-made foreign liquor, excise on opium, and general stamps should be transferred to the Centre. The recommendation regarding said excises on liquor and opium was rejected by the Government in view of administrative difficulties involved. Similarly, owing to stiff opposition from the Provinces, the proposal to centralise general stamps was dropped and only duties on documents of commercial nature were transferred to the Central Government. The proposal of the Committee to give the provinces a small share of the receipts of the corporation tax was also rejected by the Government.

A major recommendation of the Committee pertained to the distribution of income tax revenue between the Centre and the Provinces. Prior to 1919, income tax was a *divided head* of revenue. However, the Montague-Chelmsford Reforms resulted in a complete separation of Central and Provincial finances, and income tax became a part of the Central revenues.

The Todhunter Committee expressed itself against giving the Provinces power to levy and administer an income tax as well as against the imposition by the Centre of surcharges for the benefit of the Provinces. It suggested that the most appropriate solution for this problem was the assignment to the Provinces of a share of the tax. In regard to its distribution, the Committee proposed that this should be based primarily on the principle of domicile. It proposed to give the Province the proceeds of a basic rate on personal incomes, graduated proportionally to the general rate. Under its scheme, collection on incomes not pertaining to residents in particular Provinces (such as the tax on undistributed dividends of companies or on incomes of persons' resident outside the Province or the country) and the whole of super tax would be retained by the Centre. In addition to the allotment made on the basis of personal incomes, the allocation of which would be based entirely on domicile, the Committee also recommended a partial recognition of the principle of origin by assigning to each Province a small portion of the receipts of the corporation profits tax. It contemplated that this might be distributed on the basis of the collections of each Province.

In short, the Todhunter Committee opined that in the event of any division of taxes between the Centre and the Provinces, the choice of income tax as the main balancing factor was inevitable. The Government of India Act, 1935, did assign to the Provinces a part of the net proceeds of income tax levied by the Centre.

2.7.5 Indian Statutory Commission, 1930: In its report submitted in 1930, this Commission accepted the general principles of the scheme drawn up by its Financial Assessor, Sir Walter Layton, for the divisions of resources between the Central and Provincial Governments. Layton envisaged the use of income tax as the main balancing factor in the reallocation of revenues between the Centre and the Provinces. He suggested that in order to meet the claims of the industrial Provinces a substantial part of the revenue from income tax should be assigned to the Provinces. He endorsed the general method of division proposed by Todhunter Committee and recommended that one-half of the income tax paid by residents of a Province (including tax on dividends received by them from companies carrying on operations outside the Province) be assigned to the Province concerned. Super tax would remain entirely Central, subject to reconsideration after 10 years. The Provincial Governments were also to have the option of levying a surcharge on tax collected on the incomes of residents in the Province limited to half the tax transferred to them, i.e. one-fourth of the total tax. Significantly, the Commission also suggested that the exemption of agricultural incomes from income tax should be abolished by definite stages and the whole of the proceeds of the taxation of these incomes should be assigned to the Province of origin.

Sir Layton further recommended that a Provincial Fund be formed out of the proceeds of certain new excises on such commodities as cigarettes and matches and, when the centre budgetary position permitted, the duty on salt, for distribution among the Provinces on a per capita basis. The Commission endorsed this proposal.

2.7.6 Peel Committee I, 1931: The Federal Structure Committee of the Second and Third Round Table Conferences appointed two sub-committees to consider the problem of allocation of resources between the Centre and the Provinces. Both the sub-committees were presided over by Viscount Peel. The first sub-committee (Peel Committee I) submitted its report in 1931. Report of the second sub-committee (Peel Committee II) came in 1932. In between these two reports was submitted in 1932 the report of an Expert Committee presided over by Lord Percy.

Peel Committee I suggested that all income tax proceeds should be transferred to the Provinces with collection and administration being in federal hands. It suggested, though obliquely, that federal tax revenues should be mostly derived from indirect taxation. Any resultant federal deficit could be met from provincial contributions which would be gradually terminated over a 10 to 15 year period. Later, if any permanent federal surplus were to materialise, the federal government should be free to allocate the surplus to the Provinces as an alternative preferable to reduction of taxation. The Committee suggested that it was desirable that the Constitution itself should lay down the proportions in which funds thus available should be divided among the Provinces, whether according to respective revenues or to population or to some other criteria. It recommended that an expert committee should advise on this aspect as also on the criteria by which the proceeds of income tax should be allocated among the Provinces.

2.7.7 Percy Committee, 1932: Accordingly, the Percy Committee was appointed to examine the issues raised by Peel Committee I. The basis of distribution of income tax among the Provinces was considered in detail by Percy Committee. It held that a proper basis of distribution of income tax receipts should satisfy the following three tests:

1. It should be simple, easily understood and administratively workable.
2. It should give results likely to be accepted as fair between Province and Province.
3. It should be compatible with the idea of a federation of autonomous units.

It opined that an allocation on the basis of collections would lead to gross injustice as between Province and Province and ruled it out. While distribution by population had equally no scientific basis it could be adopted with advantage for the distribution of taxes on certain forms of income not easily assignable to any locality. Theoretically, the basis of origin had much to commend it, but it would be administratively unworkable unless the allocations were made on arbitrary lines. Hence, the Committee did not recommend the adoption of this basis. Finally, it expressed itself in favour of the basis of residence in one of two forms, either the basis of personal income assessed or assessable in each Province or the amount of income tax attributable to each Province.

As regards the question of distribution of income tax between the Centre and the Provinces, the Percy Committee expressed the view that if the entire proceeds of income tax were transferred, the Centre would be faced with a substantial deficit. It, therefore, proposed the following scheme:

1. Corporation tax (super tax on companies), tax paid by residents in federally administered areas and tax paid on salaries of federal officers should be retained by the Centre.
2. Of the remainder of the net proceeds, a Province should receive the amount of personal super tax on the basis of collections from residents, an estimated amount of personal income tax creditable to it, and a share on the basis of population of the tax on non-residents and undistributed profits of companies, both to be taken as an estimated percentage of the total collections.

In order to ensure stability of provincial budgets, it suggested that the share of income tax due to the Provinces should not be altered from year to year even if the data for this were readily available on the basis suggested by it. Instead, it should be fixed for a term of years, subject to revision every 5 years in the light of data of personal income tax for the previous quinquennium. The federal government would have the power to impose a surcharge, for its own purposes, on any tax levied by it for the benefit of the Provinces. Federal grants, if and when they became feasible, should be made on population basis as the Committee believed that the surplus would arise mostly from taxes on consumption.

2.7.8 Peel Committee II, 1932: It proposed a two-fold division of the proceeds of taxes on income: (a) share which would be assigned as a permanent constitutional arrangement to the federal government, and (b) share which would be assigned as a permanent constitutional arrangement to the Provinces. The federal government would be entitled to a share based on the proceeds of heads of tax which were not derived solely from the residents in British India, such as corporation tax, tax on federal officers, tax in federal areas, tax on Government of India securities and taxes on the incomes of persons not resident in British India.

The whole of the remaining proceeds from income tax were to be assigned to the Provinces. However, the federal government should retain a block amount out of the provincial share of income tax until sufficient time had elapsed for the development of new sources of revenue. The Committee was in favour of the federal government having the power to levy for its own purposes a surcharge on the heads of income tax permanently assigned to the Provinces. Most of the members of the Committee were also agreed that the Provinces should have a right to levy a surcharge on the personal tax levied on its residents under the heads permanently allocated to the Provinces, subject to a maximum of 12.5 percent. The Committee also proposed subventions from the Centre to deficit Provinces in approved cases and on certain conditions, to enable them to balance their budgets on the basis of providing for bare necessities.

2.7.9 White Paper on Indian Constitutional Reforms, 1931: The White Paper issued by Government in December 1931 contemplated that a prescribed percentage, not being less than 50 percent nor more than 75 percent, of the net revenue derived from taxes on income, other than agricultural income, except taxes on the income of companies should be assigned to the Provinces on a prescribed basis. It also proposed that the federation should retain for the first 3 years a prescribed sum out of the provincial share which would continue to be retained for a further period of 7 years with a reduction of one-eighth of the original sum in each successive year. Both the federation and the Provinces were to have power to levy surcharges on income tax for their own purposes.

Proposals contained in the White Paper introduced two new features into the plan for the division of sources of revenue. Firstly, the federal legislature was to be empowered by a law to assign to the units the whole or part of the yield of salt duties, excise duties, other than those specifically assigned to the units, and export duties. Secondly, it also suggested that in respect of certain taxes, including terminal taxes and death duties, while the power to levy the tax would be vested solely in the federation, the proceeds would be distributed to the Provinces. However, the federation would have the right to impose a surcharge for federal purposes.

2.7.10 Joint Parliamentary Committee on Indian Constitutional Reforms, 1934: This Committee was, by and large, in agreement with the proposals contained in the White Paper. It left the provincial share of income tax to be prescribed by an Order-in-Council, but could not visualise any prospect of the Provinces' share of income tax exceeding half of the net revenue from the source. The Committee did not favour the proposal to empower the Provinces also to impose surcharges on personal income tax. The modified proposals relating to income tax and other matters were incorporated in the Government of India Act, 1935.

It is noteworthy that the idea of devolving the whole of income tax to the Provinces leaving the Centre to cover the consequent deficit by provincial contributions was abandoned, and a measure of elasticity in the distribution of income tax was introduced by limiting the provincial share to a part of the net proceeds and giving the Centre power to retain, for a transitional period, a fixed amount out of the provincial share to give it time to adjust its finances.

2.7.11 Government of India Act, 1935: The Government of India Act, 1935 was a watershed in the evolution of Centre-State financial relation. To quote, "While under all the previous Government of India Acts, the Government of India was unitary, the Act of 1935 prescribed a federation, taking the Provinces and the Indian States (i.e. Princely States) as Units. But it was optional for the Indian States to join the federation; and since the Rulers of the Indian States never gave their consent, the Federation envisaged by the Act of 1935 never came into being". [20] Nevertheless, the Act was a step towards consolidation and enhancement of Provincial autonomy in matters of resources and functions. It laid the foundations for the structure of Centre-State relations as incorporated in the present Constitution of India. The Act divided taxation heads into the following three broad categories.

1. Taxes levied by and meant exclusively for the Central Government.
2. Taxes levied by and meant exclusively for Provincial Governments.
3. Taxes levied by the Centre but shared with the Provinces or completely assigned to them.

The Act also provided for grants-in-aid from the Centre to the Provinces in need of assistance.

The main provisions of the Act of 1935 relating to the subject under study were as follows.

1. Agricultural income tax was included in the list of Provincial subjects.
2. Provision was made under Section 138 of the Act for the assignment to Provinces of a percentage of the net proceeds of taxes on income other than agricultural income.
3. Section 140 of the Act provided that duties on salt, Central duties of excise, and export duties, while levied and collected by the Centre would, if an Act of Central legislature so provided, be assigned wholly or in part to the Provinces.
4. Under Section 142 provision was made for the payment of grants-in-aid of the revenues of such Provinces as might be in need of assistance.
5. The Act also provided for the levy by Central legislation of duties in respect of succession to property other than agricultural land, stamp duties, terminal taxes on goods and passengers carried by railway or air and taxes on railway

fares and freights, and for the distribution of net proceeds to the Provinces.

2.7.12 Indian Financial Enquiry Report, 1936: Fiscal arrangements of the Act of 1935 left several questions to be decided and Sir Otto Niemeyer was appointed to make recommendations on matters which under Sections 138(1) and (2), 140(2) and 142 of the Act had to be prescribed or determined by Order-in-Council and on certain other ancillary matters. The scope of the enquiry was made comprehensive by a supplementary reference which enabled it to be extended to cover a review of the existing liabilities of the Provincial Governments to the Centre.

In respect of income tax, having regard to the dual considerations of the necessity of safeguarding the financial stability of the Centre and the obvious future needs of the Provinces, Sir Otto Niemeyer felt it was desirable that the maximum practicable distribution should be achieved. He recommended that 50 percent of the net proceeds of income tax should be assigned to the Provinces.

As regards the distribution of the provincial share, he expressed the view that the mere accident of place of collection was an unsuitable guide and that the residence of the individual though it might be a convenient practical dividing line for the avoidance of double taxation between separate political units, was not in itself a very scientific criterion, particularly in a federation. Even supposing it were practicable to ascertain to what part of the country particular fractions of income and the incidence of the taxation burden properly adhered, it was, he pointed out, still arguable that in a federation other considerations also were involved, particularly if the benefits and incidence of other forms of common taxation were unequally divided as between the various partners.

After a consideration of the various elements of the problem, he came to the conclusion that substantial justice would be done by fixing the scale of distribution partly on residence and partly on population. He recommended distribution among the Provinces according to the fixed percentages given in Table 2.4.

Sir Otto Niemeyer also recommended that the Centre should retain for the first 5 years out of the provincial money a sum equivalent to the amount by which the central share plus the contribution from Railways fell short of ₹ 13 crore a year and that the amount retained from the provincial share should be surrendered to the Provinces over a further period of 5 years. As part of the assistance he contemplated for the jute-growing Provinces, Sir Otto Niemeyer recommended that the provinces' share of the jute export duty be raised by 12.5 percent to 62.5 percent of the net proceeds of the duty.

In short, his main recommendations as contained in the Indian Financial Enquiry Report 1936 were the following.

Table 2.4: Distribution of Provinces' Share in Income Tax among the Provinces Recommended by Sir Otto Niemeyer

Province	**Percent**
Madras	15
Bombay	20
Bengal	20
United Provinces	15
Punjab	8
Bihar	10
Central Provinces	5
Assam	2
North-West Frontier Province	1
Orissa	2
Sind	2
Total	**100**

Source: *Report of the Finance Commission,* 1952, p. 20.

1. That 50 percent of the net proceeds of income tax should be assigned to the Provinces.
2. That the share of jute-growing Provinces in the jute export duty be raised by 12.5 percent to 62.5 percent of the net proceeds of the duty.
3. The outstanding debts (to the Centre) of Bengal, Bihar, Assam, North-West Frontier Province, and Orissa, contracted prior to April 1, 1936 be cancelled, and the outstanding debt of the Central Provinces be reduced.
4. Annual grants of varying amounts were also recommended for United Provinces, Assam, North-West Frontier Province, Orissa, and Sind (Table 2.5).

Table 2.5: Annual Grants to the Provinces Recommended by Sir Otto Niemeyer

(₹ lakh)

United Provinces	25 for a fixed period of 5 years
Assam	30
North-West Frontier Province	100 subject to consideration at the end of 5 years.
Orissa	40 with ₹ 7 lakh additional in the first and ₹ 3 lakh additional in each of the next 4 years.
Sind	105 for 10 years, with ₹ 5 lakh additional in the first year, and thereafter falling until the grant ceased in about 45 years time

Source: *Report of the Finance Commission,* 1952, p. 21.

The aforesaid recommendations were accepted by the authorities and embodied in the Government of India (Distribution of Revenues) Order, 1936. This Order, subject to a change made in 1940, continued to regulate the allocation of resources between the Centre and the units until the partition of the country in August 1947.

Following the outbreak of Second World War, and the increasing expenditure it entailed on the Centre, steps had to be taken to strengthen Central finances. It was decided that for the duration of the war, the Centre should be permitted to retain a fixed sum of ₹ 4.5 crore out of the provincial share of income tax. The Order-in-Council was amended accordingly to secure this and the modified provision regulated the distribution of the tax from 1940-41 to 1945-46. In each of the next 4 years the sum retained by the Centre from the provincial share was reduced by ₹ 75 lakh a year over the previous year, and the full provincial share was restored to the Provinces in 1950-51.

Endnotes

1. For historical details of income tax in India, see: (a) Government of India, *Report of the Indian Taxation Enquiry Committee* (President: Sir Charles Todhunter), 1924-25, chapter 9, pp. 189-191; (b) Government of India, *Income Tax Investigation Commission* (Chairman: Sir Srinivasa Varadachariar), 1947, pp. 1-4; (c) Government of India, Ministry of Finance, *Report of the Taxation Enquiry Commission* (Chairman: John Matthai), 1953-54, Volume II, chapter 1.
2. *Report of the Indian Taxation Enquiry Committee*, 1924-25, op. cit., Volume 1, para 259.
3. *Report of the Taxation Enquiry Commission,* 1953-54, op. cit., Volume II, chapter 1, p. 16.
4. Government of India, *Report of the Indian Taxation Enquiry Committee,* 1924-25, op. cit., Volume I, para 168.
5. One *anna* was equal to 1/16th of a rupee before the introduction of the metric system of currency from April l, 1957.
6. Government of India, *Report of the Indian Taxation Enquiry Committee*, 1924-25, op. cit., Volume I, para 155.
7. Government of India, Ministry of Finance, *Report of the Central Excise Reorganisation Committee* (Chairman: A.K. Chanda), 1963, p. 4.
8. D.T. Lakdawala and K.V. Nambiar, *Commodity Taxation in India* (Ahmedabad: Sardar Patel Institute of Economic and Social Research), 1972, p. 41.
9. Government of India, *Report of the Indian Fiscal Commission* (Chairman: Ibrahim Rahimatoola), 1921-22, p. 87.
10. K.T. Shah, *Sixty Years of Indian Finance* (London: P.S. King and Son Ltd., 1927), pp. 282-283.
11. Government of India, *Report of the Indian Taxation Enquiry Committee,* 1924-25, op. cit. Volume I, para l57.
12. Government of India, *Report of the Indian Fiscal Commission*, 1921-22, op. cit., pp. XV and XVI.
13. *Report of the Indian Taxation Enquiry Committee,* 1924-25, op. cit., para l52.

14. Government of India, *Report of the Indian States Enquiry Committee* (Financial), 1932 (Chairman: J.C.C. Davidson), para 240.
15. Walter Mahler, *Sales and Excise Taxation in India* (New Delhi: Orient Longman Ltd., 1970), p. 151.
16. It may be noted that Princely States enjoyed internal financial autonomy and therefore did not form part of the structure of public finances of British India. They had separate budgets and separate sources of revenue. After Independence, the former Princely States were integrated into the fiscal and financial system of the country.
17. Gyan Chand, *The Essentials of Federal Finance: A Contribution to the Problem of Financial Re-adjustment in India* (Humphrey Milford, Oxford University Press, 1930), p. 42.
18. Government of India, *Report of the Indian Taxation Enquiry Committee*, 1924-25, Volume I (President: Sir Charles Todhunter), p. 372.
19. *Report of the Fourth Finance Commission*, 1965, pp. 6-7.
20. Durga Das Basu, *Introduction to the Constitution of India* (New Delhi: Prentice-Hall of India Pvt. Ltd., 1987), p. 9.

Part II: Post-Independence Tax Policy

3

Constitutional Provisions Pertaining to Taxes

This chapter explains the complex nature of constitutional provisions pertaining to taxation powers of different tiers of government in India. The Constitution makes elaborate and complex arrangements relating to the distribution, between the Union and the States, of taxes, the power of borrowing, and provision for grants-in-aid by the Union to the States. The underlying philosophy of these arrangements is to place at the disposal of the two tiers of Government adequate financial resources to enable them to discharge their respective responsibilities under the Constitution.

3.1 Nature of Indian Federation

The Constitution of India adopted on November 26, 1949, became operative on January 26, 1950. It provides for two layers of Government, one at the Central level, and the other at the level of the States. A federal polity of this kind requires division of powers and responsibilities between the Centre and the States and generally brings in its wake problems and conflicts in Centre-State relations. Other important countries of the world with federal set up of government are: US, Canada, Australia, Brazil, and Nigeria.

Why did the framers of the Constitution opt for a federal set up? Answering this question, the Commission on Centre-State Relations, 1988, observed, "In a country too large and diverse for a unitary form of Government, they envisaged a system which would be worked in co-operation by the two levels of government —national and regional—as a common endeavour to serve the people. Such a system, it was conceived, would be most suited to Indian conditions as it would at once have the advantages of a strong unified central power, and the essential values of federalism". [1]

The very first Article of the Constitution defines India as a Union of States. Though the word federation has been deliberately avoided in the Indian Constitution, the fiscal structure created under it is essentially federal in nature.

The political system introduced by India's constitution possesses all the essentials of a federal polity.

India's constitution is the supreme organic law of our land. Both the Centre and State Governments derive their authority from the constitution. The States are not allowed to secede from the union.

There is a division of legislative, administrative and financial powers and functions between the Union and the State Governments. Under Article 246 read with Seventh Schedule of the Constitution, these powers and functions have been defined through precise entries in the three lists in the Schedule. Thus, the Centre has exclusive powers to legislate in respect of matters contained in List I (Union List) such as defence, foreign affairs, citizenship, railways, posts and telegraph, telephones, broadcasting, airways, banking, coinage and currency. Entries 82 to 92C of this list pertain to taxation powers. Similarly, the States enjoy the power to legislate on matters mentioned in List II (State List) such as public order, police, public health, local government, agriculture and fisheries. Entries 45 to 63 of this list relate to taxation powers of the States. The Parliament and the State Legislatures have concurrent powers to make laws on any matters in List III (Concurrent List). The framers of the Constitution recognised that there was a category of subjects of common interest which could not be allocated exclusively either to the Union or the States. Some of the items included in the Concurrent List are: marriage and divorce, forests, economic and social planning, population control and family planning, legal, medical, and other professions. This list does not contain any head of taxation which means the Centre and the States have no concurrent powers of taxation. Residuary powers of legislation including taxation belong to the Centre as per Entry 97 of List I.

The foregoing three-fold division of subjects of legislation rests on the ground that matters of national concern are placed in the Union List and those of purely State or local significance in the State List. Matters of common Centre-State interest are included in the Concurrent List.

The Supreme Court stands at the head of our judiciary to guard this distribution of powers and to invalidate any action which violates the limitations imposed by the Constitution.

According to Article 254 of the Constitution of India, if any provision of a State law is repugnant to any provision of a Central law, then the Central law shall prevail and the law made by the State shall be void to the extent of repugnancy.

The most common application of Article 254 arises when both the Central and State Governments enact legislation on the same matter contained in List III (Concurrent List) of the Seventh Schedule of the Constitution. In such a situation, if there is repugnancy then Central law prevails over the State law.

It is, of course, true that the Indian constitution has a strong Central bias. The financial powers of the Central Government are overwhelming. According to some scholars the constitution of India is neither purely federal nor purely unitary but is a combination of both. India's constitution is sometimes described as federal in times of peace and unitary in times of war.

3.2 Centrally Biased Constitution and its Justification

From its very inception, the Constitution is loaded in favour of the Centre. Constitutional amendments effected subsequently have tilted the balance further in favour of the Centre. The concept of a strong Centre has been incorporated in the anatomy of the Constitution through a variety of devices, among which the following are noteworthy.

3.2.1 Supremacy of Union Legislative Power: Article 246(2) and (3), and Article 254(1) establish the supremacy of Union legislative power. Thus, where with respect to a matter, there is irreconcilable conflict or overlapping as between the three lists of the Seventh Schedule, the legislative power of the States must yield to that of the Union. This is how the non-obstante provisions of clauses (1) and (2) of Article 246 are interpreted. Similarly, Article 254(1) states that a law made by a State legislature, repugnant to a law made by the Parliament or an existing law applicable in that State, in regard to any matter enumerated in the Concurrent List, shall be void to the extent of repugnancy.

3.2.2 Union Control over State Legislation: Articles 200 and 201 establish control of the Union executive over State legislation. Article 200 provides that a Bill passed by a State Legislature shall be presented to the Governor who may give his assent, withhold his assent or return the same for reconsideration by the legislature. However, if it is again passed by the State legislature, with or without amendment, he shall not withhold his assent. The Governor may also reserve the Bill for consideration of the President (in effect the Union Council of Ministers) who may in turn signify his assent, withhold the same or return it for reconsideration. However, in contrast to the position of the Governor, the President need not give his assent when such a Bill is returned with or without amendment after reconsideration by the legislature of the State (Article 201).

3.2.3 Emergency Provisions: Articles 352 and 360 provide for certain emergency provisions. Article 352 provides for proclamation by the President of a grave emergency whereby the security of India is threatened by war or external aggression or armed rebellion. When such a proclamation is in operation, the Union may assume for its organs all the legislative and executive powers of the States. A proclamation of emergency has the effect of converting the State List into Concurrent List and, therefore, if the Parliament legislates on any subject in the State List, the State laws, to the extent of repugnancy, shall be null and void and the law made by the Parliament shall prevail.

Article 360 envisages yet another type of emergency, i.e. financial emergency. If the President is satisfied that a situation has arisen whereby the financial stability or credit of India or of any part of its territory is threatened, he may proclaim a financial emergency. When such an emergency is in operation, the executive authority of the Union extends to directing any State for the purpose of securing observance of canons of financial propriety.

3.2.4 Restrictions on Taxation Powers of the States: Constitution also imposes certain restrictions on the taxation powers of the States. Although a State legislature enjoys the power to levy any of the taxes mentioned in List II, in the case of certain taxes, this power is subject to restrictions imposed by substantive provisions of the Constitution. Some examples of these restrictions are as follows.

1. The power to impose taxes on the sale or purchase of goods other than newspapers belongs to the States vide Entry 54 of List II. However, Article 286 ensures that sales taxes imposed by the States do not interfere with imports and exports or inter-State trade and commerce which are matters of national importance. In view of this, Article 286 places the following restrictions on the power of the States to enact sales tax legislation.

(a) No law of a State shall impose a tax on the sale or purchase of goods where such sale or purchase takes place: (i) outside the State; or (ii) in the course of import into or export out of the territory of India; (b) with regard to inter-State trade, there are two restrictions: (i) the power to tax sales taking place in the course of inter-State trade and commerce belongs to the Union vide Entry 92A of List I in the Seventh Schedule, and (ii) the sales tax on intrastate sales of *declared goods* (i.e. goods of special importance in inter-State trade) is subject to certain restrictions in terms of the nature of the levy and the rate of tax.

2. A State legislature is empowered to levy a tax on professions, trade, calling or employment vide Entry 60 of List II. However, the total amount payable in respect of any one person to the State by way of such tax is not to exceed ₹ 2,500 per annum [Article 276(2)].

3.2.5 Restrictions on Borrowing Powers of the States: Under Article 292 the executive power of the Centre extends to borrowing, either within or outside India, upon the security of the Consolidated Fund of India, within such limits, if any, as may from time to time be fixed by Parliament. However, the borrowing power of a State (Article 293) is subject to a number of restrictions: (i) it cannot borrow outside India; (ii) it can borrow within the territory of India subject to the following conditions: (a) limitations as may be imposed by the State Legislature, (b) consent of the Union Government to raise fresh loan if the Union has guaranteed an outstanding loan of the State, and (c) consent of the Union to raise fresh loan if a Union loan to the State remains outstanding. Since all the States are in debt to the Centre, they have to obtain Centre's permission for raising loans. These restrictions are meant to avoid uncontrolled borrowings by the States and thus to prevent the possibility of any State becoming defaulter or insolvent.

3.2.6 President's Rule: Lastly, there is the controversial Article 356. According to it, if the President on receipt of a report from the Governor of a State, or otherwise, is satisfied that a situation has arisen in which the Government of the State cannot be carried on in accordance with the provisions of the Constitution, he may by proclamation assume to himself all or any of the functions of the State Government. He may also declare that the powers of the Legislature of the State shall be exercised by or under the authority of the Parliament.

In view of the above provisions of the Constitution, some experts call it unitary in extraordinary situations, such as war (or emergency), and federal in normal times. It is also called as a quasi-federal Constitution.

Similarly, a scrutiny of the taxation powers contained in the Union List and the State List reveals that major and elastic sources of tax revenue belong to the Centre while relatively inelastic sources of revenue come under the purview of State Governments. Moreover, the Centre enjoys almost unlimited powers to borrow from internal and external sources while the borrowing powers of the States are subject to various restrictions.

Why is there a need for a strong Centre? According to the Commission on Centre-State Relations, 1988, "The primary lesson of India's history is that, in this vast country, only that polity or system can ensure and protect its unity, integrity and sovereignty against external aggression and internal disruption, which ensures a strong Centre with paramount powers, accommodating, at the same time, its traditional diversities. This lesson of history did not go unnoticed by the framers of the Constitution. Being aware that, notwithstanding the common cultural heritage, without political cohesion, the country would disintegrate under the pressure of fissiparous forces, they accorded the highest priority to the ensurance of the unity and integrity of the country". [2] Moreover, the founding fathers were aware that several regions or areas of India were economically and industrially far behind in relation to others, a situation which exists even today. Revenue-raising capacities and revenue needs of various States also differ. To reduce these economic disparities, a policy of regional balanced development was necessary, and which could be effectively implemented by a financially and otherwise strong Centre.

3.3 Constitutional Provisions Pertaining to Taxes

The Constitution makes elaborate and complex arrangements relating to the distribution, between the Union and the States, of taxes, the power of borrowing, and provision for grants-in-aid by the Union to the States. The underlying philosophy of these arrangements is to place at the disposal of the two tiers of Government adequate financial resources to enable them to discharge their respective responsibilities under the Constitution.

3.3.1 Distribution of Taxation Powers: Article 265 of the Constitution specifically states that no taxes shall be levied or collected except by the authority of law. Entries 82 to 92B of List I in the Seventh Schedule refer to the taxation powers of the Union Government (Table 3.1). Entries 45 to 63 of List II in the same Schedule specify the taxation powers of the State Governments (Table 3.2). List III does not contain any head of taxation which means the Union and the States have no concurrent powers of taxation. The absence of joint occupancy of tax fields is meant to avoid duplication in tax administration, and minimise tax rivalry between the Centre and the States, and among the States themselves. [3] The residual powers of taxation, as in general legislation, belong to the Union vide Entry 97 of List I in the Seventh Schedule. For example, gift tax (abolished in 1998) was imposed by the Union Government under these residual powers. Similarly, prior to the Constitution (Eighty-eighth Amendment) Act, 2003, service tax was imposed under these residual powers.

The Constitution does not provide for any taxation powers to local governments. However, the implication of Article 276 is that the taxes on professions, trades, callings or employment are for the benefit of a State or of a municipality, district board, local board or any other local authority. The States on their own may assign any of the taxes in the State List to the local bodies. The taxes generally assigned to local governments are property taxes, octroi, and taxes on vehicles.

The property of the Centre is exempt from State taxation under Article 285(1). Likewise, the property and incomes of the States are exempt from Union taxes [Article 289(1)], except that Parliament may by law provide for Central taxation of any trading activities of a State which are not incidental to the ordinary functions of Government [Article 289(2)]. As regards Union Territories, the Parliament has the power to impose any tax included in the State List.

3.3.2 Restrictions on the Taxation Powers of the States: see section 3.2.4 of this chapter.

3.3.3 Rationale for Constitutional Arrangements: Constitutional division of taxation powers between the Union and the States rests on economic and administrative considerations. Taxes with an inter-State base, and those in the case of which uniformity in rates is desirable, are vested in the Central Government. Also, taxes which the taxpayer can evade by shifting his habitat, or where the place of residence is not a correct guide to the true incidence of the tax, belong to the Centre. Taxes which are location-specific and relate to subjects of local consumption are with the States.

Table 3.1: Taxes within Union Jurisdiction as Enumerated in List I in the Seventh Schedule of the Constitution of India

S. No.	Entry No. in List I	Description of the Tax/Duty
1.	82	Taxes on income other than agricultural income.
2.	83	Duties of customs including export duties.
3.	84	Duties of excise except on alcoholic liquors and narcotics but including medicinal and toilet preparations containing alcohol.
4.	85	Corporation tax.
5.	86	Taxes on the capital value of assets, exclusive of agricultural land, of individuals.
6.	87	Estate duty in respect of property other than agricultural land.
7.	88	Duties in respect of succession to property other than agricultural land.
8.	89	Terminal taxes on goods and passengers carried by railway, sea or air; taxes on railway fares and freights.
9.	90	Taxes other than stamp duties on transactions in stock exchanges and future markets.
10.	91	Rates of stamp duty in respect of bills of exchange, cheques, promissory notes, bills of lading, letters of credit, policies of insurance, transfer of shares, debentures, proxies, and receipts.
11.	92	Taxes on the sale or purchase of newspapers and on advertisements published therein.
12.	92A*	Taxes on the sale or purchase of goods other than newspapers, where such sale or purchase takes place in the course of inter-State trade or commerce.
13.	92B**	Taxes on the consignment of goods (whether the consignment is to the person making it or to any other person), where such consignment takes place in the course of inter-State trade or commerce.
14.	92C***	Taxes on services.
15.	97	Any tax not enumerated in List II or List III of the Seventh Schedule.

* Inserted by the Constitution (Sixth Amendment) Act, 1956.
** Inserted by the Constitution (Forty-sixth Amendment) Act, 1982.
*** Inserted by the Constitution (Eighty-eighth Amendment) Act, 2003.
Source: Government of India, Ministry of Law, Justice and Company Affairs, *The Constitution of India,* Seventh Schedule, List I.

Table 3.2: Taxes within State Jurisdiction as Enumerated in List II in the Seventh Schedule of the Constitution of India

S. No.	Entry No. in List II	Description of the Tax/Duty
1.	45	Land revenue.
2.	46	Taxes on agricultural income.
3.	47	Duties in respect of succession to agricultural land.
4.	48	Estate duty in respect of agricultural land.
5.	49	Taxes on lands and buildings.
6.	50	Taxes on mineral rights subject to any limitations imposed by Parliament by law relating to mineral development.
7.	51	Duties of excise on alcoholic liquors and narcotics manufactured or produced in the State but not including medicinal and toilet preparations containing alcohol.
8.	52	Taxes on the entry of goods into a local area for consumption, use or sale therein.
9.	53	Taxes on the consumption or sale of electricity.
10.	54*	Taxes on the sale or purchase of goods other than newspapers, subject to the provisions of Entry 92A of List I.
11.	55**	Taxes on advertisements other than advertisements published in the newspapers (and advertisements broadcast by radio or television).
12.	56	Taxes on goods and passengers carried by road or on inland waterways.
13.	57	Taxes on vehicles, whether mechanically propelled or not, suitable for use on roads, including tram-cars subject to the provisions of Entry 35 of List III.
14.	58	Taxes on animals and boats.
15.	59	Tolls.
16.	60***	Taxes on professions, trades, callings and employment.
17.	61	Capitation taxes.
18.	62	Taxes on luxuries, including taxes on entertainment, amusements, betting and gambling.
19.	63	Rates of stamp duty in respect of documents other than those specified in the provisions of List I with regard to rates of stamp duty.

*Substituted by the Constitution (Sixth Amendment) Act, 1956: ** The words 'and advertisements broadcast by radio or television' inserted by the Constitution (Forty-second Amendment), Act, 1976: *** The scope of these taxes is spelt out in Article 276, the clause (2) of which fixes the amount payable by a person on account of these taxes.

Source: Government of India, Ministry of Law, Justice and Company Affairs, *The Constitution of India*, Seventh Schedule, List II.

Broadly speaking, taxes on production, with some exceptions, are levied by the Centre, and taxes on sales by the State Governments. The distribution of taxation powers between the Centre and the States is meant to minimise tax problems in a federal set up such as double taxation, tax rivalry among States, duplicate tax administration, and tax evasion.

Commenting upon the soundness of the constitutional arrangements regarding division of taxation powers, the Commission on Centre-State Relations, 1988, observed, "A well balanced distribution of heads of taxation based on economic and administrative rationale between the Union and the States and adequate arrangements for sharing of resources is vital for the proper functioning of the two-tier polity. We are of the firm view that the basic scheme of the Constitution dividing the field of taxation between the Union and the States and incorporating adequate arrangements for sharing of resources between them, is sound and no major modifications in it are called for". [4]

Similarly, the Sixth Finance Commission made the following observations in this regard, "We must bear in mind that the country as a whole and every part thereof has gained significantly from the maintenance of a vast unified market within which there is free movement of goods and men. Having regard to the trends all over the world even for independent political entities to come together to forge closer economic links in the form of common markets and economic groupings, our best hopes of accelerated economic development lie in the further strengthening of our national market and in the promotion of fiscal arrangements that are most conducive to the effective functioning of this market. Given this basic fact, there can be no room for argument that the levy and administration of taxes with wide economic base such as income tax, corporation tax, Union excise duties and of course also import and export duties will have to remain with the Union Government. In fact the architects of our Constitution drew on the experience of some of the other federations in which the assignment of taxes with wide economic base to units had led to intractable problems of conflicting tax jurisdictions. They wisely averted the possibility of such conflicts by assigning such taxes right from the beginning to the Union Government. At the same time, the framers of our Constitution rightly allocated to the States' subjects such as agriculture, education, medical care, public health, irrigation and law and order that touch intimately the lives of the people. These can be efficiently administered in a vast country only by the State Governments which are closer to the people and are more keenly alive to their problems and needs. The heads of revenue and responsibilities were distributed on the basis of whether the Centre or the State was better equipped to deal with the particular head". [5]

3.3.4 Sharing of Central Taxes: Although the taxation powers allocated to the Union and the States are mutually exclusive, all the taxes and duties levied by the Union are not meant entirely for the purpose of the Union. Revenues from certain taxes and duties leviable by the Union are totally assigned to or shared with the States to supplement their revenues in accordance with their needs. It is a tribute to the foresight of the founding fathers that they realised that the sources of revenue allocated to the States may not prove sufficient in view of their growing welfare, maintenance, and developmental activities. Hence, specific provisions were made to set apart a portion of Central revenues for the benefit of States. These provisions indicate the flexibility of India's Constitution in terms of distribution of financial resources between different layers of the Government. They also make a distinction between the legislative power to *levy* a tax and the power to *appropriate* the proceeds of a tax so levied.

Prior to the Eightieth Amendment of the Constitution, two main Central taxes were shared with the states, namely income tax other than corporation tax and the Union excise duties. The sharing of the income tax was mandatory under Article 270 while that of the Union excise duties was discretionary under Article 272. There were also two tax rental arrangements with the States, where the Union Government collected the tax on behalf of the States and then distributed the proceeds among the States on the basis of criteria recommended by the Finance Commission. These were: (i) additional duties of excise in lieu of sales tax on textiles, tobacco and sugar, and (ii) grant in lieu of tax on railway passenger fares.

The Constitution (Eightieth Amendment) Act, 2000, significantly changed the manner of distribution of Central tax collections between the Central and State Governments. Following this amendment, all central taxes were brought into a shareable pool and it became mandatory to assign a share from each central tax to the States. The amended article 270 provided for the sharing of all central taxes except taxes under Articles 268 and 269, earmarked cesses, and surcharges under Article 271. Only *net proceeds* are to be shared, and as such *cost of collection* has to be deducted to obtain the net proceeds as prescribed under Article 279. The proceeds are to be distributed among the States where the central taxes are *leviable* in *that year*. Article 269 was also amended and it now contains only central sales tax and consignment tax, which is not levied.

The objective of the Constitution (Eightieth Amendment) Act, 2000 was to construct a pool of all central taxes for sharing so that a holistic view can be taken and both sides could share in the aggregate buoyancy of the central tax revenues.

Furthermore, Constitution (Eighty-eighth Amendment) Act, 2003 placed service tax under the Union List in the Seventh Schedule and was brought under the purview of Article 268A which provides as follows:

"(1) Taxes on services shall be levied by the Government of India and such tax shall be collected and appropriated by the Government of India and the States in the manner provided in clause (2).

(2) The proceeds in any financial year of any such tax levied in accordance with the provisions of clause (1) shall be:

(a) collected by the Government of India and the States; and

(b) appropriated by the Government of India and the States;

in accordance with such principles of collection and appropriation as may be formulated by Parliament by law".

Thus, Article 268A specifies that the principles of collection and appropriation of taxes on services will be determined by Parliament. Prior to Eighty-eighth Amendment, the Central Government levied the service tax on specific services under its residual powers (vide Entry 97 of List I in the Seventh Schedule). The sharing of this revenue was on the basis of the recommendations of the Finance Commission, as applicable to other central taxes. However, revenue from taxation of services which are taxed by the centre under Article 268A rather than under Article 270 is now excluded from the purview of the Finance Commission.

In this connection, the Twelfth Finance Commission remarked, "With service taxes having been excluded from the ambit of the recommendations of the finance commission, the idea of an overall shareable pool of central taxes appears to be in the process of being reversed. While service taxes are likely to prove highly buoyant in the near future, these will not be subjected to sharing with the states under the Constitution, although other statutory arrangements can be made, which can include sharing as well as assignment. It may be noted that hitherto items under Articles 268 and 269 were subjects that were generally of inter-state nature with limited revenue importance. These were wholly assigned to the states. In this context, it needs to be stressed that any legislation passed by Parliament with respect to appropriation of service tax proceeds must take care to ensure that the revenue accruing to the states through any proposed changes should not be less than the share that would accrue to them, had the entire service tax proceeds been part of the shareable pool". [6]

After the Constitution (Eighty-eighth Amendment) Act, 2003, the Central taxes can be classified into the following categories.

1. **Duties Levied by the Union but Collected and Appropriated by the States (Article 268):** These include duties of excise on medicinal and toilet preparations containing alcohol, and stamp duties on bills of exchange etc. as mentioned in Entries 84 and 91 of the Union List respectively.

2. **Service Tax Levied by the Union and Collected and Appropriated by the Union and the States (Article 268A).** This is self-explanatory.
3. **Taxes Levied and Collected by the Union but Assigned to the States (Article 269):** These are: taxes on the sale or purchase of goods other than newspapers, where such sale or purchase takes place in the course of inter-State trade or commerce, and taxes on the consignment of goods (whether the consignment is to the person making it or to any other person), where such consignment takes place in the course of inter-State trade or commerce. These taxes correspond to Entries 92A and 92B in the Union List. [7]
4. **Taxes Levied and Distributed Between the Union and the States (Article 270):** All taxes and duties referred to in the Union List shall be levied and collected by the Government of India and shall be distributed between the Union and the States with the following exceptions: (a) duties and taxes referred to in Articles 268 and 269, (b) surcharge on taxes and duties referred to in Article 271, and (c) any cess levied for specific purposes under any law made by the Parliament.

3.3.5 Philosophy of Articles 268 and 269: Taxation arrangements under Articles 268 and 269 of the Constitution are of special importance. They place under the charge of the Union the taxes and duties which have inter-State character and require uniformity in rate structure for the smooth conduct of business and trade activities throughout the country. These two Articles mention taxes/duties which shall be levied by the Centre but assigned completely to the States within which they are leviable.

A. Duties under Article 268: Article 268 mentions duties which shall be levied by the Union but collected and appropriated by the States within which they are leviable. These are duties of excise on medicinal and toilet preparations containing alcohol, and stamp duties, and correspond respectively to Entries 84 and 91 of the Union List with corresponding qualification of Entry 51 of the State List in the Seventh Schedule of the Constitution. The Eighth Finance Commission was asked for the first time to examine the scope for enhancing revenues from these duties.

Duties on medicinal and toilet preparations are imposed under the Medicinal and Toilet Preparations (Excise Duties) Act, 1955. It includes a range of medicinal items which are important from the viewpoint of public health policy. They have inter-State significance and therefore uniformity in regard to taxation is in larger national interest. Since the rates of duty on these preparations were increased in 1982 (the year in which the Commission was constituted), the Commission did not find any scope for enhancing this duty at that time.

Stamp duties are leviable on bills of exchange, cheques, promissory notes, bills of lading, letters of credit, policies of insurance, transfer of shares, debentures, proxies, and receipts. These documents are executed in the course of business and trade and they find place in the Union List to ensure uniformity of rates throughout the country for the smooth conduct of commercial and related transactions. Inter-State disparities in their rates and tax regulations can hinder, and even disrupt, the free flow of trade and commercial activities. The levy and collection of stamp duty is governed by the Indian Stamp Duty Act, 1899 which was last amended in 1976 when rates of stamp duty on certain instruments were revised.

After ascertaining the views of States and other relevant agencies, the Eighth Finance Commission did not think it desirable to raise the rates of stamp duty on bills of exchange, promissory notes, life insurance policies, transfer of shares, debentures, proxies, and receipts. Raising duty on these instruments was considered to be detrimental to the growth of trade and industry. The Commission also disfavoured re-imposition of stamp duty on cheques. [8] However, the Commission opined that scope for raising the rates of duty exists in respect of bills of lading, letters of credit, and policies of general insurance.

B. Taxes and Duties under Article 269: Article 269 mentions taxes which shall be levied and collected by the Union but assigned completely to the States, in which they are leviable. These taxes are: (a) taxes on the sale or purchase of goods other than newspapers, where such sale or purchase takes place in the course of inter-State trade or commerce, and (b) taxes on the consignment of goods where such consignment takes place in the course of inter-State trade or commerce. These taxes correspond to Entries 92A and 92B in the Union List in the Seventh Schedule of the Constitution. It is noteworthy that out of these two taxes only one is being levied at present, viz. inter-State sales tax (Entry 92A).

3.3.6 Taxes and Duties in the Union List not being Levied at Present: These taxes/duties are discussed below individually along with the logic for retaining them with the Centre.

A. Entries 87 and 88: These two entries pertain to estate duty, and succession duty in respect of property other than agricultural land respectively. Since the incidence of both estate duty, and succession duty is on the same object, viz. property passing on the death of the owner to his successors, they are essentially similar in nature. However, while in the case of the estate duty, the value of the whole estate, even if situated in more than one State, is the base for taxation, the succession duty is relatable to the value of individual shares (i.e. parts of an estate) passing on to the successors.

The desirability of retaining both these duties with the Centre is self-evident. An individual may have properties located in more than one State and a total assessment of his estate can better be undertaken by the Union Government.

Similarly, if succession duty is levied by the States, the persons inheriting properties in different States will have to deal with different tax rates and procedures. Moreover, if estate/succession duties are levied by the States, it may trigger unhealthy competition among the States, resulting into harassment of the assessees and hence litigation. On efficiency criterion (i.e. cost of collection) also it is desirable if these duties are levied and administered by the Union, thus avoiding duplication of tax administration. Moreover, the Union has better access to information and otherwise also it is in larger national interest to ensure uniformity with respect to these duties. It may be noted that estate duty was first imposed in India in 1953 when the Estate Duty Act of that year imposed a duty on the capital value of all property passing on the death of any person on or after October 15, 1953. It was abolished with effect from March 16, 1985.

B. Entry 89: It relates to terminal taxes on goods and passengers carried by railway, sea or air. However, by virtue of entry 52 of List II, States are competent to impose octroi (terminal tax) on Entry of goods into a local area for consumption, use or sale. Likewise, under Entry 56 of List II, States are empowered to levy taxes on goods and passengers carried by road or on inland waterways. Thus, the taxation powers in regard to the services of the major means of transport rest with the Union.

In a developing and diversifying economy like India, the importance of transport sector is self-evident. The growth of this vital infrastructure enlarges the size of the market and determines, *inter alia*, the level of private enterprise. Lest the free flow of inter-State trade should be hampered by differential State levies, the taxation of transport services is, by and large, with the Union Government. The Fifth and the Eighth Finance Commissions examined the scope for levying these taxes but expressed themselves against their imposition on grounds of administrative difficulties and meagre revenue potential. It is noteworthy that there already exists a terminal tax on passengers carried by railway from or to certain places of pilgrimage or where fairs or exhibitions are held. The proceeds of the tax are credited to the Consolidated Fund of the concerned States. The tax is restrictive and limited in scope and not a general terminal tax on passengers carried by railways to all places.

Entry 89 also refers to taxes on railway fares and freights. The Eighth Finance Commission favoured levying tax on railway passenger fares but not until the present arrangement of giving grants in lieu of such a tax continues to exist.

C. Entry 90: It pertains to 'taxes other than stamp duties on transactions in stock exchanges and future markets'. Since stock exchanges and future markets [9] are at a formative stage and have an inter-State character therefore it is desirable to retain these taxes with the Union. The Eighth Finance Commission did not think it advisable to levy taxes on transactions in stock exchanges and future markets.

D. Entry 92: It refers to 'taxes on the sale or purchase of newspapers and on advertisements published therein'. This tax is retained with the Union to protect the freedom of the press, and avoid undue tax burden on newspaper industry, particularly the regional language newspapers. Since newspaper reading habit is not sufficiently developed and widespread in the country, it is not desirable to impose a tax on the sale or purchase of newspapers.

Both the Fifth and the Eighth Finance Commissions did not recommend a tax on the sale or purchase of newspapers. However, both the Commissions opined that there was scope for tax on advertisements published in newspapers. The Eighth Commission cautioned that a tax on advertisement, if levied, should be borne by the advertisers themselves and not passed on to the newspapers and journals.

3.3.7 Freedom as to Payment of Taxes for Promotion of any Particular Religion: According to Article 27 of the Constitution of India, "No person shall be compelled to pay any taxes, the proceeds of which are specifically appropriated in payment of expenses for the promotion or maintenance of any particular religion or religious denomination".

Endnotes

1. Government of India, *Report of the Commission on Centre-State Relations* (Chairman: Justice R. S. Sarkaria) Part I, 1988, p. 8.
2. *Ibid.*, p. 7.
3. Concurrent taxation powers are a characteristic feature of federal set up in USA, Canada, and Australia. Most tax fields in these countries are jointly occupied by the federal and provincial governments. The overlapping taxation powers have often caused frictions not only between the federal and provincial governments but also among the provinces *inter se.* Tax problems owing to joint occupancy of tax fields are solved through tax rental and tax sharing negotiations and agreements.
4. *Report of the Commission on Centre-State Relations*, Part I, 1988, op. cit., p. 271.
5. *Report of the Sixth Finance Commission*, 1973, p. 5.
6. Report of the Twelfth Finance Commission (2005-10), November 2004, pp. 15-16.
7. Prior to the Eightieth Amendment of the Constitution, provisions of Article 269 were as follows.

   Taxes Levied and Collected by the Union but Assigned to the States (Article 269): These were: (a) duties in respect of succession to property other than agricultural land, (b) estate duty in respect of property other than agricultural land, (c) terminal taxes on goods or passengers carried by railway, sea or air, (d) taxes on railway fares and freights, (e) taxes other than stamp duties on transactions in stock exchanges and future markets, (f) taxes on the sale or purchase of newspapers and on advertisements published therein, (g) taxes on the sale or purchase of goods other than newspapers, where such sale or purchase takes place in the course of inter-State trade or commerce, and (h) taxes on the consignment of goods (whether the consignment is to the person making it or to any other person), where such consignment takes place in the course of inter-State trade or commerce. These taxes corresponded to Entries 87, 88, 89, 90, 92, 92A and 92B in the Union List.

8. Stamp duty was payable on cheques prior to 1927 but was withdrawn in that year.
9. Future trading refers to contracts for sale and purchase of goods at a future date primarily with a view to avoid price fluctuations. Presently, future trading is allowed at specific centres in respect of four commodities, viz. jute products, paper, turmeric, and *gur*.

4

Socio-economic Objectives of Tax Policy

The Indian tax system has undergone major structural changes since Independence in 1947. It has become comprehensive and complicated over the years. It has successfully mobilised resources to finance administrative, welfare and developmental activities of public authorities. Besides being the main source of revenue, both for the Central and State Governments, it is an effective instrument to realise various socio-economic objectives of national policies. Restructuring of the tax system has constituted a major component of fiscal reforms initiated since 1991. The main focus of the tax reforms has been on simplification and rationalisation of both direct and indirect taxes with the objective of augmenting revenues and removing anomalies in the tax structure. Tax reforms of recent years have brought the tax system much closer to international tax practices.

Furthermore, tax policy—as an integral part of the fiscal policy of a country—is an important determinant of the investment climate in a country. Rates of direct taxes determine the incentives to work, save and invest, while the level and structure of indirect taxes influences the aggregate demand and thus the scale of operations on the one hand and relative prices of different goods and services on the other. Concerted efforts to simplify the tax system, moderate tax rates and avoid cascading of taxes have improved the investment climate in India.

Tax laws in India are replete with various exemptions, concessions, deductions, allowances, tax credits etc. to promote a host of desirable economic and social activities. These tax incentives [1] encourage individuals and business entities to undertake activities desired by the government.

4.1 Health, Education and Housing

4.1.1 Health: Improvement in the health status of the population has been one of the major thrust areas in social development programmes of India since Independence. Over the past six decades, India has built up a vast health infrastructure and manpower at primary, secondary and tertiary care levels in the government, voluntary and private sectors manned by professionals and para-medicals. India has invested massive amounts under the successive Five Year Plans in medical education, training and research which has ensured large manpower from the super-specialists to the auxiliary midwives.

Income Tax Act, 1961 allows deductions from gross total income in respect of the following: (a) deduction in respect of medical insurance premia (Section 80D), (b) deduction in respect of medical treatment and deposit made for maintenance of handicapped dependents (Section 80DD), and (c) deduction in respect of medical treatment (Section 80DDB).

4.1.2 Education: Education has been a thrust sector ever since India attained Independence in 1947. Right from the inception of planning, the crucial role of education in economic and social development has been recognised and emphasised. Efforts to increase people's participation in education and to diversify educational programmes in order to promote knowledge and skills required for nation-building have characterised successive Five Year Plans. Despite a series of problems that the country faced soon after Independence, it has been possible to create a vast educational infrastructure in terms of large enrolments and teaching force and massive capabilities for management, research and development.

Under Section 80E of the Income Tax Act, 1961, deduction from gross total income is allowed in respect of interest on loans taken for higher education.

4.1.3 Housing: Housing is an activity that is typically labour intensive and, therefore, fits in well with the pattern of development envisaged for India. The provision of shelter is a basic need which must be met. Housing construction also creates much-needed employment for the unskilled and, therefore, income for the relatively poor.

Income Tax Act, 1961 allows deduction from gross total income in respect of home loan repayment (Section 80C) and in respect of interest on loan taken for residential house property (Section 80EE).

4.2 Tax Holiday Schemes

These schemes of the Indian Income Tax Act exempt certain incomes from the purview of income tax for specified periods of time.

For details, see section 12.3.4 of chapter 12 of this book.

4.3 Tax Incentives for Infrastructure Development

4.3.1 Justification: The magnitude of resources needed for the infrastructure sector is of such dimensions that the requisite investments would need to be funded eventually by raising resources from the domestic and international capital markets. In the initial stages, support from the financial institutions and commercial banks could be relied upon to a degree. However, there is clearly a limit to the extent of resources that could be accessed through the existing financial system.

In a liberalised economic regime, it is inevitable that all sectors would need to compete for capital. It is only those sectors that provide attractive rates of return that would eventually be successful in this resource-raising exercise. Projects in the infrastructure sector would need to compete for resources from the capital market and be perceived by investors as being as attractive as conventional manufacturing projects. It is, thus, desirable that such projects be brought to the centre stage of capital market flows to attract investments from a wider pool of lenders, including financial institutions, the corporate sector and in the medium term, retail investors.

Initial encouragement is needed from the Government to induce a sectoral flow of savings to the infrastructure sector. Once the initial clutch of projects of this genre is established successfully on commercial principles, fiscal benefits may no longer be needed to the same degree.

It can be demonstrated that the economic rate of returns from infrastructure projects is well in excess of the financial rate of returns. The higher economic rates of return stem from monetary as well as social factors including reduction in pollution levels, savings in time, and the ancillary economic activities that such projects generate.

The case for attracting FDI is significantly strengthened through the provision of an adequate level of infrastructure. There is thus adequate economic rationale for encouraging the sponsorship of infrastructure projects and to facilitate investments in this sector.

The commercialisation of infrastructure projects is typically formulated on the basis of recovery of investments through a system of user charges. Such user charges bear a direct relation to the specific benefits that the facility provides to the user. For example, a toll road would provide the user savings in terms of time, fuel, vehicular maintenance etc. The user would then compare the user charge to the benefits and savings realised. The level of user charges does not encompass the secondary and tertiary levels of economic benefits stemming from the implementation of the project and which flow to society at large. Typically, such benefits are a multiple of project cost. These externalities arise without government contributing to project expenditure.

To this extent, it can be argued that the provision of fiscal benefits is not a subsidy, but a contribution from government that is supported by benefits accruing from the externalities of the project. In the absence of such contribution, the private investment flows may not take place at all. Thus, such fiscal benefits have the effect of mobilising private resources in the financing of projects.

The fundamental premise of commercialisation is a shift of the burden of funding from government to a structure where public savings are channelised to create infrastructure facilities. Significant growth in the Indian capital market and the appetite of investors for financial assets received a fillip after specified fiscal incentives were provided by government for investments in the shares of newly promoted companies. Public savings were thus channelised towards the creation of productive capacities. A similar initiative is needed today from government to create a shift in savings towards investment in infrastructure.

Infrastructure projects in the targeted sectors are not readily amenable to attracting public savings. Typically, these projects have a long gestation period and are not readily understood by retail and other investors. Hence, there is a need to position such investments as an attractive option vis-à-vis other competing opportunities. An investor today needs an inducement to shift a part of his portfolio from conventional projects to projects in the targeted sections. There is hence a need to consider the provision of specific fiscal benefits to infrastructure projects that are deemed to be of public interest.

Once a project is defined to an adequate degree, an array of fiscal benefits could be considered on a project-specific basis. The array of benefits could be defined under four generic heads:

1. Tax-free status for the project entity.
2. Benefits to the sponsor.
3. Benefits to the wholesale investor.
4. Benefits to the retail investor.

4.3.2 Income Tax Incentives under Section 80-IA: Section 80-IA of Income Tax Act, 1961 provides for deduction from profits and gains of industrial undertakings/enterprises engaged in infrastructure development. The deduction is available to the following:

1. An enterprise owned by a company or consortium of companies or by an authority or a board or a corporation or any other statutory body, carrying on the business of: (i) developing, (ii) operating and maintaining, or (iii) developing, operating and maintaining, any infrastructure facility under an agreement with the Central/State Government or a local authority etc. which starts operating and maintaining the infrastructure facility on or after April 1, 1995. Infrastructure facility means the following: (a) a road including toll road, a bridge or a rail system, (b) a highway project including housing or other activities being an integral part of the highway project, (c) a water supply project, water treatment system, irrigation project, sanitation and sewerage system or solid waste management system, and (d) a port, airport, inland waterways or inland port or navigational channel in the sea.
2. An undertaking which starts providing telecommunication services (basic or cellular), including radio paging, domestic satellite services or network of

trunking and electronic data interchange services, during April 1, 1995 to March 31, 2005.

3. (a) An undertaking which develops or develops and operates or maintains and operates an industrial park notified by the Ministry of Commerce and Industry, during April 1, 1997 to March 31, 2011. (b) An undertaking which develops, develops and operates, or maintains and operates a special economic zone notified by the Government for the period April 1, 1997 to March 31, 2006.
4. An undertaking set up in any part of India for the generation, or generation and distribution of power, which begins to generate power during April 1, 1993 to March 31, 2014.
5. An undertaking which starts transmission or distribution by laying a network of new transmission or distribution lines, during April 1, 1999 to March 31, 2014.
6. An undertaking which undertakes substantial renovation and modernization of the existing network of transmission or distribution lines, during April1, 2004 to March 31, 2014.
7. An undertaking owned by an Indian company (formed before November 30, 2005 and notified before December 31, 2005) and set up for reconstruction or revival of a power generating plant, which begins to generate or transmit or distribute power before March 31, 2011.

Amount of Deduction: The deduction is allowable for 10 consecutive assessment years (A.Ys) as under:

(i) In the case of an undertaking providing telecommunication services
For the initial 5 A.Ys : 100 percent of the profits and gains
For the next 5 A.Ys: 30 percent of the profits and gains

(ii) In the case of other eligible undertakings and enterprises.
For 10 consecutive A.Ys: 100 percent of the profits and gains

The assessee may opt for any 10 consecutive years out of 15 years beginning with the year in which the undertaking starts the eligible activity.

In the case of an enterprise providing an infrastructure facility (except a port, airport, inland waterways, inland port or navigational channel in the sea), the assessee may opt for any 10 consecutive years out of 20 years beginning with the year in which it begins providing such infrastructure facility.

Experts have recommended several changes to be made in Section 80-IA which are crucial to the commercialisation of the country's infrastructure services.

1. The Section gives a restricted meaning to 'infrastructure facility' covering infrastructure relating to transport, such as surface transport, air, waterways

and rail. Infrastructure, however, includes other services such as land area development, establishment of township, water and sewerage systems, social welfare like education and healthcare. These sectors have not been included in the definition. Therefore, the scope of infrastructure facility should be expanded to include all these sectors.

2. The Section also specifies that the infrastructure facility should be *new*. Accordingly, it may not include projects which involve remaking or expansion. Most infrastructure projects would involve acquisition of existing facility to meet the increased demands, e.g. a surface transport project could involve remaking the existing road and extending or converting two lanes into four lanes. Similarly, water and sewerage projects could involve taking over the existing distribution system or treatment facilities and building additional facilities to augment increased requirements. In most cases, it is necessary to capture revenues from existing facilities to make the expansion viable. Hence, the scope of definition should be extended to include projects involving expansion or remaking of existing facilities.
3. The Section requires the infrastructure facility to be owned by an enterprise. In many infrastructure projects, it may not be feasible to own all the facilities. As a financing strategy some of the equipment may be procured under a leasing or other financing arrangement. It is, therefore, necessary to clarify that the scope of this section extends to include cases where part of the infrastructure facility is procured under a lease or any other financing arrangement.
4. The benefits under the Section are available only to enterprises owned by a company—or a consortium of companies—incorporated in India. Given the nature of infrastructure projects, it would be necessary to have access to technological and financial participation from international sources. It is therefore necessary to extend the benefits to all enterprises including those where majority of shareholding is held by foreign companies.
5. In most infrastructure projects, it would be necessary to consider the grant of rights from the government to develop ancillary facilities such as land for building townships, developing adjacent areas or operating utilities like petrol pumps, restaurants etc. The current meaning of Section 80-IA defines tax holiday on profits derived from infrastructure business. Accordingly, the revenue authorities could argue that revenues or profits derived from such ancillary development are not eligible for tax holiday. However, in that case, the project would not be in a position to claim the tax holiday benefit on income purely derived from the user charges of infrastructure facilities because these revenues will not generate significant profits. A clarification

should be provided in Section 80IA stating that the entire project income inclusive of income from any ancillary development will qualify for tax holiday benefit.

4.3.3 Tax-free Bonds: In order to facilitate the creation of urban infrastructure, the Finance Minister in his 2007-08 budget speech allowed the issue of tax-free bonds through State Pooled Finance Entities formed for raising funds for a group of urban local bodies.

4.4 Tax Concessions for Labour Welfare

4.4.1 Income Tax Concessions: The Indian Income Tax Act, 1961, provides various incentives for promoting labour welfare activities. Section 10 of the Act describes incomes which are absolutely exempt from the purview of income tax, i.e. tax free incomes. These exemptions are meant to serve various socio-economic objectives through the medium of tax policy. The important types of income altogether excluded from the scope of tax under various clauses of Section 10 of the Act and which have bearing on labour welfare are the following.

A. Leave Travel Concession: Value of any leave travel concession or assistance received by an employee from the employer for himself and his family in connection with his proceeding on leave to any place in India is exempt from tax [Section 10(5)]. For the purpose of this section, 'family' in relation to an individual means: (a) the spouse and children of the individual, and (b) the parents, brothers and sisters of the individual dependent on him. Furthermore, the amount exempt under this section can in no case exceed the expenditure actually incurred for the purpose of such travel.

B. Death-cum-Retirement Gratuity: Exemption from tax is available to gratuity payments up to the following prescribed limits [Section 10(10)].

1. In the case of Government employees, any death-cum-retirement gratuity received by Government employees is wholly exempt from tax. Government employees mean employees of Central Government, State Governments, and Local Authorities.
2. In the case of employees covered by the payment of Gratuity Act, 1972, any gratuity received by an employee is exempt from tax to the extent of the least of the following: (a) 15 days salary (based on salary last drawn) for every completed year of service or part thereof in excess of six months, (b) ₹ 1,00,000 or (c) gratuity actually received.
3. In the case of any other employee, any gratuity received by him is exempt from tax to the extent of the least of the following: (a) ₹ 10 lakh, (b) half month's salary for each completed year of service, or (c) gratuity actually received.

C. Commutation of Pension: Pension received by a Government employee as well as non-Government employee is taxable as salary under Section 15 of the Act. However, any commuted pension received by a Government employee is wholly exempt from tax under Section 10(10). In the case of payment in commutation of pension received by a non-Government employee, the following provisions apply: (a) where the employee receives gratuity, the commuted value of one-third of the pension is exempt from tax, and (b) in any other case, the commuted value of one-half of such pension is exempt from tax. It may be noted that pension is a periodic payment received by an employee after his retirement while commuted pension is a lump sum payment in lieu of periodic pension payment.

D. Leave Salary: Under Section 10(10AA), any amount received by an employee of Central/State Government as the cash equivalent of leave salary in respect of period of earned leave at his credit at the time of his retirement is exempt from tax. In the case of a non-Government employee, leave salary is exempt from tax to the extent of the least of the following: (a) cash equivalent of the leave salary in respect of the period of earned leave to the credit of employee at the time of his retirement or (b) eight month's average salary or (c) the amount specified by the Government (₹ 2,40,000 if the date of retirement is on or after July 1, 1997), or (d) leave encashment actually received at the time of retirement.

E. Retrenchment Compensation: Under Section 10(10B), compensation received by a workman at the time of retrenchment is exempt from tax to the extent of the lower of the following: (a) An amount calculated in accordance with the provisions of Section 25F (b) of the Industrial Disputes Act, 1947 (these provisions entitle a workman to retrenchment compensation equal to 15 days average pay for every completed year of service or any part thereof in excess of six months), or (b) such amount (not being less than ₹ 5,00,000) as notified by the Government.

F. Voluntary Retirement Compensation: Under Section 10(10C), compensation received by an employee at the time of voluntary retirement is exempt from tax subject to certain conditions.

G. Income of Fund Established for Welfare of Employees: Section 10(23AAA) provides exemption from tax on any income received by any person on behalf of a fund established for the welfare of employees or their dependents and of which fund such employees are members.

H. Income of Trade Unions: Under Section 10(24), any income chargeable under the heads *income from house property* and *income from other sources* of a trade union is exempt from tax. The trade union must be registered under the Indian Trade Union Act, 1926 formed primarily for the purpose of regulating the relations between workmen and employers. Similarly, tax exemption is available to an association of trade unions.

I. Health Insurance of Employees: Under Section 36(1), an employer can claim deduction in respect of premia paid by him by cheque for insurance on the health of his employees.

J. Bonus to Employees: Under Section 36(1), bonus or commission paid to an employee is allowable as deduction subject to certain conditions.

K. Employer's Contribution to Gratuity Fund: Under Section 36(1), employers' contribution towards an approved gratuity fund created by him exclusively for the benefit of his employees under an irrevocable trust is allowable as deduction.

L. Family Planning Expenditure: Any bonafide expenditure incurred by a company for the purpose of promoting family planning among its employees is allow-able as deduction. If such expenditure is of a capital nature, one fifth of it is allowable as deduction for the year in which it was incurred and the balance is deductible in equal instalments in the next four years [Section 36(1)(ii)].

M. Provident Fund: Employer's contribution towards recognised provident fund or an approved superannuation fund is allowable as deduction subject to certain limits [Section 36 (1)(iv)].

4.4.2 Wealth Tax Concessions: It is notable that Indian Wealth Tax Act, 1957, also contains provisions which facilitate the employment of labour. One such provision exempts from wealth tax the value of any building belonging to the assessee if the building is exclusively used for the purpose of the residence of persons employed by him in any plantation or industrial undertaking belonging to him. The exemption is subject to the condition that the annual salary of each such employee is ₹ 10,000 or less [Section 5(i)(XXXa)].

4.4.3 Excise Duty Concessions: Excise exemptions and concessions are particularly important in promoting labour-intensive technology and small-scale industries. Central excise law contains provisions the sole objective of which is employment generation. Products of a number of industries are exempt from excise duty if they are manufactured without the aid of power. Duty differentials have been used to discourage mechanisation in certain industries.

Similarly, concessions are available to the handloom sector of the textile industry. Processed *khadi* cloth woven on handloom wholly from hand spun cotton yarn or in admixture with similar silk and/or woollen yarn enjoys full exemption since 1969. Cotton fabrics manufactured on handlooms and processed by a factory owned by a registered handloom co-operative society enjoy full exemption from duty.

The Expert Committee on Tax Measures to Promote Employment, 1980, made estimates of the annual cost of protecting or subsidising employment through concessions in excise duties. It found that the annual cost of protecting or subsidising employment through concessions in excise duties was ₹ 523 per full-time worker in the handloom industry, ₹ 881 in *khandasari*, and ₹ 2,669 in the cottage sector of the match industry. [2]

In line with Government's policy of encouraging small-scale industries, a wide range of concessions and exemptions from excise duty is available to small producers to enable them to stand in competition with large-scale manufacturers. Also, relatively simple and concessional procedures are followed for the assessment and collection of excises from the small-scale sector.

4.5 Fiscal and Financial Incentives for Protection of Environment

4.5.1 Income Tax Concessions: These are as under:

A. Concessions under Section 35-CCB: Following types of concessions under Section 35-CCB of the Indian Income Tax Act, 1961 are available to taxpayers carrying on business or profession.

1. Sums paid by a taxpayer to any association or institution, which has as its object the undertaking of programmes of conservation of natural resources, to be used for such programmes, are allowed as deductions in the computation of taxable profits. The deduction under this provision is not allowed unless the association or institution, as also the programme of conservation of natural resources for which such sums are paid have been approved by the prescribed authority (i.e. Secretary, Department of Environment, Government of India). The prescribed authority will not approve an association or institution for this purpose for more than three years at a time.
2. Sums paid to an association or institution which has as its object the undertaking of any programme of afforestation are allowed as deduction in the computation of taxable profits. For this purpose, both the association/institution and the programme of afforestation will have to be approved by the prescribed authority.
3. Any payment made to a notified Fund for Afforestation will also qualify for deduction under Section 35-CCB. A National Fund for Afforestation and Wasteland Development has been set up. Donations from individuals as well as corporate/non-corporate bodies are eligible for 100 percent deduction.

B. Long-term Capital Gains: Under Section 54-G of the Indian Income Tax Act, 1961, long-term capital gains made from the transfer of machinery, plant, land, and building etc., forming part of an industrial undertaking are exempt from taxation where transfer is effected for the shifting of the industrial undertaking from an urban area to any other area, provided these are reinvested in approved relocation schemes within one year before or three years after the date of transfer. The amount of exemption is equal to the amount so utilised or the amount of capital gains, whichever is less. Apparently, the purpose of this exemption is to encourage industries to shift out of congested urban areas to reduce pollution and other hazards.

C. Depreciation Allowance: Depreciation allowance at the rate of 100 percent is granted for installing pollution control equipment. Pollution control equipment has been given the benefit of accelerated depreciation for corporate tax computation. In the 1993-94 budget, 100 percent of written down capital cost of such equipment is exempted from the corporate tax.

In his 1998-99 budget, the Finance Minister allowed 100 percent deduction, subject to a ceiling of ₹ 5 lakh, to undertakings engaged in the collection or processing of biodegradable waste. Similarly, activities which encourage the production of bacteria induced fertilisers were made eligible for 100 percent deduction under Section 35-AC of the Income Tax Act.

4.5.2 Excise Duty Concessions: These are as under:

1. Production of building material using fly ash and phospho-gypsum in 25 percent or more quantities as raw material is exempt from excise duty.
2. Bricks and tiles manufactured using red mud in 25 percent or more quantities as raw material are exempt from excise duty.
3. Excise duty at the low rate of 5 percent is levied on manufactured goods that are used for pollution control.

4.5.3 Customs Duty Concessions: Customs waive off is provided by the Government to encourage the installation of appropriate pollution abatement equipment.

1. Exemption from customs duty is allowed on the import of equipment, machinery, and capital goods required for the production of building materials, using fly ash/phosphor-gypsum, such as bricks, light weight aggregates and light weight concrete elements.
2. Customs duty is levied at the reduced rate of 35 percent on equipment and spares for pollution control.
3. Customs duty is levied at the reduced rate of 25 percent on kits required for conversion of petrol driven vehicles to compressed natural gas driven vehicles.

As a measure of environmental protection, the Finance Minister in his 1998-99 budget reduced the import duty on sawn wood and certain other varieties of wood from 30 percent to 25 percent, on bio-pesticides (which are eco-friendly) from 30 percent to 5 percent and on membrane electrolysers and parts from 25 percent to 10 percent.

4.5.4 Financial Assistance: It is provided in the following manner:

1. Under the Scheme for Promotion of Common Effluent Treatment Plants in clusters of small industries (aided by World Bank), financial assistance towards capital investment up to 50 percent or ₹ 1 crore, whichever is less, is given as a subsidy.
2. Central Government assistance up to 40 percent or a maximum of ₹ 1.5 crore is provided for setting up demonstration projects in the areas of waste minimisation, clean technologies, and waste recycling.
3. Assistance is provided to large and medium scale units to install effluent treatment plants aimed at waste minimisation, resource recovery, and pollution abatement.

The policy of the Government of India on environment has been guided by the principles of Agenda 21 which was adopted at the Earth Summit in Rio de Janeiro in June 1992 and which aims at integrating environmental imperatives with developmental aspirations. The principles of Agenda 21 find reflection in the policy statements of the Government of India on forestry, abatement of pollution, national conservation strategy and environment and development. India is a signatory to the Montreal Protocol for phasing out ozone depleting substances, the Convention on biological diversity and other international treaties.

In India, Government has taken various measures, preventive as well as promotive, to improve environment. However, it has not used pollution taxes for environmental protection. The currently levied cess on the consumption of water for industrial activities is not a pollution tax. Its objective is to raise revenue for the pollution control boards but not to control pollution. Pollution taxes are levied in many countries with public support. Thus, Brazil, Colombia, and Venezuela charge a forestry tax when tree harvesting is not compensated by equivalent reforestation. Similarly, landfill tax [3] is imposed in many Western countries including Britain.

The policy in India has focused on providing pollution subsidies (i.e. tax concessions) to industries in various forms. These subsidies have not proved effective in controlling pollution. They do not force the polluters, as do pollution taxes, to adopt pollution abatement technologies. Similarly, there has been a lack of an appropriate price policy for the use of natural resources.

4.6 Tax Incentives for Non-resident Indians: See section 25.7 of chapter 25 of this book.

Endnotes

1. Tax incentives, an integral part of tax systems the world over, are designed to promote a wide

spectrum of socio-economic objectives. If judiciously used, they can become an effective tool of economic change on desired lines.

Individuals: Tax incentives related to individuals promote equity. Examples in this category are exemption of an initial slice of income from tax, and allowances related to dependants. Two individuals with equal incomes may have to support families of different sizes and it would be justifiable to extract less from the individual with a larger family size. However, these considerations are more relevant at low income levels. Apart from equity, promotion of individual savings, contributions towards charitable purposes are other commonly promoted objectives. Tax incentives for these purposes are usually in the form of deductions from taxable base or tax credits against savings/investments in specified channels.

Business Organisations: Tax incentives related to business sector are meant to induce business enterprises to undertake activities which they would otherwise shirk. Thus, these incentives are designed to encourage investment in general or in preferred industries or in preferred geographical areas (industrially backward regions). Such incentives take a variety of forms such as investment allowance, accelerated depreciation of fixed assets, and exemption of profits from tax for specified initial years of business (tax holiday).

General Purpose Incentives: These are meant to provide flexibility to the tax system to deal with changing market situations. They are used as a corrective mechanism to stabilise demand, production, and profits of different industries. Thus, tax incentives may be given to boost sluggish demand for idle-capacity industries. Similarly, incentives are given for the promotion of sports, cultural and social welfare organisations. Tax incentives are also given to promote exports, scientific research, and desired type of technology (e.g. labour-intensive technology in labour surplus economies). Thus, a tax system, apart from raising revenue, may be used to promote activities deemed vital by society, though it is controversial as to which activities are vital and require governmental support.

2. Government of India, Ministry of Finance, *Report of the Expert Committee on Tax Measures to Promote Employment* (Chairman: V.M. Dandekar), 1980, pp. 91, 113 and 117.
3. Landfill tax is a fiscal innovation of recent origin, necessitated by world-wide concern for depleting environmental resources. It is a tax on producers who dump their industrial waste in the landfills. It can also be levied on municipal authorities for dumping city waste in the landfills. Such a tax, it is argued, encourages recycling and treatment of various types of waste by producers and local authorities. By following proper waste management practices, polluters can avoid the tax and hence contribute to cleaner environment. The tax, thus, acts as a deterrent on dumping industrial and other wastes in the landfills. The tax may distinguish between active waste and inert waste, the former being more harmful and therefore taxed at a higher rate. For example, in Britain (where the tax was introduced in 1996) active waste is taxed at £10 per tonne as compared to £7 per tonne for inert waste. The tax has gained popularity in the West and needs to be adopted in India where concern for environmental degradation is growing day by day.

5

Tax Reforms since 1991

5.1 Approach to Tax Reforms

It may be recalled that the external payments crisis of 1991, which led to the initiation of economic reforms in India, was the result of deteriorating fiscal situation during the latter half of 1980s. This period was marked by high and persistent fiscal deficits, accompanied by large revenue deficits. This had led to a significant enlargement of Government borrowings from financial intermediaries and increased financing of Government deficit through automatic monetisation which aggravated price rise. When the Indian economy faced an unprecedented macroeconomic crisis in 1991, fiscal consolidation constituted a major objective of the policy response. This consolidation was to be achieved through reduction in the size of budget deficit and public debt in relation to GDP. For this purpose, it became necessary to: (a) enhance tax and non-tax revenue, (b) curtail current expenditure growth, (c) restructure public sector undertaking, including disinvestment, (d) improve fiscal-monetary co-ordination, and (e) deregulate financial system.

Apart from these reforms aimed at fiscal consolidation, a number of institutional measures were also taken during the 1990s. Public sector restructuring and disinvestments were undertaken with a view to increase the efficiency of the public sector undertakings and also to provide additional resources to the Government. The need for improvements in budgetary practices led to the enactment of the Fiscal Responsibility and Budget Management (FRBM) Act, 2003 which ushered the Indian economy in an era of fiscal consolidation based on fiscal policy rules.

The financing of fiscal deficit is another area, which has undergone significant changes in the post-reform period. With the discontinuation of *ad hoc* 91-day Treasury Bills in April 1997, automatic monetisation of deficits was eliminated. Greater reliance on borrowing at market-related interest rates since 1992 led to a substantial lowering of statutory pre-emption of institutional resources for the Government. This has also facilitated development of the market for Government securities, which has witnessed remarkable changes since the latter half of the 1990s.

Restructuring of the tax system has constituted a major component of fiscal reforms initiated since 1991. The main focus of the tax reforms has been on simplification and rationalisation of both direct and indirect taxes with the objective of augmenting revenues and removing anomalies in the tax structure. Tax reforms since 1991 have brought the tax system much closer to international tax practices. Government's concern with tax reforms is reflected in the appointment of a number of committees in recent years to review the tax system. These have, *inter alia*, included:

1. Tax Reforms Committee (Chairman: Raja Chelliah), 1991.
2. Advisory Group on Tax Policy and Tax Administration for the Tenth Plan (Chairman: Parthasarathi Shome), 2001.
3. Inter-ministerial Working Group on Customs Tariff (Chairman: Arvind Virmani), 2002.
4. Task Force on Direct Taxes (Chairman: Vijay Kelkar), 2002.
5. Task Force on Indirect Taxes (Chairman: Vijay Kelkar), 2002.
6. White Paper on State-Level Value Added Tax (Chairman: Asim Kumar Dasgupta), 2005.
7. Rationalisation of Customs and Excise Duties on Edible Oils and Oilseeds (Chairman: Ashok Lahiri), 2006.

In fact, tax reforms are a part of the package to liberalise and globalise the Indian economy. The post-1991 period has witnessed a sharp decline in the rates of income tax, excise duty and customs tariff. The theory that high rates of duty lead to higher revenue collection has been discarded in favour of lower rates with fewer exemptions and concessions.

Tax reforms undertaken by the Government in tandem with economic reforms since 1991 have helped to rationalise and simplify the tax system considerably. The rates have been moderated and many exemptions and concessions have been weeded out.

5.2 Income Tax

Prior to reforms, rates of income tax were quite high, almost punitive. For example, in 1973-74, the maximum marginal rate of individual income tax was as high as 97.7 percent. When high rates proved counter-productive from revenue angle, the Government initiated a series of rate reductions with the result that the present (financial year 2015-16) top rate for individual taxpayers is 30 percent. Pursuant to the recommendations of the Tax Reforms Committee (Chairman: Raja Chelliah), 1991, the scheme of capital gains tax was drastically recast by the Finance Act, 1992. A system of indexation was introduced for the first time under which long-term capital gains are now computed by allowing the cost of acquisition and the cost of improvement of the asset to be adjusted for general inflation. Similarly, a new Section 112 was inserted in the Income Tax Act, 1961 to provide that long-term capital gains would be subject to a flat rate of income tax. The rate of tax is 20 percent. Presently, concessionary treatment to long-term capital gains is given through inflation indexing, relatively low flat rate of tax, and a set of exemptions.

Prior to the assessment year 1993-94, taxation of partnership firms was rather cumbersome. For example, the method of taxation differed according to whether the firm was registered or not under the Income Tax Act. Taxation of partnership firms was drastically modified through the Finance Act, 1992. The chief feature of these changes was to avoid double taxation of profits of firms. Thus, from the assessment year 1993-94 a partnership firm is taxed as a separate entity. Like a company, it is liable to income tax however small its income may be. There is no distinction between registered and unregistered firms. Similarly, there is no distinction between firms carrying professions or business. The procedure for registration of firms has been abolished. A new procedure for the assessment of a firm as a firm has been prescribed in Section 184. In order to be assessed as a firm, the partnership should be evidenced by an instrument of partnership, specifying the individual shares of the partners and a copy of the same certified in writing by all the partners should be filed along with the first return of the firm. [1]

5.3 Wealth Tax

Prior to the enactment of the Finance Act, 1992, the term *assets* as described in Section 2(e) of the Wealth Tax Act, 1957 included property of every description, movable and immovable, such as cash, bank balances, shares, jewellery, and other assets. The term *assets* was of widest import and sufficiently comprehensive. However, various provisions of the wealth tax law were drastically restructured by the Finance Act, 1992. In order to encourage the taxpayers to invest in productive assets such as shares, securities, bonds, bank deposits, mutual funds etc., these financial assets were exempted from wealth tax. In short, the basis of taxation was shifted from wealth to unproductive assets.

The maximum marginal rate of wealth tax, applicable to net wealth above ₹ 15 lakh, was quite high at 8 percent till the year 1975-76. Presently, (financial year 2015-16) wealth tax is charged at the flat rate of 1 percent with a basic exemption of ₹ 30 lakh. In view of the meagre revenue and problems of administration and compliance, the Task Force on Direct Taxes (Chairman: Vijay Kelkar), 2002 had recommended the abolition of wealth tax. [2] In his Budget Speech to the Parliament on February 28, 2015, the Finance Minister announced the abolition of wealth tax.

5.4 Excise Duties

Prior to tax reforms initiated in 1991, excise taxation in India was an interesting example of the multitude of rates which were subject to frequent revisions. Numerous considerations contributed to the complexity of excise rates. The labyrinthine intricacies of the tariff often led to confusion and litigation amongst the taxpayers and revenue authorities.

Thus, in a landmark move, the Finance Minister announced in his 1999-2000 budget a triple rate excise structure. In other words, the then existing 11 major ad valorem rates were reduced to 3, viz. a central rate of 16 percent, a merit rate of 8 percent and a demerit rate of 24 percent. This was done by: (a) merging the existing rates of 5 percent, 10 percent and 12 percent into the existing 8 percent rate, (b) creating a new rate of 16 percent by merging the existing 13 percent, 15 percent and 18 percent rates into it, and (c) fixing a new rate of 24 percent in substitution of the existing rate of 25 percent. The initiative of the Finance Minister to rationalise the rate structure of excise system was widely appreciated. For the financial year 2015-16, the normal rate of excise duty is 12 percent. [3]

5.5 Taxation of Services

Service sector is very wide in its range. It includes, *inter alia*, health care, education, social security, leasing, entertainment, credit rating agencies, telecommunications, transport, publicity and advertising, insurance, banking, legal and financial services.

The Central Government had no specific powers to tax services when it introduced service tax on select services in 1994. It was done under its residual powers of taxation vide Entry 97 of List I (Union List in the Seventh Schedule). The collection of service tax was entrusted to the excise department.

However, the Constitution (Eighty-eighth Amendment) Act, 2003 put service tax in the Union List by inserting Entry 92C in that List. Furthermore, service tax was put under Article 268A of the Constitution which specifies that the principles of collection and appropriation of taxes on services will be determined by Parliament. In other words, revenue from service tax is outside the purview of the Finance Commission.

Presently, service tax is levied on as diverse services such as credit rating on the one hand and mechanised slaughter houses on the other. It is clear that service sector in India constitutes a tax base with vast potential which has not been exploited as yet. For the financial year 2015-16, the standard rate of service tax is 14 percent. [4]

5.6 Customs Duties

Prior to tax reforms initiated in 1991, import tariff had a variety of rates for different items, and even for the same item depending on its end use. Such a cumbersome system led to legal disputes pertaining to import classifications and encouraged corruption in the administration of customs tariff.

In India, about 99 percent of customs revenue is derived from import duties which are levied on a wide range of commodities. Apart from revenue function, import duties act as policy instrument to provide protection to domestic industry, conserve and ration scarce foreign exchange, and frame external trade policy of the Government. Export duties, accounting for the rest of 1 percent revenue, are imposed on a few commodities, namely coffee, mica, black pepper, hides and skins, and leather. Government has generally refrained from levying export duties in order to ensure competitiveness of India's exports in the world market.

Radical reforms have been introduced in the import tariff since 1991. These reforms were necessary because the customs tariff had become, over the years, very complicated in terms of multiple rates, innumerable exemptions, excessive controls, and elaborate procedures. These infirmities of the customs tariff often led to delays, harassment, corruption, and litigation. Moreover, rationalisation and simplification of the customs duties was needed to move towards a market economy, freedom of trade, and opening up the Indian economy to the outside world. The country has moved towards moderate rates of taxation with a view to improve compliance and reduce litigation.

In mid-l991, Government began the process of reducing import duties. The Finance Act (No. 2), 1991, reduced the *ad valorem* rate of basic plus auxiliary duties of customs to a maximum of 150 percent where it was more than that. Thus, tariff peaks above 150 percent were eliminated with the exceptions of duty on imported alcoholic beverages and passenger baggage. The Finance Act, 1992, lowered the peak level of import duties to 110 percent with the exception of passenger baggage and alcoholic beverages. The Finance Act, 1993, made a significant simplification in the import tariff by merging auxiliary duty with basic duty, and also by reducing the maximum rate of import duty from 110 percent to 85 percent. After successive downward revisions, the peak rate of import duty on non-agricultural products stands at 10 percent at present (financial year 2015-16). [5]

5.7 State Level Sales Tax/VAT

Under the Constitution, the right to levy sales tax belongs to the State Governments. Each State is, therefore, empowered to collect tax on the sale of goods within its territory according to the rules framed by it. Prior to tax reforms initiated in early 1990s, sales tax was characterised by a multiplicity of tax rate and exemptions, lack of uniformity across States, large number of exemptions and concessions, and differing procedures for tax collection. In mid-1990s, most states had agreed to phase out the incentive related exemptions and implement floor rates of sales tax. As part of the nation wide efforts to redesign commodity taxation and the implementation of CENVAT at the level of the Centre, many States have modified their sales tax regimes to launch a state level VAT under the scheme prepared by the Empowered Committee for this purpose.

At a meeting of the State Finance Ministers with the Union Finance Minister on June 18, 2004, it was decided that all States would introduce a uniform VAT from April 1, 2005 to replace sales tax. After missing many deadlines, VAT has been finally introduced in all the States. Broadly speaking, the experience of implementing VAT has been quite encouraging. The new system has been received well by all the stakeholders, and the transition has been quite smooth. [6]

5.8 Direct Taxes Code (DTC)

In the Central Government Budget for 2009-10, the importance of continuing the process of structural changes in direct taxes was reiterated and a comprehensive code to this effect was envisaged. The Government signalled its intention to consolidate and comprehensively amend the existing Income Tax Act 1961 and Wealth Tax Act 1957 through a single legislation, by releasing a draft Direct Taxes Code (DTC) and a Discussion Paper for public comments in August 2009. Based on analysis of the numerous inputs received from stakeholders, a Revised Discussion Paper was released in June 2010 followed by the introduction of the Direct Taxes Code Bill, 2010 in Parliament in August 2010. It was proposed to make it effective from April 1, 2012.

However, the Union Finance Minister informed the Parliament in his budget speech for 2012-13 that the Government received the Report of the Parliamentary Standing Committee on March 9, 2012. Enactment of DTC would take place after the report is examined. [7] In his Budget Speech to the Parliament on February 28, 2015, the Finance Minister saw 'no great merit in going ahead with the Direct Tax Code as it exists today'.

5.9 Goods and Services Tax (GST)

GST is a part of the proposed tax reforms to evolve an efficient and harmonized consumption tax system in the country. Presently, there are parallel systems of indirect taxation at the central and state levels. Each of the systems needs to be reformed to eventually harmonize them.

GST is proposed to be a comprehensive indirect tax levy on manufacture, sale and consumption of goods as well as services at the national level. GST would give India a world class tax system and improve tax collections. It would end the long standing distortions of differential treatment of manufacturing and service sector. The introduction of GST will lead to the abolition of various central and state indirect taxes and eliminate the cascading effects of multiple layers of taxation. It is claimed that GST will facilitate seamless credit across the entire supply chain and across all states under a common tax base.

The changeover to GST will be a game-changing tax reform measure which will significantly contribute to the buoyancy of tax revenues, acceleration of growth, and generation of many positive externalities.

Once the integrated GST across the country is introduced, it will simplify tax administration and eliminate cascading of taxes. It will lead to reduction in the distortions in the structure of production, consumption and exports and further to a more efficient allocation of resources. The demand for manufactured goods can be expected to grow significantly. [8]

To sum up, tax reforms introduced by the Government since mid-1991 have helped to build a structure which is simple, relies on moderate tax rates but with a wider base and better enforcement. Tax reforms since 1991 have helped in correcting•structural imbalances in the tax system. They are *soft* on industry with a view to create new investment climate and make India internationally competitive. By lowering the tax rates, the Government expects speedy industrial development and hence buoyancy in tax revenues.

The country is keenly awaiting implementation of Direct Taxes Code (DTC) and Goods and Services Tax (GST). GST is India's most ambitious indirect tax reform. Lack of political consensus is holding up progress and implementation of GST.

In his Budget Speech to the Parliament on February 28, 2015, the Finance Minister resolved to implement GST from April 1, 2016.

Endnotes

1. See chapter 12 of this book for more details.
2. See chapter 13 of this book for more details.
3. See chapter 14 of this book for more details.
4. See chapter 15 of this book for more details.
5. See chapter 16 of this book for more details.
6. See chapter 21 of this book for more details.
7. See chapter 17 of this book for more details.
8. See chapter 18 of this book for more details.

Part III: Combined (Centre and States) Tax Revenue

6

Trends in Tax-GDP Ratio

6.1 Tax-GDP Ratio: Meaning and Significance

The primary objective of tax policy in developing countries is to mobilise resources for the public sector to finance welfare and developmental plans. The extent to which tax policy is used for this purpose is a matter of interest for national policymakers and foreign aid donors. Foreign governments and international organisations usually assess the efforts made by recipient countries to raise resources domestically.

Level of taxation in a country is traditionally judged in terms of the ratio which taxes bear to some measure of national income. This ratio is called tax-GDP ratio and the change in it is determined by variations in both the numerator (total tax revenue) and the denominator (national income).

Tax-GDP ratio is generally regarded as an index of relative tax burden in a country over a period of time (time-series analysis) or when countries are compared for the same period (cross-section analysis). To describe tax burden in terms of tax-GDP ratio can be misleading because taxes, though burden for individuals, are used to finance vital governmental activities and to make transfers to needy sections of society.

What does then tax-GDP ratio signify? Since tax-GDP ratio indicates the percentage of national income that is compulsorily transferred from private pockets to public exchequer, and hence the relative share of government in the disposition of national income, it signifies the economic role of a government in the national economy. The ratio, however, does not reflect the importance of government sector as a final purchaser of goods and services because a part of tax revenue is returned to the private sector in the form of transfer payments like pensions and scholarships. If such transfer payments are deducted from the total tax revenue, the ratio of the remaining tax revenue to GDP will show importance of government as a final purchaser of goods and services. Since tax-GDP ratio reflects movements in both tax receipts and GDP, any significant revision in GDP figures will affect the ratio. Such revisions are not uncommon, particularly in developing countries, and therefore they indicate a limitation of the use of tax-GDP ratios. These cautions must be kept in mind while interpreting tax ratios.

6.2 Trends in Tax-GDP Ratio

In 1950-51, total tax collections in India were a mere 6.03 percent of GDP. With the launching of the Five Year Plans in 1951, and expansion in administrative and welfare activities of the Government at different levels, the need for revenue increased and it was met mainly by additional tax efforts. Consequently, tax-GDP ratio started increasing from decade to decade, being 7.52 percent in 1960-61, 9.98 percent in 1970-71 and 13.26 percent in 1980-81. It stood at 14.96 percent in 1990-91 and 14.08 percent in 2000-01. For the year 2013-14, it was estimated at 17.87 (Table 6.1).

Table 6.1: Combined Tax Revenue as Percent of GDP: Selected Years

(₹ crore)

Year	Combined tax revenue*	Col. 2 as % of GDP	Year	Combined tax revenue*	Col. 5 as % of GDP
1	2	3	4	5	6
1950-51	627	6.03	1990-91	87,722	14.96
1955-56	768	6.75	1995-96	1,75,259	14.29
1960-61	1,350	7.52	2000-01	3,05,320	14.08
1965-66	2,922	10.13	2005-06	5,87,688	15.91
1970-71	4,752	9.98	2010-11	12,71,666	16.31
1975-76	11,182	12.90	2011-12	14,67,891	16.29
1980-81	19,844	13.26	2012-13	17,26,549	17.22
1985-86	43,267	14.94	2013-14	20,32,489	17.87

* Total tax revenue of the Central and State Governments.
2012-13 = Revised estimates; 2013-14 = Budget estimates.
Note: The ratios to GDP at market prices are based on CSO's National Accounts 2004-05 series.
Source: Rearranged data from Government of India, Ministry of Finance, *Indian Public Finance Statistics, 2013-2014*, Tables 1.7 and 1.8. For full time series data from 1950-51 to 2013-14, see Table 1 in Part VIII of this Book.

A slippage in tax-GDP ratio from 14.96 to 14.08 is noticeable between 1990-91 and 2000-01. The slippage in tax-GDP ratio was noted by the Twelfth Finance Commission. To quote, "Taking the 15-year period from 1987-88 to 2001-02, and comparing three-year averages at both ends, that is for 1987-90 and 1999-2002, we note that the tax-GDP ratio fell from a level of about 16 percent relative to GDP by 1.6 percentage points to reach an average level of 14.4 percent of GDP". [1] Stating the reasons for the slippage, the Commission noted, "As a result of tax reforms, the indirect taxes relative to GDP started coming down whereas that of direct taxes started increasing. But the magnitude of increase in the direct taxes was less than the fall in indirect taxes. In consequence, the overall tax-GDP ratio fell from its peak in 1987-88 to 14.4 percent in 2001-02". [2] It is noteworthy that rates of excise and customs duties have gradually been lowered during the post-1991 period.

Emphasising the need to increase tax-GDP ratios, the Commission suggested ratios for the year 2009-10 (Table 6.2).

Table 6.2: Tax-GDP Ratios Suggested by the Twelfth Finance Commission for the Year 2009-10

	2004-05	2009-10
Combined tax revenue	15.6	17.6
Centre's gross tax revenue	9.7	10.9
States' own tax revenues	5.9	6.8

Source: Report of the Twelfth Finance Commission (2005-10), November 2004, Tables 4.12 and 4.13 (excerpted).

6.3 Tax-GDP Ratios in Developed and Developing Countries

There has been a good deal of literature on ranking countries according to tax ratio relative to their taxable capacity to measure national tax performance. These inter-country comparisons of tax levels have been attempted by individual scholars, and international agencies from time to time. Much of the research work in this area has been done by the Fiscal Affairs Department of the International Monetary Fund. [3]

Tax-GDP ratio is generally high in developed countries as compared to developing countries. In Denmark, the tax-GDP ratio was as high as 48.15 percent in 2011. For the same year, it was 37.35 percent in Sweden, 35.06 percent in Norway, and 31.28 percent in Australia. Table 6.3 records tax-GDP ratios for important developed countries of the world and compares them with tax-GDP ratios in some developing countries. It is found that tax-GDP ratios in developing countries are far low as compared to developed countries. From the foregoing analysis it can be inferred that the level of taxation is linked with the stage of development. More specifically, tax-GDP ratio is positively related to per capita income, i.e. higher the per capita income, greater is the tax-GDP ratio and *vice versa*. In poor countries, the taxpaying capacity of the people is less owing to low levels of per capita income.

6.3.1 Limitations of Inter-country Tax Comparisons: Are inter-country comparisons of taxation levels meaningful? Some fiscal experts have sharply criticised these attempts. [4] According to critics, the economic, political, and institutional characteristics of individual countries are so different that neither theoretical nor empirical studies provide useful information of policy relevance. Tax-GDP ratios do not consider the fact that some countries are more favourably placed to levy and collect taxes than others. For example, Lotz and Morss [5] analysed a sample of 72 developed and developing countries to examine the relationship between tax ratio variations and differences in per capita income and degree of openness. The sample included a wide spectrum of dissimilar economies ranging from Nepal to Singapore. It is *prima facie* erroneous to compare Nepal's traditional rural and agricultural economy with a highly commercial and industrial city state of Singapore.

Table 6.3: Tax-GDP Ratios in Selected Developed and Developing Countries: 2011 (in percent)

Countries (in descending order of tax-GDP ratio)	Tax-GDP ratio	Countries (in descending order of tax-GDP ratio)	Tax-GDP ratio
Developed countries		**Developing countries**	
1. Denmark	48.15	1. Malaysia	18.87
2. Sweden	37.35	2. Thailand	17.39
3. Norway	35.06	3. Mauritius	17.21
4. Australia	31.28	4. India	16.43
5. Italy	29.58	5. Nepal	9.72
6. United Kingdom	29.26		
7. Canada	28.88		

Sources: International Monetary Fund, *Government Finance Statistics Yearbook* 2012. For India, Government of India, Ministry of Finance, *Indian Public Finance Statistics*, 2012-13, Table 1.8.

According to critics, the actual tax-to-income ratio is a vague concept because the definitions of numerator and denominator are debatable. In spite of these limitations, international tax comparisons are useful so far as they process and condense a large amount of otherwise incomprehensible information. However, it must be emphasised that such comparisons are more meaningful if attempted among countries having similar socio-economic circumstances.

Endnotes

1. *Report of the Twelfth Finance Commission* (2005-10), November 2004, p. 22.
2. Ibid., p. 63.
3. Studies pertaining to international tax comparisons conducted by International Monetary Fund include: (i) Jorgen R. Lotz and Elliott R. Morss, 'Measuring 'Tax Effort' in Developing Countries', *IMF Staff Papers*, Vol. 14, November 1967, pp. 478-499; (ii) Raja J. Chelliah, 'Trends in Taxation in Developing Countries', *IMF Staff Papers*, Vol. 18, July 1971, pp. 254-331; (iii) Roy W. Bahl, 'A Regression Approach to Tax Effort and Tax Ratio Analysis', *IMF*

Staff Papers, Vol. 18, November 1971, pp. 570-612; (iv) Roy W. Bahl, 'A Representative Tax System Approach to Measuring Tax Effort in Developing Countries', *IMF Staff Papers*, Vol. 19, March 1972, pp. 87-123; (v) Raja J. Chelliah, Hessel Bass and Margaret Kelly, 'Tax Ratios and Effort in Developing Countries, 1969-71', *IMF Staff Papers*, Vol. 22, March, 1975, pp. 187-205; (vi) Alan Tait, Wilfrid Gratz, and Barry Eichengreen, 'International Comparisons of Taxation for Selected Developing Countries, 1972-76', *IMF Staff Papers*, Vol. 26, March 1979; (vii) Vito Tanzi, 'The Impact of Macroeconomic Policies on the level of Taxation and the Fiscal Balance in Developing Countries', *IMF Staff Papers*, Vol. 36, No. 3, September 1989, pp. 633-656.

4. See contributions of R.M. Bird, B.R. Bolnick, and A.R. Prest in J.F.J. Toye (ed.), *Taxation and Economic Development,* London: Frank Cass and Company.
5. See Lotz and Morss in endnote 3.

7

Trends in the Relative Revenue Significance of Direct and Indirect Taxes

7.1 Direct versus Indirect Taxes

A direct tax is one the ultimate burden of which falls on the person on whom it is levied. In other words, it is a tax that cannot be shifted from the original payer to someone else. It is contrasted with indirect tax which can be shifted from the original payer to the ultimate consumer of the commodity or service taxed.

John Stuart Mill, the celebrated British economist of the 19th century, distinguished between direct and indirect taxes as follows. "A direct tax is one which is demanded from the very person who, it is intended or desired, should pay it. Indirect taxes are those which are demanded from one person in the expectation and intention that he shall indemnify himself at the expense of another". [1]

Income tax, wealth tax, and estate duty are generally considered direct taxes. Import duties, excise levies, and sales taxes are generally regarded as indirect taxes. Thus, an excise duty on cigarettes levied on producers is usually passed on to the consumers in the form of higher prices.

Direct taxes, though administratively inconvenient, are preferred because they: (a) can be related to ability-to-pay, (b) satisfy the principle of certainty, and (c) create civic consciousness.

Indirect taxes (also called hidden taxes) are convenient to collect but lack equity attribute. They do not allow considerations for the personal circumstances of taxpayers as do direct taxes. It is not possible to grant exemptions or allow deductions or to have a progressive rate schedule. Indirect taxes are borne in relation to the consumption expenditure which constitutes a higher percentage of income for lower income groups than for persons in higher income brackets. It is true that incidence of indirect taxes depends on: (a) the selection of commodities for taxation, and (b) the rate of tax on them. It is desirable that luxuries and comforts are chosen for heavy taxation with necessities of life either exempted or moderately taxed. However, in poor countries the demand for luxury items is limited apart from being price elastic. Conversely, the demand for necessities is vast and price inelastic, obliging tax authorities to extend the tax net to daily needs. This has a tendency to fuel inflation.

In short, it is almost universally accepted that indirect taxes are inferior to direct taxes in terms of equity attribute. The distribution of indirect tax burden is often, though not always, regressive and even the poorest of the poor are made to contribute to public exchequer. The chief advantage of indirect taxes is that they are convenient to collect.

The distinction between direct and indirect taxes has been a subject of long-drawn debate in public finance literature. Some economists believe that it is possible to pass on certain direct taxes under special circumstances. Corporate income tax, a supposedly direct tax, is known to be shifted to consumers in many countries. [2]

The demarcation between direct and indirect taxes is ambiguous because of conflicting empirical evidence of tax incidence studies. Direct taxes can be shifted under certain circumstances while taxes on commodities may stick on the producers finally. [3]

There is no legal definition of direct and indirect taxes in India. Taxes under the charge of Central Board of Direct Taxes are direct taxes while those administered by the Central Board of Excise and Customs are indirect taxes. The classification adopted in this book is the same as followed in the documents of the Government of India.

7.2 Trends Prior to Tax Reforms (i.e. Pre-1991 Period)

In 1950-51, direct taxes accounted for a sizeable 36.8 percent of total tax collections: ₹ 231 crore out of ₹ 627 crore. Within a span of 35 years the proportionate share dropped to less than half at 14.4 percent in 1985-86, and stood at 14.0 percent in 1990-91. The declining trend of direct taxes led to a rising share of indirect taxes. The ratio between direct and indirect taxes which stood at 36.8:63.2 in 1950-51 worsened with every passing decade, recording 29.8:70.2 in 1960-61, 21.2:78.8 in 1970-71, 16.5:83.5 in 1980-81 and 14.0:86.0 in 1990-91 (Table 7.1).

It is customary to explain the limited role of direct taxes in developing countries in terms of their peculiar circumstances which include large agricultural sector of subsistence nature, small-scale industrial activities, lack of monetisation and accounting practices, and low levels of income. Even a modest exemption limit of personal income tax keeps the vast majority of income earners outside the income tax net. In addition to these underlying reasons, a host of specific factors also contributed to the reduced role of direct taxes. These included, *inter alia*, the following: (a) scaling down rates of direct taxes, (b) plethora of exemptions and concessions, (c) abolition of estate duty in 1985, and (d) large-scale tax evasion.

However, the declining share of direct taxes was not consistent with the norms of tax theory. It is well-known that as an economy experiences modernisation, diversification, and expansion of corporate sector, the scope for direct taxes widens. [4]

Table 7.1: Combined Tax Revenue, Breakdown between Direct and Indirect Taxes with Percentage Shares: Selected Years

(₹ crore)

Year	Combined tax revenue* (3+4)	Direct taxes	Indirect taxes	Col. 3 as % of Col. 2	Col. 4 as % of Col. 2
1	2	3	4	5	6
1950-51	627	231	396	36.8	63.2
1955-56	768	259	509	33.7	66.3
1960-61	1,350	402	948	29.8	70.2
1965-66	2,922	734	2,188	25.1	74.9
1970-71	4,752	1,009	3,743	21.2	78.8
1975-76	11,182	2,493	8,689	22.3	77.7
1980-81	19,844	3,268	16,576	16.5	83.5
1985-86	43,267	6,252	37,015	14.4	85.6
1990-91	87,722	12,260	75,462	14.0	86.0
1995-96	1,75,259	35,777	1,39,482	20.4	79.6
2000-01	3,05,320	71,762	2,33,558	23.5	76.5
2005-06	5,87,688	1,67,635	4,20,053	28.5	71.5
2010-11	12,71,666	4,50,822	8,20,843	35.6	64.4
2011-12	14,67,891	5,01,395	9,66,496	34.2	65.8
2012-13	17,26,549	5,74.681	11,51,868	33.3	66.7
2013-14	20,32,489	6,79,298	13,53,192	33.4	66.6

* Total tax revenue of the Central and State Governments.
2012-13 = Revised estimates; 2013-14 = Budget estimates.
Note: The ratios to GDP at market prices are based on CSO's National Accounts 2004-05 series.
Source: Rearranged data from Government of India, Ministry of Finance, *Indian Public Finance Statistics, 2013-2014*, Tables 1.7 and 1.8. Columns 5 and 6 calculations own. For full time series data from 1950-51 to 2013-14, see Table 1 in Part VIII of this Book.

The declining share of direct taxes caused concern in Government circles and this feeling was expressed in official documents. The Long Term Fiscal Policy (LTFP), 1985 while seeking to correct the imbalance maintained, "While the predominance of indirect taxes in the present situation is unavoidable, it cannot be gainsaid that a certain balance has to be maintained between direct and indirect taxes. Taxes like the personal income tax have an important role in the tax structure and cannot be substituted by taxes on commodities. It is not easy to tailor commodity taxes to the circumstances of the taxpayers in the same way as is possible with the personal income tax. Hence, although reliance on indirect taxation cannot be avoided in the foreseeable future, it is necessary to make a transition to a system whereby income tax makes a larger contribution to revenue. Such transition is not possible without a distinct improvement in the buoyancy of the income tax in response to growth in incomes. An important objective of fiscal policy must be to reverse the decline in the share of direct taxes over the long term". [5]

7.3 Post-Tax Reforms Period

After the tax reforms initiated in 1991, the decline in the relative share of direct taxes has not only been arrested but reversed. The ratio between direct and indirect taxes which stood at 14.0:86.0 in 1990-91 gradually improved to 23.5:76.5 in 2000-01, to 35.6:64.4 in 2010-11 and was estimated at 33.4:66.6 for the year 2013-14, showing a marginal decline (Table 7.1).

Stating the reasons for fall in the share of indirect taxes and increase in the share of direct taxes, the Tenth Five Year Plan (2002-07) observed, "The reasons for this steep fall in the indirect tax revenue are obvious. The structural and administrative reforms in the Indian tax system during the Nineties characterised by scaling down of the tax rate, reduction in number of slabs, introduction of modified value added tax system, etc., among others, were not necessarily aimed at raising revenue productivity. Rather, the purpose was to improve efficiency in production and trade by removing market distortion. The analysis of data in the post -reform period exposes several issues worth mentioning. First, the value of imports has not responded to tariff reduction in equal proportion, i.e. import elasticity with respect to tariff has not been very high. Second, a host of tariff exemptions still exists on substantial proportion of imports ranging from 60 percent to 80 percent. Third, the excise duty has not been structured to lead to a revenue-neutral tax system under MODVAT/CENVAT. Fourth, the tax base for excise revenue (manufacturing sector) is gradually shrinking as a proportion of GDP. Our projections of the tax buoyancy for the Tenth plan have considered all these issues.

The improvement in direct tax collection, which has been experienced despite the scaling back of income tax rates in India during the post-reform period, could be attributed to expansion in the tax base through introduction of innovative schemes, extension of the base for tax deduction at source and improvement in direct tax administration etc. Continuous efforts towards improvement in the direct tax administration and its re-structuring, and introduction of information technology on a large scale to facilitate tax administration are expected to further enhance revenue collection under direct tax". [6]

7.4 Equity Implications

Though, of late, the share of direct taxes has increased, they are still far below the contribution made by indirect taxes. The subdued role of direct taxes or the dominance of indirect taxes in India's tax structure has serious equity implications, because the burden of direct taxes falls solely on the well-off while the burden of indirect taxes is shared by all sections of the society. It is noteworthy that in the combined (Centre and the States) tax revenue, the tilt in favour of indirect taxes is mainly because of the overwhelming contribution of indirect taxes in States' own tax revenue. Direct taxes (land revenue and agricultural income tax) contribute very little to revenue raised through taxes by the State Governments. [7]

It is also notable that a substantial amount of indirect taxes is paid by the Government to itself. Broadly speaking, public expenditure at all levels forms one-fourth of the total spending in India. Customs duties, excise levies, and sales taxes and the hikes in them entail additional expenditure on the part of Central and State Governments to maintain their existing command over real resources of the economy. Commodities like motor vehicles, petrol, air conditioners, water coolers, and steel furniture are favourite items for heavy and additional taxation and these are also the items extensively used by civil and defence establishments of the Government. Therefore, a substantial part of indirect tax revenue including the additional tax effort is merely a book transfer and does not reflect increase in real resources at the command of the Government. This argument can also be extended to increase in the prices of goods produced by public sector enterprises. Any such increase and the resultant additional proceeds may improve the finances of an individual public enterprise but not necessarily of the Government of India because the various Ministries and Departments will be required to spend more to purchase the same volume of goods and services from the concerned enterprise. Thus, in any reform of indirect tax structure it is important to emphasise, apart from quantity, the quality of revenue, i.e. who pay the taxes to the Government.

With the growth of corporate sector and the rise in income levels, India is showing signs of modernisation, reflecting increased scope for direct taxes. For widening the direct tax base, effective measures are needed to tap the unincorporated industrial sector and the affluent agricultural class.

Endnotes

1. *Collected Works of John Stuart Mill,* University of Toronto Press, 1965, Vol. III, Book V, chapter 3, p. 825.

2. For United States, see M. Krzyzaniak and R.A. Musgrave, *The Shifting of the Corporation Income Tax* (Baltimore: John Hopkins University Press, 1963); For India, see G.S. Laumas, 'The Shifting of Corporation Income Tax: A Study with Reference to Indian Corporations', *Public Finance*, Vol. 21, No. 4, 1966, pp. 462-473.
3. For a detailed discussion on the distinction between direct and indirect taxes, see: (i) Ursula K. Hicks, "The Terminology of Tax Analysis," in *Readings in the Economics of Taxation,* The American Economic Association, (London: George Allen and Unwin Ltd., 1959), pp. 214-216; (ii) D. Walker, "Direct versus Indirect Taxes", in *Public Finance* edited by D.W. Houghton, (England: Penguin Books Ltd., 1972), pp. 349-375.
4. According to a study conducted by Raja Chelliah and others for a group of 47 developing countries for the average of the period 1969-71, the average share of indirect taxes was 64 percent of the total tax revenue. As for developed economies, the share of indirect taxes ranged between 45-50 percent of the total tax revenues. [See R.J. Chelliah, H.J. Bass, and M.R. Kelly, "Tax Ratios and Tax Efforts in Developing Countries, 1969-71", *I.M.F. Staff Papers,* Vol. 22, No. 1, March 1975, Table 2]. It is noteworthy that in India the proportion of indirect taxes stood at 78.8 per cent in 1970-71, much higher than the international average of the developing world.
5. Government of India, Ministry of Finance, *Long Term Fiscal Policy,* December 1985, p. 23.
6. Government of India, Planning Commission, *Tenth Five Year Plan* (2002-07), Vol. I, p. 61.
7. See chapter 19 of this book for details.

8

Buoyancy and Elasticity of Tax Revenue

8.1 Conceptual Framework

High degree of responsiveness of tax yield to changes in national income is a desirable characteristic of any tax system. If a government depends on tax revenue to finance a large part of its expenditure, then it is necessary to ensure that an increasing proportion of national income flows into the public treasury as taxes. In other words, the requirement is to increase the incremental tax ratio. Computation of tax buoyancy and elasticity becomes relevant in this context.

8.1.1 Automatic Response versus Discretionary Changes: Tax revenue may change through *automatic* response of the tax yield to changes in national income and/or through the imposition of new taxes, revision of the rates and/or the bases of the existing taxes, tax amnesties, stricter tax compliance and other administrative measures backed by legal action. Changes in the tax yield resulting from modifying such tax parameters (i.e. rate, base etc.) are called *discretionary changes* which are the result of legislative action.

With tax parameters held constant (i.e. discretionary changes being removed), automatic changes in the tax yield resulting from variations in the national income measure the elasticity or built-in-flexibility of a tax or a tax system. It is computed by dividing percentage change in tax revenue (adjusted for discretionary changes) to the percentage change in national income. Changes in the tax yield flowing from the combined effect of automatic response and discretionary changes measure the buoyancy of a tax. It is computed by dividing the percentage change in tax revenue by the percentage change in the national income. [1]

Buoyancy coefficient compares the actual growth of tax revenue with the growth in national income. It assesses the overall success of government measures to increase tax revenue. Elasticity coefficient, on the other hand, indicates the inherent responsiveness of a tax system to changes in national income. It reflects the revenue potential of the tax system.

If a tax system lacks elasticity, the government will have to make frequent changes in tax laws to boost revenue. This will cause legal complications, reduce administrative efficiency and prove to be politically inexpedient. Therefore, while casting the tax net, tax bases should be so selected and rate structure so designed that reasonable degree of elasticity is imparted to the tax system.

Buoyancy and elasticity attributes of a tax system assume varying importance during the course of development process. As economic activities pick up and monetisation spreads, more and more tax bases become available to the government. To extend and intensify the tax structure, new taxes are imposed, rates of existing taxes are revised, tax bases are widened and administrative machinery is toned up. These discretionary changes, which are part of the buoyancy concept, play the dominant role and in a sense initiate the process towards higher tax-to-national income ratio. When tax revenue forms quite a high ratio of national income, further legislative action becomes politically disadvantageous in view of tax payers' resistance. Moreover, frequent changes in tax parameters create confusion and uncertainty harming the smooth growth of trade and industry. Thus, discretionary changes, though never coming to a halt in an expanding economy, lose significance in course of time. Elasticity of the tax system becomes more important at this stage. If a tax system is sufficiently elastic, the process initiated by discretionary changes will be kept up automatically.

8.2 Various Estimates of Buoyancy and Elasticity of Tax Revenue

Several studies have computed the buoyancy and elasticity attributes of the Indian tax system since Independence. Estimates of some of these studies are summarised in Table 8.1.

In the early 1960s, G.S. Sahota made the first systematic and comprehensive attempt to compute buoyancy and elasticity of the tax revenue. For the period 1951-52 to 1957-58, Sahota estimated the buoyancy of Union and State taxes taken together at 1.69 while for Union taxes taken separately at 2.39. The crucial elasticity coefficient for the same period was found to be 0.83 for Union and State taxes considered together and 0.61 for Union taxes considered separately.

Another notable study was undertaken by V.G. Rao who estimated the buoyancy and elasticity of all Central and State taxes at 1.22 and 0.82, all Central taxes at 1.22 and 0.74, and all State taxes at 1.27 and 1.01 respectively for the period 1960-61 to 1973-74.

The computations of the Indirect Taxation Enquiry Committee (ITEC), 1978, also revealed poor elasticity of the indirect tax system, except import duties. For the Union excise duties, accounting for nearly half of Centre's total tax collections, the Committee estimated the buoyancy and elasticity coefficients at 1.31 and 0.75 respectively for the period 1963-64 to 1974-75.

In another study, I.K. Khadye estimated the buoyancy and elasticity of combined tax revenue (Centre and States) at 1.25 and 0.88 respectively for the period 1960-61 to 1978-79. For the same period, the buoyancy and elasticity coefficients of Central taxes taken separately were found to be 1.25 and 0.83 respectively.

Table 8.1: Buoyancy and Elasticity of Tax Revenue in India in Relation to National Income

Author	Period for which computations made	Tax group	Buoyancy	Elasticity
G.S. Sahota	1951-52 to 1957-58	1. All Central and State taxes 2. All Central taxes	1.69 2.39*	0.83 0.61
V.G. Rao	1960-61 to 1973-74	1. All Central and State taxes 2. All Central taxes 3. All State taxes	1.22 1.22 1.27	0.82 0.74 1.01
Indirect Taxation Enquiry Committee, 1978	1963-64 to 1974-75	1. Union excise duties	1.31	0.75
I.K. Khadye	1960-61 to 1978-79	1. All Central and State taxes 2. All Central taxes	1.25 1.25	0.88 0.83
M.M. Sury	1950-51 to 1964-65 and 1965-66 to 1980-81	1. Union excise duties	3.02 and 1.27	1.86 and 0.73
Tenth Finance Commission (1995-2000)	1983-84 to 1992-93	1. Union excise duties 2. Income tax 3. Corporation tax 4. Customs duties	1.01 1.10 1.31 1.38	--- --- --- ---
Eleventh Finance Commission (2000-05)	1980-81 to 1989-90 and 1990-91 to 1998-99	1. Central taxes: Gross revenues 2. States own tax revenues 3. Combined tax revenues	1.15 and 0.91 1.12 and 1.04 1.14 and 0.96	--- --- ---
Tenth Five Year Plan (2002-07)	8th Plan, 9th Plan and 10th Plan	1. Central tax revenue 2. Direct taxes 3. Indirect taxes 4. Customs 5. Excise	0.9, 0.8, and 1.26 1.3, 1.3, and 1.5 0.7, 0.6, and 1.1 0.9, 0.1, and 0.96 0.6, 1.0, and 1.16	--- --- --- --- ---

Contd...

Twelfth Finance Commission (2005-2010)	1950-51 to 2001-2002	1. Central taxes: Gross revenues	1.14	---
		2. States own tax revenues	1.17	---
		3. Combined tax revenues	1.15	---

* For the period 1953-54 to 1957-58.

Sources: (i) G.S. Sahota, *Tax Structure and Economic Development,* (Bombay: Asia Publishing House, 1961), Tables IV and VI; (ii) V.G. Rao, *Responsiveness of the Indian Tax System,* 1960-61 to 1973-74 (New Delhi: Allied Publishers Pvt. Ltd., 1979), Tables 4.1 and 4.4; (iii) Government of India, Ministry of Finance, *Report of the Indirect Taxation Enquiry Committee,* Part II, January 1978, p. 399; (iv) I.K. Khadye, "The Responsiveness of Tax Revenue to National Income in India, 1960-61 to 1978-79", RBI *Occasional Papers,* Vol. 22, No. 1, June 1981; (v) M.M. Sury, "Buoyancy and Elasticity of Union Excise Revenue in India: 1950-51 to 1980-81", *Margin,* Vol. 18, No. 1, October, 1985, p. 55; (vi) *Report of the Tenth Finance Commission,* December 1994, p. 168; (vii) *Report of the Eleventh Finance Commission,* June 2000, p. 10; (viii) Government of India, Planning Commission, *Tenth Five Year Plan* (2002-07), Vol. I, Table 2.25, p. 61; (ix) *Report of the Twelfth Finance Commission* (2005-10), November 2004, Table 4.9, p. 64.

In yet another attempt, M.M. Sury estimated buoyancy and elasticity of Union excise duties for two sub-periods, 1950-51 to 1964-65, and 1965-66 to 1980-81 separately. For the period 1950-51 to 1964-65, the buoyancy and elasticity coefficients turned out to be 3.02 and 1.86 respectively. However, for the period 1965-66 to 1980-81, the values of both the buoyancy and elasticity coefficients were relatively low at 1.27 and 0.73 respectively. It is noteworthy that these estimates (1.27 and 0.73) were very close to the estimates of ITEC (1.31 and 0.75) for Union excise duties for the period 1963-64 to 1974-75.

The buoyancy estimates of various Central taxes made by the Tenth Finance Commission (1995-2000) for the period 1983-84 to 1992-93 were as follows: Union excise duties (1.01), income tax (1.10), corporation tax (1.31), and customs duties (1.38).

Eleventh Finance Commission (2000-05) also estimated buoyancy coefficients for Central taxes, States' own tax revenue, and combined tax revenue for the periods 1980-81 to 1989-90 and 1990-91 to 1998-99. In its own words, "The buoyancy of gross tax revenue of the Centre with respect to GDP works out to 0.91 during the nineties, as compared to 1.15 in the eighties. In the case of the States, the buoyancy coefficients were 1.04 in the nineties as against 1.12 in the eighties. The slump in the buoyancy of Central taxes in the nineties occurred despite a smart rise in the growth of revenue from direct taxes, as the revenue growth from the two major indirect taxes—customs and Union excises—sharply decelerated. Tax reform, while no doubt helping to introduce some rationality in the tax structure apparently had a dampening effect on the Centre's revenue, as the impressive growth of direct taxes could not fully compensate for the drop in customs and Union excises that took place in the post-reform period. On the States' side, the dip in tax buoyancy occurred as revenue from sales tax, the principal component of their own tax sources, showed a declining growth trend owning to tax competition among the States to attract trade and industry". [2]

For more recent periods, two estimates of buoyancy of tax revenue in India are noteworthy: one by the Tenth Five Year Plan (2002-07) and the other by the Twelfth Finance Commission (2005-10).

Tenth Plan estimated the buoyancy of Central tax revenue at 0.9, 0.8 and 1.26 for Eighth Plan, Ninth Plan, and Tenth Plan respectively. Buoyancy of direct tax revenue of the Centre was estimated at 1.3, 1.3 and 1.5 for the three Plans respectively. For the same Plans, buoyancy estimates for other categories of taxes were as follows: Centre's indirect taxes (0.7, 0.6, 1.1); customs duties (0.9, 0.1, 0.96); and excise duties (0.6, 1.0, 1.16).

Buoyancy estimates of the Twelfth Finance Commission (2005-10) of various groups of taxes for the period 1950-51 to 2001-02 were as follows: gross Central taxes (1.14), States own tax revenue (1.17) and combined tax revenue (1.15).

The relatively high buoyancy of the tax system revealed by the foregoing estimates indicates the success of tax policy as a tool of resource mobilization in India. However, the same studies show a relatively low elasticity of the tax system, indicating lack of inherent response of tax yield to changes in national income. Weakness of the elasticity characteristic of the tax system is generally attributed to lax administration and large-scale tax evasion.

Endnotes

1. If there are several discretionary changes of revenue significance during the reference period, the elasticity coefficient would be much lower than the buoyancy coefficient.
2. Report of the Eleventh Finance Commission, June 2000, p. 11.

9

Distribution of Tax Burden (Tax Incidence)

9.1 Meaning of Tax Incidence

Incidence in economics refers to the distributional effects of a fiscal measure. Thus, tax incidence means *who bears the burden of taxes* while expenditure incidence means *who benefits from public expenditure*? Similarly, budget incidence relates to the combined effects of an equal increase in tax and public expenditure on the distribution of income. It is also called net incidence and is obtained by summing, algebraically, both the tax incidence (negative) and expenditure incidence (positive) for each of the income/expenditure classes.

Incidence of a tax is on the person who ultimately pays it, i.e. who cannot shift it any further. Hence, tax incidence relates to the final resting place of the tax burden as against the impact which means the first place where a tax is imposed. Due to economic transactions, a tax percolates through many parts of the economy and the burden of it can be shifted, forward or backward, by the original taxpayer to other entities.

9.2 Methodological Issues

Analysis of the incidence of direct taxes is comparatively simple because the burden by income groups is indicated by the schedule of rates. Moreover, in poor countries direct taxes cover a very small fraction of the community so that in a classification of the population into a few broad income categories, the class of direct taxpayers will easily belong to the highest income category. In the case of indirect taxes, the problem is difficult. To analyse the incidence, one has to trace the consumption of taxed commodities to the family budgets of people in different income/expenditure classes. Income distribution data are required to estimate the liability of households for direct taxes while expenditure data are needed for ascertaining the burden of indirect taxes on households.

A tax incidence study aims at obtaining a quantitative basis for examining equity attribute of a tax system. For example, we may like to know the distribution of the money burden of excise duties among different economic classes in India in a particular year. The following points need to be kept in view before surveying tax incidence studies in India.

1. It is generally assumed that commodity taxes levied on the producers are

shifted in full to the consumers who bear them in proportion to their consumption of the various commodities taxed. However, the theory of tax incidence states that the burden of a commodity tax is shared between the consumers and producers in the ratio of elasticity of supply to elasticity of demand of the taxed commodity.

The full shifting assumption would be valid if the supply of the taxed commodity is perfectly elastic. This is not likely to be the case in the short-run in view of certain fixed costs of production. However, in the long-run when all costs become variable (i.e. factors of production can move in and out of the industry freely), the supply can be assumed to be perfectly elastic. The whole burden of the tax will get shifted to the consumers.

2. Evasion of commodity taxes (customs duties, excise levies and sales taxes) by importers, manufacturers and sellers is not uncommon in India. For example, while producers evade excise duty, in part or in full, they nevertheless 'recover' the same from the consumers. It means excise duty paid by consumers is not reflected, in such cases, in the tax collections of the Government. Estimates of tax incidence are understated to this extent.
3. A part of actual collection of commodity taxes represents tax element in the Government's consumption expenditure. This part of collections is a mere book adjustment and should be excluded from the purview of the study to avoid overestimation of tax burden. For this purpose the share of Government (at all levels) in the consumption of taxed commodities has to be found out so that that portion of revenue which the Government pays to itself could be taken out. [1] It means the money burden of commodity taxes is taken to be equivalent to revenue collections realised from non-Government sector.
4. It is desirable if the incidence analysis estimates the burden of commodity taxes on rural and urban sectors separately. This inter-sectoral approach provides a measure of horizontal equity of the tax under consideration. The rural-urban classification is important because it reflects the nature of economic activity in which people are engaged—the former primarily in agriculture and the latter in industry and services.
5. For the purpose of the study of tax incidence, researchers generally use the consumer expenditure data collected by the National Sample Survey (NSS) periodically. The NSS data splits total expenditure of a class into cash and non-cash expenditure. The important items in which non-cash expenditure (for which values are imputed) predominates are foodgrains, pulses, milk and milk products, fuel and light. These items are supplied from own-farms, kitchen gardens or free sources. The ratio of non-cash expenditure to total expenditure is high in rural sector as compared to urban sector due to obvious

reasons. The non-cash expenditure is not subject to taxation.

Should incidence of taxation he expressed in relation to cash consumer expenditure only or to total consumer expenditure? One view can be that since only cash purchases are subject to taxation therefore the burden of the latter should be expressed in relation to the total cash purchases. Relating tax burden to total expenditure, will underestimate the incidence in cases where the ratio of cash purchases to total expenditure is lower as, for example, in rural areas. The other view is that since total consumption expenditure and not cash expenditure only is the appropriate index of taxpaying capacity therefore tax burden should be related to the total expenditure. As already pointed out, non-cash expenditure mainly pertains to the value imputed to consumption of home produce, goods supplied in kind (e.g. to agricultural workers) and articles acquired by barter.

6. Another issue is whether to work out incidence per capita or per household in urban and rural areas. Though estimates are available for both per household and per capita expenditure, there is no standard definition of a household in NSS data. NSS defines household as a group of persons normally living together and taking food from common kitchen. Now the ratio of tax incidence for each income/expenditure class represents the 'average' burden on that class. If these classes consist of families with different sizes, there would naturally be variations in the tax incidence on the households within each class. Therefore, the Indirect Taxation Enquiry Committee preferred monthly per capita expenditure groups "because the relative economic positions of different households are more accurately reflected by per capita expenditure levels". [2]
7. Should the burden of commodity taxes be related to income or expenditure of various economic classes? Preferably, it should be estimated with reference to both income and expenditure to present a comparative view of tax progressivity. While expenditure data are actuals as provided by NSS, income data could be derived with the help of available saving estimates of different classes.

Estimates of various studies regarding incidence of indirect taxes in India during the post-Independence period are presented below. The findings of these studies are helpful in assessing the equity attribute of the Indian tax system.

9.3 All-India Level Studies

9.3.1 Findings of the Taxation Enquiry Commission (Chairman: John Matthai), 1953-54: Taxation Enquiry Commission (TEC), 1953-54, was the first to undertake a systematic and comprehensive study of the incidence of Central and State indirect taxes on rural and urban households in different expenditure groups. [3] TEC study was based on the consumer expenditure data collected by the National Sample Survey (NSS) in the 4th round (April-September 1952). These data were assumed to hold good for the year 1953-54 for which TEC worked out the incidence of indirect taxes. The burden of indirect taxes was worked out in terms of percentages of expenditure in different monthly expenditure classes by rural and urban areas. In the absence of data on income distribution, the expenditure was assumed to be equal to income and this presumption constituted a serious limitation of the study. The main findings of the TEC study were: (a) 3.6 percent of consumer expenditure was paid in indirect taxes by all households in the country, (b) urban households paid twice the proportion of consumer expenditure paid in indirect taxes by rural households, and (c) among different expenditure groups in rural and urban households, the money burden of indirect taxes was mildly progressive (Table 9.1).

9.3.2 Studies by the Ministry of Finance: The incidence of Central and State indirect taxes in India was examined twice later by the Union Ministry of Finance. The first study which may be called in short as MF-I related to the year 1958-59 [4], and the second called MF-II to the year 1963-64. [5]

MF-I study was based on the NSS data on consumer expenditure collected in the 13th round (September 1957 to May 1958). Similarly, MF-II study was based on NSS data on consumer expenditure collected during the 18th round (February 1963 to January 1964). Results of these two studies are summarised in Table 9.1.

MF-I provided a comparative analysis of the distribution of money burden of all indirect taxes among rural and urban households in different expenditure groups during 1953-54 and 1958-59. The comparison brought out the change in the distribution of tax burden produced by the increase in indirect taxation during the period between the mid-points of the First and the Second Five Year Plans. The main findings of MF-I study were as follows: (a) In 1953-54, indirect taxes accounted for 3.6 percent of consumer expenditure of all households in the country. By 1958-59, the proportion went up to 5.7 percent, mainly on account of expansion of Central excises, and sales taxes; (b) This was true for both rural and urban households. The proportion of consumer expenditure paid in indirect taxes by rural households increased from 2.9 percent in 1953-54 to 4.4 percent in 1958-59, and by urban households from 5.9 percent to 9.3 percent over the same period; (c) In 1953-54, urban households paid twice the proportion of consumer expenditure paid in indirect taxes by rural households while by 1958-59 the proportion paid by urban households became 2.1 times that paid by rural households, implying a slightly higher relative burden on urban households; (d) the distribution of money burden of indirect taxes among different expenditure groups was progressive both in 1953-54, and 1958-59; and (e) In 1958-59, the distribution of money burden of indirect taxes among different expenditure groups was more progressive at the all-India level and also separately for rural and urban households.

Table 9.1: Indirect Taxes as Percent of Consumer Expenditure

	TEC 1953-54			MF-I 1958-59			MF-II 1963-64		
Monthly Household Expenditure Groups (₹)	Rural	Urban	All-India	Rural	Urban	All-India	Rural	Urban	All-India
1-50	2.2	3.3	2.4	2.5	5.8	3.1	5.8	11.1	6.5
51-100	2.3	4.4	2.7	3.6	7.1	4.3	6.1	11.6	7.0
101-150	2.7	5.1	3.1	4.1	8.0	5.1	6.8	12.6	8.0
151-300	2.8	5.1	3.3	4.8	9.0	5.9	8.8	14.0	10.1
301 and above	4.4	8.3	5.6	6.9	13.8	9.3	11.9	24.6	16.6
All households	2.9	5.9	3.6	4.4	9.3	5.7	8.0	16.6	10.1

Note: In the MF-II study, the lowest monthly group consisted of ₹ 0-50 and the highest ₹ 501 and above whereas in the case of the earlier studies the lowest group comprised ₹ 0-50, and the highest ₹ 301 and above. To facilitate comparison, groups ₹ 301-500 and ₹ 501 and above in the MF-II study were combined and the results for the merged group ₹ 301 and above are set out in the above table.

Sources: For TEC, Government of India, Ministry of Finance, *Report of the Taxation Enquiry Commission, 1953-54,* Volume I, p. 69, Table 7; for MF-I, Government of India, Ministry of Finance, *Incidence of Indirect Taxation, 1958-59,* (New Delhi, 1961), p. 10; and for MF-II, Government of India, Ministry of Finance, *Incidence of Indirect Taxation, 1963-64,* (New Delhi, 1969), Table VI.

MF-II study pertained to the incidence of indirect taxes for the year 1963-64. According to MF-II study, the proportion of indirect taxes in the total consumer expenditure increased from 3.6 percent in 1953-54 to 5.7 percent in 1958-59, and 10.1 percent in 1963-64. In the case of urban households, the tax element as a percentage of per capita consumer expenditure rose from 5.9 percent in 1953-54 to 9.3 percent in 1958-59, and further up to 16.6 percent in 1963-64. In the case of rural households, the corresponding increase in the tax element was from 2.9 percent in 1953-54 to 4.4 percent in 1958-59, and 8.0 percent in 1963-64. Thus, as in the case of TEC and MF-I studies, the tax incidence on the urban households in 1963-64 was a little more than two times the incidence on rural households. Finally, the incidence of indirect taxation continued to remain progressive in 1963-64, both in the case of urban and rural households, judging by the proportion paid in indirect taxes by the households in different expenditure groups.

9.3.3 Estimates of Indirect Taxation Enquiry Committee (Chairman: L.K. Jha), 1978: Indirect Taxation Enquiry Committee (ITEC), 1978, undertook a comprehensive study of the incidence of indirect taxes for the year 1973-74. It was based on NSS data of consumer expenditure collected in the 28th round (October 1973 to June 1974). [6] Taking into account all indirect taxes which amounted to 11.2 percent of national income in 1973-74, the ITEC arrived at the following main conclusions, "of this 11.2 percent, 1.65 percentage points could be said to have fallen on the Government sector and on the investors, and the rest to have been shifted to the private consumers. The portion falling on the consumers is estimated to have amounted to 10.54 percent of household consumption expenditure. This is an average of the burden on rural and urban households, which differed considerably in percentage terms. While the burden on rural households amounted only to 8.0 percent of their consumption, that on the urban households amounted to 18.0 percent. The rural sector accounted for 77 percent of private consumption, and bore 57 percent of the indirect taxes allocable to consumers. The share of rural sector in total population is estimated to have been 80.1 percent in that year". [7]

Table 9.2 shows indirect taxes paid as percent of consumer expenditure by different per capita expenditure groups ranging from the poorest group with a monthly per capita expenditure not exceeding ₹ 15 to the highest expenditure group with a monthly per capita expenditure above ₹ 100.

Table 9.2: Indirect Taxes as Percent of Total Expenditure by Per Capita Expenditure Groups (1973-74)

Monthly Per Capita Expenditure Group (₹)	Taxes as Percent of Total Expenditure		
	Rural	Urban	All-India
0-15	2.91	3.63	2.96
15-28	3.33	6.31	3.63
28-43	4.45	7.36	4.89
43-55	6.18	9.66	6.85
55-75	6.71	11.86	7.92
75-100	10.02	14.80	11.40
100 and above	16.17	30.19	21.96
All Households	8.03	17.96	10.54

Source: Government of India, Ministry of Finance, *Report of the Indirect Taxation Enquiry Committee,* Part II (January 1978), p. 90 (excerpted).

Table 9.2 reveals a progressive distribution of the tax burden in terms of percentage of total expenditure at the all-India level. It increases progressively from 2.96 percent for households with per capita monthly expenditure not exceeding ₹ 15 to 21.96 percent for the group with per capita expenditure of ₹ 100 and above. Thus, even the poorest section of the society was found to be paying about 3 percent of its expenditure as taxes to the Government.

Table 9.2 further reveals that the incidence of indirect taxes on different per capita expenditure groups in both rural and urban households was progressive but more so in urban than in rural area. In rural area, the lowest expenditure group (₹ 0-15) paid 2.91 percent of its expenditure as indirect taxes and the highest expenditure group (₹ 100 and above) paid 16.17 percent. In urban area, the proportion varied from 3.63 percent (for ₹ 0-15) to 30.19 percent (for ₹ 100 and above). The higher burden of taxes on urban households was explained by differences in the pattern of consumption between rural and urban households and also by the higher proportion of non-cash expenditures of rural households.

The ITEC study concluded also that per capita indirect tax payment per annum for urban and rural households was ₹ 174.50 and ₹ 57.30 respectively in 1973-74, giving an approximate ratio of 3:1(Table 9.3).

Apart from the combined burden of indirect taxes, ITEC studied also the incidence of individual taxes on various expenditure groups. Table 9.3 shows the relative incidence of Central indirect taxes vis-à-vis State indirect taxes as also the incidence of Central excise duties. The last column of the table reveals that Central taxes accounted for a larger share of incidence in both urban and rural sectors. Out of 8.03 percent, Central taxes accounted for 4.99 percentage points in rural areas and in urban areas their share was 12.03 percentage points out of a total tax burden of 17.96 percent of expenditure. It is also observed that Central indirect taxes were more progressive than State taxes.

The share of Central excises hovered around half of the total incidence of indirect taxes. Their burden on the lowest expenditure group (₹ 0-15), middle expenditure group (₹ 43-55) and the highest expenditure group (₹ 100 and above) was estimated to be 1.47 percent 3.31 percent and 11.55 percent of expenditure respectively at all-India level; 1.42 percent, 2.92 percent and 7.87 percent for rural sector; and 2.42 percent, 4.94 percent and 16.78 percent for urban sector. The incidence of Central excises was quite progressive (Table 9.3).

In a first attempt of its kind in India, ITEC worked out the incidence of indirect taxes on major types of goods separately. The goods subject to taxes were classified into three main groups according to the nature of use, viz.: (a) consumption goods, (b) intermediate goods, and (c) capital goods.

Table 9.3: Per Capita Per Annum Consumer Expenditure, Indirect Tax Burden and Indirect Tax Burden as Percent of Consumer Expenditure, 1973-74

				Rural				
Monthly per capita expenditure group (₹)	0-15	15-28	28-43	43-55	55-75	75-100	100 and above	All Households
Per capita per annum total CE* (₹)	164.6	311.2	478.5	653.0	855.1	1146.4	1907.8	713.7
Indirect taxes per capita per annum (₹)	4.7	10.3	21.2	40.3	57.3	114.8	308.4	57.3
Central taxes	2.7	5.8	12.3	24.0	36.3	72.4	196.4	35.5
Central excises	2.3	4.6	9.6	19.0	27.9	55.5	150.1	27.4
States taxes	2.0	4.5	8.9	16.3	21.0	42.3	111.9	21.7
Tax as % of CE								
All indirect taxes	2.9	3.3	4.4	6.1	6.7	10.0	16.1	8.0
Central taxes	1.6	1.8	2.5	3.6	4.2	6.3	10.3	4.9
Central excises	1.4	1.5	2.0	2.9	3.2	4.8	7.8	3.8
States taxes	1.2	1.4	1.8	2.5	2.4	3.7	5.8	3.0
				Urban				
Per capita per annum total CE (₹)	166.7	329.4	497.0	671.7	879.7	1179.3	2164.4	971.8
Indirect taxes per capita per annum (₹)	6.0	20.8	36.5	64.8	104.3	174.5	653.3	174.5
Central taxes	4.0	12.3	22.6	40.1	66.9	110.9	454.3	116.8
Central excises	4.0	10.2	18.6	33.1	55.0	91.6	363.1	94.5
States taxes	2.0	8.4	13.9	24.7	37.3	63.6	199.0	57.6
Tax as % of CE								
All indirect taxes	3.6	6.3	7.3	9.6	11.8	14.8	30.1	17.9
Central taxes	2.4	3.7	4.5	5.9	7.6	9.4	20.9	12.0
Central excises	2.4	3.1	3.7	4.9	6.2	7.7	16.7	9.7
States taxes	1.2	2.5	2.8	3.6	4.2	5.4	9.2	5.9
				All India				
Per capita per annum total CE (₹)	164.7	312.9	481.2	656.5	860.7	1156.7	2006.0	765.1
Indirect taxes per capita per annum (₹)	4.8	11.3	23.5	45.0	68.1	131.8	440.4	80.6
Central taxes	2.8	6.4	13.8	27.1	43.3	83.3	295.1	51.7
Central excises	2.4	5.1	10.9	21.7	34.1	65.8	231.6	40.8
States taxes	2.0	4.9	9.6	17.9	24.7	48.4	145.3	28.8
Tax as % of CE								
All indirect taxes	2.9	3.6	4.8	6.8	7.9	11.4	21.9	10.5

Contd...

Central taxes	1.7	2.0	2.8	4.1	5.0	7.2	14.7	6.7
Central excises	1.4	1.6	2.2	3.3	3.9	5.6	11.5	5.3
States taxes	1.2	1.5	2.0	2.7	2.8	4.1	7.2	3.7

*CE = Consumer expenditure;

Source: Government of India, Ministry of Finance, *Report of the Indirect Taxation Enquiry Committee*, Part II, January 1978, Appendix 10, Table 1 (excerpted).

Table 9.4 shows that out of the total incidence of 10.54 percent of consumption expenditure for all households at all-India level, the share of consumption goods was 5.34 percentage points, amounting to half of the total incidence. Intermediate goods accounted for 4.53 percentage points and the remaining 0.63 percentage point was accounted for by capital goods. In sharp contrast to this pattern, the incidence of Central excises according to type of goods showed a totally different distribution. Intermediate goods claimed the largest share of the incidence of Central excises i.e. out of a total incidence of 5.34 percent of consumption expenditure attributable to Central excises in respect of all households at all-India level, the incidence of Central excises on intermediate goods accounted for 2.95 percentage points which was 55 percent of 5.34 percent.

Table 9.4: Burden of all Indirect Taxes and Central Excises as percent of Consumer Expenditure According to Type of Goods

	Monthly Per Capita Expenditure Groups (₹)							
	0-15	15-28	28-43	43-55	55-75	75-100	100 and above	All House -holds
All India All Indirect Taxes	2.95	3.63	4.89	6.85	7.92	11.40	21.96	10.54
1. Consumption Goods	1.32	1.66	2.31	3.58	3.91	6.10	11.11	5.34
2. Intermediate Goods	1.47	1.75	2.30	2.91	3.59	4.75	9.17	4.53
3. Capital Goods	0.16	0.22	0.28	0.36	0.42	0.55	1.68	0.67
Central Excises	1.47	1.66	2.27	3.31	3.97	5.69	11.55	5.34
1. Consumption Goods	0.41	0.46	0.74	1.37	1.63	2.62	5.03	2.25
2. Intermediate Goods	1.06	1.19	1.52	1.92	2.31	3.01	6.01	2.95
3. Capital Goods	---	0.01	0.01	0.02	0.03	0.06	0.51	0.14

Source: Compiled from Government of India, Ministry of Finance, *Report of the Indirect Taxation Enquiry Committee*, Part II, (January 1978), Chapter 6, Tables 3 and 4, pp. 96 and 98.

The ITEC also estimated the distribution of the burden of indirect taxes on certain selected commodities among various expenditure groups of urban household. It is interesting to note that the expenditure group ₹ 15-28 was made to pay 1.77 percent of its total expenditure as tax on the six commodities (Table 9.5, col. 3, last row) while the burden on the highest expenditure group (₹ 100 and above) was just 1.57 percent of its expenditure (col. 8, last row). It points to the regressive nature of indirect taxes on commodities listed in Table 9.5.

Table 9.5: Distribution of the Burden of Indirect Taxes on Certain Selected Commodities among Various Expenditure Groups of Urban Households as Percent of Total Consumption Expenditure (1973-74)

	Monthly Per Capita Expenditure Groups (₹)							
Commodities	0-15	15-28	28-43	43-55	55-75	75-100	100 and above	All Households
	Percentages							
Total Incidence for All Indirect Taxes	3.63	6.31	7.36	9.66	11.86	14.80	30.19	17.96
Foodgrains and *Atta**	0.30	0.37	0.36	0.33	0.28	0.24	0.18	0.26
Sugar	0.61	0.46	0.60	0.55	0.54	0.51	0.38	0.47
Vegetable product, oil and fats	0.00	0.33	0.46	0.52	0.50	0.50	0.40	0.47
Kerosene	0.00	0.48	0.51	0.54	0.51	0.50	0.45	0.50
Matches	0.00	0.05	0.07	0.10	0.09	0.06	0.05	0.07
Soaps and detergents	0.00	0.08	0.11	0.11	0.12	0.12	0.11	0.11
Total for the 6 items	0.91	1.77	2.11	2.15	2.04	1.93	1.57	1.88

*Taxes on these commodities are levied only by the State Governments.
Source: Compiled from Government of India, Ministry of Finance, *Report of the Indirect Taxation Enquiry Committee*, Part II (January 1978), Chapter 6, Table 7, pp.102-103.

A. Critical Assessment: The estimates of incidence by ITEC indicated that the overall indirect tax structure was quite progressive. However, before drawing any conclusions the following points should be noted. In its study, all households with per capita monthly expenditure of ₹ 100 and above were lumped together into one class. This was too broad a group to understand the distribution of tax burden on the middle and the rich classes.

Furthermore, the study expressed the burden of indirect taxes as a ratio of expenditure, rather than income of different economic groups. It is generally accepted that income of an individual is a better index of his ability-to-pay taxes. What percentage of income do people surrender as taxes shows the real sacrifice on their part. The law of marginal propensity to consume states that consumption expenditure, as a proportion of income, tends to fall as one moves up the income scale. Thus, at very low levels of income, consumption might be as much as the income whereas it might account for an insignificant proportion of income at high income levels. For instance, it can safely be assumed that for the lowest two or three expenditure groups the distinction between income and expenditure is not significant in view of the high marginal propensity to consume amongst these groups.

Therefore, the percentage of consumption expenditure paid as taxes virtually represents the percentage of income. This, however, is not true at higher levels of income where the amount of taxes forms a higher percentage of expenditure but quite a low percentage of income. Thus, a progressive system of taxation with reference to expenditure may turn out to be less progressive or even regressive when related to income. Or, putting it differently, the studies which relate tax burden to expenditure overstate the progression (or understate the regression) of the tax system. Therefore, it is difficult to conclude on the basis of ITEC findings whether the indirect tax system is equitable or not.

9.3.4 Findings of the Study by National Institute of Public Finance and Policy (NIPFP): This study of incidence of indirect taxes in India was sponsored by the Ministry of Finance, Government of India. It was conducted at the National Institute of Public Finance and Policy (NIPFP) by Pawan K. Aggarwal. The study, which has recently been published in the form of a book [8], estimated the incidence of major indirect taxes, viz. customs duties and excise duties levied by the Central Government, and sales taxes levied by the State Governments.

Major findings of the study which pertained to the fiscal year 1989-90 are the following: "(i) a large variation in the tax incidence across commodities with high incidence of tax on some commodities, (ii) moderately high tax incidence on necessities, (iii) substantial input taxation (accounting for more than 30 percent of tax incidence on most commodities), (iv) sales tax contributing the highest to input taxation, (v) tax incidence on consumers in rural areas lower than that in urban areas, (vi) progresssivity of taxes in rural areas higher than that in urban areas, (vii) tax incidence on food items lower than that on non-food items, and (viii) tax incidence on cereals lower than that on other food items". [9]

Based on the consumer expenditure data of the National Sample Survey in the 44th round (July 1988-June 1989), the study estimated the combined effective tax rates for rural and urban areas at 11.2 percent and 12.2 percent respectively, indicating lower tax burden on consumers in rural areas than in urban areas. The distribution of tax burden with reference to consumer expenditure was found to be progressive in both rural and urban areas, though tax progressivity was higher in rural areas vis-à-vis urban areas. The effective tax rate increased along low to high expenditure classes from 9.8 percent to 13.7 percent in rural areas, and from 10.2 percent to 13.4 percent in urban areas (Table 9.6).

By relating tax burden to monthly per capita expenditure, the study repeated the mistake committed by the Indirect Taxation Enquiry Committee. Hence, its conclusions suffer from limitations. By its own admission, the study observed "It may, however, be noted that the tax progressivity would not have been so pronounced if it was viewed with reference to income instead of expenditure as the rich has a lower propensity to spend. If we assume zero savings by an average person in the lowest expenditure class and a 30 percent savings rate for an average person in the top expenditure class, then their effective tax rates with respect to income will be approximately equal even in the rural areas". [10] More appropriately, the expenditure classes should have been converted into income classes by using estimates of savings of different income groups, periodically brought out by NCAER. This was actually done by the Orissa Taxation Enquiry Committee while estimating incidence of taxation in that State.

Table 9.6: Combined Effective Rates of Major Indirect Taxes by 5 Expenditure Classes: 1988-89

		All Commodities		
S. No.	Monthly Per Capita Expenditure (₹)	Rural Areas	Urban Areas	All Areas
1.	< 110	9.81	10.25	9.85
2.	110-160	10.27	10.82	10.36
3.	160-215	10.94	11.21	11.00
4.	215-385	11.74	11.78	11.75
5.	Above 385	13.75	13.45	13.59

Source: Pawan K. Aggarwal, *Who Pays the Tax,* (Gayatri Publications, Delhi, 1998), p. 63, Table 5.3 (excerpted).

9.4 State-Level Studies

Among the State-level tax incidence studies, the following are noteworthy: one by the Orissa Taxation Enquiry Committee [11] and two studies by National Council of Applied Economic Research (NCAER) for the States of Gujarat, and Mysore (now Karnataka). [12]

9.4.1 Orissa Taxation Enquiry Committee: The Orissa Taxation Enquiry Committee was appointed by the Government of Orissa in 1959 under the chairmanship of P.S. Lokanathan. One of the terms of reference of the Committee was, 'to assess and advise on the incidence of the present structure and level of taxation on the people of different classes with particular reference to conditions in other States'.

For analysing the tax burden vis-à-vis the pattern of consumption expenditure of different income groups in the rural and urban sectors in Orissa, the Committee conducted a family budget enquiry in 1960 on the basis of stratified sampling. Households were classified and calculations of incidence made on the basis of monthly expenditure, instead of on the basis of monthly income. However, a procedure was devised to compute average income of each of the expenditure groups so that the burden of taxation could be related to income rather than expenditure of the household. It was assumed that the three expenditure groups (Table 9.7) did not have any savings, i.e. their income was the same as expenditure. In regard to the remaining groups it was assumed that there were some savings, and the higher the group the greater would be the rate of saving. The average propensity to save would be different for urban and rural households in the same expenditure level. Generally speaking, urban households can save less than their counterparts in rural areas in the same expenditure group. On the advice of NCAER, the average propensity to save in Orissa was assumed to be 5 percent in rural areas and 11 percent in urban areas. The rate of saving assumed for each group may be seen in Table 9.7.

Table 9.7: Incidence of Taxes in Orissa, 1960

Monthly Expenditure Group (₹)	Taxes as % of Consumption Expenditure		Average Propensity to Save		Taxes as % of Income	
	Rural	Urban	Rural	Urban	Rural	Urban
1-50	1.9	3.6	---	---	1.9	3.6
51-100	2.2	4.1	--	---	2.2	4.1
101-150	2.7	4.3	---	--	2.7	4.3
151-300	3.3	4.7	7.0	7.0	3.1	4.3
301-500	3.0	5.7	12.0	10.0	2.7	3.2
501-1,000	2.8	8.2	25.0	20.0	2.3	6.8
1,000 and above	2.6	14.6	35.0	25.0	1.9	11.7
All Groups	2.6	5.8	5.0	11.0	2.5	5.2

Source: Government of Orissa, *Orissa Taxation Enquiry Committee Report*, Bhubaneshwar, 1961.

The following information was revealed by the Orissa Committee: (a) Incidence of direct taxes per person per year was ₹ 1.56 in the rural areas against ₹ 8.64 in the urban areas. This disparity was due to the fact that income tax did not touch the rural taxpayers; (b) among indirect taxes, those of Central origin were found to claim a larger share than State taxes in rural as well as urban sectors. Rural incidence was ₹ 5.40 per annum while the urban incidence was ₹ 13.68; (c) by relating tax burden to income, the Committee found that in rural areas people paid 2.5 percent of their income towards taxes against 5.2 percent in urban areas; (d) the Committee found that the more well-to-do households in rural areas pay comparatively less tax than their counterparts in the urban areas or even the poorer households in the rural areas.

9.4.2 NCAER Study on Gujarat: The NCAER study of tax incidence in Gujarat pertained to the year 1967-68. It was an attempt to estimate the incidence of all taxes (Central and State) on households by income/expenditure groups. In order to measure the distribution of the burden of taxation among different income/expenditure classes of households, a sample survey was specially designed to collect data regarding family budgets and incomes of households. The actual tax liability of each household was calculated by applying the tax rates to the expenditure and income data collected through the survey.

The distribution of the money burden of the tax system as a whole was found to be progressive. Taxes as a proportion of income increased from 8 percent in the lowest income group (less than ₹ 1,200 per annum) to 22 percent in the highest group (above ₹ 24,000 per annum). This progression was attributed to the Central income tax, particularly at the higher income levels. The Study, however, found the incidence of individual taxes on commodities and services, such as Union excise and sales tax, to be regressive throughout the income ranges. The incidence of taxes on commodities and services was also studied with reference to expenditure. It was found that the overall burden of these taxes did not vary significantly at lower expenditure ranges although it became markedly progressive in the higher expenditure groups mainly due to the Central excise duty and State sales tax.

Two limitations of this study may particularly be noted. The Gujarat study was confined to the urban sector of that State. This partial analysis robbed the study much of its usefulness. Not only this, the survey sample (1,000 households in five towns) was too inadequate for a State like Gujarat. Moreover, the incidence of Union excises on consumer goods only was taken into account, i.e. the duty on producer goods used for the production of consumer goods was not covered due to difficulties of calculating the tax element in the prices of consumer goods that might have been shifted from the excise duties on raw materials and other intermediate goods.

9.4.3 NCAER Study on Mysore (Now Karnataka): The NCAER study of tax incidence for the State of Mysore related to the year 1968-69. It examined the tax burden in relation to household income and analysed the pattern of its distribution among different income groups, both in the urban and in the rural sectors of the State of Mysore. A representative sample survey of incomes and expenditures of households, stratified separately for urban and rural areas was undertaken to collect the necessary data.

For estimating the incidence of income tax, the tax revenue realised in the State from incomes arising during the year 1968-69 was allocated to the different income classes in the proportion of their tax liability calculated on the basis of the survey data. For indirect taxes, incidence was calculated separately for taxes on final consumer goods and producer goods.

The study showed contrasting effects of the tax system on the urban and the rural sectors. The tax system as a whole was found to be progressive in the urban sector but regressive in the rural sector (Table 9.8). Thus, in the urban sector, the tax-income ratio was found to rise from 10.1 percent in the lowest income class to 18.3 percent in the highest income group. Conversely, the ratio declined from 9.0 percent to 5.7 percent in the rural sector. The regressivity of the tax system in the rural sector was attributed to the absence of a progressive income tax. A marked disparity between the tax incidence on the urban and the rural sectors was also noticed throughout the entire range of household incomes.

Table 9.8: Incidence of Tax System as a whole in the State of Mysore (now Karnataka), 1968-69

Annual Household Income Groups (₹)	Urban (%)	Rural (%)	Ratio of Urban/Rural Tax Incidence
Up to 1,200	10.1	9.0	1.12
1,201-2,400	9.0	6.5	1.37
2,401-4,800	8.8	6.6	1.35
4,801-9,000	9.3	7.0	1.33
9,001-18,000	10.3	7.1	1.46
18,001-36,000	14.1	5.7	2.47
Over 36,000	18.3	5.7	3.21
All Groups	11.4	6.7	1.70

Source: National Council of Applied Economic Research, *Incidence of Taxation in Mysore State* (1972), p. 6.

The inter-sectoral disparity was found to increase sharply with increase in income and the tax burden on the highest income class in the urban sector was more than three times that on the comparable level in the rural sector (18.3:5.7). However, the average incidence on households in the urban areas was less than twice than in the rural sector (11.4:6.7). It was observed that even in the urban sector the tax system was not strictly progressive throughout the range of household incomes. It was regressive in the lowest income classes due to exemption from income tax at that income level. [13]

9.5 Sectoral Studies

Tax incidence studies pertaining to particular sectors of the Indian economy have also been attempted. Agricultural sector has received the maximum attention owing to the long-standing controversy regarding tax burden on Indian agriculture. The controversy was further aggravated by the Report of the Committee on Taxation of Agricultural Wealth and Income. [14] The Committee recommended the levying of agricultural holdings tax (AHT) on operational holdings and on a family basis. Incidence studies on Indian agriculture have been of all-India as well as State-level character. [15]

Most of the tax incidence studies have pointed out that the agricultural sector is relatively under-taxed and thus has the potential to bear a larger share of the tax burden. However, it must be noted that aggregative estimates of tax incidence of these studies have not taken into account the pattern of distribution of income in the two sectors. The greater the unequal distribution of income, the higher the tax yield under a system of progressive taxation. Furthermore, differences in the incidence of indirect taxes on the same expenditure groups in the rural and in the urban sectors are not due to deliberate manipulations in the tax system but are the result of differing characteristics of the two sectors. As Anand P. Gupta observed, "But what must be noted is that this horizontal inequity in the incidence of Central taxes is not due to any formal bias of these taxes in favour of the expenditure groups in the rural areas. In effect, the reasons for the inequitable incidence of Central indirect taxes, which are formally uniform throughout the country, lie in (a) the differences in the relative shares of cash and non-cash expenditures in the total consumer expenditures, with the ratio of cash purchases to total consumer expenditures for the same expenditure groups being lower in the rural sector than in the urban sector and (b) the differences in the expenditure patterns of the same rural and urban expenditure groups and the failure of the tax system to adapt itself to these differences". [16]

Incidence of individual taxes has also attracted a lot of attention, the prominent being the corporation tax which has become an issue of fierce controversy as regards the possibility of its being shifted to consumers. Traditionally, this tax, on the earnings of companies, has been accepted as a direct tax but lately this belief has come in for sharp criticism in view of the empirical evidence produced by some studies. [17] While V.D. Lall and G.S. Laumas have concluded that company taxes are shifted to consumers, Ved. P. Gandhi has come to the opposite conclusion that company taxes are not shifted to the consumers. In view of the conflicting evidence, the issue can be regarded as wide open.

Endnotes

1. Government here means Government Administration as defined in Account 1 of the economic classification of the Central Government budget. In other words, departmental and non-departmental industrial and commercial activities of the Government are not considered. This distinction is important because all Governmental activities do not have the same economic significance. Thus, expenditure of Government administration is in the nature of consumer outlays and represents demand for goods and services for final consumption. Contrarily, expenditure of public sector undertakings is intermediate expenditure forming part of the prices of goods and services supplied by them.
2. Government of India, Ministry of Finance, *Report of the Indirect Taxation Enquiry Committee,* (Chairman: L.K. Jha), Part II, 1978, p. 105.
3. Government of India, Ministry of Finance, *Report of the Taxation Enquiry Commission,* (Chairman: John Matthai), 1953-54, Vol. I, chapters 4 and 5.
4. Government of India, Ministry of Finance, *Incidence of Indirect Taxation, 1958-59,* (New Delhi, 1961).
5. Government of India, Ministry of Finance, *Incidence of Indirect Taxation, 1963-64,*(New Delhi, 1969).
6. The procedures adopted by the National Sample Survey (NSS) to collect consumer expenditure data in the 28th round are explained hereunder.

   NSS collected in its 28th round (October 1973 to June 1974) data on *consumer expenditure per person* for 30 days on *broad groups of items by monthly per capita expenditure classes* in rural and urban areas. It also prepared estimates of quantity of consumption of cereals per person for 30 days by the same expenditure classification. The information was collected both at State and all-India level. The period of 30 days for which data were collected preceded the date of survey. No account was taken of any expenditure incurred towards the productive enterprises of the household. The survey extended over the whole of the rural and urban areas of the Indian Union except certain inaccessible parts like Ladakh or disturbed areas like parts of Tripura. The survey period of 9 months was divided into 3 sub-rounds of 3 months each.

   Some of the important concepts and definitions followed in the 28th round were as follows:

   Household: A household was defined as a group of persons normally living together and taking food from common kitchen. A boarding house, a hotel or a hostel was treated as a cluster of households, where each individual boarder formed a separate household. Households maintained and fed directly by government such as those in prisons, police quarters, cantonments, hospitals, relief camps were excluded from the scope of the enquiry.

   Cash Purchase: This referred to all cash purchases except for enterprise purposes of the household during the reference period. Only such purchases as were made for non-productive domestic purposes were considered for this purpose.

   Home-grown Stock: Home-grown stock included commodities produced at home like from kitchen garden and household livestock products and produce from household industries. Produce brought from village home was also included in this. Home-grown stocks were imputed ex-farm price or ex-factory rate which was free from distribution cost or middle man's profit or other trade margins.

Household Consumer Expenditure: Consumer expenditure of a household comprised all expenditure incurred by the household during a reference period of 30 days preceding the date of survey exclusively towards its non-productive domestic consumption. Transfer payments in *kind* like loans advanced, charities, gifts and other payments in kind, if any, were not considered as consumer expenditure. But any consumption out of transfer receipts in kind like borrowing, gifts, charities, perquisites received by the household, free collection and other receipts in kind, if any, were considered for determining total consumption of the household.

Data on consumer expenditure were collected by NSS for a large number of items. But in presenting the results similar items were merged to form homogeneous groups (21 such groups were formed in the 28th round).

The results were presented in the form of detailed tables in respect of rural and urban areas for each State and Union Territory, all-India, Union Territories pooled, and for four big cities (Bombay, Calcutta, Delhi and Madras) separately and combined.

The following information was provided by the 28th round.

(a) Distribution of sample households, percentage distribution of estimated number of households and estimated number of adult males, adult females and children per household *by monthly per capita expenditure classes.*

(b) Consumer expenditure (in ₹) per person for a period of 30 days by broad groups of items and by monthly per capita expenditure classes.

(c) Quantity (in kg.) and value (in ₹) of consumption per person for a period of 30 days on items cereals, gram and cereal substitutes by monthly per capita expenditure classes.

The general sample design in the NSS 28th round was stratified with two-stage selection within each stratum; the first stage units were villages/blocks in the rural/urban areas and the second stage units the households. The sample design was made self-weighting for all the household schedules at stage level separately by rural and urban sectors.

In the sample there were 8,730 villages in rural areas and 4,944 blocks in urban areas.

Rural Sample Design: The sampling frame used for selection was the list of villages as per 1971 population census stratification. The whole of India was divided into a number of basic strata so that the basic strata did not cut across district boundaries. Districts with more than 1.5 million 1971 Census rural population were divided into two or more basic strata by grouping contiguous tehsils, homogeneous as far as possible with respect to density of rural population and crop pattern, so that the population of each basic stratus was less than 1.5 million. Each district with less than 1.5 million 1971 Census rural population formed one basic stratum by itself. Basic strata so formed were treated as basic strata both for rural and urban sectors.

Allocation: Within each State and Union Territory, the allocated number of villages was distributed over the constituent basic strata in proportion to their rural population.

Selection of Villages: The 1971 Census list of villages was used as the sampling frame for selection of villages. Sample villages within each basic stratum were selected with probability proportional to 1971 population and with replacements.

Selection of household: All households in a sample village were arranged into six classes on the basis of their means of livelihood and visit to health centre or not. From the arranged frame in a village, a sample of households was selected linear systematically using the intervals and random starts specified for the purpose. The list of 1971 Census enumeration blocks was used as the sampling frame.

Stratification: Basic strata as described in rural sample design were treated as basic strata for urban sector also.

Allocation: Within each State and Union Territory, the allocated number of blocks was distributed over the constituent basic strata in proportion to their urban population.

Selection of Households: All households in a sample block were arranged into six classes by occupations. From the arranged frame in a block a sample of households was selected linear systematically with specified interval and random start.

7. Government of India, Ministry of Finance, *Report of the Indirect Taxation Enquiry Committee,* (Chairman: L.K. Jha), Part II, January 1978, p. 89.
8. Pawan K. Aggarwal, *Who Pays the Tax*?, (Delhi: Gayatri Publications, 1998).
9. *Ibid.*, pp. i-ii.
10. *Ibid.*, p. 61.
11. Government of Orissa, *Report of the Orissa Taxation Enquiry Committee,* Bhubaneshwar, 1961.
12. National Council of Applied Economic Research, *Incidence of Taxation in Gujarat,* (New Delhi, 1970); and *Incidence of Taxation in Mysore State,* (New Delhi, 1972). See also A.C. Angrish, "Agricultural and Non-Agricultural Taxation: An Estimate of Their Burden in Rajasthan', in *Economic and Political Weekly*, Vol. V, January 10, 1970.
13. It is a general phenomenon that the tax system as a whole is regressive in the lowest ranges, proportional in the middle ranges and progressive in the upper ranges of income. Thus, continuous progressivity is a rare occurrence when both direct and indirect taxes are taken into account.
14. Government of India, Ministry of Finance, *Report of the Committee on Taxation of Agricultural Wealth and Income*, (Chairman: K.N. Raj), October 1972.
15. Major among these are: Ved P. Gandhi, *Tax Burden on Indian Agriculture* (Cambridge, Massachusetts, 1966); Mahesh T. Pathak and Arun S. Patel, *Agricultural Taxation in Gujarat* (Bombay: Asia Publishing House, 1970); Hemlata Rao, "Tax Incidence on Agricultural Sector in Uttar Pradesh", in *Economic and Political Weekly*, Vol. VI, September 11, 1971; S.L. Shetty, "An Inter-Sectoral Analysis of Taxable Capacity and Tax Burden", in *Indian Journal of Agricultural Economics,* (Bombay), Vol. XXVI, July-September 1971 and "Inter-Class Incidence of Taxation in Farm and Non-Farm Sectors in India", in *Economic and Political Weekly,* (Bombay), Vol. VI, December 25, 1971; C.H. Hanumantha Rao, *Taxation of Agricultural Land in Andhra Pradesh,* (Bombay, Asia Publishing House, 1964).
16. Anand P. Gupta, *Fiscal Policy and Employment Generation in India,* (New Delhi: Tata McGraw-Hill, 1977), p. 37.
17. The chief among these are: Ved P. Gandhi, *Some Aspects of India's Tax Structure,* (Bombay: Vora and Co., 1970); A. Ambirajan, *The Taxation of Corporate Income in India,* (Bombay: Asia Publishing House, 1964); V.D. Lall, "Shifting and Incidence of Direct Taxes on Companies", *Fiftieth Annual Conference Papers of Indian Economic Association*, Part III, (Bombay, 1967); Gurcharan S. Laumas, "The Shifting of the Corporation Income Tax: A Study with Reference to Indian Corporations", in *Public Finance*, Vol. 21, 1966; V. Ganapathi Rao and K.S. Hanumantha Rao, "The Incidence of the Corporate Income Tax in the Short Run: The Case of Indian Corporations", in *Public Finance*, Vol. 26, 1971.

10

Tax Evasion

10.1 Tax Evasion: Meaning

Tax evasion exists in all countries, though in varying degrees. It is a serious problem in developing countries which are in the process of evolving their tax systems.

Tax evasion is an illegal attempt to reduce the tax payable by deliberately under-reporting or not reporting taxable incomes or concealing one's true *state of affairs* from tax authorities. Tax evasion is a criminal offence and if detected is punishable by financial penalties or even by imprisonment or both.

10.1.1 Tax Evasion and Tax Avoidance: Tax avoidance means preventing or reducing one's tax liability through manipulations within the framework of existing tax legislation. Tax avoidance, as against tax evasion, is legally permissible and hence a legitimate aim of taxpayers.

Tax avoidance is resorted to through such devices as formation of holding companies to claim artificial deductions, constitution of trusts and family partnerships, transfer of income earning assets to one's wife and children for fractioning income for tax purposes, investing in provident funds and life insurance policies, and manipulation of capital gains.

Since tax avoidance has a colour of legality about it, clever taxpayers do their best to avoid or keep down tax payments. This may force the government to raise tax rates, making the less clever assessees bear a disproportionate tax burden.

Tax laws in many countries incorporate anti-tax avoidance provisions under which certain incomes are included in an assessee's total income, though such incomes legally belong to other persons. For example, in India, Sections 60 to 65 of the Income Tax Act, 1961, deal with instances where an assessee may attempt to reduce his tax liability either by transferring his assets in favour of his family members or by arranging his sources of income in such a manner that tax incidence falls on others, whereas benefit of income, directly or indirectly, is derived by the assessee himself. Thus, income arising to the spouse, minor child, son's wife, son's minor child and certain other persons are clubbed with the assessee's income in certain circumstances. In this regard, the Indian income tax law deviates from the general principle that a person can be assessed in respect of his own income.

10.2 International Tax Avoidance and Evasion

While it is true that international business operations are exposed to the risk of being subject to double taxation, it cannot be gainsaid that such activities provide opportunities for tax avoidance/evasion. Following are the devices generally applied for the purpose.

10.2.1 Transfer Pricing: It refers to the price attached to transactions between the divisions (e.g. branches or subsidiaries) of a company. Transfer pricing is usually considered in a global context, particularly in relation to cross-frontier transactions within a multinational company.

Determination of transfer price has significance in relation to such matters as taxation, exchange restrictions, and currency fluctuations. The incentive for transfer price manipulations is provided by varying rates of taxation in countries where a multinational company operates. Thus, where goods are being transferred from a company in a low tax country to a subsidiary company in a high tax country, there is a clear tax incentive if a high transfer price is ensured to maximise profit within the low tax country.

Similarly, sales of a multinational group may be routed through a specially formed tax haven distribution company. The tax haven company purchases goods from affiliated companies at the lowest possible prices and sells to independent purchasers at the full market price, ensuring that most or all of the profit from the transaction is earned in the tax haven.

Due to the inherent difficulties in determining a fair or market price for inter-company transactions, a multinational company has always the option to fix artificial transfer prices.

A. Arm's Length Price: It refers to market price that would have been negotiated by unrelated parties engaged in the same or similar transactions under the same or similar conditions. Arm's length standard is used to prevent the use of transfer pricing technique for tax avoidance. Many countries exercise their right to adjust reported transfer prices to conform to an arm's length criterion. Implementing the arm's length principle is a difficult task for tax authorities.

10.2.2 Tax Treaty Shopping: It is a situation where a person resident in a third country seeks to obtain benefits of a double tax treaty between two other countries. A double tax treaty confers substantial benefits on the residents of treaty countries. Let us suppose that Mr. Wilson, resident in country A, wants to invest in country B. Assuming that there is no double tax treaty between country A and country B, any income received by Mr. Wilson will be subject to full rates of taxation in country B. In such a situation, Mr. Wilson may find it advantageous to channel his investment to country B through a company in country C because country C has double tax treaties with countries A and B. For example, Mauritius is a popular treaty shopping haven for many foreign companies for channelling investments into India because of favourable tax treaty provisions.

To prevent the misuse of tax treaties through tax treaty shopping, many countries take care to include anti-treaty abuse provisions in these agreements. For example, there is a specific clause in the double tax treaty between India and US under which benefits of the treaty are available only to genuine residents of either country. In other words, the treaty restricts the use of US as a treaty shopping centre for investments in India.

10.3 Causes of Tax Evasion

10.3.1 High Level of Tax Rates: Among the host of causes of tax evasion and hence the generation of black money, the level of tax rates is probably the most crucial. It is widely believed that higher the rate of tax, the greater is the tendency to evade taxes. High tax rates make tax evasion more tempting. Tax evaders readily take greater risks if they know that in the event of success the reward is high. Per contra, it can be expected that low tax rates improve tax compliance and broaden the tax base.

10.3.2 Less Respect for Government and its Laws: Tax evasion is more in countries where there is general apathy on the part of people towards the government and its laws. People will have less respect for tax laws if they perceive the tax system to be unfair in terms of level of taxation (tax-GDP ratio) [1] and/or distribution of tax burden among various classes (i.e. tax equity). [2] Similarly, there can be a feeling among taxpayers that government is indulging in wasteful expenditure (e.g. digging the roads too often), spending excessively on government functionaries, permitting loan waivers, maintaining perpetually sick public undertakings, and granting unnecessary subsidies. Tax evasion by politicians sends wrong signals to the general public that non-compliance is acceptable.

It is necessary to change the attitude of the people towards Government and its laws. In this connection, the Indian Tax Reforms Committee, 1991, observed, "...there is a widespread feeling among the electorate that there is considerable waste in government expenditure, that there is excess staff and that the tail to teeth ratio is unduly high. And with it all, it is generally felt that the public which pays the taxes gets poor service and members of the public are treated often not as masters who pay but as supplicants". [3]

10.3.3 Lenient Penal Action: Lenient penal action in case violation of law is detected also encourages tax evasion. In general, countries with relatively poor implementation of regulations tend to have a higher share of unaccounted economy, whereas countries with properly implemented regulations and sound deterrence have smaller *black* economies.

10.3.4 Nature of the Economy: The problem of tax evasion in underdeveloped countries is associated with the peculiar characteristics of their economies which, in most cases, are agriculture-based in the sense that a substantial part of national income originates from and the majority of the work force is engaged in agriculture. Moreover, there is widespread illiteracy, lack of accounting practices, limited monetisation and shortage of administrative resources in these countries. A regime of controls, licences, and shortages also breeds tax evasion and black money.

10.4 Consequences of Tax Evasion

The nexus between tax evasion and black money and its distortion of the redistributive role of tax policy was noted by India's Seventh Five Year Plan (1980-85) as follows, "With a sizeable proportion of income and wealth evading taxation, the redistributive impact of progressive taxation had been severely blunted. A reduction in the scale of black income generation would improve distribution of income and wealth after taxation. Besides, if the magnitude of tax evasion is significantly reduced, there would be a greater volume of tax revenue, and a greater volume of public expenditure benefiting the poorer section of the population would become possible". [4]

Black money in social, economic and political space of the country has a debilitating effect on the institutions of governance and conduct of public policy in the country. Governance failure adversely affects the interests of vulnerable and disadvantaged sections of society. The success of an inclusive growth strategy [5] critically depends on the capacity of society to root out the evil of corruption and black money from its very foundations. Undoubtedly, India needs a speedy transition towards a more transparent and result-oriented economic system.

The effects of tax evasion, resulting in black money, on an economy are indeed disastrous. Some of these are listed below:

1. Tax evasion cuts at the very root of the revenue potential of a tax system and therefore hinders the resource mobilisation efforts of a government. Lack of funds may distort implementation of development plans and force a government to resort to deficit financing in case public expenditure is inelastic.
2. Tax evasion may interfere with the declared economic policies of a government by distorting saving/investment patterns and availability of resources for various sectors of the economy. For instance, government may impose credit restrictions to discourage certain activities (e.g. speculation) but money saved through tax evasion may finance and encourage the same activities.
3. Evasion of tax seriously undermines the equity attribute of a tax system. Honest

taxpayers, who are obliged to bear disproportionate tax burden, feel demoralised and tempted to join the tax evaders' camp.

4. Tax evasion leads to the creation of black money which in turn is a menace to the economy in its own way. Tax evasion and black money encourage concentration of economic power in the hands of undesirable groups in the country.
5. Tax evasion eats into the time and energy of tax administration which is obliged to unravel the intricate manipulations of tax dodgers.
6. Tax evasion leads to degradation of social and moral standards. Social abuses like bribery, intimidation, blackmailing, tampering with official records, submitting fake documents etc. all go with tax evasion.

With liberalisation of restrictions on cross-border flow of goods and services and relaxation of foreign exchange control, new opportunities have opened up for tax evasion through tax havens, misuse of transfer pricing, and other sophisticated methods. Globalisation has reduced the cost of these sophisticated methods thereby facilitating generation of black money and its transfer across the border. These changes require new strategies to curb black money.

The fight against generation and accumulation of black money is far more complex and prolonged, requiring stronger intervention of the state. It needs a robust legal framework, commensurate administrative set up, and a very strong resolve to fight the menace.

10.5 Devices Adopted to Evade Taxes

Various devices are adopted to evade taxes domestically and internationally.

10.5.1 Evasion of Specific Taxes:

A. Income Tax: Income tax is evaded through non-reporting, under-reporting and misreporting of income (e.g. showing non-agricultural income as agricultural income). [6]

The following devices are generally employed to evade income tax:

1. Non-reporting/under-reporting of taxable income.
2. Maintaining multiple set of account books, fraudulent changes in account books, and keeping transactions out of account books.
3. Opening and operating bank accounts under assumed names.
4. Doing business in the name of dummies.
5. Over-reporting expenses.
6. Fragmenting income to reduce tax liability.
7. Under-invoicing sales and other transfer pricing manipulations.

Although evasion of tax is a common tendency among people belonging to different groups, opportunities for it vary according to the nature of income earned by taxpayers. In the case of income from salaries and interest from deposits, evasion is less likely because of proper recording and auditing of transactions, and deduction of tax at source. However, opportunities for tax evasion are very large in the case of self-employed in business and professions. Doctors, lawyers, architects, property dealers, individual contractors can evade taxes more easily than others. They can insist on their customers to pay them in cash or accept invoices which underestimate the payment.

B. Excise Duties: Excise evasion is generally resorted to by adopting, *inter alia*, following malpractices:

1. Incorrect accountal of goods.
2. Undervaluation of goods.
3. Flouting the conditions subject to which any goods may be exempted from duty.

C. Value-Added Tax (VAT): The proponents of VAT claim that evasion under it is difficult and minimal. The tax credit method ensures cross-checking of the records of taxpayers through invoices. Buyer firms insist on supplier firms to furnish invoices which help the former to claim tax credit. Since tax liability of a single taxpayer under VAT is only a fraction of the total amount of tax, the incentive for evasion is relatively weak. Even a successful evasion would mean less revenue loss as compared to the one suffered under a system of turnover tax on gross value (excise duty or sales tax).

Despite the self-policing nature of VAT, opportunities do exist under it for evasion and fraud. In fact, VAT provides opportunities for fraud (fictitious claims for refunds) which are not available under other forms of commodity taxation. The methods commonly applied to defraud tax authorities under VAT include, *inter alia,* the following.

1. Use of fake invoices to claim tax credit.
2. Tax credit claims on purchases for personal use.
3. Over-reporting of sales of zero-rated goods.
4. Secret deals between buyers and sellers as regards issuance of receipts.
5. Formation of fake companies which sell receipts to traders to enable them to claim tax credit on inputs.

Thus, VAT is as susceptible to evasion and fraud as any other tax. An efficient tax machinery capable of cross-checking a large number of invoices through an elaborate computer system is a pre-requisite for the successful implementation of VAT.

D. Customs Duties: Evasion of customs duties takes place through following malpractices:

1. Invoice misclassification.
2. Manipulation of documents.
3. Suppression of quantities imported.

10.5.2 Tax Havens: The term *tax haven* has been widely used since the 1950s. However, there is no precise definition of the term. The expression is used to describe any country or locality which levies very low taxes, or none at all, on foreigners. Tax havens can be broadly classified into three categories based on the degree of tax concessions.

1. Where there is no tax at all, e.g. Bahamas, Bermuda, and Cayman Islands.
2. Where only a low rate of tax is imposed, e.g. British Virgin Islands, Hong Kong, Isle of Man.
3. Where the tax system favours particular activities or entities, e.g. Luxembourg, Panama, and Switzerland.

Tax havens are used in a number of ways to avoid/evade high taxes of non-tax haven countries. The commonest device is to use a tax haven only as a conduit for transactions the real economic impact of which is located elsewhere. Thus, international transactions between two high tax rate countries may be channelled through a tax haven company so that any resulting profit is realised in the tax haven with a consequent minimisation of tax.

The Organization for Economic Co-operation and Development (OECD) initially defined tax havens as being characterised by no or very low taxes, lack of effective exchange of information, and lack of transparency about substantial activities. It listed 35 countries/jurisdictions as tax havens in the year 2000.

A. Offshore Financial Centres: Some of the old tax havens have adopted the more benign designation of *offshore financial centre* (OFC) and tend to describe themselves as financial centres specializing in non-residential financial transactions. However, with their array of secrecy provisions that lack regulation, zero or near zero taxation imposed by them, and lack of adequate capital controls, they are logical extensions of the traditional tax havens. The International Monetary Fund (IMF) has defined OFCs as centres where the bulk of financial sector transactions on both sides of the balance sheet are with individuals or companies that are not residents, where the transactions are initiated elsewhere, and where the majority of the institutions involved are controlled by non-residents. Thus, many OFCs have the following characteristics:

1. Jurisdictions that have financial institutions engaged primarily in business with non-residents.
2. Financial systems with external assets and liabilities out of proportion to domestic financial intermediation.
3. Centres which provide some or all of the following opportunities: (a) low or zero taxation, (b) moderate or light financial regulation, and (c) banking secrecy and anonymity.

Various studies on tax havens have shown that tax havens are typically small countries/jurisdictions, with low or nil taxation for foreigners who decide to come and settle there. They usually also offer strong confidentiality or secrecy regarding wealth and accounts, making them very attractive locations for safe keeping of unaccounted wealth. They also offer a very liberal regulatory environment and allow opaque existence, where an entity can easily be set up without indulging in any meaningful commercial activity and yet claim to be a genuine business unit, merely by getting itself incorporated or registered in that jurisdiction. This makes them highly desirable locations for multinational entities wishing to reduce their global tax liabilities. These multinational entities — consisting of a network of several corporate and non-corporate bodies—may set up conduit companies in tax havens and artificially transfer their income to such conduit companies in view of the low tax regime there. There is increasing global awareness and concern about the role of tax havens and their facilitation of certain abusive and undesirable arrangements that result in significant fiscal challenges to other countries and also pose a threat in terms of potential financing of terrorism and other activities that threaten peace and security.

The role of tax havens has gradually come under scrutiny globally. With near-zero tax regimes, banking secrecy, and weak financial regulations, these tax havens facilitate hiding of money accumulated through tax evasion and other illegal means in addition to creating risks of terrorist financing and money laundering. At the G-7 summit in Lyons in 1996, a call was given to the OECD to prepare a report to address these issues with a view to establishing a multilateral approach under which countries could operate individually and collectively to limit the extent of these practices. The OECD came up with a report in 1998 and called for action against tax havens. The report envisaged blacklisting of and internationally coordinated sanctions against havens that persisted in luring other states' tax bases.

10.5.3 Participatory Notes (PNs): A participatory note (PN) is a derivative instrument issued in foreign jurisdictions, by a foreign institutional investor (FII)/or one of its associates, against underlying Indian securities.

PNs are popular among foreign investors since they allow these investors to earn returns on investment in the Indian market without undergoing the significant cost and time implications of directly investing in India. These instruments are traded overseas outside the direct purview of Securities and Exchange Board of India (SEBI) surveillance thereby raising many apprehensions about the beneficial ownership and the nature of funds invested in these instruments. Concerns have been raised that some of the money coming into the market via PNs could be the unaccounted wealth camouflaged under the guise of FII investment. SEBI has been taking measures to ensure that PNs are not used as conduits for black money or terrorist funding.

10.5.4 Investment through Complex Derivative Instruments: With increasing sophistication of derivative instruments [7], new opportunities for investing and making profits without being subjected to taxes and regulations are also opening up. Such innovative means can also be misused by unscrupulous parties to generate unaccounted income. Some such instruments like participatory notes may not be adequately covered by regulatory mechanisms and their oversight and hence have potential for misuse.

10.6 Various Estimates of Tax Evasion in India

Widespread tax evasion is a perennial problem of the Indian tax system. The history of taxation law amendments in India is essentially a history of plugging loopholes, as and when discovered, to prevent leakages of revenue.

10.6.1 Early Attempts: The problem of tax evasion and generation of black money is not new. As far back as 1936, the Ayers Committee, while reviewing the income tax administration in India suggested large-scale amendments to secure the interests of the honest taxpayer and effectively deal with fraudulent evasion.

The Income Tax Investigation Commission was appointed in 1947 to investigate tax evasion and suggest measures for preventing it in future.

Soon after Independence in 1947, the Indian Income Tax Investigation Commission, 1948, investigated all matters relating to taxation of income, with particular reference to preventing evasion and avoidance. The Commission recommended several changes in the law to plug loopholes in the income tax system. It recommended, *inter alia*, that the law should be amended so as to allow speculative losses to be set off only against speculative gains.

Since early 1950s, various commissions, committees and individual scholars have made estimates of tax evasion in India, particularly evasion of income tax. The findings of these studies are summarised below chronologically.

10.6.2 Taxation Enquiry Commission (TEC) [Chairman: John Matthai], 1953-54: TEC which dealt at length with the administration of income tax, found staggering levels of tax evasion. To quote, "It is observed from statistics in connection with the Disclosure Drive that income as originally included in the returns sent to the income tax department by assessees who made disclosures was grossly understated, the difference between the income as originally returned and that disclosed later to the department being, on the average, as much as 600 percent. Such other statistics as have been made available to us by the Central Board of Revenue also give evidence of the fact that evasion is prevalent on a considerable scale". [8] The Commission maintained that improvement and strengthening of the enforcement machinery was the only way to tackle evasion effectively.

10.6.3 Estimates of Nicholas Kaldor: Nicholas Kaldor, a British economist, made the first systematic estimates of income tax evasion in India in the mid-1950s. He estimated income tax loss through tax evasion at ₹ 200 to ₹ 300 crore for the year 1953-54. [9] The estimates of Kaldor were based on certain tentative figures relating to national income provided to him by the Central Statistical Organisation (CSO). Kaldor made it clear in his report that his estimates were tentative and should be interpreted with caution. His recommendations resulted in several amendments to the Income Tax Act and new legislations like the Wealth Tax Act.

10.6.4 Central Board of Revenue: Another study by the Central Board of Revenue for the same year (1953-54) recorded a much lower estimate of tax evasion at ₹ 20 to ₹ 30 crore, almost one-tenth of Kaldor's estimate. [10] One main reason for the wide divergence between the two estimates was the inclusion in Kaldor's estimate of what the Central Board of Revenue counted as avoidance rather than evasion.

Kaldor himself had admitted while tendering oral evidence before Direct Taxes Administration Enquiry Committee, 1958-59, that his estimate represented the loss of tax not only through evasion but also through avoidance. [11] Therefore, it is generally agreed that the estimates of income tax evasion by Kaldor were on the high side.

10.6.5 Direct Taxes Enquiry Committee (DTEC) [Chairman: Justice K.N. Wanchoo], 1971: DTEC [12] was appointed in 1971 to examine and suggest legal and administrative measures for unearthing black money and countering evasion and checking avoidance. It comprehensively dealt with the causes of and methods of tackling tax evasion and made a number of recommendations for strengthening tax administration.

It estimated assessable non-salary income for the year 1961-62 at ₹ 2,686 crore and non-salary income actually assessed to tax to be of the order of ₹ 1,875 crore. Accordingly the income which escaped income tax was of the order of ₹ 811 crore. After making rough adjustments for exemptions and deductions, the Wanchoo Committee found that "the estimated income on which tax has been evaded (black income) would probably be ₹ 700 crore and ₹ 1,000 crore for the years 1961-62 and 1965-66 respectively". "Projecting this estimate further to 1968-69 on the basis of percentage increase in national income from 1961-62 to 1968-69, the income on which tax was evaded for 1968-69 was estimated as ₹ 1,800 crore".

10.6.6 National Institute of Public Finance and Policy (NIPFP): In its study conducted in 1985, NIPFP defined *black money* as the aggregate of incomes which were taxable but which were not reported to tax authorities. The study made use of a range rather than a single figure of underestimation. While preparing the estimate of *black* income, the study excluded incomes generated through illegal activities like smuggling, black market transactions, and acceptance of bribes and kickbacks.

NIPFP study estimated the ratio of tax-evaded income to GDP in the range of 3.7 percent to 5.7 percent in 1975-76, and 4.2 percent to 8.6 percent in 1980-81. [13]

10.6.7 Tax Reforms Committee (TRC) [Chairman: Raja Chelliah], 1991: According to TRC, "not more than 30-35 percent of legally taxable income is being disclosed, on the average". [14] In this context it observed, "it would be fair to say that the income tax department which is in-charge of all the Central Government direct taxes is in shambles. It cannot complain of lack of manpower, but the majority of personnel is constituted by inspectors and clerks who are not adequately trained and are paid fairly low salaries". [15]

Apart from the foregoing estimates, some evidence of general nature also suggests widespread non-reporting and under-reporting of taxable income in India. In this connection, the Finance Minister in his 1997-98 budget speech observed, "It is inexplicable that in a country of over 900 million people, only 12 million people are assessed to income tax and what is worse, only about 12,000 assessees are in the tax bracket of income above ₹ 10 lakh". [16]

It is noteworthy that tax evasion is not confined to income tax only, rather it is widely practised for other direct taxes also like wealth tax. The ridiculously low yield from these taxes is partly due to plethora of exemptions/concessions and also due to widespread evasion. In India, economic inequalities have been caused mainly by the inequitable ownership of wealth and the failure of the wealth tax to make a headway in lessening inequalities is indeed regrettable.

It may be recalled that in 1957 and 1958, three new taxes were introduced, viz. wealth tax, expenditure tax, and gift tax. Estate duty was already in operation since 1953. The basic philosophy underlying the introduction of the system of integrated direct taxes was to prevent evasion and avoidance of direct taxes and thereby to reduce inequalities of income and wealth. However, the yield from wealth tax, expenditure tax, gift tax, and estate duty has never been of much significance in the Central tax structure. The meagre revenue collection ultimately led to the abolition of expenditure tax, estate duty and gift tax in 1966, 1985 and 1998 respectively. Wealth tax continues to be in operation.

Wealth tax liability is computed by applying the rate schedule to net wealth (i.e. taxable wealth). Till recently, (financial year 2014-15), wealth tax was charged at the flat rate of 1 percent in the case of all assessees having taxable wealth exceeding ₹ 30 lakh. In view of the meagre revenue and problems of administration and compliance, the Task Force on Direct Taxes (Chairman: Vijay Kelkar), 2002 recommended the abolition of wealth tax. Wealth tax was abolished in the 2015-16 budget.

Estimation of evasion of indirect taxes in India has always remained a hard task even for the officially appointed committees. For example, the Central Excise (Self-Removal Procedure) Review Committee, 1973, made extensive studies of excise evasion, both sector-wise and commodity-wise. However, it could not quantify the total magnitude of evasion. It observed, "we have reached the conclusion that evasion is considerable and, in certain sectors, pervasive. This is an inference we have drawn from the totality of what we have seen, heard and investigated". [17]

10.7 Agencies for Enforcement of Tax Laws

10.7.1 Central Board of Direct Taxes (CBDT): The CBDT, New Delhi, is part of the Department of Revenue in the Ministry of Finance. While the CBDT provides essential inputs for policy and planning of direct taxes in India, it is also responsible for administration of direct tax laws through its Income Tax Department. The CBDT is a statutory authority functioning under the Central Board of Revenue Act 1963. The officials of the Board in their ex-officio capacity also function as a Division of the Ministry dealing with matters relating to the levy and collection of direct taxes.

The Income Tax Department is primarily responsible for combating the menace of black money. For this purpose, it uses the tools of scrutiny assessment as well as information-based investigations for detecting tax evasion and penalising the same as per provisions of the Income Tax Act, 1961 with the objective of creating deterrence against tax evasion. In doing so, it plays one of the most important roles in preventing generation, accumulation, and consumption of unaccounted black money.

The investigation wing of the Income Tax Department deals with investigations to detect tax evasion and carries out operations like surveys and searches to collect evidence of such evasion. Such operations are usually carried out after detailed preliminary investigations.

A. Directorate of Criminal Investigation (DCI): The tax administration in India did not have a separate set-up for targeted investigation into criminal cases. On May 30, 2011, a notification was issued by the Government of India for creation of a Directorate of Income Tax (Criminal Investigation) or DCI in the

Central Board of Direct Taxes, Department of Revenue, Ministry of Finance. The DCI is mandated to perform functions in respect of criminal matters having any financial implication punishable as an offence under any direct taxes law.

The DCI, in discharge of its responsibilities under the direct tax laws, is required to perform the following functions:

1. Seek and collect information about persons and transactions suspected to be involved in criminal activities having cross-border, inter-state, or international ramifications that pose a threat to national security and are punishable under the direct tax laws.
2. Investigate the sources and uses of funds involved in such criminal activities.
3. Cause issuance of show cause notices for offences committed under any direct tax law.
4. File prosecution complaints in the competent court under any direct tax law relating to a criminal activity.
5. Hire the services of special prosecutors and other experts for pursuing a prosecution complaint filed in any court of competent jurisdiction.
6. Execute appropriate witness protection programmes for effective prosecution of criminal offences under the direct tax laws, i.e. to protect and rehabilitate witnesses who support the state in prosecution of such offences so as to insulate them from any harm to their person.
7. Coordinate with and extend necessary expert, technical, and logistical support to any other intelligence or law enforcement agency in India investigating crimes having cross-border, inter-state or international ramifications that pose a threat to national security.
8. Enter into agreements for sharing of information and other cooperation with any central or state agency in India.
9. Enter into agreements for sharing of information and other cooperation with such agencies of foreign states as may be permissible under any international agreement or treaty.
10. Any other matter relating to the above.

The DCI is headed by a Director General of Income Tax (Criminal Investigation) and functions under administrative control of the CBDT.

The head office of the DCI is located at New Delhi and it has eight regional offices all over India.

B. Exchange of Information (EoI) Cell: The Government of India has set up an EoI Cell in CBDT. The EoI works on the basis of mutual cooperation. The competent authorities of different countries provide different forms of administrative assistance to each other based on the provisions of Double Tax Avoidance Agreements (DTAAs) or the Multilateral Convention for Mutual

Administrative Assistance. Administrative assistance under these instruments of EOI, depending on the terms of the agreement, may take the form of: (a) specific exchange of information, (b) spontaneous exchange of information, (c) automatic exchange of information, (d) tax examination abroad, (e) simultaneous exchange of information, (f) service of documents, and (g) assistance in collection of tax.

C. Income Tax Overseas Units (ITOUs): With increased scope for international cooperation in areas of exchange of information, transfer pricing, and taxation of cross-border transactions, Government of India decided to create a network of ITOUs. In addition to the existing two ITOUs at Singapore and Mauritius, eight more have been opened. The objectives of these ITOUs are as under:

1. Monitor DTAA-related issues.
2. Assist the authorities in handling issues arising out of international taxation and transfer pricing.
3. Assist the authorities in frequent revision of existing DTAAs.
4. Assist the authorities in negotiation of TIEAs.
5. Expedite the exchange of information by the competent authorities (as per DTAAs and TIEAs) of these countries as required by the competent authority in India.
6. Assist the authorities in collection of taxes.
7. Assist the authorities in work relating to Mutual Agreement Procedure under DTAAs.
8. Maintain liaison with various departments of the respective countries especially Income Tax Department, Registrar of Companies, Department of Banking Services, and Administrators of Financial Services.
9. Maintain liaison with investors investing in India from these countries.
10. Impart information about domestic laws of India to foreign investors.
11. Maintain liaison with Indian investors in these countries to assess any tax-related problems arising for these investors.
12. Assist the Mission in any other commercial/economic work assigned to the officer by the Head of the Mission.
13. Any other work assigned to the officer by the CBDT, Department of Revenue.

Opening of the new ITOUs and presence of tax officers in the ITOUs also acts as effective deterrence against tax evasion.

10.7.2 Central Board of Excise and Customs (CBEC): The CBEC is a part of the Department of Revenue under the Ministry of Finance, Government of India. It deals with the tasks of formulation of policy concerning levy and collection of customs and central excise duties, prevention of smuggling, and administration of matters relating to customs, central excise and narcotics to the extent under the CBEC's purview. The Board is the administrative authority for its subordinate organizations, including Custom Houses, Central Excise Commissionerates, and the Central Revenues Control Laboratory.

The Directorate General of Central Excise Intelligence (DGCEI) is the apex intelligence organization functioning under the CBEC. It is entrusted with the responsibility of detecting cases of evasion of central excise and service tax. The Directorate develops intelligence, especially in new areas of tax evasion through its intelligence network across the country and disseminates information in this respect by issuing Modus Operandi Circulars and Alert Circulars to apprise field formations of the latest trends in duty evasion. Wherever found necessary, DGCEI on its own, or in coordination with field formations, organises operations to unearth evasion of central excise duty and service tax.

10.8 Regulatory Authorities for Supervision and Policing

10.8.1 Central Bureau of Investigation (CBI): CBI, functioning under the Department of Personnel, Ministry of Personnel, Pension and Public Grievances, Government of India, is the premier investigating police agency in India. It handles a broad category of criminal cases including cases of corruption and fraud committed by public servants, economic crimes, and other specific crimes involving terrorism, bomb blasts, sensational homicides, kidnappings and the underworld. The CBI plays an important role in international cooperation relating to mutual legal assistance and extradition matters. The Ministry of Home Affairs is the central authority for mutual legal assistance in criminal matters and the Ministry of External Affairs the nodal agency for extradition matters.

10.8.2 Financial Intelligence Unit (FIU): The FIU-IND was established by the Government of India on November 18, 2004 for coordinating and strengthening efforts for national and international intelligence by investigation and enforcement agencies in combating money laundering and terrorist financing. FIU-IND is the national agency responsible for receiving, processing, analysing, and disseminating information relating to suspect financial transactions. It is an independent body reporting to the Economic Intelligence Council headed by the Finance Minister. For administrative purposes, the FIU-IND is under the control of the Department of Revenue, Ministry of Finance.

10.8.3 Narcotics Control Bureau (NCB): It functions under the Ministry of Home Affairs, Government of India. It was established on March 17, 1986 and its functions include co-ordination of actions by various offices, state governments, and other authorities under the Narcotics Drugs and Psychotropic Substances (NDPS) Act 1985, Customs Act, Drugs and Cosmetics Act, and any other law for the time being in force in connection with the enforcement provisions of the

NDPS Act. It is assigned the task of counter measures against illicit drugs traffic under the various international conventions and protocols, and also assists concerned authorities in foreign countries and concerned international organisations dealing with prevention and suppression of this traffic.

10.9 Co-ordinating Agencies

10.9.1 Central Economic Intelligence Bureau (CEIB): The CEIB functioning under the Ministry of Finance is responsible for coordination, intelligence sharing, and investigations at national as well as regional levels amongst various law enforcement agencies. The existing coordination mechanism in the CEIB consists of Regional Economic Intelligence Councils (REICs) at regional level and the Group on Economic Intelligence and meetings of the heads of investigating agencies under the Department of Revenue at the centre. While the Group on Economic Intelligence is focused on matters relating to intelligence sharing, the REICs and heads of agencies meetings cover both intelligence and investigations.

10.9.2 National Investigation Agency (NIA): It is a specialised and dedicated investigating agency set up under the National Investigation Agency Act to investigate and prosecute scheduled offences, in particular offences under the Unlawful Activities (Prevention) Act, including Financing of Terrorism. The NIA has concurrent jurisdiction with the individual states, thereby empowering the Central Government to probe terror attacks in any part of the country. Officers of the NIA have all powers, privileges, and liabilities which police officers have in connection with investigation of an offence.

The Central Government has the power to suo moto assign a case to the NIA for investigation. The NIA Act also provides for setting up of special courts and trials to be held on a day-to-day basis. The NIA Act can investigate offences under the specific Acts mentioned in the Schedule to NIA Act, including the Atomic Energy Act, 1962, Unlawful Activities (Prevention) Act, 1967, Anti-Hijacking Act, 1982, Suppression of Unlawful Acts against Safety of Civil Aviation Act, 1982, SAARC Convention (Suppression of Terrorism) Act, 1993, Suppression of Unlawful Acts against Safety of Maritime Navigation and Fixed Platforms on Continental Shelf Act, 2002, Weapons of Mass Destruction and Their Delivery Systems (Prohibition of Unlawful Activities) Act, 2005, and offences under Chapter VI and Sections 489-A to 489-E of the Indian Penal Code.

10.10 Other Agencies

10.10.1 Central Bureau of Narcotics (CBN): It supervises the cultivation of opium poppy in India and issues necessary licences for manufacture, export and import of narcotics drugs and psychotropic substances. It monitors India's implementation of the United Nations Drug Control Conventions and also interacts with the International Narcotics Control Board (INCB) in Vienna and the competent authorities of other countries to verify the genuineness of a transaction prior to authorising shipments.

10.10.2 Serious Frauds Investigation Office (SFIO): It functions under the Ministry of Corporate Affairs and takes up for investigation complex cases having inter-departmental and multidisciplinary ramifications and substantial involvement of public interest, either in terms of monetary misappropriation or in terms of persons affected. It also takes up cases where investigation has the potential of contributing towards a clear improvement in systems, laws, or procedures.

10.10.3 Registrar of Companies (ROCs): It is the Registry for companies and limited liability firms and is established under the Ministry of Corporate Affairs. The Ministry of Corporate Affairs has a three-tier organisational set-up consisting of a Secretariat in New Delhi, Regional Directorates in Mumbai, Kolkata, Chennai and Noida, and field offices in all states and union territories.

10.10.4 Registrar of Societies (ROSs): The Registrars of non-profit societies are within State Government's purview and most of the states have an ROS office. The Society Registration Act is a Central Act but many states have adopted it with some state amendments and are registering non-profit societies under their respective Acts. Some state assemblies have enacted completely separate legislation on the subject. The ROS offices are reservoirs of data on societies and also function as their regulator.

10.10.5 Economic Intelligence Council (EIC): It came into existence in 2003 and is chaired by the Finance Minister and comprises senior functionaries of various ministries and intelligence agencies, including the Governor of the Reserve Bank of India (RBI) and the Chairman of the Securities and Exchange Board of India (SEBI). The EIC meets at least once a year to discuss and take decisions regarding trends in economic offences and strategies on intelligence sharing, coordination etc. The implementation of decisions taken by the EIC is monitored by the Working Group on Intelligence Apparatus, set up for this purpose within the EIC.

10.10.6 National Crime Records Bureau (NCRB): It was set up with the objective of empowering the Indian police services with information technology and criminal intelligence with a view to enabling them to effectively and efficiently enforce the law. It therefore creates and maintains a secured national database on crimes, criminals, property, and organised criminal gangs for use by law enforcement agencies.

The NCRB also processes and disseminates fingerprint records of criminals, including foreign criminals, to establish their identity.

10.10.7 State Police Agencies: Under the Constitution of India, police and public order are state (provincial) subjects. Every State/Union Territory has its own police force, which performs not only normal policing duties but also has specialised units to combat economic offences.

The Economic Offences Wing (EOW) of the police functioning under the administrative control of states (provinces) is entrusted with the responsibility of investigation of serious economic offences and offences having inter-state ramifications.

10.11 Measures Adopted to Curb Tax Evasion

Direct Taxes Enquiry Committee (Chairman: Justice K.N. Wanchoo), 1971, had suggested various measures to fight the evil of black money and tax evasion. Some of the measures suggested were as follows.

1. Reduction in tax rates.
2. Minimisation of controls and licences.
3. Regulation of donations to political parties.
4. Creating confidence among small taxpayers.
5. Substitution of sales tax by excise duty.
6. Vigorous prosecution policy.
7. Compulsory maintenance of accounts.

To give effect to the recommendations made by the Committee, the Government enacted the Taxation Laws (Amendment) Act, 1975. This Act, *inter alia,* provided stringent punishment for tax evaders.

In cases where tax evasion exceeded ₹ 1 lakh or prosecution was for the second or subsequent offence, the maximum punishment prescribed was 7 years rigorous imprisonment. Also, the discretionary powers to courts to award monetary punishment as an alternative to imprisonment or to reduce the term of imprisonment less than the minimum period, was withdrawn.

Efforts have been made to curb tax evasion and control black money through various measures: Some of these are described below.

1. Lowering of tax rates.
2. Tax amnesties.
3. Advance tax payment.
4. Withholding tax [or tax deduction at source (TDS)].
5. Presumptive tax for small traders.
6. Permanent account number (PAN) or general index register number (GIR).
7. Survey of income tax.
8. Summons, and search and seizure.

9. Restrictions on the transfer of high value immovable properties.
10. Penalties and prosecutions.

10.11.1 Lowering of Tax Rates: The Report of the Direct Taxes Enquiry Committee (DTEC), 1971, was a milestone in the area of income tax rates. The Committee made a number of far-reaching suggestions for unearthing black money, preventing evasion and avoidance of taxes, and reducing arrears. One important recommendation of the Committee related to reduction in the rates of direct taxes which in its view were mainly responsible for tax evasion because they made tax evasion profitable and attractive. The rates of individual income tax were quite high till the year 1973-74. These high rates, necessitated by contingencies like drought and war, when combined with the prevailing shortages, resulted in controls and licences, and thereby provided further incentives for evasion of taxes. It was largely in this economic environment that generation of black money became highly prevalent and acquired serious proportions.

However, pursuant to the recommendations of the DTEC, the Government initiated a series of rate reductions in individual income tax. The top marginal rate of tax was reduced from 97.7 percent in 1973-74 to 77 percent in 1974-75, and further down to 66 percent in 1976-77. It is noteworthy that DTEC had recommended a maximum marginal rate of 75 percent. [18]

The downward trend in the rate of income tax was temporarily reversed during the brief Janata Government rule at the Centre. The top marginal rate of income tax was increased from 66 percent in 1976-77 to 69 percent in 1977-78, and further up to 72 percent in 1979-80. However, the policy of low direct tax rates started by the Congress Government in 1974 and carried forward in 1976 was further reinforced after it came back to power at the Centre in 1980. After a series of revisions, the maximum marginal rate of individual income tax was 54 percent (including employment surcharge of 8 percent), applicable from the financial year 1990-91.

Consequent upon the recommendations contained in the Interim Report of the Tax Reforms Committee (Chairman: Raja Chelliah), 1991, the top marginal rate was fixed at 44.8 percent (including surcharge) from the financial year 1992-93. The Finance Act, 1994 abolished the surcharge of 12 percent and hence the maximum marginal rate of tax was 40 percent from the financial year 1994-95. From the same year it was made applicable on incomes over ₹ 1,20,000. It may be recalled that the top marginal rate of income tax applied to incomes above ₹ 1 lakh from 1967-68 to 1993-94. The ₹ 1 lakh of 1967-68 was approximately equivalent to ₹ 5.5 lakh of 1993-94. This showed the laxity of the administration in adjusting tax brackets for inflation. It is noteworthy that Tax Reforms

Committee had recommended 40 percent maximum rate inclusive of surcharge for income exceeding ₹ 2 lakh.

The maximum marginal rate of personal income tax was further reduced from 40 percent to 30 percent in the 1997-98 budget. In another significant move, it was made applicable to incomes above ₹ 1,50,000.

Low tax rates are welcome provided they improve compliance and revenue yield. However, to expect that lowering of rates would improve compliance automatically is unrealistic because tax evasion occurs at all levels of income. As the Indian Direct Taxation Administration Enquiry Committee, 1958-59, observed, "While we cannot deny that the higher the rate of tax, the greater will be the temptation for evasion and avoidance, we feel that the tax rates by themselves are not to blame for the large extent of evasion in the country. Even if the rates of tax are reduced, evasion will still continue, because it exists at all levels of income". [19]

10.11.2 Tax Amnesties: Government may provide opportunity, from time to time, to tax evaders to declare their past concealments of income and wealth without fear of being prosecuted. Tax amnesty (or impunity) is granted only for the past in order to secure better compliance and thus higher tax yield in the present and future. Tax amnesties (or voluntary disclosure schemes) bring concealed money in the open, broaden the base of investment and hence accelerate economic development.

However, tax amnesties are criticized on the grounds that they provide a premium on dishonesty and are unfair to honest taxpayers. Tax amnesties set bad precedents and encourage tax evaders in the hope that they will be let off leniently for their past sins any time in the future. Practically, the same group of tax evaders takes advantage of tax amnesties announced by the government. The honest taxpayers are demoralised and the tax enforcement machinery also loses respect in the eyes of the common man.

In India, tax amnesties with varied characteristics have been offered from time to time to unearth black money. These amnesties provided taxpayers immunity from interest, penalty, investigation or prosecution in exchange for disclosures of incomes which did not pay tax.

In 1951, a voluntary disclosure scheme was announced under which penal provisions of tax laws were relaxed to persuade tax evaders to disclose their unaccounted incomes.

Under another scheme, announced in 1965, tax evaders were required to pay 60 percent of the disclosed income by way of tax and allowed to bring into books of account the remaining 40 percent.

Another scheme announced in 1975 provided for clubbing together of all black income irrespective of the years over which it was earned and treated as a block separately from other taxable income for the purpose of income tax liability. It provided for a concessional rate of tax ranging from 25 percent to 60 percent on income disclosed under the scheme.

A. Special Bearer Bonds: In 1981, Government offered Special Bearer Bonds to the public. The Bonds were redeemable after 10 years (i.e. in 1991) and carried 2 percent per annum simple rate of interest. The Bonds were marketable and the holders were not required to explain their origin. On their redemption, the holders were allowed to bring them into their books. The value of the Bonds and interest thereon were exempt from income tax and wealth tax till their redemption.

B. Voluntary Deposit Scheme, 1991: This scheme to mobilise unaccounted money was announced through the Voluntary Deposits (Immunities and Exemptions) Act, 1991. Under this scheme, any person could make a deposit with the National Housing Bank on or before January 31, 1992. Thereupon, 40 percent of such deposit was deducted and set apart as a special levy for financing slum clearance and low cost housing for the poor. The balance of 60 percent was credited to the depositor's account which he was allowed to withdraw in one or more instalments for any purpose specified by him. Persons who made deposits under this scheme were not required to disclose the sources of funds from which the deposits were made. Hence, the money deposited was completely immune from all sorts of inquiry and investigation.

C. Gold Bond Scheme, 1993: This scheme was introduced through the Gold Bonds (Immunities and Exemptions) Ordinance, 1993, promulgated by the President on January 31, 1993. The objective of the scheme was to mobilise idle gold reserves of the country to supplement official reserves and thereby strengthen the credit position of the country in the international market. The scheme allowed amnesty from the provisions of direct tax laws to induce persons to legitimise their unaccounted holding of gold.

The scheme remained open for subscription from March 15, 1993 to June 14, 1993. Subscription to the Gold Bonds was made in the form of gold only. The minimum limit for subscription was 500 grams of gold. There was no maximum limit. A subscriber was not required to disclose, for any purpose whatsoever, the nature and source of acquisition of the gold subscribed for the Gold Bonds, including the money with which the gold was acquired.

The Bonds matured after 5 years from the date of issue and were repaid in the form of gold. Besides, a lump sum interest of ₹ 40 per gram of gold for the period of 5 years was paid on maturity.

D. Voluntary Disclosure of Income Scheme (VDIS), 1997: In his 1997-98 budget speech, the Finance Minister announced the introduction of a Voluntary Disclosure Scheme to harness black money for productive purposes. The scheme was rechristened as Voluntary Disclosure of Income Scheme, 1997 by the Finance Minister while moving amendments to the Finance Bill in the Lok Sabha on May 7, 1997.

VDIS, 1997 announced by the Central Board of Direct Taxes on June 18, 1997 had the following provisions.

1. The scheme came into force from July 1, 1997. Any eligible person could make a disclosure of income on or after this date. The last date for making the disclosure was December 31, 1997. Thus, the scheme lasted for six months.
2. A person could make a disclosure in respect of income chargeable to tax under the Indian Income Tax Act, 1961 for any assessment year.
3. The particulars furnished by a declarant were kept a secret. Nothing contained in any declaration was used against the declarant for the purpose of any proceedings relating to imposition of penalties or launching of prosecution under the Income Tax Act, 1961, Wealth Tax Act, 1957, Foreign Exchange Regulation Act, 1973 or the Companies Act, 1956.
4. The tax payable on the disclosed income in respect of any assessment year was at the rate of 35 percent in the case of companies and 30 percent in the case of other assessees including individuals.
5. The tax payable under the scheme was to be paid before the filing of the declaration. In other words, the declaration was accompanied by the proof of payment of tax. In case a person was not in a position to pay the tax before the filing of the declaration, he was allowed to do so within three months of the date of filing of the declaration. In such a case, a simple interest at the rate of 2 percent was charged for every month or part of a month beginning from the date of filing of the declaration to the date of payment of the tax.
6. The declaration was made to the commissioner of income tax in his area and was in a prescribed format. The declaration was signed in the case of an individual by the individual himself. In the case of a Hindu Undivided Family, company, firm etc. the declaration was signed and verified by persons specified in Section 65 of the Finance Act, 1997.
7. Where voluntarily disclosed income was represented by jewellery, the value of the jewellery or bullion was substantiated by a registered valuer's certificate. In case the jewellery declared was from a period before the financial year 1987-88, the value for purposes of declaration was taken to be value as on April 1, 1987.
8. The disclosure made in respect of any assessment year did not affect the

finality of any completed assessment.

9. The voluntarily disclosed income was not added to the total income of the declarant if the declarant credited such amount in his books of account and intimated the credit so made to the Assessing Officer.
10. VDIS did not apply to the following categories of persons: (a) those on whom an *order of detention* had been served under the Conservation of Foreign Exchange and Prevention of Smuggling Activities Act, 1974 in certain circumstances, (b) those punishable under the Narcotic Drugs and Psychotropic Substances Act, 1985, (c) those punishable under the Terrorists and Disruptive Activities (Prevention) Act, 1987, (d) those notified under Section 3 of the Special Court (trial of offences relating to transaction in securities) Act, 1992, and (e) those on whom notices under Section 142 or 148 had been served.
11. A person was not eligible for the income disclosure benefit if that income was before or for a year when a search had been initiated under Section 132 or a requisition made under Section 132A. However, persons surveyed under Section 133A of the Income Tax Act were barred from making a declaration only for income in the year of the survey.
12. State Governments got 77.5 percent of the total resources secured under the scheme. The remaining portion, being share of the Central Government, was used entirely to finance the Basic Minimum Services Programme and infrastructure needs.

At a press conference on January 3, 1998, Finance Minister P. Chidambaran announced that VDIS netted ₹ 10,050 crore towards tax revenue. The total disclosure of black money in the six-month-long campaign was ₹ 33,000 crore and an estimated 4.6 lakh declarations were made under the VDIS.

10.11.3 Advance Tax Payment: Though the regular assessment in respect of any income is made in a later assessment year, the tax on such income is payable by way of advance payment or deduction at source. Section 208 of the Income Tax Act, 1961 makes it obligatory to pay advance tax in every case where the advance tax payable is ₹ 10,000 or more.

10.11.4 Withholding Tax [or Tax Deduction at Source (TDS)]

There are provisions under various sections of the Act regarding tax deduction at source (TDS) [20], e.g. deduction of tax from salaries (Section 192). Other incomes covered under the scheme of TDS include fees for professional or technical services, interest, rent from real estate, commission from insurance, sale of lottery tickets, and winnings from lotteries, crossword puzzles and horse racing.

In recent years, improvement in the percentage share of direct taxes (mainly income tax) has taken place due to widening of the tax base, presumptive taxation and broadening the scope of TDS. In this context, the Ninth Five Year Plan (1997-2002) observed, "The share of TDS in gross collection of income tax increased from about 23 percent in 1980-81 to about 37 percent in 1989-90, but declined subsequently to about 31 percent in 1994-95. One of the major loopholes which contributes to the decline in revenue from TDS relates to the branch-wise threshold of ₹ 10,000 for the purpose of deducting income tax at source from interest on time deposits with banks. Further, the provision for TDS does not apply to non-banking financial companies. Other deficiencies from which the TDS scheme suffers arise from lack of proper monitoring and scrutiny". [21]

10.11.5 Presumptive Tax for Small Traders [22]: In its Interim Report, submitted in December 1991, the Tax Reforms Committee examined the problems and possibilities of taxing the small business sector. The Committee suggested two new presumptive taxes on small businesses:

1. A fixed tax on businesses whose turnover was less than ₹ 5 lakh.
2. An estimated income scheme on small businesses with a turnover above ₹ 5 lakh but less than ₹ 25 lakh.

The schemes envisaged profit to be a certain percentage of turnover depending on the type of activity from which it was earned. The Government introduced the first scheme through the Finance Act, 1992, but deferred its decision to introduce the second scheme.

The presumptive tax system for persons engaged in retail trade with an annual turnover up to ₹ 5 lakh was introduced on an experimental basis. The scheme was in operation initially for two assessment years 1993-94 and 1994-95. It was continued after the expiry of these two years. The objective of the new simplified procedure for taxation was to widen the tax base by encouraging shopkeepers (including those engaged in vocations like tailoring, typewriting, photocopying, repair work etc.) and other small retail traders to pay taxes. The scheme had the following features:

- The scheme was optional and open to individuals not assessed to tax earlier and who had an income from the business of retail trade having an annual turnover up to ₹ 5 lakh.
- Persons opting for the scheme were deemed to have a turnover of ₹ 5 lakh and their total income was deemed to be ₹ 35,000 (₹ 37,000 for A.Y. 1994-95) on which the tax worked out to ₹ 1,400 after allowing for the basic exemption of ₹ 28,000 (₹ 30,000 for A.Y. 1994-95).
- A retail trader opting for the scheme had only to file the simplified statement

(name, address, nature of business etc.) and pay a tax of ₹ 1,400 by 15th March of the financial year in which the income was earned.

The scheme was optional to avoid objection on constitutional grounds. If presumptive tax results in a higher tax burden than the one on the basis of book profit, it can be said to violate Article 14 of the Constitution which guarantees equality before law. Thus, the taxpayer had the option to pay presumptive tax or ask for regular assessment of his income, whichever he thought was advantageous to him.

Unfortunately, the scheme of presumptive taxation did not gain popularity with small traders and self-employed entrepreneurs. In 1992-93, the first year of the operation of the scheme, 1,16,644 persons opted for the scheme and paid a total tax of ₹ 16.4 crore, as against the anticipated revenue collection of ₹ 140 crore. [23] This was by no means a significant addition to the existing 70 lakh individual assessees under the income tax net. The number of shopkeepers and other small traders was much higher. The scheme touched only the tip of the iceberg.

The Government introduced through the Finance Act, 1994 two new schemes for estimating the income from the business of civil construction and plying or hiring trucks. The Finance Act, 1994 introduced Sections 44AD and 44AE in the Income Tax Act to provide for a method of estimating income from these businesses.

While the section for civil construction applied to all assessees whose gross receipts from the business did not exceed ₹ 40 lakh, the section for plying trucks applied to businessmen owning not more than 10 trucks. Under Section 44AD, the income from these businesses was estimated at 8 percent of the gross receipts paid or payable to an assessee. Income of truck owners is assessed at ₹ 3,500 p.m. per heavy vehicle and at ₹ 3,150 p.m. per medium and light vehicle.

In the 1997-98 budget, the Finance Minister discontinued the presumptive scheme under Section 115K as it failed to yield the desired results. In its place, he introduced a new estimated income scheme for retail traders. The new scheme is applicable to persons engaged in the business of retail trade of any goods or merchandise having a total turnover of less than ₹ 40 lakh. The income of the trader will be estimated at 5 percent of the total turnover. A trader with a turnover of less than ₹ 10 lakh is exempted given the present exemption limit of ₹ 50,000. Assessees who file a return showing an income less than 5 percent of turnover are required to maintain books of account and get their accounts audited.

A. Estimated Income Scheme for Small Businesses: This scheme, applicable for assessment year 2011-12 and onwards, applies to assessees engaged in any eligible business whose total turnover or gross receipts do not exceed ₹ 1 crore during a year. The scheme, under Section 44AD, is compulsory for all eligible assessees. Under the scheme, the income of an assessee from the eligible business is estimated at 8 percent of the total turnover in the previous year.

B. Estimated Income Scheme for Truck Owners: This scheme, provided under Section 44AE, applies to assesses engaged in business of plying, leasing or hiring trucks, owning not more than 10 trucks, at ant time during the previous year. The income is estimated at ₹ 5,000 p.m. for each heavy goods vehicle and ₹ 4,500 p.m. for each vehicle other than heavy goods vehicle.

10.11.6 Permanent Account Number (PAN) or General Index Register Number (GIR): In order to strengthen the efforts at enforcement, the Finance Minister in his 1998-99 budget made it obligatory for assessees to quote their PAN or GIR mandatorily in respect of the following high value transactions: purchase and sale of immovable property; purchase and sale of motor vehicles; transactions in shares exceeding ₹ 10 lakh; opening of new bank accounts; fixed deposits of more than ₹ 50,000; applications for allotment of telephone connections; and payments to hotels exceeding ₹ 25,000.

10.11.7 Survey of Income Tax: Income tax authorities may conduct, from time to time, a shop to shop or house to house survey to rope in new assessees. Potential assessees are required to fill up a questionnaire in Form 45-D. Officials conducting the survey cannot seize any books of account, cash, or articles. If any person fails to comply with a notice under Section 133B requiring the survey information in Form 45-D, he is liable to pay a penalty up to ₹ 1,000 (Section 272AA of Income Tax Act, 1961).

10.11.8 Summons, and Search and Seizure:

A. Summons: Under Section 131 of the Income Tax Act, an authorised income tax officer can issue summons when he has reasons to suspect that any income has been concealed by any person within his jurisdiction. Summons is issued to enforce attendance of any person for the purpose of examining him. The person concerned may be examined to verify the authenticity of various types of transactions, the following being the common ones.

(a) Capital Contributions: Summons can be issued to owners of a business (i.e. proprietors, partners, and shareholders) to verify their capital contributions and sources of money thereof. Borrowed funds can be sources of money for capital contributions.

(b) Business Transactions: An assessee makes claim in his return of income regarding purchases, sales, revenue expenditure, and capital outlays. To verify such claims, the assessing officer can issue summons to suppliers, buyers, and recipients of commissions, salaries, rent etc.

(c) Borrowing of Funds: An assessee may borrow funds from institutional and/or non-institutional sources for various purposes. Borrowings from non-institutional sources (e.g. private moneylenders, relatives, friends etc.) may need to be confirmed by income tax authorities. Hence, summons can be issued to persons who have lent money to explain sources of money lent.

(d) Investment Transactions: Summons can be issued to any person who has made substantial investments in shares, securities, land, buildings, and costly consumer durables. The person so summoned is expected to explain with documentary evidence the sources of his funds. These sources may include borrowings, gifts received, property inherited, sale of jewellery etc. However, documentary evidence is necessary to prove these sources of money. It is advisable to reveal correct factual information which can be cross-verified.

B. Search and Seizure: To conduct search (popularly called raid) and seizure, an authorisation in the prescribed form is issued by the competent income tax authority under his signature and seal. Income tax officials are vested with considerable powers to carry out search operations.

Thus, they can: (a) enter and search any building, place or vehicle in occupation of the person being searched, (b) break the lock and examine any box, locker, almirah etc., and (c) seize any books of account, other documents, money, bullion, jewellery etc.

Books of account and other documents impounded cannot be retained beyond 180 days without obtaining approval of the Commissioner. However, the assessee can have copies made out of the original books impounded by the authorities (Sections 132, and 132A of the Income Tax Act, 1961).

10.11.9 Penalties and Prosecutions: These are as under:

A. Penalties: Income Tax Act contains provisions under which penalties are imposed for various defaults committed by the taxpayers. The important provisions in this regard are summarised in Table 10.1.

B. Prosecutions: Income Tax Act contains provisions under which prosecution proceedings can be started for different offences committed by taxpayers. The important provisions in this regard are summarised in Table 10.2.

C. Penal Provisions: A Comment: There are quite a few sections in the Income Tax Act which confer discretionary powers on income tax officers. Thus, Section 273A of the Act allows income tax officers to reduce or waive penalties for tax evasion if it is voluntarily disclosed before being discovered by the assessing officer. According to the Act, this can be done only once in the life time of a taxpayer. However, in practice it is likely that the penalty is waived several times for the same taxpayer even when the disclosure criterion is not met. The possibility of misuse of Section 273A cannot be ruled out.

Table 10.1: Select Penalty Provisions for Different Defaults under Income Tax Act, 1961

Section	Nature of default	Penalty
271(1)(C)	Concealment of particulars of income	Not less than the amount of tax sought to be evaded and not exceeding three times the amount of tax sought to be evaded
271A	Failure to keep or maintain books of account as required under Section 44AA	₹ 25,000
271C	Failure to deduct tax at source	Amount equal to tax which he failed to deduct or pay
271F	Failure to furnish return of income under Section 139(1) i.e. persons owning immovable property, motor vehicle, telephone etc.	₹ 5,000
272B	Failure to apply for allotment of permanent account number (PAN)	₹ 10,000

Table 10.2: Select Prosecution Provisions for Various Offences under Income Tax Act, 1961

Section	Nature of offence	Punishment
276B	Failure to deposit tax deducted at source or tax collected at source	Rigorous imprisonment up to 7 years (not less than 3 months) and fine
276C(2)	Wilful attempt to evade the payment of any tax, penalty or interest	Rigorous imprisonment up to 2 years (not less than 3 months) and fine
276CC	Wilful failure to furnish in due time return of income or return of fringe benefits	(a) Rigorous imprisonment up to 7 years (not less than 3 months) and fine if the amount sought to be evaded exceeds ₹ 25,00,000 (b) Imprisonment up to 2 years (not less than 3 months) and fine in other cases
277	Making a false statement in verification or delivering a false account	(a) Rigorous imprisonment up to 7 years (not less than 6 months) and fine if the amount sought to be evaded exceeds ₹ 25,00,000 (b) Rigorous imprisonment up to 2 years (not less than 3 months) and fine in other cases

Similarly, Section 273A(4) of the Act allows tax officers to reduce or waive penalty on grounds of genuine hardships.

Furthermore, under Section 279(2) of the Act tax officers are empowered to compound an offence either before or after the institution of prosecution proceedings. These powers are discretionary and cannot be challenged in a court of law.

Endnotes

1. Level of taxation in a country is traditionally judged in terms of the ratio which taxes bear to some measure of national income. This ratio is called tax-GDP ratio and the change in it is determined by variations in both the numerator (total tax revenue) and the denominator (national income).
2. Tax equity refers to *fair* or *just* or *equitable* distribution of tax burden among taxpayers. Though fairness and justness in taxation are universally accepted, these terms are rarely defined rigorously and can be interpreted in various ways. Hence, there is no unanimity of opinion as to the type of tax system which results in the most equitable distribution of tax burden.
   There are two main approaches to tax equity in tax literature: the Benefit Principle of Taxation which states that tax payments should be proportional to the benefits derived from government services, and the Ability-to-Pay Principle of Taxation which holds that each taxpayer should contribute to the public exchequer in line with his ability-to-pay.
3. Government of India, Ministry of Finance, *Interim Report of the Tax Reforms Committee* (Chairman: Raja Chelliah), December 1991, p. 44.
4. Government of India, Planning Commission, *The Seventh Five Year Plan (1985-90)*, Volume I, p. 71.
5. Inclusive growth may be defined as growth that promotes equal opportunities and increases access to these opportunities, i.e. growth that allows all members of society to participate in and contribute equally to development efforts, regardless of individual circumstances. This concept appears in Asian Development Bank's (ADB), *Strategy 2020,* that examines the extent of inequality of opportunities and to what extent it can be overcome by different types of growth process. The main idea in the ADB's approach is to focus on productive employment as an important element of inclusive growth.
   Inclusive growth, defined in a broader sense has three dimensions: (a) Equity among all sections of the society; (b) Equity among all sectors of the economy, and (c) Equity among all regions in the country.
   Thus, inclusive growth means inter-group, inter-sector as well as inter-regional equity. Growth is inclusive when it creates economic opportunities along with ensuring equal access to them.
6. Agricultural income is exempt from tax under Section 10(1) of the Income Tax Act, 1961.
7. Derivative in mathematics means a variable derived from another variable. The term *derivative* indicates that it has no independent value, i.e. its value is entirely *derived* from the value of the underlying asset. The underlying asset can be security, commodity, bullion, currency, live stock or anything else. In other words, derivative means a forward, future, option or any other hybrid contract of pre-determined fixed duration, linked for the purpose of contract fulfilment to the value of a specified real or financial asset of an index of securities. Similarly, in the financial sense, a derivative is a financial product, which has been derived from a market for another product. Without the underlying product, derivatives do

not have any independent existence in the market.

Derivative instruments are defined by the Indian Securities Contracts (Regulation) Act, 1956 to include: (i) a security derived from a debt instrument, share, secured/unsecured loan, risk instrument or contract for differences, or any other form of security, and (ii) a contract that derives its value from the prices/index of prices of underlying securities.

In other words, derivatives are financial instruments/contracts whose value depends upon the value of an underlying. Since their value is essentially derived out of an underlying, they are financial abstractions whose value is derived mathematically from the changes in the value of the underlying.

The International Monetary Fund (IMF) defines derivatives as "financial instruments that are linked to a specific financial instrument or indicator or commodity and through which specific financial risks can be traded in financial markets in their own right. The value of a financial derivative derives from the price of an underlying item, such as an asset or index. Unlike debt securities, no principal is advanced to be repaid and no investment income accrues".

8. Government of India, Ministry of Finance, *Report of the Taxation Enquiry Commission,* (Chairman, John Matthai), 1953-54, Vol. II, p. 189.
9. Nicholas Kaldor, *Indian Tax Reform: Report of a Survey,* Government of India, Ministry of Finance, 1956, p. 105.
10. Quoted by Government of India, Ministry of Finance, *Report of the Direct Taxes Administration Enquiry Committee,* (Chairman: Mahavir Tyagi), 1958-59, p. 148.
11. *Ibid.,* p. 148.
12. Government of India, Ministry of Finance, *Final Report of Direct Taxes Enquiry Committee,* (Chairman, Justice K.N. Wanchoo), December 1971.
13. Government of India, Ministry of Finance, *Aspects of the Black Economy in India*, March 1985, p. 161.
14. Government of India, Ministry of Finance, *Interim Report of the Tax Reforms Committee,* (Chairman, Raja Chelliah), December 1991, p. 47.
15. *Ibid.,* p. 37.
16. Government of India, Ministry of Finance, *Budget 1997-98, Speech of the Finance Minister*, Part B, p. 25.
17. Government of India, Ministry of Finance, *Report of the Central Excise (Self-Removal Procedure) Review Committee,* (Chairman: B. Venkatappiah), 1973, p. 65.
18. Government of India, Ministry of Finance, *Final Report of Direct Taxes Enquiry Committee,* (Chairman: Justice K.N. Wancoo), 1971, para 2.52.
19. Government of India, Ministry of Finance, *Report of the Direct Taxes Administration Enquiry Committee,* (Chairman: Mahavir Tyagi), 1958-59, p. 149.
20. TDS is a system of collecting income tax whereby money is periodically deducted by the employers, financial institutions, and others from wages of employees, returns on securities, and other payments. Thus, intermediaries (or third parties) do the job on behalf of the government as regards assessment of the taxable base and the collection of tax thereon.

    Generally, a fixed percentage is withheld from the payment made and the same is deposited in government's account. At the time of filing the return of income, the taxpayer encloses withholding tax receipts and in case of overpayment he can claim refund of tax.

    Tax withholding system (also called tax deduction at source or Pay-As-You-Earn) satisfies the canon of convenience both for the fiscal authorities and the taxpayers. It is beneficial for the government because it reduces the possibility of tax evasion, ensures prompt tax payment, and simplifies tax collection. It does not allow any lag between the time of receiving income and the time of tax payment. For the taxpayer, it is an instalment plan of taxation and hence convenient.

However, tax withholding involves additional paper work on the part of tax deductors. It also adds to the burden of taxpayers who have to obtain tax deduction certificates from deductors, fill additional tax forms, and wait for refunds.

21. Government of India, Planning Commission, *Ninth Five Year Plan* (1997-2002), Vol. I, p. 168.

22. Presumptive Tax: In every country, there are some soft-to-tax and hard-to-tax sources of income. Wages and salaries are properly recorded and therefore it is easy to assess and collect taxes on them through the Pay-As-You-Earn (PAYE) system. Similarly, income from securities paid through banks can easily be subjected to deduction at source.

Contrarily, the three hard-to-tax classes of the non-corporate sector are: (a) unincorporated commercial and industrial units, (b) self-employed professionals, and (c) rich peasantry. The problem of taxing the first two categories relates to accounting difficulties while in the case of third category, it is essentially the lack of political will. Non-reporting and under-reporting of income is quite sizeable in these sectors. The growing small business sector is a tax haven. It is very difficult to enforce a reliable system of book-keeping to assess earnings of this sector. Pragmatically, a system of lump sum taxation may be tried in place of taxation of profits.

Presumptive tax relates to the use of appropriate indicators of income, wealth etc. instead of the actual records of these tax bases. In the case of income tax, a presumptive tax is imposed on the basis of an estimated taxable income. Presumptive income is exogenously determined. The base for the presumptive income tax is fixed and does not depend on the behaviour of individual entrepreneurs. In essence, a presumptive income tax works like a lump sum tax and therefore does not impose marginal tax burden on actual income. Varying methods of presumptive taxation are in operation in Israel, Argentina, Chile and Columbia. The French *forfait* system is a typical example of presumptive taxation. The chief advantage of presumptive taxation is its simplicity, both for the tax collectors and the taxpayers. It is, therefore, cost-effective for the administration. The simplicity attribute may also encourage tax compliance. Presumptive taxation particularly suits the developing countries with a large unorganised business sector consisting of small retail establishments, and self-employed professionals. It is easy to administer this tax which can become an effective source of revenue. It also promotes horizontal equity.

The French forfait system has several features. Firstly, the taxable profit of a given business unit is agreed upon mutually between the tax authorities and the assessee. Secondly, the assessment remains valid for a limited number of years. Finally, the taxpayer is required to submit a set of simple facts to the authorities, namely the amount of his purchases and sales, the wage bill, the value of his inventory, and the number of employees. Alternatively, small businesses may be subject to a system of licence fee charged in accordance with some well-defined criteria such as the location of business and its size.

23. Government of India, *Economic Survey*, 1993-94, p. 26.

Part IV: Structure of Central Taxes

11

Trends in the Level and Composition of Central Taxes

This chapter describes the composition and trends in Central tax revenues. Central taxes account for about two-thirds of total tax collections in India. [1] The relative significance of various taxes in Central revenues has undergone major changes since Independence. Income tax and wealth tax are the direct taxes while excise levies and customs duties are the indirect taxes of the Central Government.

11.1 Central Taxes as Percent of GDP

In 1950-51, gross central taxes accounted for 3.89 percent of GDP. With the widening and deepening of the tax net to raise resources for development projects, the percentage started increasing with every passing decade. It increased to 4.99 in 1960-61, to 6.73 in 1970-71 and stood at 8.81 in 1980-81.

In 1990-91, when the process of economic reforms was initiated, gross Central taxes accounted for 9.82 percent of GDP. However, as a result of tax reforms initiated since then, this percentage started falling and it became as low as 8.70 in 2000-01. Stating the reasons for this fall, the Twelfth Finance Commission noted, "The impact of these reforms on direct and indirect taxes was diametrically opposite. While the direct taxes showed, even with the lower rates, a rising tax-GDP ratio, this ratio for the indirect taxes kept sliding down. The indirect taxes had a larger share in the total tax revenues of the centre and the fall in the indirect tax to GDP ratio could not be compensated by a rise in the direct taxes. As a result, the overall central tax-GDP ratio fell". [2]

Of late, however, recovery is noticeable in the tax-GDP ratio at the level of Central Government. For the year 2013-14, it was estimated at 10.87 (Table 11.1).

11.2 Direct and Indirect Taxes

As in the case of combined (Centre and States) tax revenues, tax structure at the Central level also evolved around indirect taxes during the post-Independence period. The ratio between direct and indirect taxes in gross Central taxes declined from 43.4:56.6 in 1950-51 to 32.6:67.4 in 1960-61, to 27.1:72.9 in 1970-71 and to 22.7:77.3 in 1980-81. Resultantly, indirect taxes came to occupy a dominant place in Central finances.

Table 11.1: Gross Central Tax Revenue as Percent of GDP: Selected Years

(₹ crore)

Year	Gross Central Taxes*	Col. 2 as % of GDP	Year	Gross Central Taxes	Col. 5 as % of GDP
1	2	3	4	5	6
1950-51	405	3.89	1990-91	57,577	9.82
1955-56	485	4.27	1995-96	1,11,224	9.07
1960-61	895	4.99	2000-01	1,88,603	8.70
1965-66	2,061	7.14	2005-06	3,66,151	9.91
1970-71	3,206	6.73	2010-11	7,93,072	10.17
1975-76	7,609	8.78	2011-12	8,88,898	9.87
1980-81	13,179	8.81	2012-13	10,38,037	10.35
1985-86	28,670	9.90	2013-14	12,35,870	10.87

* Before transferring States' share in Central taxes.
2012-13 = Revised estimates; 2013-14 = Budget estimates.
Note: The ratios to GDP at market prices are based on CSO's National Accounts 2004-05 series.
Source: Rearranged data from Government of India, Ministry of Finance, *Indian Public Finance Statistics, 2013-2014*, Tables 1.7 and 1.8. For full time series data from 1950-51 to 2013-14, see Table 2 in Part VIII of this book.

In the wake of reforms initiated in the early 1990s, rates of both corporate and personal income tax were substantially reduced. Following better compliance, the decline in the relative share of direct taxes was reversed. Direct taxes as a percentage of Centre's total tax collections rose from 19.2 percent in 1990-91 (pre-reform period) to 36.2 percent in 2000-01. The figure stood at 55.7 percent in 2010-11 and was estimated at 53.5 for the year 2013-14 (Table 11.2).

11.3 Composition of Direct Taxes

11.3.1 Income Tax: In the case of corporation tax, the relative contribution was 9.9 percent in 1950-51 while in 1990-91 it was 9.3 percent. In the intervening period, however, moderate changes are noticeable in the percentage share of corporation tax. As in the case of personal income tax, the percentage share of corporation tax in Centre's gross tax revenues has increased sharply during the post-1991 period. In 2000-01, it accounted for 18.9 percent and increased sharply to 37.7 percent in 2010-11. In the budget estimates for 2015-16, its share was 32.5 percent (Table 11.3).

In 1950-51, personal income tax accounted for almost one-third (32.7 percent) of Central tax collections. However, the relative contribution declined over the years and was less than one-tenth (9.3 percent) in 1990-91. After the tax reforms initiated since early 1990s, the share of personal income tax in gross tax revenues of the Central Government increased sharply. In 2000-01, it accounted for 16.8 percent, and increased to 18.5 in 2010-11. In the budget estimates for 2015-16, its share stood at 22.6 percent (Table 11.3).

Table 11.2: Gross Central Tax Revenue, Breakdown between Direct and Indirect Taxes with Percentage Shares: Selected Years

(₹ crore)

Year	Gross Central Taxes*(3+4)	Direct Taxes	Indirect Taxes	Col. 3 as % of Col. 2	Col. 4 as % of Col. 2
1	2	3	4	5	6
1950-51	405	176	229	43.4	56.6
1955-56	485	171	314	35.2	64.8
1960-61	895	292	603	32.6	67.4
1965-66	2,061	598	1,463	29.0	71.0
1970-71	3,206	869	2,337	27.1	72.9
1975-76	7,609	2,205	5,404	29.0	71.0
1980-81	13,179	2,997	10,182	22.7	77.3
1985-86	28,670	5,620	23,050	19.6	80.4
1990-91	57,577	11,030	46,547	19.2	80.8
1995-96	1,11,224	33,564	77,660	30.2	69.8
2000-01	1,88,603	68,305	1,20,298	36.2	63.8
2005-06	3,66,151	1,62,337	2,03,814	44.3	55.7
2010-11	7,93,072	4,38,515	3,54,556	55.7	44.3
2011-12	8,88,898	4,88,160	4,00,738	54.9	45.1
2012-13	10,38,037	5,59,677	4,78,360	53.9	46.1
2013-14	12,35,870	6,61,396	5,74,474	53.5	46.5

* Before transferring States' share in Central taxes.
2012-13 = Revised estimates; 2013-14 = Budget estimates.
Note: The ratios to GDP at market prices are based on CSO's National Accounts 2004-05 series.
Source: Rearranged data from Government of India, Ministry of Finance, *Indian Public Finance Statistics, 2013-2014*, Tables 1.7 and 1.8. Columns 5 and 6 calculations own. For full time series data from 1950-51 to 2013-14, see Table 2 in Part VIII of this book.

It is noteworthy that both personal and corporate income taxes were rationalized as part of the package of economic reforms initiated in 1991. The number of rate categories, as well as the marginal income tax rates, was substantially reduced.

Income tax is discussed separately in chapter 12 this book.

11.3.2 Wealth Tax: This so-called capital tax of the Central Government is without much revenue significance. Chapter 13 of this book deals with it in some detail. Wealth tax was abolished in the 2015-16 budget.

Table 11.3: Trends in the Level and Composition of Gross Tax Revenues* of the Central Government: 1950-51 to 2015-16 (Selected Years)

(₹ crore)

Central taxes	1950-51	1960-61	1970-71	1980-81	1990-91	2000-01	2010-11	2015-16
A+B Gross tax revenues	404 (100.0)	888 (100.0)	3,206 (100.0)	13,179 (100.0)	57,576 (100.0)	1,88,603 (100.0)	7,93,072 (100.0)	14,49,490 (100.0)
A. Direct taxes of which	174 (43.1)	290 (32.6)	870 (27.1)	3,004 (22.8)	11,025 (19.1)	68,306 (36.2)	4,45,962 (56.2)	7,97,995 (55.1)
1. Corporation tax	40 (9.9)	11 (12.5)	371 (11.6)	1,310 (9.9)	5,235 (9.3)	35,696 (18.9)	2,98,688 (37.7)	4,70,628 (32.5)
2. Personal income tax	132 (32.7)	166 (18.7)	473 (14.8)	1,506 (11.4)	5,371 (9.3)	31,764 (16.8)	1,46,587 (18.5)	3,27,367 (22.6)
3. Other taxes**	2 (0.5)	13 (1.5)	26 (0.8)	188 (1.4)	319 (0.5)	846 (0.5)	687 (0.1)	0 (0.0)
B. Indirect taxes of which	229 (56.7)	599 (67.5)	2,337 (72.9)	10,175 (77.2)	46,552 (80.9)	1,20,297 (63.8)	3,47,110 (43.8)	6,51,495 (44.9)
1. Customs duties	157 (38.9)	170 (19.1)	524 (16.3)	3,409 (25.8)	20,644 (35.8)	47,542 (25.2)	1,35,813 (17.1)	2,08,336 (14.4)
2. Union excises	68 (16.8)	414 (46.6)	1,759 (54.9)	6,500 (49.3)	24,514 (42.6)	68,526 (36.3)	1,38,299 (17.4)	2,29,808 (15.9)
3. Service tax	-	-	-	-	-	-	71,016 (9.0)	2,09,774 (14.4)
4. Other taxes***	4 (1.0)	15 (1.7)	54 (1.7)	266 (2.0)	1,394 (2.4)	4,229 (2.2)	1,982 (0.2)	3,577 (0.2)

* Before transferring States' share in Central taxes; 2015-16 Budget estimates.

** These are wealth tax (abolished in the 2015-16 budget) and some other taxes of minor revenue significance.

*** These are State excise duties, taxes on vehicles, sales tax, octroi, duties on electricity, stamp and registration, entertainment tax (all from Union Territories without legislature) and foreign travel tax.

Figures in parentheses are corresponding percentages of total tax collections.

Sources: Government of India, Ministry of Finance, *Explanatory Memorandum on the Budget of the Central Government* (various years); *Receipts Budget* (various years); and *Budget at a Glance*, 2015-16.

11.4 Composition of Indirect Taxes

11.4.1 Union Excise Duties: In the post-Independence period (1950-70), a major change in the Indian tax system pertained to the phenomenal rise in the relative revenue significance of Union excise duties. In 1950-51, excise revenue accounted for a modest 16.8 percent of total Central tax collections: ₹ 68 crore out of ₹ 404 crore. Within a span of 20 years, the proportionate share shot up to 54.9 percent in 1970-71. It declined to 49.3 percent in 1980-81 and 42.6 in 1990-91. In 2000-01, it was recorded at 36.3 percent which further declined to 17.4 percent in 2010-11. In the 2015-16 budget, the contribution of excise duties in gross tax revenues of the Centre was estimated at 15.9 percent (Table 11.3). The relative contribution of excise revenue has declined due to reduction in the average tax rates (without a compensatory rise in the tax base), evasion, and litigation.

Union excise duties are examined in detail in chapter 14 of this book.

11.4.2 Service Tax: In view of the need for additional resources and the rising contribution of service sector to GDP, a modest effort was made in the 1994-95 budget when a 5 percent tax was imposed on the services of telephones, non-life insurance, and stock brokers with effect from July 1, 1994. Since then the coverage of service tax has been extended to a host of other services and it is considered as the tax of the future. In 2010-11, its contribution to gross tax revenues of the Centre was 9.0 percent which was estimated at 14.4 percent in the budget estimates for 2015-16 (Table 11.3).

Service tax is discussed separately in chapter 15 of this book.

11.4.3 Customs Duties: During pre-Independence days and even during the early post-Independence period, customs duties formed the mainstay of Central tax revenues. However, the relative share of customs duties started declining from early 1950s in view of a protective trade policy and dwindling foreign exchange reserves. The share of customs revenue in Centre's total tax collections dropped from 38.9 percent in 1950-51, to 19.1 percent in 1960-61, and to as low as 16.3 percent in 1970-71. After that customs revenue maintained an upward swing, accounting for 25.8 percent in 1980-81 and 35.8 percent in 1990-91. This upward trend was attributable to a changed emphasis from physical to fiscal controls to regulate imports, a policy reiterated in the Long-Term Fiscal Policy of December 1985.

However, during the post-liberalisation period (i.e. 1991 onward), a sharp fall is noticeable in the relative share of customs duties in gross tax revenues of the Central Government. The relative share fell to 25.2 percent in 2000-01 and further down to 17.1 percent in 2010-11. This is due to drastic reductions in the tariff rates across the rate categories including the peak rate in the wake of WTO commitments and the policy to become globally competitive. In the 2015-16 budget, the share of customs revenue was estimated at 14.8 percent (Table 11.3).

Customs duties are discussed separately in chapter 16 of this book.

Endnotes

1. Tax collections (or gross tax revenues) of the Central Government are different from its net tax revenues because a part of the proceeds from taxes is transferred to State Governments under tax sharing arrangements of the Constitution.
2. *Report of the Twelfth Finance Commission* (2005-10), November 2004, p. 31.

12

Income Tax

Besides being the main source of direct tax revenue for the Government, income tax is an effective instrument to realise various socio-economic objectives of national policies. This chapter explains the legal framework, and describes the present system of income tax in India. [1]

12.1 Constitutional Provisions and Legal Framework

12.1.1 Constitutional Provisions: Taxation of income in India may be classified into two broad categories: (a) taxation of non-agricultural income, a Central subject, and (b) taxation of agricultural income, a matter for State legislation. The two relevant entries in List I (Union List) of the Seventh Schedule of the Constitution which empower the Parliament to levy income tax are: Entry 82, "taxes on income other than agricultural income", and Entry 85, "corporation tax". According to Article 366(6) of the Constitution "corporation tax means any tax on income, so far as that tax is payable by companies".

For the purpose of taxation of non-agricultural incomes, the enactment is the Indian Income Tax Act, 1961 which is amended from time to time by the annual Finance Act and other legislations pertaining to direct taxes. Entities chargeable to tax under the Act are of two types: (i) non-corporate entities, and (ii) corporate entities. Non-corporate entities mainly consist of individuals and firms and their taxation is called personal income tax.

The States are empowered to make laws with respect to taxes on agricultural income vide entry 46 of List II (State List) of the Seventh Schedule of the Constitution. Therefore, agricultural income is exempt from Central income tax. However, from the assessment year 1974-75, agricultural income is taken into account to determine the rate of tax on non-agricultural income if agricultural income exceeds ₹ 5,000. Although the power to impose tax on agricultural income is vested in State Governments, in practice very few States have imposed this tax and wherever it is imposed the revenue is negligible.

Till recently, the proceeds from income tax were shareable with the States under Article 270(1) of the Constitution. The Finance Commission recommended the formula for the distribution of income tax revenue between the Centre and the States and the distribution of States' share among the States themselves. Thus, income tax played an important role not only in Central finances but also in the finances of the State Governments.

The Constitution (Eightieth Amendment) Act, 2000 substituted a new Article for Article 270 under which States are now given a percentage share of all Central taxes and duties. However, the surcharge levied for purposes of the Union under Article 271 is excluded from the divisible pool.

12.2 Revenue Significance of Income Tax

Income tax is the only notable source of direct tax revenue in India. Companies (corporations) and individuals are the two main taxpaying entities. In the case of corporation tax, the relative contribution was 9.9 percent in 1950-51 while in 1990-91 it was 9.3 percent. In the intervening period, however, moderate changes are noticeable in the percentage share of corporation tax. As in the case of personal income tax, the percentage share of corporation tax in Centre's gross tax revenues has increased sharply during the post-1991 period. In 2000-01, it accounted for 18.9 percent and increased sharply to 37.7 percent in 2010-11. In the budget estimates for 2015-16, its share was 32.5 percent (Table 12.1).

In 1950-51, personal income tax accounted for almost one-third (32.7 percent) of Central tax collections. However, the relative contribution declined over the years and was less than one-tenth (9.3 percent) in 1990-91. Lamenting the sharp decline in the relative revenue significance of personal income tax, the Tax Reforms Committee, 1991, observed, "It is a matter for concern that the share of taxes on income particularly personal income tax has registered a sharp decline over the years and despite efforts to raise more revenue from these taxes, no appreciable improvement seems to have come about". [2]

After the tax reforms initiated since early 1990s, the share of personal income tax in gross tax revenues of the Central Government increased sharply. In 2000-01, it accounted for 16.8 percent, and increased to 18.5 in 2010-11. In the budget estimates for 2015-16, its share stood at 22.6 percent (Table 12.1).

12.3 Income Tax Act, 1961: Main Provisions

The present law of income tax in India is governed by the Income Tax Act, 1961 (hereinafter called the Act), which is amended from time to time by the annual Finance Act and other legislations pertaining to direct taxes. The Act which came into force on April 1, 1962, replaced the Indian Income Tax Act, 1922, which had remained in operation for 40 years. Furthermore, a set of rules known as Income Tax Rules, 1962 have been framed for implementing the various provisions of the Act. [3] The law of income tax is stated here as applicable for the financial year 2015-16 (i.e. assessment year 2016-17).

Table 12.1: Trends in the Relative Significance of Income Tax in Gross Tax Revenues* of the Central Government: Selected Years

(₹ crore)

Central taxes	1950-51	1960-61	1970-71	1980-81	1990-91	2000-01	2010-11	2015-16
A+B Gross tax revenues	404 (100.0)	888 (100.0)	3,206 (100.0)	13,179 (100.0)	57,576 (100.0)	1,88,603 (100.0)	7,93,072 (100.0)	14,49,490 (100.0)
A. Direct taxes of which	174 (43.1)	290 (32.6)	870 (27.1)	3,004 (22.8)	11,025 (19.1)	68,306 (36.2)	4,45,962 (56.2)	7,97,995 (55.1)
1. Corporation Tax	40 (9.9)	11 (12.5)	371 (11.6)	1,310 (9.9)	5,235 (9.3)	35,696 (18.9)	2,98,688 (37.7)	4,70,628 (32.5)
2. Personal income tax	132 (32.7)	166 (18.7)	473 (14.8)	1,506 (11.4)	5,371 (9.3)	31,764 (16.8)	1,46,587 (18.5)	3,27,367 (22.6)
B. Indirect taxes	229 (56.7)	599 (67.5)	2,337 (72.9)	10,175 (77.2)	46,552 (80.9)	1,20,297 (63.8)	3,47,110 (43.8)	6,51,495 (44.9)

* Before transferring States' share in Central taxes; 2015-16 Budget estimates.
Figures in parentheses are corresponding percentages of gross tax revenues.
Sources: Government of India, Ministry of Finance, *Explanatory Memorandum on the Budget of the Central Government* (various years); *Receipts Budget* (various years); and *Budget at a Glance*, 2015-16.

12.3.1 Meaning of Income: Section 4 of the Act deals with the basis of charge of income tax. Thus, income tax is an annual tax on income charged on every person. It is levied on the *total income* of every assessee computed in accordance with the provisions of the Act. *Total income* means the income for which an assessee is chargeable to tax. [4] As in most other countries, income is exemplified rather than defined. The Act does not define the term *income*, but Section 2(24) of the Act describes the various receipts as income which include, *inter alia*, the following: profits and gains, dividends, voluntary contributions received by a charitable trust, the value of any perquisite or profit in lieu of salary, any capital gains, any winnings from lotteries, crossword puzzles etc.

Apart from the aforesaid receipts, any other receipt is taxable under the Act if it comes within the general and natural connotation of the term *income*. Thus, the law brings under charge various types of income which may be classified as follows: (a) income received, (b) income deemed to be received (Section 7), e.g. annual accretion to the account of an employee participating in a recognised provident fund, dividend declared by the company but not yet received by the individual shareholders etc., (c) income accrued [Section 5(1)(b)], and (d) income deemed to have accrued (Section 9). Income is said to be received when it reaches the assessee. It is said to accrue or arise when the right to receive the income becomes vested in the assessee. In short, the description of the term *income* in Section 2(24) is inclusive and not exclusive.

It is indeed very difficult to reduce the concept of income to a precise and unambiguous definition. Various forms of imputed and accrued incomes pose serious practical difficulties of measurement and guidance is sought from judicial pronouncements on the subject. The Taxation Enquiry Commission, 1953-54, opined, "It will be impracticable to reduce the principles evolved by judicial decisions in the leading cases on this subject (income) into an exhaustive and self-contained definition of income in our taxation Act. We are also of the opinion that perhaps more harm than good may result from including in the taxation Act a rigid definition of income. We think that guidance in this matter should continue to be drawn in the future as heretofore, from the extensive case law in the subject". [5]

12.3.2 Residential Status: Income which is subject to charge of tax varies according to the residential status of taxpayer. In the case of a person *resident* in India, all income derived from whatever source is within the scope of taxation. Thus, he is liable to pay tax in respect of his income received or deemed to be received by him in India, income accruing or deemed to accrue to him in India, and income accruing or arising to him outside India. In short, a resident is charged to income tax on his world income, subject to a double taxation relief in respect of foreign incomes taxed abroad. However, in the case of a *non-resident*, tax liability extends only to income which: (a) is received or is deemed to be received in India by or on behalf of the non-resident, or (b) accrues or arises, or is deemed to accrue or arise, to the non-resident in India. It is evident that income which accrues or arises outside India (i.e. foreign income) is beyond the scope of tax liability in India in the case of a non-resident. However, if he is a *resident but not ordinarily a resident*, his liability in respect of such income arises only if it is from a business controlled or a profession set up in India. There are elaborate rules for ascertaining the residential status of an assessee. These are given in Sections 5 and 6 of the Act. For details, see section 25.6 of chapter 25 of this book.

12.3.3 Incomes Exempt from Tax: Section 10 of the Act describes incomes that are completely or partially exempt from income tax, i.e. tax free incomes. These exclusions are meant to serve various socio-economic objectives through the medium of tax policy. [6]

12.3.4 Tax Holiday Schemes: These schemes are extensions of the provisions which exempt certain incomes from the purview of income tax.

A. Tax Holiday for Newly Established Industrial Undertakings in Free Trade Zones, Electronic Hardware Technology Parks, or Software Technology Parks or Special Economic Zones: This scheme provides for a complete tax exemption in respect of the profits and gains of an industrial undertaking set up in any free trade zone, electronic hardware technology park, or software technology park or special economic zone as specified by the Central

Government for the purpose of Section 10A. Complete tax exemption can be claimed for a period of 10 consecutive assessment years beginning from the first year of production. From the assessment year 2003-04, the amount of deduction is 90 percent of export profits for the first 10 consecutive assessment years.

This tax concession is available to all categories of taxpayers. The tax holiday is in lieu of all other tax concessions available in the Income Tax Act. Assessees availing this tax holiday scheme are not entitled to various benefits and deductions under various sections of the Act. However, the assessees have the option to choose either the complete tax holiday under section l0A or all other tax concessions available under the Act.

B. Tax Holiday for New Special Economic Zone (SEZ) Units: Under Section10AA, profits and gains derived by an entrepreneur from a unit in SEZ, manufacturing or producing any article or thing or providing any service (including computer software) are eligible for deduction for 15 consecutive assessment years, beginning from the first year of production.

C. Tax Holiday for Newly Established 100 Percent Export-Oriented Undertakings: Under provisions of Section l0B, any profits and gains made by an assessee from a 100 percent export-oriented undertaking are not included in the total income of the assessee. This benefit is available to the assessee in respect of 10 consecutive assessment years beginning with the initial assessment year in which the undertaking begins to manufacture or produce articles. From the assessment year 2003-04, the amount of deduction is 90 percent. Assessees availing this tax holiday scheme are not entitled to other tax concessions available in the Act.

D. Tax Holiday for Exporters of Wood-based Handicraft Items: Under provisions of Section 10BA, any profits and gains derived by an undertaking from the export of wood-based handicraft items, manufactured without the use of imported raw materials, are deductible as per rules.

12.3.5 Heads of Income: Income tax is a composite tax on the aggregate of incomes from various sources. However, taxable income is first computed under different heads of income and then aggregated. From the aggregated amount certain deductions are made to arrive at taxable income. Section l4 of the Act prescribes five broad heads under which the income of an assessee is classified for purposes of computation of total income and the charge of income tax. These are: salaries, income from house property, profits and gains of business or profession, capital gains, and income from other sources. These five heads of income are mutually exclusive. If any income falls under one head, it cannot be considered under any other head.

The method of computing income and the permissible deductions differ with each head of income. The heads of income are intended to indicate the classes of income to which different rules of computation are applied. The aggregate of income under these heads is termed as *gross total income* which, when reduced by the deductions available under Sections 80C to 80U (also called Chapter VI-A deductions) gives total income on which the charge is applied. A brief explanation of the different rules governing the computation of taxable income under each of the above-mentioned heads is as follows.

A. Salaries: Those payments which are connected with employment are taxable under the head *salaries*. The existence of employer-employee relationship is essential for taxing income under this head. Under Section 17(1), salary is defined to include, *inter alia*, the following: (i) wages, (ii) any annuity or pension, (iii) any fees, commissions, bonus, (iv) any advance of salary, and (v) any arrears of salary. It also includes perquisites, i.e. the value of any benefit or amenity provided by the employer like rent-free accommodation. However, Section 17 provides for exemption from tax in respect of perquisites in the form of medical facilities provided by the employer. Broadly speaking, whatever is received from the employer is salary.

The Act allows some relief in respect of salary paid in arrears or in advance in lump sum. The computation of relief is governed by Section 89(1) and Rule [21A(2)].

From the aggregate amount of salary, a standard deduction was allowed (Section 16) till recently to account for the expenditure incidental to the employment of an assessee. [7] However, it was withdrawn by the Finance Act, 2005.

B. Income from House Property: The scope of income charged under this head is defined by Section 22 and the computation of income under this head is explained by Sections 23 to 27. Income tax is payable by an assessee on the annual value of property consisting of buildings and land appurtenant thereto of which he is the owner. The annual value of such property, called house property, is deemed to be the sum for which the property might reasonably be expected to let from year to year. The annual value is ascertained by taking into consideration all relevant facts such as rent received, terms of the lease, the municipal valuation, and rent paid for similar property in the locality. The concept of taxation under this head does not extend to properties used for the purpose of any business or profession pursued by the owner of the property because house property is regarded as any other business asset. One house used by the owner for his own residence is exempt from tax. Prior to the assessment year 1987-88, income from owner-occupied houses used to be assessed notionally subject to a maximum of 10 percent of the total income. However, from that year onward, no income is imputed from owner-occupied houses due to valuation problems.

From the annual value of the house property, various deductions are allowed in computing the net annual value of a house property. Deduction is first made in respect of municipal taxes. Presently (financial year 2015-2016), a deduction of 30 percent of annual value of house property is allowed for repairs etc. Similarly, deduction is allowed in respect of the current interest liability on money borrowed for the acquisition, construction, repair or renewal of the property.

As a result of various deductions, taxpayers in many cases showed negative income from house property which was then set off against income from other sources such as salaries, business or professional income. The Finance Act, 1992, provided that the loss from house property will not be allowed to be set off against income under any other head of income from the assessment year 1993-94. Further, the carry forward of losses of any year from house property will be allowed to be set off only against income from house property of subsequent years.

C. Profits and Gains of Business or Profession: This head of income is beset with complicated rules of computation, often leading to controversies and litigation. According to Section 2(13), business includes any trade, commerce, or manufacture or any adventure in the nature of a trade, commerce, or manufacture. A profession, under Section 2(36), is an occupation requiring purely intellectual skill or manual skill such as that of a lawyer, accountant, engineer, surgeon, author etc. Section 28 defines various incomes which are chargeable to tax under the head profits and gains of business or profession. Sections 30 to 44D specify the method of computation of income under this head by describing the nature and amount of permissible and non-permissible deductions. Broadly speaking, all expenses that are wholly or exclusively laid out or expended for the purpose of business and that are not of capital nature are deductible.

(a) Deductions Expressly Allowed. There is a long list of deductions expressly allowed while computing taxable income under this head. The important ones are listed below with relevant Sections mentioned in parentheses.

1. Rent, taxes, repairs and insurance for building (30). In respect of premises owned by the assessee, no deduction is allowed. However, amount spent on current repairs is allowed. In respect of premises taken on rent, actual rent paid is admissible as deduction. Insurance premium against the risk of damage or destruction of the business premises is also allowable as business deduction.
2. Repairs and insurance of machinery, plant, and furniture (31).
3. Depreciation allowance (32). The Act provides for different rates of depreciation for different categories of assets. Depreciation is not allowed in

respect of any motor car manufactured outside India unless it is used in a business of running it on hire for tourists.

Where an asset is acquired during the previous year and is used for less than 180 days in that previous year, the depreciation allowable in respect of such asset is restricted to 50 percent of the amount normally allowable.

Unabsorbed depreciation can be carried forward and claimed by the assessee in the following years against income from 'profits and gains of business or profession'. Any amount remaining still unabsorbed can be carried forward till it is finally set off.

4. Expenditure on scientific research (35).
5. Expenditure on acquisition of patent rights and copyrights (35A).
6. Expenditure on know-how (35AB).
7. Expenditure on eligible projects or schemes for promoting social and economic welfare (35AC).
8. Payments to associations and institutions for carrying out rural development programmes (35CCA).
9. Payment to associations and institutions for carrying out programmes of conservation of natural resources (35CCB).
10. Amortisation of preliminary expenses (35D). Certain preliminary expenses incurred before or after the commencement of business in connection with the extension of an industrial undertaking or setting up a new industrial unit qualify for amortisation. The amount is allowed against the profits of the assessee in ten equal instalments over a period of ten years. The aggregate amount of the qualifying expenditure should not exceed 2.5 percent of the cost of project. Some of the heads of qualifying expenditure specified for the purpose are: expenditure in connection with preparation of a feasibility report, conducting a market survey, legal charges for drafting the memorandum and articles of association of the company, printing expenses of the memorandum and articles of associations, and expenses in connection with the public issue of shares.
11. Insurance premium [36(1)(i)]. The amount of any premium paid in respect of insurance against risk of damage or destruction of stocks or stores used for the purpose of business is admissible as deduction.
12. Bonus or commission to employees [36(1)(ii)]. Bonus or commission paid to an employee is allowable as deduction subject to certain conditions.
13. Interest on borrowed capital [36(1)(iii)].
14. Employer's contribution to recognised provident fund and approved superannuation fund [36(1)(iv)].
15. Contribution towards approved gratuity fund [36(1)(v)].

16. Bad debts [36(1)(vii)].
17. General deductions (37). In order to claim deduction under this section, the expenditure should not be of the nature described under Sections 30 to 36. A variety of expenses are allowed under the residuary Section 37 and it is not possible to draw an exhaustive list. A few instances of such expenses are: entertainment expenditure, expenses on advertisements, travelling expenses, litigation expenses in protecting trade or business, commission paid to selling agents, salary and perquisites to employees, expenses incurred on the occasion of *diwali* and *mahurat* subject to the satisfaction of the income tax officer, and expenses on registration of trade marks.

(b) Expenses Expressly Disallowed. The following expenses, *inter alia,* are expressly disallowed (with relevant sections mentioned in parentheses) while computing taxable income under this head.

1. Expenditure on advertisement in any souvenir, brochure etc. of a political party [37(2B)].
2. Any interest or salary payable outside India from which due tax has not been deducted at source; any tax calculated on the basis of profits or gains of business or profession [40(a)].
3. Payment to partner [40(b)].

D. Capital Gains: Under Section 45 of the Act, any profits or gains arising from the transfer of a capital asset are chargeable to tax under the head capital gains. Taxation of capital gains has been discussed separately in section 12.8 of this chapter.

E. Income from Other Sources: Income of every kind, which is not chargeable to tax under any of the other four heads and which is not to be excluded from the total income, is chargeable to tax under the residuary head *income from other sources*. Section 56 defines the scope of income chargeable under this head and Sections 57 and 58 lay down the basis of computation of such income. Some examples of incomes included under this head are: (i) dividends, (ii) winnings from lotteries, crossword puzzles, races including horse races, card games, gambling or betting, (iii) income from machinery, plant or furniture belonging to an assessee and let on hire, (iv) interest on bank deposits and loans, and (v) interest on securities issued by the Government; and interest on debentures and other securities issued by a local authority, a company, or a public sector corporation.

The following deductions are allowed under Section 57 in computing income chargeable to tax under this head: (i) In the case of dividends any reasonable sum paid by way of commissions etc. for the purpose of realising the dividend. (ii) In the case of income from machinery, plant or furniture let on hire, current repairs, depreciation, and unabsorbed depreciation etc. (iii) Any other expenditure (not being a capital expenditure) expended wholly and exclusively for the purpose of making or earning such income. In computing income from securities etc., a taxpayer may deduct: (a) any reasonable sum expended by him for the purpose of realising such interest, and (b) any interest payable on moneys borrowed for the purpose of investment in securities by the assessee.

12.3.6 Clubbing of Income: To counteract practices of tax avoidance, the Act contains provisions under which income of other persons is included in an assessee's income. Sections 60 to 64 of the Act deal with instances where an assessee may attempt to reduce his tax liability either by transferring his assets in favour of his family members or by arranging his sources of income in such a manner that tax incidence falls on others whereas the benefit of income, directly or indirectly, is derived by the assessee himself. To counter such attempts, the Act incorporates provisions under which certain incomes are included in the assessee's total income, though such incomes legally belong to other persons. In other words, incomes arising to the spouse, minor child, son's wife, son's minor child and other persons are clubbed with the assessee's income in certain circumstances. In this respect, the Act deviates from the general principle that a person can be assessed in respect of his own income.

12.3.7 Set Off and Carry Forward of Losses: As already noted, income chargeable under the Act is computed under five different heads. The aggregation of *gross total income* is relatively easy if income under each head and from each source is positive. However, loss may be sustained in one or more sources under one or more heads of income. Therefore, in the computation of *gross total income* of an assessee, appropriate adjustments should be made of the losses suffered by him. Sections 70 to 80 of the Act deal with provisions concerning set off of losses and their carry forward. The following three steps may be followed to understand the procedure of set off and carry forward of losses: (a) Inter-source adjustment under the same head of income; (b) Inter-head adjustment in the same assessment year. Provisions of (b) are applied only if a loss cannot be set off, fully or partly, under (a); and (c) Carry forward of loss. Provisions of (c) are applied only if a loss cannot be set-off, fully or partly under (a) and (b).

The purpose of these provisions is to mitigate the disincentive effects of fluctuating income. Under a system of progressive income tax based on yearly assessment, a taxpayer whose income fluctuates from year to year will surrender a larger proportion of his income in tax than a taxpayer with the same average income more evenly distributed over the years. To prevent this violation of the principle of horizontal equity, some form of income averaging method is necessary. Set off and carry forward provisions are proxy for income averaging principle.

12.3.8 Deductions from Gross Total Income: Gross total income of an assessee is obtained by adding up incomes under different heads. While computing incomes under various heads, certain deductions are allowed, which are in the nature of expenses incurred in earning the specific incomes under different heads. These have already been discussed while dealing with various heads of income.

The Act provides certain special deductions under Sections 80C to 80U (Chapter VI-A) and these are intended to promote various national policy objectives like industrialisation of backward areas, encouragement to small-scale industries, export promotion, and helping an assessee in meeting certain essential expenditures. These deductions are made from the gross total income of an assessee and not from any particular head of income.

The aggregate amount of deductions allowable cannot exceed the gross total income. No such deduction is allowed against long-term capital gains. Thus, where the gross total income includes long-term capital gains, the gross total income is reduced by such long-term capital gains for the purpose of deductions. These deductions are allowed under various clauses of Section 80 of the Act (i.e. Sections 80C to 80U), and are arranged alphabetically. The following select list shows the deductions which are available to an individual assessee.

A. Deductions for Individuals in Respect of Certain Payments: Deductions under this category relate to certain kinds of payments made by an assessee. These payments are not made in connection with earning of any income chargeable to tax. Some of these are of the following types with relevant sections mentioned in parentheses.

1. Deduction is allowed in respect of life insurance premia, deferred annuity, contributions to provident funds, subscriptions to certain equity shares or debentures (80-C).
2. Deduction in respect of contribution to pension fund of Life Insurance Corporation (LIC) of India or of any other insurance company (80-CCC).
3. Deduction in respect of contribution to new pension scheme (80-CCD).
4. Deduction in respect of investment in equity savings scheme (80-CCG).
5. Deduction in respect of medical insurance premia (80-D).
6. Deduction in respect of medical treatment and deposit made for maintenance of handicapped dependents (80-DD).
7. Deduction in respect of interest on loan taken for higher education (80-E).
8. Deduction in respect of interest on loan taken for residential house property (80EE).
9. Deduction in respect of rent paid (80-GG).
10. Deduction in respect of royalty of authors (80-QQB).

11. Deduction in respect of interest on saving account deposits (80-TTA).
12. Deduction for blind/physically handicapped/mentally retarded persons (80U).

B. Deductions in Respect of Certain Incomes from Specified Businesses: Deductions are allowed, *inter alia*, in respect of the following kinds of income of an assessee, with relevant sections mentioned in parentheses.

1. Deduction in respect of profits and gains from industrial undertakings or enterprises engaged in infrastructure development etc. (80-IA). There are elaborate rules for claiming deduction under this section.
2. Deduction in respect of developer of special economic zone (80-IAB).
3. Deduction in respect of profits and gains from certain industrial undertakings other than infrastructure development undertakings (80-IB0). There are elaborate rules for claiming deduction under this section.
4. Deductions in respect of profits and gains from certain undertakings or enterprises in the States of Himachal Pradesh, Uttrakhand, Sikkim and North-Eastern States (80-IC). There are elaborate rules for claiming deduction under this section.
5. Deductions in respect of new hotels and convention centres in National Capital Region or World Heritage sites (80-ID).
6. Deduction in respect of specified undertakings in North-Eastern States (80-IE).
7. Deduction in respect of profits and gains from the business of collecting and processing of bio-degradable waste (80-JJA).
8. Deductions in respect of donations to political parties (80-GGB and 80-GGC).
9. Deductions for co-operative societies (80-P).
10. Deductions for donations (80-G).

12.3.9 Rebates: Till recently, the Act provided for a rebate (or tax credit) on tax liability for investment in specified schemes (Section 88), for senior citizens (Section 88-B), for women assessees (Section 88-C) and for small assessees. However, all these rebates were withdrawn by the Finance Act, 2005. [8] However, tax rebate for small taxpayers was introduced from financial year 2013-14. Thus, a resident individual having total income up to ₹ 5 lakh is entitled to a tax rebate from his income tax liability. The amount of rebate is equal to the amount of income tax payable or ₹ 2,000, whichever is less.

12.3.10 Computation of Total Income: According to Section 2(45), the total income of an assessee means the income for which he is chargeable to tax on the basis of his residence. It is computed in the following manner:

1. Ascertain the residential status of the assessee and find out which income is chargeable in his hands. For a resident assessee, the whole of his world

income is chargeable to tax while for a non-resident assessee, his Indian incomes only are taxable.

2. Compute such incomes under different heads of income after allowing deductions relevant to each head of income and total them up (an individual may earn income from all the heads but a company can earn income from all the heads except salaries).
3. Add others' incomes with the assessee's income wherever applicable (Sections 60 to 64).
4. Allow set off and carry forward of losses. The resultant figure is known as *gross total income* of the assessee.
5. From the *gross total income* make the deductions allowed under Sections 80-C to 80-U (Chapter VI-A) on account of certain payments and in respect of certain incomes. The balance is called *total income,* i.e. the base for charging income tax.
6. Compute tax liability on total income.
7. From the tax liability so determined, deduct tax already paid to arrive at net tax liability. The procedure for computation of income and determination of tax liability is summarised in Table 12.2.

12.3.11 Units of Assessment: There are seven categories of persons (i.e. units of assessment or taxable entities) chargeable to tax under the Act. According to Section 2(31) the word *person* includes: (i) an individual, (ii) a Hindu undivided family, (iii) a company, (iv) a firm, (v) an association of persons or a body of individuals whether incorporated or not, (vi) a local authority, and (vii) every artificial juridical person, not falling within any of the preceding categories. [9]

However, individuals and companies are the two main taxpaying entities. Depending upon the residential status, companies are classified into *domestic* and *foreign* companies.

12.3.12 Basic Exemption: A company is liable to income tax however small its income may be while a basic exemption is allowed to individual taxpayers. Basic exemption is allowed to permit a minimum standard of living or some level of income which does not reflect the taxpaying capacity of a person.

Presently (financial year 2015-16), the basic exemption limit is ₹ 2,50,000 in the case of individual taxpayers who are below the age of 60 years. For senior citizens (60 years and above) it is ₹ 3,00,000 and for very senior citizens (80 years and above) it is ₹ 5,00,000. Tax credit of ₹ 2,000 is available to every person who has a total income up to ₹ 5,00,000.

Table 12.3 records trends in the basic exemption limit for individual income taxpayers during the post-Independence period.

Table 12.2: Computation of Income and Determination of Tax Liability

1. Income from salary
2. Income from house property
3. Profits and gains of business/profession
4. Income from capital gains
(a) Short-term capital gains
(b) Long-term capital gains
5. Income from other sources
Aggregate of Incomes
[Total of 1+2+3+4+5]
Add: Others' incomes with the assessee's income wherever applicable.
Less: Adjustments for set off and carry forward of losses
Gross Total Income
Less: Deductions under chapter VI-A [Sections 80-C to 80-U]
Total Income (or taxable income)
Tax on long-term capital gains
Add: Tax on taxable income less long-term capital gains.
Total Tax
Less: Rebates/reliefs, if any
Net Tax
Add: Surcharge, if any
Total Tax Payable
Less: Tax deducted at source
Less: Advanced tax paid
Balance: Tax payable/refundable

The exemption limit has generally been raised from time to time to make adjustments for inflation. Only once it was actually reduced from ₹ 4,200 to ₹ 3,000 in 1957-58. Proposing the reduction the Finance Minister remarked, "The minimum limit had been raised over the past few years mainly for administrative reasons. An income of ₹ 4,200, modest though it is in absolute terms, is quite a large multiple of the average level of incomes in the country. It is reasonable to expect that those with an income over ₹ 3,000 should also make their contribution, however small, to the public exchequer, and should come within the range of direct taxation". [10]

12.3.13 Rate Structure of Income Tax: Prior to 1916, income tax was levied at a flat rate of 5 *pies* in a rupee on all incomes above ₹ 2,000. With a rupee containing 192 *pies*, the rate of tax worked out to 2.6 percent approximately. It was in 1916 that the income tax came to be levied at graduated scale and this principle has been followed since then. In 1945-46, the maximum rate of income tax was 57 pies in a rupee (29.7 percent). In 1946-47, there was a steep rise in the maximum rate of income tax to 15.5 *annas* in a rupee (96.9 percent). The Taxation Enquiry Commission, 1953-54, recommended 92 percent rate of tax (including surcharge) on the highest slab of income.

Table 12.3: Basic Exemption Limit for Individual Income Taxpayers: 1947-48 to 2015-16

Financial Year	Basic Exemption Limit (₹)	Financial Year	Basic Exemption Limit (₹)
1947-48	2,500	1990-91 and 1991-92	22,000
1948-49 to 1950-51	3,000	1992-93	28,000
1951-52 and 1952-53	3,600	1993-94	30,000
1953-54 to 1956-57	4,200	1994-95	35,000
1957-58 to 1965-66	3,000	1995-96 to 1997-98	40,000
1966-67 to 1969-70	3,500	1998-99 to 2004-05	50,000
1970-71 to 1973-74	5,000	2005-06 and 2006-07	1,00,000
1974-75 and 1975-76	6,000	2007-08	1,10,000
1976-77	8,000	2008-09	1,50,000
1977-78 to 1979-80	10,000	2009-10 and 2010-11	1,60,000
1980-81	12,000	2011-12	1,80,000
1981-82 to 1984-85	15,000	2012-13 to 2013-14	2,00,000
1985-86 to 1989-90	18,000	2014-15 to 2015-16	2,50,000

Source: Government of India, *Budget Papers* (various years).

Rates of income tax in India were quite high, almost punitive, till mid-1970s. For example, in 1973-74, the maximum marginal rate of individual income tax was as high as 97.7 percent which proved counter-productive from revenue angle.

The Report of the Direct Taxes Enquiry Committee (DTEC) [Chairman: Justice K.N. Wanchoo], 1971, was a milestone in the area of income tax rates. The Committee made a number of far-reaching suggestions for unearthing black money, preventing evasion and avoidance of taxes, and reducing arrears. One important recommendation of the Committee related to reduction in the rates of direct taxes which in its view were mainly responsible for tax evasion because they made tax evasion profitable and attractive. The rates of individual income tax were quite high till the year 1973-74. However, following the recommendations of the DTEC, the Government initiated a series of rate reductions in individual income tax.

The rate of tax was reduced from 97.7 percent in 1973-74 to 77 percent in 1974-75, and further down to 66 percent in 1976-77. It is noteworthy that DTEC had recommended a maximum marginal rate of 75 percent. [11]

The downward trend in the rate of income tax was temporarily reversed during the brief Janata Government rule at the Centre. The top marginal rate of income tax was increased from 66 percent in 1976-77 to 69 percent in 1977-78, and further up to 72 percent in 1979-80.

However, the policy of low direct tax rates started by the Congress Government in 1974 and carried forward in 1976 was further reinforced after it came back to power at the Centre in 1980. After a series of revisions, the maximum marginal rate of individual income tax was 54 percent (including employment surcharge of 8 percent), applicable from the financial year 1990-91.

Consequent upon the recommendations contained in the Interim Report of the Tax Reforms Committee (Chairman: Raja Chelliah), 1991, the number of income tax rates was reduced and the rates themselves were scaled down. The maximum marginal rate was fixed at 44.8 percent (including surcharge) from the financial year 1992-93. The Finance Act, 1994, abolished the surcharge of 12 percent and hence the maximum marginal rate of tax was 40 percent from the financial year 1994-95. From the same year it was made applicable on incomes over ₹ 1,20,000. It may be recalled that the top marginal rate of income tax applied to incomes above ₹ 1 lakh from 1967-68 to 1993-94. The ₹ 1 lakh of 1967-68 was approximately equivalent to ₹ 5.5 lakh of 1993-94. This showed the laxity of the administration in adjusting tax brackets for inflation. It is noteworthy that the Tax Reforms Committee had recommended 40 percent maximum rate inclusive of surcharge for income exceeding ₹ 2 lakh.

Table 12.4 summarises the decline in the maximum marginal rate of income tax beginning with the year 1974-75.

The maximum marginal rate of personal income tax was further reduced from 40 percent to 30 percent in the 1997-98 budget. In another significant move, it was made applicable to incomes above ₹ 1,50,000. After further revisions, the maximum rate (inclusive of surcharge) stood at 30.75 percent for the financial year 2007-2008.

The philosophy of low tax rates presupposes improved tax compliance to control the growth of black money, and broadening of the tax base. It is argued that high tax rates increase premium on tax evasion which, in turn, generates black money. Low tax rates are welcome provided they improve compliance and revenue yield. However, to expect that lowering of rates would improve compliance automatically is unrealistic because tax evasion occurs at all levels of income.

Broadly speaking, the present system of income tax is *global* in nature in that it does not discriminate between different sources of income. Income from various sources is pooled together for determining tax liability. Elements of schedular system (under which different sources of income are taxed differently) exist insofar as agricultural income is excluded from the tax base, and long-term capital gains, though included in the definition of income, are given special concessions.

Table 12.4: Trends in the Maximum Marginal Rate of Individual Income Tax: 1973-74 to 2015-2016

(percent)

Financial Year	Top Marginal Rate	Surcharge, if any	Rate Including Surcharge
1973-74	85	15	97.7
1974-75 and 1975-76	70	10	77.0
1976-77	60	10	66.0
1977-78 and 1978-79	60	15	69.0
1979-80	60	20	72.0
1980-81 to 1982-83	60	10	66.0
1983-84	60	12.5	67.5
1984-85	55	12.5	61.9
1985-86 and 1986-87	50	Nil	50.0
1987-88 and 1988-89	50	5	52.5
1989-90	50	8	54.0
1990-91 and 1991-92	50	12	56.0
1992-93 and 1993-94	40	12	44.8
1994-95 to 1996-97	40	Nil	40.0
1997-98 and 1998-99	30	Nil	30.0
1999-00	30	10	33.0
2000-01	30	15	34.5
2001-02	30	2	30.6
2002-03	30	5	31.5
2003-04 and 2004-05	30	10	33.0
2005-06 to 2007-08	30	2.5	30.75
2008-09 to 2015-16	30	3	30.9

Note: The maximum marginal rate of individual income tax was applicable on income above ₹ 1,00,000 up to the financial year 1993-94. From 1994-95, it was made applicable on income above ₹ 1,20,000;.from 1997-98 on income above ₹ 1,50,000; from 2005-06 on income above ₹ 2,50,000; from 2008-09 on income above ₹ 5,00,000; from 2010-11 on income above ₹ 8,00,000; and from 2012-13 on income above ₹ 10,00,000.
Source: Government of India, *Budget Papers* (various years).

As already noted, income tax revenue originates mainly from two taxpaying entities, viz. companies, and individuals. Although the concept of taxable income and the procedure for its computation is the same, except for minor differences, for all taxable entities, the income tax rates vary among different entities. From the standpoint of differential tax treatment, the tax on companies (also referred to as corporation tax) and firms is essentially a proportional tax while the tax on non-corporate entities (also referred to as personal income tax) is basically a progressive income tax. The different constituents of the non-corporate entities, viz. individuals, Hindu undivided families etc., are subject to varying rates of income tax. Likewise, the rate of tax on corporate entities differs depending on whether a company is *domestic* or *foreign*. In general, a domestic company is taxed at a lower rate than a foreign company.

Prior to the enactment of the Finance Act, 1994, a distinction existed among domestic companies, viz. widely-held companies, and closely-held companies. Widely-held companies were subject to lower tax rates as compared to closely-held companies. Again, prior to the enactment of Finance Act, 1991, domestic companies were categorised into industrial and trading companies. The industrial companies were taxed at a lower rate than the non-industrial companies.

A. Surcharge: A notable feature of the rate structure is the imposition of surcharge on income tax wholly for the purpose of the Centre. Article 271 was retained in its existing form (after Eightieth Amendment of the Constitution) which means that Parliament can now levy surcharge on all Union taxes and not merely on income tax and the taxes specified in Article 269 as was the position before the Eightieth Amendment to the Constitution. Surcharge is generally levied for the purpose of meeting the expenditure for providing relief to the affected population at the occurrence of a calamity of rare severity.

Rates of income tax are fixed by the annual Finance Act and not by the Income Tax Act. (In the case of other direct taxes, e.g. wealth tax, the rates are specified in a schedule to the Act imposing the tax). Rates of income tax applicable to various entities for the financial year 2015-16 are given in Table 12.5.

12.3.14 Advance Payment of Tax: Though the regular assessment in respect of any income is made in a later assessment year, the tax on such income is payable by way of advance payment. Section 208 of the Act makes it obligatory to pay advance tax in every case where the advance tax payable is ₹ 10,000 or more. Furthermore, every income (including capital gains, winnings from lotteries, crossword puzzles etc.) is liable for payment of advance tax. Thus, all assessees are required to pay tax in advance on incomes which they expect to earn during the current financial year. For instance, for the financial year 2015-16 advance tax is payable in instalments during the financial year 2015-16 itself. The advance tax so paid is adjusted when assessment takes place in 2016-17.

Table 12.5: Rates of Income Tax for Various Entities: Financial Year 2015-16

Individuals (other than resident senior and very senior citizens), Hindu undivided families, association of persons etc.		
Slab of Income (₹)		Rate of Income Tax
From	To	
0	2,50,000	Nil
2,50,000	5,00,000	10 percent of the amount exceeding ₹ 2,50,000
5,00,000	10,00,000	₹ 25,000 plus 20 percent of the amount exceeding ₹ 5,00,000
10,00,000 and above		₹ 1,25,000 plus 30 percent of the amount exceeding ₹ 10,00,000
Companies and Partnership Firms		
Domestic companies and partnership firms		30 percent*
Foreign companies		40 percent

*In the 2015-16 budget, the Finance Minister proposed to reduce the rate of corporate tax from 30 percent to 25 percent over the next 4 years.

12.3.15 Tax Deduction at Source: There are provisions under various sections of the Act regarding tax deduction at source (TDS), e.g. deduction of tax from salaries (Section 192). Other incomes covered under the scheme of TDS include fees for professional/technical services, interest, dividends, rent from real estate, commission from insurance, sale of lottery tickets, winnings from lotteries, crossword puzzles and horse racing etc.

Persons responsible for making payments of such specified incomes are liable to deduct tax at source on such payments and deposit the same with the Government within the stipulated time. Select payments subject to tax deduction at source along with rates are given in Table 12.6.

12.4 Taxation of Companies

Companies have been treated as separate taxable units from the very beginning. In the 1886 Act, profits of a company were taxed at a flat rate. In 1916, companies with an income of less than ₹ 1,000 were exempted from paying income tax. The Act of 1918 inserted a new provision under which dividends received by a shareholder were included in his total income for the purpose of determining the rate of tax on his other income. The dividends as such continued to be exempt in the hands of the shareholders. Under the differentiation principle introduced in 1948, companies with a total income not exceeding ₹ 25,000 were required to pay income tax of only 2.5 *annas* in a rupee (15.5 percent) as against 5 *annas* in a rupee (31.2 percent) on other companies.

Table 12.6: Select Payments Subject to Tax Deduction at Source (TDS) under the Income Tax Act, 1961

Nature of Income	Relevant Section of the Act	Rate of TDS (percent)
Salaries	192	Average rate of income tax
Interest on time deposits with a banking company where the interest (payable by each branch) exceeds ₹ 10,000 per annum.	194A	10
Winnings from lotteries and crossword puzzles exceeding ₹ 10,000	194B	30
Winnings from horse races exceeding ₹ 5,000	194BB	30
Payments to contractors exceeding ₹ 20,000 for carrying out any work	194C	1 and 2*
Commission to insurance agents exceeding ₹ 20,000	194D	10
Commission, remuneration or reward on sale of lottery tickets exceeding ₹ 1,000	194G	10

*1 percent in the case of payment to individuals and 2 percent in the case of payment to companies.

Prior to the year 1960-61, a company was deemed to have paid income tax on behalf of its shareholders on dividends declared out of income on which the company had paid income tax. Each shareholder was entitled for a tax credit against his income tax liability to the tune of the tax deemed to have been paid on his behalf by the company. The tax credit entitlement of a shareholder was determined on the basis of gross dividend income, instead of net dividend income, and the rate at which the tax deemed to have been paid by the company was the rate applicable to companies in that given year in which the dividend was declared or paid. If, for example, a shareholder received net dividend of ₹ 900 paid entirely out of the profits of a company, and the income tax rate (including surcharge) applicable to the company in that year was 40 percent, the gross dividend was calculated by the formula $G = N/(1-R)$, where G = gross dividend, N = net dividend, and R = income tax rate. For the above example $G = 900/(1-0.4)$, or $G = 1500$. The difference between G and N, i.e. ₹ 600 was taken to be the tax payment made by the company on behalf of the shareholders.

However, the super tax paid by companies was assumed as paid by a company on its own behalf. Thus, there was an important distinction between income tax and super tax paid by companies, the former on behalf of shareholders and the latter on its own behalf. The super tax was often called the real corporation tax. The distinction was rendered irrelevant when beginning with the year 1960-61, a company was deemed to have paid income tax on its own behalf.

The scheme of tax credit to shareholders was discontinued with effect from the financial year 1960-61, making dividends received by shareholders subject to personal income tax.

Prior to the enactment of Finance Act, 1994, a distinction existed among domestic companies, viz. widely-held companies, and closely-held companies. Widely-held companies were subject to lower tax rates as compared to closely-held companies. Again, prior to the enactment of Finance Act, 1991, domestic companies were categorised into industrial and trading companies. The industrial companies were taxed at a lower rate than the non-industrial companies.

The 1994-95 budget abolished the distinction between widely-held domestic companies and closely-held domestic companies and introduced a single tax rate of 40 percent for all types of domestic companies.

12.4.1 Main Features of Company Taxation: These are the following.

As already noted, income tax revenue originates mainly from two taxpaying entities, viz. companies, and individuals. Although the concept of taxable income and the procedure for its computation is the same, except for minor differences, for all taxable entities, the income tax rates vary among different entities. From the standpoint of differential tax treatment, the tax on companies (also referred to as corporation tax) and firms is essentially a proportional tax while the tax on non-corporate entities (also referred to as personal income tax) is basically a progressive income tax. The rate of tax on corporate entities differs depending on whether a company is *domestic* or *foreign*. A domestic company is taxed at a lower rate than a foreign company.

1. Under the Indian income tax law, a company is regarded as a separate entity for the purpose of income tax. Till recently, dividends were taxed twice, first in the hands of the company, and second in the hands of the shareholders. This was an example of double taxation of a source of income, viz. dividends. Business community had often demanded that dividends should be totally exempted from tax and treated as an allowable expenditure in the hands of a company. Hence, from the financial year 1997-98, tax on dividends in the hands of the shareholder was abolished. Instead, a tax on distributed profits at

the rate of 10 percent on the amount so distributed was levied. In the 2002-03 budget, dividends on shares were again made taxable in the hands of the recipients (i.e. share holders).

2. Corporate assesses pay tax on their total income which in the case of resident companies is the total world income and in the case of non-resident companies total Indian income.
3. The total income of a company is arrived at with reference to its profits shown in its profit and loss account. To such profits (or losses) are added those expenses which, though actually incurred by the company, are disallowed, partially or wholly, under the Act. From this total, the amount of tax concessions is deducted to arrive at the base for company taxation.
4. Prior to the assessment year 1984-85, the rate structure of company tax was progressive. However, from that year a flat rate is charged depending upon the domicile and nature of a company. This single rate formula provides strong inducement to companies to close their books showing a marginal loss. Such malpractices can be discouraged by introducing a two-tier rate structure, e.g. 25 percent rate of tax for the initial slab of income and 40 percent for the remaining income.
5. Under the income tax law, a parent (or a holding) company and its subsidiary company are separate legal entities and are, therefore, taxed separately. Thus, if a holding company receives dividends from its subsidiary, the former has to pay tax on such dividends. Taxation of inter-corporate earnings is designed to prevent concentration of economic power in the hands of corporate giants. However, this provision is said to give rise to treble taxation of such dividends: first in the hands of the earning company, then in the hands of the receiving company, and finally in the hands of individual shareholders. The law provides certain concessions to facilitate inter-corporate investment. Thus, under section 80M of the Act any domestic company is allowed deduction of the amount of dividend received from another domestic company, subject to the maximum of the amount of dividend distributed by the recipient company.
6. Income tax laws throughout the world generally provide for a number of tax concessions. A profit-making clever company may arrange its affairs in such a manner that the cumulative effect of all tax concessions is to reduce its income declared in the tax return to zero. Minimum Alternate Tax (MAT) is a device to keep a zero tax company within the tax net. In the 1996-97 budget, an effort was made to tackle the phenomenon of zero tax companies (having substantial book profits) by bringing them under MAT.

12.4.2 Compulsory Filing of Returns by Companies: According to sub-section (1) of Section 139 of the Income Tax Act, every person, if his total income during the previous year exceeded the maximum amount which is not chargeable to income tax, is required to file a return of such income. It was observed that a number of companies which incurred losses were not filing returns on the plea that they had not earned any income. Therefore, the Finance Act, 2001 amended Section 139(1) to provide that every company is required to file a return of income, even if it incurs a loss. The amendment became effective retrospectively from April 1, 2001.

12.5 Taxation of Partnership Firms

Prior to the assessment year 1993-94, taxation of partnership firms was rather cumbersome. For example, the method of taxation differed according to whether the firm was registered or not under the Income Tax Act. Following the recommendations contained in the Interim Report of the Tax Reforms Committee (Chairman: Raja Chelliah), 1991, the taxation of partnership firms was drastically modified through the Finance Act, 1992. The chief feature of these changes was to avoid double taxation of profits of firms. Thus, from the assessment year 1993-94 the scheme of taxation of firms and their partners is as follows.

1. A partnership firm is taxed as a separate entity. Like a company, it is liable to income tax however small its income may be. There is no distinction between registered and unregistered firms. Similarly, there is no distinction between firms carrying professions or business. The procedure for registration of firms has been abolished. A new procedure for the assessment of a firm as a firm has been prescribed in Section 184. In order to be assessed as a firm, the partnership should be evidenced by an instrument of partnership, specifying the individual shares of the partners and a copy of the same certified in writing by all the partners should be filed along with the first return of the firm.
2. The share of the partner in the income of the firm is not included in computing his total income, i.e. it is fully exempt from income tax [Section 10(2A)].
3. Any payment of salary, bonus, commission, remuneration etc. to any partner under the terms of the partnership deed is allowed as a deduction in the computation of the total income of the firm subject to certain restrictions. Thus, salary can be paid only to a working partner.
4. Interest paid by a firm to any partner is deductible from its income. However, 12 percent per annum is the maximum rate at which interest can be allowed to a partner. Interest paid must be in accordance with the terms of the

partnership deed [Section 40(b) (ii) and (iii)].

12.6 Tax Treatment of Small Traders (Presumptive Tax) See section 10.11.5 of chapter 10 of this book.

12.7 Taxation of Non-residents in India: See section 25.6 of chapter 25 of this book.

12.8 Taxation of Capital Gains

A tax on capital gains was in operation in India for a short period in respect of capital gains which arose during the period April 1, 1946 to March 31, 1948. Following the recommendations of British economist Nicholas Kaldor, the tax was revived in 1956 and made applicable on capital gains arising on or after April 1, 1956. It is levied within the framework of Indian Income Tax Act, 1961. Section 14 of the Act prescribes five broad heads under which the income of an assessee is classified for purposes of computation of total income and the charge of income tax. These are: salaries, income from house property, profits and gains of business or profession, capital gains, and income from other sources. Sections 45 to 55A of the Act relate to the taxation of capital gains. Since capital gains are not annual accruals from a given source but represent appreciation in the market value of assets over a period of time, they are treated on a different footing. The preferential treatment is given to long-term capital gains only.

12.8.1 Meaning and Scope of Capital Gains Tax: According to Section 45 of the Act any profits or gains arising from the transfer of a capital asset are chargeable to tax under the head 'capital gains'. The term 'capital asset' means property of any kind, movable or immovable, held by an assessee but it does not include the following: stock-in-trade, consumable stores or raw materials held for the purpose of his business or profession, personal effects, i.e. movable property (clothes, motor car, furniture etc., but excluding jewellery) held for personal use, and agricultural land in India [Section 2(14)]. The gains on transfer of assets in relation to which there is no cost of acquisition like self-generated goodwill of a business are also liable to capital gains tax.

12.8.2 Transactions Regarded as *Transfer*: The act of transfer has special and extended meaning under the law [Section 2(47)]. Besides the sale of the asset or its exchange for another asset, it includes: relinquishment of the asset, extinguishment of any rights in the asset, compulsory acquisition of the asset under any law, conversion of the asset into stock-in-trade, handing over the possession of an immovable property in part performance of a contract for the transfer of that property, and transactions which have the effect of transferring, or enabling the enjoyment of any immovable property.

However, certain transactions, though falling within the foregoing meaning of transfer, are not regarded as transfers. These are: transfers under a gift, will, or an irrevocable trust, transfer of shares of the amalgamating company in consideration of allotment of shares in an Indian amalgamated company, and transfer of works of art, books, manuscripts etc., to the government, a university or any other notified museum or institution.

Prior to the assessment year 1988-89, distribution of assets on the dissolution of a firm, body of individuals or other association of persons was also not regarded as a transaction resulting in taxable capital gains. However, for and from the assessment year 1988-89 the position has changed and such transactions are now regarded as transfers resulting in taxable capital gains.

12.8.3 Year of Taxability: As regards the year of taxability, the basic rule is that capital gains are deemed to be income of the previous year in which the transfer giving rise to the gains takes place. Thus, the year of charge is the year in which the sale, exchange, relinquishment etc., takes place. In case of conversion of a capital asset into stock-in-trade, the gains are deemed to arise in the year in which such stock-in-trade is sold or otherwise transferred.

12.8.4 Short-term versus Long-term Capital Gains: The incidence of tax on capital gains depends upon whether such gains arise from the transfer of a short-term or a long-term capital asset. Under Section 2(42A), a short-term capital asset is one which is held by the assessee for less than 36 months from the date of its acquisition. (However, in order to improve the mobility of capital, equity shares, units of the Unit Trust of India and other mutual funds are treated as short-term capital assets if they are held for less than 12 months). If the asset is held for more than 36 months, it is regarded as a long-term capital asset.

Capital gains arising from the transfer of a short-term capital asset are taxable like an ordinary income in the case of all assessees. However, capital gains relating to long-term capital assets are taken as a separate block and get lenient tax treatment (flat rate of 20 percent).

12.8.5 Computation of Short-term Capital Gains: Under Section 48, the procedure to compute capital gains involves the following steps: Firstly, the full value of consideration received or accruing as a result of the transfer is ascertained. If the transaction is in cash the full value of consideration is the cash payment received. In case the consideration for transfer is in the form of another asset, the fair market value of the asset received as consideration is ascertained. Also, the value of any debt settled by way of consideration is included in the full value of consideration. It is likely that the consideration is not paid in cash but by way of promise to pay after a period. In such cases the full value of consideration will be the present value of the amount to be paid at maturity discounted at the market rate.

Secondly, the following deductions are made from the full value of consideration: (a) cost of acquisition of the asset including cost of any improvements made to the asset, and (b) expenditure incurred in connection with the transfer of such asset such as brokerage paid for arranging the deal, legal expenses incurred for preparing transfer documents, cost of inserting advertisement in newspapers for sale of the asset, and commission paid to auctioneer. However, it is necessary that the expenditure should be incurred wholly and exclusively in connection with the transfer. The balance is the amount of short-term capital gain to be included in the gross total income of the assessee.

12.8.6 Computation of Long-term Capital Gains: Following the recommendations contained in the Interim Report of the Tax Reforms Committee (Chairman: Raja Chelliah), 1991, the scheme of capital gains tax was drastically recast in the following manner by the Finance Act, 1992: (a) The cut-off date for valuation of assets acquired in earlier years was shifted from April 1, 1974 to April 1, 1981, (b) a system of indexation was introduced for the first time under which long-term capital gains are now computed by allowing the cost of acquisition and the cost of improvement of the asset to be adjusted for general inflation, and (c) a new section 112 was inserted in the Income Tax Act to provide that long-term capital gains would be subject to a flat rate of income tax. The rate of tax is 20 percent. Presently, concessionary treatment to long-term capital gains is given through inflation indexing, relatively low flat rate of tax, and a set of exemptions.

In fact, the assessee has two options as regards the computation of long-term capital gains: (a) calculate the difference between the cost of acquisition and the sale price and pay the tax on the same at a flat rate of 10 percent, or (b) adjust the cost of the asset sold for inflation and pay tax at the rate of 20 percent.

A. Inflation Indexing: This new procedure to compute long-term capital gains effective from the assessment year 1993-94 is as follows. The full value of consideration received as a result of the transfer is ascertained. From the full value of consideration, the Indexed Cost of Acquisition (I.C.A.) and the Indexed Cost of Improvement (I.C.I.) are deducted. Also, from the full value of consideration the expenditure incurred in connection with such transfer is deducted. Indexed cost of acquisition is actual cost of acquisition multiplied by Cost Inflation Index (C.I.I.) for the year of transfer and divided by C.I.I. for the year of purchase. Thus,

$$\text{I.C.A.} = \frac{\text{Cost of acquisition} \times \text{C.I.I. for the year of transfer}}{\text{C.I.I. for the year of acquisition}}$$

and,

$$\text{I.C.I.} = \frac{\text{Cost of improvement} \times \text{C.I.I. for the year of transfer}}{\text{C.I.I. for the year of improvement}}$$

With 1981-82 as the base year (i.e. 1981-82 = 100) the Central Government notifies each year the C.I.I. having regard to 75 percent of average rise in consumer price index for urban non-manual employees. C.I.I. notified by the Government from time to time is given in Table 12.7. The cost of acquisition is adjusted with reference to the rate applicable for the relevant year. There is similar indexation of cost of improvement.

The index factors are applied uniformly to all assets without making any distinction between shares, buildings, and machinery. The new procedure is related to the period of time for which the asset is held and takes into account the inflation that may have crept in over time.

Table 12.7: Cost Inflation Index Notified by the Income Tax Authorities from Time to Time

Financial Year	C.I.I.	Financial Year	C.I.I.
1981-82	100	1998-99	351
1982-83	109	1999-00	389
1983-84	116	2000-01	406
1984-85	125	2001-02	426
1985-86	133	2002-03	447
1986-87	140	2003-04	463
1987-88	150	2004-05	480
1988-89	161	2005-06	497
1989-90	172	2006-07	519
1990-91	182	2007-08	551
1991-92	199	2008-09	582
1992-93	223	2009-10	632
1993-94	244	2010-11	711
1994-95	259	2011-12	785
1995-96	281	2012-13	852
1996-97	305	2013-14	939
1997-98	331	2014-15	1024

The cost of acquisition of an asset is the amount for which it was originally acquired by the assessee. However, where the capital asset became the property of the assessee before April 1, 1981, he has the option to substitute for the actual cost the fair market value of asset as on April 1, 1981. Furthermore, where the capital asset became the property of the assessee by succession, inheritance, or under a gift or a will etc., the cost of acquisition of the asset in the hands of the assessee is the cost for which the previous owner of the asset had acquired it. In case the asset was acquired by the previous owner prior to April 1, 1981, the assessee enjoys the option to substitute the fair market value of the asset as on April 1, 1981 for the cost of the asset to the previous owner. Any expenditure of a capital nature incurred by an assessee to increase the value of the asset is to be added to the cost of acquisition by way of cost of improvement.

Deductions under chapter VI-A (Sections 80C to 80U) are not available in respect of long-term capital gains. Prior to the assessment year 1993-94, income arising under the head *capital gains* was included in the gross total income of the assessee and after allowing deductions under chapter VI-A, the total income was subject to tax and surcharge at the rates in force. Rebate under Section 88 was available from the tax computed on the total income in respect of deposits/payments made in approved schemes and instruments. As already noted, the Finance Act, 1992 inserted a new Section 112 in the Income Tax Act to provide that long-term capital gains will be subject to a flat rate of income tax. The rate of tax is 20 percent. Hence, deductions under chapter VI-A and rebate under Section 88 were withdrawn in respect of long-term capital gains.

B. Certain Long-term Capital Gains Exempt from Tax: Exemptions available to an assessee with regard to certain long-term capital gains are as under:

(a) Capital Gains from Transfer of a Residential House: Capital gains arising from the transfer of a residential house enjoy exemption if the assessee has purchased a new residential house within a period of 1 year before the date of transfer or within 2 years after the date of transfer or has constructed a residential house property within a period of 3 years after the date of transfer (Section 54). The amount of exemption available is equal to the amount so utilised or the amount of capital gain, whichever is less.

(b) Capital Gains from Transfer of Agricultural Land: Capital gains arising from the transfer of agricultural land are exempt from tax if the assessee has purchased another land for agricultural purposes within a period of 2 years from the date of such transfer (Section 54-B).

(c) Capital Gains from Compulsory Acquisition of Industrial Undertaking: Where an industrial undertaking is to be shifted as a result of compulsory acquisition of its land or buildings by the Government, the capital gain arising from the payment of compensation is exempt from tax if the assessee has purchased any other land or building forming part of industrial undertaking within a period of 3 years from the date of acquisition (Section 54-D).

(d) Capital Gains from Shifting of an Industrial Undertaking from Urban Area to Rural Area: Capital gains made from the transfer of machinery, plant, land, and building etc., forming part of an industrial undertaking are exempt where transfer is effected for the shifting of the industrial undertaking from an urban area to any other area, provided these are reinvested in approved relocation schemes within 1 year before or 3 years after the date of transfer (Section 54-G). The amount of exemption is equal to the amount so utilised or the amount of capital gain, whichever is less. The purpose of this exemption is to encourage industries to shift out of congested urban areas to reduce pollution and other hazards.

(e) Capital Gains from an Asset other than Residential House: Capital gains on the transfer of a long-term capital asset other than a house property are tax-exempt if the net consideration for the transfer is invested in a residential house (Section 54-F). This exemption is available to an individual assessee provided he does not own any residential house on the date of transfer of the original asset. The investment in residential house must be made in case of purchase within 1 year before or 2 years after the date of transfer and in case of construction within 3 years of such transfer.

Meanwhile, the amount of net consideration or the unutilised part of it must be kept in the Deposit Account like in other cases discussed above. If the cost of the newly acquired house is less than the net consideration in respect of the asset transferred, the exemption is allowed only in respect of part of the capital gain proportionate to ratio of the amount invested to the net consideration. In other words, the amount of exemption shall be equal to:

$$\frac{\text{Capital gains} \times \text{Cost of new residential house}}{\text{Amount of net consideration}}$$

If the assessee transfers the newly acquired residential house within a period of three years of its purchase or construction, then the amount of capital gains arising from the transfer of the original asset which was not charged to tax, will be deemed to be the income from capital gains for the year in which the new asset is transferred. In addition to this, there is another circumstance when exemption granted may be withdrawn. This happens if the assessee within the time for acquiring new house (within 2 years of the transfer of original asset in case of purchase or within 3 years in case of construction) purchases or constructs another residential house in addition to the new house. In that case, the capital gains earlier exempted from tax are charged to tax as income of the year in which that second house is purchased or constructed.

(f) Capital Gains Invested in Certain Bonds: Any long-term capital gain is exempt if the whole of amount of such capital gain is invested in long-term specified assets (e.g. bonds issued by National Highway Authority of India (NHAI) and Rural Electrification Corporation Ltd.) within a period of 6 months from the date of transfer [Section 54-EC].

(g) Capital Gains from Shifting of an Industrial Undertaking from Urban Area to Special Economic Zone (SEZ): Any capital gains arising from the transfer of machinery, plant, land or building, in the course of shifting of an industrial undertaking in an urban area, to any SEZ, are exempt if the assessee has, within a period of 1 year before or 3 years after the date of transfer, purchased new plant or machinery, acquired or constructed land or building, shifted the original assets and transferred the establishment, to the SEZ [Section 54-GA].

(h) Capital Gains from the Transfer of a Residential Property Invested in a Manufacturing Small or Medium Enterprise: Any long-term capital gain from the transfer of a residential property effected up to March 31, 2017 is exempt if the net consideration is invested in the equity of a new start-up small and medium enterprise (SME) company in the manufacturing sector, which in turn is utilized by such company for the purchase of new plant and machinery [Section 54-GB].

12.8.7 Capital Gains Account Scheme, 1988: This scheme is applicable to all the five types of exemptions mentioned above under Sections 54, 54B, 54D, 54F, and 54G. However, an assessee has to open a separate account under each section if he wishes to avail the benefit under more than one section. Under this scheme, if the amount of capital gain is not utilised by the assessee for purchase or construction of the new asset before the due date for furnishing the return of income for the relevant year, it must be deposited by him on or before the due date of furnishing the return of income, in the Deposit Account in any branch (except rural branch) of a public sector bank in accordance with Capital Gains Account Scheme, 1988. The amount utilised for acquiring the new asset together with the amount so deposited is deemed to be the amount utilised for acquiring the new asset. If the amount deposited is not utilised fully for purchase or construction of the new asset within the stipulated period, then the amount not so utilised is treated as the capital gain of the year in which the period specified for investment in new asset (3 years from the date of transfer of original asset) expires.

12.8.8 Set Off and Carry Forward of Capital Losses: A capital loss represents the amount by which the full value of consideration for the transfer of an asset falls short of the sum of cost of acquisition and improvement of that asset and the expenditure incurred in connection with the transfer of that asset.

From the assessment year 2003-04, the provisions are as follows:

1. Any short-term capital loss can be set off against any capital gain (both long-

term and short-term) and against no other income.

2. Any long-term capital loss can be set off only against long-term capital gain and against no other income.
3. Any short-term capital loss can be carried forward to the next 8 assessment years and set off against capital gains (both short-term and long-term) in those years.
4. Any long-term capital loss can be carried forward to the next 8 assessment years and set off only against long-term capital gain in those years.

It is noteworthy that if there is loss under any head, it can be set off against income from long-term capital gain and the balance of long-term capital gain is subject to tax at the rate of 20 percent.

12.8.9 A Critique: How has the scheme of inflation indexing worked? There is a widespread feeling that introduction of inflation indexing for capital gains has unnecessarily complicated the income tax law.

The argument in favour of inflation indexing is that capital gains resulting from inflation are illusory in real terms. To offset the inflationary rise in the value of an asset, it is rational to increase the acquisition cost by the rate of inflation in the period between acquisition and realisation. True, an inflation-proof tax system is more certain and equitable in an inflationary economy but this is an ideal situation for all sources of income and not only for capital gains alone. Surprisingly, salary incomes which suffer the most due to inflation are left out and only capital gains are accorded the coveted treatment of inflation adjustment. Experience suggests that real estate prices move upward more quickly than the general index of prices while wage level adjustments not only lag but fall short of the rate of inflation.

The solution to the inflation problem lies in revision of exemptions and allowances for various types of income. Thus, the Finance Act, 1992, shifted the cut-off date for valuation of assets acquired in earlier years from April 1, 1974 to April 1, 1981. It means an assessee has the option of substituting the fair market value as on April 1, 1981 for the cost of acquisition where the asset had been acquired prior to that date. This concession itself offsets, though partially, the inflationary effect on capital gains.

Prior to the assessment year 1993-94, a basic exemption of ₹ 15,000 and a further deduction of 50/60 percent depending on the category of asset was provided to individual assessees in computing long-term capital gains. This concession gave relief, particularly to assessees in the lower income group. It also provided a kind of incentive for new entrants to the capital market. Revival of the basic exemption would make the capital gains tax more equitable.

The flat rate of 20 percent for capital gains as compared to the maximum marginal rate of 30 percent for other incomes in the case of individuals has reduced the effective progressivity of income tax besides producing differential tax liabilities at given levels of income, violating the principle of horizontal equity. Moreover, this differential will induce people to earn income in the form of capital gains (often speculative) rather than as business profits, dividends, or interest. The inducement will be stronger at higher income levels because of the high tax rates applicable thereon.

12.9 Survey, Summons, Search and Seizure See sections 10.11.7 and 10.11.8 of chapter 10 of this book.

12.10 Penalties and Prosecutions See section 10.11.9 of chapter 10 of this book.

12.11 Organisational Set Up and IT Initiatives

Work of the Ministry of Finance, Government of India is divided into 5 Departments:

- Department of Economic Affairs.
- Department of Expenditure.
- Department of Revenue.
- Department of Financial Services.
- Department of Disinvestment.

12.11.1 Department of Revenue: The Department of Revenue functions under the overall direction and control of the Secretary (Revenue). It exercises control in respect of matters relating to all the Direct and Indirect Union Taxes through two statutory Boards namely, the Central Board of Direct Taxes (CBDT) and the Central Board of Excise and Customs (CBEC). Each Board is headed by a Chairman who is also ex-officio Special Secretary to the Government of India. Matters relating to the levy and collection of all Direct taxes are looked after by the CBDT whereas those relating to levy and collection of Customs and Central Excise duties and other Indirect taxes fall within the purview of the CBEC. The two Boards were constituted under the Central Board of Revenue Act, 1963. At present, the CBDT has six Members and the CBEC has five Members. The Members are also ex-officio Additional Secretaries to the Government of India.

12.11.2 Central Board of Direct Taxes (CBDT): The CBDT, New Delhi, is part of the Department of Revenue in the Ministry of Finance. While the CBDT provides essential inputs for policy and planning of direct taxes in India, it is also responsible for administration of direct tax laws through its Income Tax Department. The Income Tax Department is primarily responsible for combating the menace of black money. For this purpose, it uses the tools of scrutiny assessment as well as information-based investigations for detecting tax evasion and penalizing the same as per provisions of the Income Tax Act, 1961 with the objective of creating deterrence against tax evasion. In doing so, it plays one of the most important roles in preventing generation, accumulation, and consumption of unaccounted black money. The Investigation Wing of the Income Tax Department deals with investigations to detect tax evasion and carries out operations like surveys and searches to collect evidence of such evasion. Such operations are usually carried out after detailed preliminary investigations and in cases involving substantial evasion of taxes.

The Income Tax Department is also engaged in the task of educating and assisting taxpayers in filing tax returns, assessing tax liability, demanding pending taxes, penalising dishonest taxpayers and disposing of tax disputes. The role of this Department in tax system of India is rapidly increasing as the share of direct taxes in the revenue of the country has registered a steady increase over the years.

12.11.3 Permanent Account Number (PAN): PAN issued by Income Tax Department is the critical element in capturing incomes and expenditures of a person. The Department identifies the assesses/persons with PAN which is a unique 10 digit alpha-numeric number. Obtaining PAN is compulsory not only for income tax purposes but also for certain other purposes/transactions. PAN is to be obtained only once for ever. An assessee need not obtain a new PAN, even if he is transferred to any other place.

The Finance Act 1998 laid down that under Section 139-A a person whose taxable income is beyond basic exemption limit or turnover exceeds ₹ 5 lakh is required to apply for PAN. Every person has to quote PAN on any document while dealing with Income Tax Department and financial transactions exceeding the specified limit. It has been made compulsory for tax deductors to quote PAN of the deductees in the return of tax deducted and certificate issued to the deductees with effect from June 1, 2001. The Finance Act, 2009 provided that if PAN is not quoted by the deductee, the TDS rate will be 20 percent instead of 10 percent. The main purpose of these amendments has been to compel people to quote PAN, so that information contained in such returns or certificates can be processed properly.

12.11.4 E-payment of Tax and E-filing of Returns: E-payment of tax is a facility provided to the taxpayers for making income tax payment through internet banking facility or through internet by using credit/debit cards. Assessees required to get their accounts audited under Section 44-AB and all companies are mandatorily required to make E-payment of tax.

While E-filing of returns through internet is mandatory for a company and a firm liable to audit under Section 44-AB, it is optional for other assessees.

Similarly, it is mandatory for corporate deductors to furnish their TDS return in electronic form.

12.11.5 Digital Signature: A person desiring to furnish his return of income electronically, may sign it digitally or manually. For signing the return digitally, he is required to obtain a digital signature. A digital signature is the electronic signature issued by the certifying authority that shows the authenticity of the person signing the same.

12.12 Recommendations of the Task Force on Direct Taxes (Chairman: Vijay Kelkar), 2002 Pertaining to Income Tax

At the time of presenting the first batch of supplementary demands for grants to Parliament in July 2002, the Finance Minister had proposed setting up of two task forces to recommend measures for simplification and rationalization of direct and indirect taxes. Accordingly, two task forces were set up in September 2002 under the chairmanship of Dr. Vijay Kelkar, Adviser to Minister of Finance and Company Affairs.

The Task Force on Direct Taxes presented its consultation paper to the Government on November 2, 2002. The discussion paper on indirect taxes was presented on November 25, 2002. These consultation papers were made public to facilitate an informed discussion on tax policy.

After taking in to account the response on the discussion papers, the Task Forces submitted their final reports to the Government in December 2002. These Task Forces have made important recommendations on toning up tax administration to put in place a system that is simple, effective and at par with international standards.

The main recommendations on direct taxes relate to raising of exemption limit of personal income tax, rationalization of exemptions, abolition of concessional treatment to long-term capital gains, and abolition of wealth tax. In respect of indirect taxes, the main recommendations relate to widening of the tax base, removal of exemptions, expansion in the coverage of service tax etc.

The Task Force on Direct Taxes was assigned the following Terms of Reference:

- Rationalisation and simplification of the direct taxes with a view to minimizing exemptions, removing anomalies and improving equity;
- Improvement in taxpayer services so as to reduce compliance cost, impart transparency and facilitate voluntary compliance;
- Redesigning procedures for strengthening enforcement so as to improve compliance of direct tax laws; and

- Any other matter related to the above points".

12.12.1 Personal Income Tax: The Task Force recommended a two rate schedule for personal income tax (Table 12.8).

Table 12.8: Rate Structure of Personal Income Tax Recommended by the Task Force on Direct Taxes

Income Level	Tax Rates
Below ₹ 1,00,000	Nil
₹ 1,00,000-4,00,000	20 percent of the income in excess of ₹ 1,00,000
Above ₹ 4,00,000	₹ 60,000 plus 30 percent of the income in excess of ₹ 4,00,000

Source: Government of India, Ministry of Finance and Company Affairs, *Report of the Task Force on Direct Taxes* (Chairman: Vijay Kelkar), December 2002, p. 71.

It recommended the abolition of surcharge on income tax. It was of the opinion that revenue gain from levy of surcharge is generally illusory since such a levy has the effect of increasing the marginal rate of tax, which adversely affects compliance.

It recommended that residents but not ordinarily residents must be subjected to tax on their global/world-wide income at par with residents. To do so, this unusual category of resident but not ordinarily resident taxpayers must be deleted. Most countries across the world provide for only two status: residents and non-residents.

It recommended that standard deduction under Section 16(1) of the Income Tax Act should be eliminated. However, the exemption of conveyance allowance subject to a ceiling of ₹ 9,600 should be continued. This should serve as a reasonable deduction for employment related expenses.

As regards tax treatment of agricultural income, the Task Force recommended as follows:

- A tax rental arrangement should be designed whereby States should pass a resolution under Article 252 of the Constitution authorizing the Central Government to impose income tax on agricultural income. The taxes collected by the Centre would however be assigned to the States.
- Tax from agricultural income for the purpose of allocation between States will be the difference between the tax on total income (including agricultural income) and the tax on total income net of agricultural income.
- Where a taxpayer derives agricultural income from different States, the revenues attributable to a State will be in the ratio of the income derived from a particular State to the total agricultural income.
- A separate tax return form should be prescribed for taxpayers deriving

income from agriculture.

It recommended the elimination of the tax incentives for savings under Sections 88, 80L, 10 (15)(i), 10 (15) (iib), 10 (15) (iic), 10 (15) (iid), 10 (15) (iv) (h) and 10 (15) (iv) (i) of the Income Tax Act. It insisted that these benefits must be immediately withdrawn and not through a sunset clause.

It recommended that the basic exemption limit for senior citizens should be ₹ 50,000 more than the exemption limit for the general class of individual taxpayers. To put it differently, the exemption limit for senior citizens should be ₹ 1,50,000 as against ₹ 1,00,000 for the general category of individual taxpayers. It further recommended that the exemption limit for senior citizens should be revised as and when the exemption limit for the general category of individual taxpayers is revised. Still further, it recommended that this benefit of higher exemption limit should also be extended to widows.

12.12.2 Corporate Tax: The Task Force on Direct Taxes made the following recommendations for the reform of corporate income tax:

1. Reduction in corporate tax rate from the existing levels of 36.75 percent to 30 percent for domestic companies and to 35 percent for foreign companies.
2. Exemption of dividend from taxation in the hands of the shareholders. There will also be no tax on distribution of dividends by a company.
3. Exemption of long-term capital gains on listed equity.
4. Elimination of Minimum Alternate Tax under Section 115-JB.
5. Removal of the distinction between unabsorbed depreciation and unabsorbed business loss.
6. Removal of the following deductions under Section 10 and Chapter VIA of the Income Tax Act with immediate effect and not by a sunset clause:

- Elimination of Sections 10-A and 10-B of the Income Tax Act for all taxpayers other than those engaged in manufacturing computer software.
- In the case of taxpayers engaged in manufacturing computer software, the Government of India must take immediate steps to negotiate with foreign governments to enter into a comprehensive totalisation agreement leading to a single point incidence of taxes.
- Section 80-IA in respect of profit and gains from industrial undertakings engaged in infrastructure development or telecommunication service or development of industrial park or special economic zones or generation, transmission or distribution of power.
- Section 80-IB in respect of profits and gains from certain industrial undertakings other than infrastructure development undertakings (this includes backward areas also).

- Section 80-JJA in respect of profits and gains from business of collecting and processing of biodegradable wastes.
- Section 80-JJAA in respect of employment of new workman.
- Section 80-M in respect of inter-corporate dividends.
- The phase out programme in respect of Sections 80-HHB, 80-HHBA, 80-HHC, 80-HHD, 80-HHE, 80-HHF, 80-O, 80-R, 80-RR and 80-RRA will continue.

7. Depreciation rates for the purposes of depreciation allowance under Section 32 should be reduced to 15 percent for the general category of plant and machinery and to appropriate lower rates for other categories of block of assets.
8. Elimination of following Sections: 33-AB (relating to tea development allowance; 33-AC (relating to reserve for shipping business); 33-B (relating to rehabilitation allowance); 35 (relating to scientific research); 35-AC (relating to expenditure on eligible projects); 35-CCA (relating to expenditure by way of payment to associations and institutions for carrying out rural development programmes); 36 (1) (iii) (in respect of interest on borrowed capital).
9. The provision for bad and doubtful debts allowable under Section 36(1)(viia) of the Income Tax Act will henceforth be restricted to the amount of provision debited to profit and loss account as audited subject to the maximum amount of provisioning permitted under the prudential guidelines issued by the Reserve Bank of India.

12.12.3 Capital Gains: The Task Force on Direct Taxes recommended that concessional treatment of long-term capital gains through a reduced scheduler rate of tax must be abolished. In other words, the long-term capital gains would be aggregated with other incomes and subjected to taxation at the normal rates.

12.13 Critical Evaluation of the Indian Income Tax System

12.13.1 Unstable Law: There is considerable instability in the income tax law of India, owing mainly to introduction, withdrawal, and reintroduction of exemptions and concessions for various purposes. According to one estimate, there were 3,300 amendments to the Income Tax Act during 1961-90. [12] As the Direct Tax Laws Committee remarked, "The instability of our tax laws is another of their worst features. The laws are riddled with uncertainties and statutory amendments are as unpredictable as they are frequent. Surely, after more than half a century of the working of income tax Acts of 1922, and 1961, it should be possible to have an enduring tax system". [13] Frequent amendments have led to uncertainty and confusion among taxpayers and tax collectors.

12.13.2 Multitude of Exemptions/Concessions: It is quite common in tax laws to incorporate provisions which exclude certain items and deduct others from the tax base. These tax preferences are referred to as *tax expenditures* in the literature and often resemble the more notorious term *tax loopholes*. As in other countries, exclusions, deductions, and rebates are integral part of the Indian income tax system designed to promote a variety of socially desirable activities. However, their wide amplitude has adversely affected revenue yield. These concessions, each with a rationale of its own, have the combined effect of eroding the tax base and impairing the progressivity of the tax system. The supposedly high statutory rates of income tax turn out to be illusory in view of the various exemptions/concessions which lower the effective rates of taxation significantly.

The plethora of exemptions/concessions has led to complexities in the income tax law, obscuring its evaluation, particularly from equity angle. Exemptions and concessions are often the result of persistent representations and pressure tactics by vested interests rather than any economic justification.

Income tax concessions are subsidy payments and need to be devised carefully. For example, there is no fundamental difference between outright subsidy payment to a newly established export-oriented undertaking and a tax holiday for it under Section 10B of the Income Tax Act, 1961. Indeed, outright subsidy payments attract public attention more readily than tax concessions which lie scattered in the cobwebs of ever-changing tax laws. For a simple and efficient income tax system, exemptions and concessions should be kept to the minimum and used selectively for very genuine purposes. A review of the whole gamut of exemptions and concessions is called for to streamline revenue and administration. Measures other than income tax concessions should also be considered to encourage activities which deserve governmental support.

12.13.3 Earned versus Unearned Incomes: Another serious lacuna in the present system of personal income tax is the non-discriminatory treatment of earned and other forms of income for tax purposes. Income of an assessee from various sources is pooled together for the purpose of computation of taxable income and tax liability determination. This so-called *global principle* of income tax does not differentiate between different sources of income.

Earned income (or employment income) is derived from actual work or service performed and includes wages, salaries, and income from professions. Unearned income (or capital income) is derived from investments, rents etc.

The Indian Taxation Enquiry Committee, 1924-25 examined, for the first time, the desirability of differentiation between earned and unearned incomes for the purpose of income tax. The Committee, however, rejected the idea, maintaining that it was premature in the context of the Indian conditions. It was in 1945 that a distinction between earned and unearned incomes was introduced when assessees were allowed to exclude from their earned incomes a fixed proportion subject to a maximum limit.

The Taxation Enquiry Commission (TEC), 1953-54, made several recommendations regarding income tax, some of which dealt with the broad structure of taxation while others related to maters of detail like inclusion and exclusion of certain categories of income from taxation, grant of concessions to promote objectives of economic policy and so on. A notable recommendation of the TEC pertained to the withdrawal of the concession relating to earned income beyond a certain level of income which it suggested should be ₹ 24,000. Agreeing with this recommendation that earned income relief should not be allowed on higher brackets of income, the Government, as a first step, reduced the allowance in the 1955-56 budget by stages on incomes in excess of ₹ 25,000, the concession ceasing when the level of ₹ 45,000 was reached. Under the recast scheme, an allowance of 20 percent subject to a maximum of ₹ 4,000 was granted to earned incomes not exceeding ₹ 25,000. For incomes in excess of this amount the allowance of ₹ 4,000 was reduced at the rate of 20 percent of the excess over ₹ 25,000 so that for an earned income of ₹ 45,000 the allowance was reduced to nil. From 1957-58, the relief was given in the form of a lower surcharge on earned income than on unearned income. The surcharge was fixed at 5 percent of the tax on earned incomes up to ₹ 1 lakh and 10 percent on incomes in excess of that sum while for unearned incomes a uniform surcharge of 20 percent was imposed. However, the distinction between earned and unearned incomes introduced in 1945 under which the earned income was treated leniently was completely abolished from April 1, 1968. This decision was widely criticised as a retrograde fiscal measure.

The present law of income tax does recognise and tax different sources of income differently, though to a limited extent. Thus, long-term capital gains enjoy special concessions under the income tax law. The Finance Act, 1992, introduced inflation indexation of the cost of acquisition of assets for computing long-term capital gains. Moreover, a flat rate tax of 20 percent was fixed on long-term capital gains arising to individuals and HUFs. It is ironical that preferential tax treatment denied to earned incomes is available to long-term capital gains which are purely accidental in nature and bear no relationship to efforts on the part of the recipient. Till 1990-91, the differentiation principle was followed in the case of company taxation when trading and investment companies were subject to a higher flat rate tax (50 percent) than industrial and other companies (45 percent).

If the distinction between earned and unearned incomes is to be revived, it may take the form of: (a) reduction in the base of earned income (for example, exclusion from income of a fixed proportion subject to a maximum limit) and/or (b) lower rate structure for earned incomes.

Endnotes

1. For historical evolution of income tax in India, see section 2.2 of chapter 2 of this book.
2. Government of India, Ministry of Finance, *Interim Report of the Tax Reforms Committee* (Chairman, Raja Chelliah), 1991, p. 20.
3. Ordinarily, the legislature enacts a bare Act and makes provision in the Act itself for details to be taken care of by the executive authority created for administration of the Act. Thus, rules and regulations concerning direct tax laws are framed by the Central Board of Direct Taxes and are referred to as delegated, subordinate or administrative law. It is noteworthy that rules made under an Act have the same force as sections of the Act itself. However, they must be within the powers given to the rule-making authority. In case of any conflict, the Act overrides the rules framed under it.
4. In the terminology of Section 3 of the Act, the year during which the income is received or otherwise earned is called the *previous year* (i.e. the income year). It is a period of twelve months starting from April 1 of every year and ending on March 31 of the next year, being also the financial year of the Government of India. The year immediately succeeding the previous year and in which the income so earned is assessed to tax is called, under Section 2(9), the *assessment year* (i.e. the tax year). For example, income for the period from April 1, 2013 to March 31, 2014 (i.e. 2013-14) is income of the previous year relevant for the assessment year 2014-15. An assessee means a person by whom any tax or other sum of money is payable under the Act.
5. Government of India, Ministry of Finance, Report of the Taxation Enquiry Commission, 1953-54, op. cit, Vol. II, chapter 3, p. 41.
6. The following is a select list of types of income that are exempt from income tax either fully or up to specified limits under various clauses (mentioned in parentheses) of Section 10 of the Income Tax Act, 1961.

- Agricultural income [10(1)].
- Receipts by a member from a Hindu Undivided Family [10(2)].
- Partner's share in the profits of a firm [10(2A)].
- Certain income from interest received by non-residents [10(4)].
- Value of any leave travel concession or assistance received by the employee from the employer in connection with the former proceeding on leave to any place in India [10(5)].
- Remuneration received by employees of foreign missions, foreign enterprises, foreign philanthropic institutions [under various sub-clauses of Section 10(6)].
- Salaries of a foreign government employee under co-operative technical assistance programme [10(8)].
- Income of a family member of a technical assistant/consultant/employee [10(9)].
- Death-cum-retirement gratuity subject to a maximum of ₹ 10,00,000 with effect from 24.5.2010 [10(10)].
- Any payment in commutation of pension received by Government or semi-government employee. Payment in commutation of pension received by private sector employee is

exempt subject to certain limits [10(10A)].

- Any payment received by an employee of Central/State Government as the cash equivalent of the leave salary in respect of the period of earned leave at his credit at the time of his retirement. In the case of other employees, the exemption is available subject to limits prescribed [10(10AA)].
- Any compensation received by a workman at the time of retrenchment or closure or transfer of undertaking subject to prescribed limits [10(10B)].
- Any payment received by an employee of a company at the time of his voluntary retirement [10(10C)].
- Any sum received under a life insurance policy, including any bonus allocated on such policy [10(10D)].
- Payment from provident fund [10(11), (12)].
- Payment from superannuation fund [10(13)].
- House rent allowance [10(13A)].
- Special allowance or benefit to employees [10(14)].
- Interest on certain securities [10(15)].
- Scholarships granted to meet the cost of education [10(16)].
- Daily allowance of Members of Parliament [10(17)].
- Any amount received in connection with an award instituted by Central/State Government [10 (17A)].
- Income of a local authority [10(20)]; a scientific research association [10(21)]; a university [10(22)]; a hospital [10(22A)]; *Khadi* or Village Industries [10(23B)]; certain national funds [10(23C)]; mutual funds [10(23D)]; trade unions [10(24)]; provident funds [10(25)]; a member of scheduled tribe [10(26)]; a body for promoting interest of scheduled castes/tribes etc. [10(26B)]; a co-operative society for promoting interest of scheduled castes/tribes [10(27)].
- Subsidy received from the Tea Board [10(30)].
- Subsidy received from commodity boards [10(31)].
- Income of minor child liable to be included in the income of his parent up to a maximum of ₹ 1,500 per minor child [10(32)].

7. Prior to the assessment year 1975-76, the computation of income under the head salaries allowed deduction of expenditure from gross salary income incurred by a taxpayer on purchase of books and for maintenance of conveyance for employment purposes. The deduction was allowed to the taxpayer only on production of proof of having incurred such expenditure. The procedure was obviously cumbersome for the salaried persons and to simplify it, the Finance Act of 1974 substituted it with a standard deduction for all types of expenditure incurred towards employment. The maximum amount of deduction allowed for this purpose was fixed at ₹ 3,500. According to the provisions of the Income Tax Act, standard deduction was granted, 'in respect of deduction incidental to the employment of the assessee'. However, this clause was deleted by an amendment introduced by the Finance (No. 2) Act, 1980. Consequently, standard deduction became claimable by an employee regardless of the fact whether or not any expenditure incidental to employment had actually been incurred. For example, a pensioner was eligible to claim it although he did not incur, under normal circumstances, any expenditure to collect his pension. Even a person who was in receipt of family pension could claim this deduction. Family pension was included under the

head 'income from other sources' and this deduction was available under Section 57(iia). Thus, standard deduction, originally envisaged as a device to arrive at an assessee's net salary income, had virtually become a blanket deduction against salary income.

Standard deduction was raised from ₹ 3,500 to ₹ 5,000 in 1981, ₹ 6,000 in 1983, ₹ 10,000 in 1986, ₹ 12,000 in 1988, and ₹ 15,000 in 1993. Thus, salaried employees were entitled to a standard deduction at the rate of 33.3 percent of salary income or ₹ 15,000 whichever was less. However, in 1996 standard deduction was raised from ₹ 15,000 to ₹ 18,000 for salaried employees having an income up to ₹ 60,000.

As a special consideration for women, the Finance Act, 1992 provided for a higher standard deduction of ₹ 15,000 (as against the general ₹ 12,000) in respect of working women having total income up to ₹ 75,000. When the general standard deduction was increased from ₹ 12,000 to ₹ 15,000 by the Finance Act, 1993, a corresponding increase from ₹ 15,000 to ₹ 18,000 was made in the case of women.

In the 1997-98 budget, a uniform standard deduction of ₹ 20,000 was introduced for all salaried taxpayers. In the 1998-99 budget, the ceiling of standard deduction was raised from ₹ 20,000 to ₹ 25,000 in the case of salary earners having income up to ₹ 1 lakh. For salary earners having income between ₹ 1 lakh and ₹ 5 lakh, the existing position (i.e. ₹ 20,000) remained unchanged. However, entitlement to standard deduction was discontinued for salary earners having income above ₹ 5 lakh. In the 2001-02 budget, standard deduction was raised to ₹ 30,000 for taxpayers earning up to ₹ 1.5 lakh, and ₹ 25,000 for those earning between ₹ 1.5 lakh and 3 lakh. The limit of ₹ 20,000 was retained for taxpayers earning between ₹ 3 lakh and 5 lakh. Denial of standard deduction to salary earners having income above ₹ 5 lakh continued. Standard deduction was completely withdrawn for all categories of salary earners by the Finance Act, 2005.

8. Till March 31, 1990, incentives to promote savings and investments were based entirely on deductions from gross total income. When a deduction is made from income, an assessee gets tax relief at the highest marginal rate of tax applicable to him. Apparently, this system confers higher amount of tax benefit to a person with higher income compared to a person with lower income. To do away with this iniquitous system, the Finance Act, 1990, introduced a new scheme of tax rebate for individuals and HUFs on gross amount of savings. The new scheme covered under Section 88 provided for a rebate (or tax credit) on tax liability to the extent of 20 percent of the sums invested in National Savings Certificates, provident funds, life insurance policies etc. The maximum amount eligible for rebate was ₹ 50,000 generally and ₹ 70,000 in the case of authors, playwrights, artists, musicians, actors, and sportsmen, thereby permitting a maximum rebate of ₹ 10,000 and ₹ 14,000 respectively.

   Under this new scheme with uniform tax rebate, all taxpayers derived the same amount of tax benefit on a given amount of savings irrespective of their levels of income. It also led to simplification in tax deduction at source by the employers. It was a good example of how equity and simplicity criteria can be combined in the tax system.

   The Finance Act, 1992, increased the maximum amount eligible for rebate for general category of investors from ₹ 50,000 to ₹ 60,000 (or the ceiling of tax rebate was increased from ₹ 10,000 to ₹ 12,000). It extended also the scope of Section 88 by including under it the National Savings Scheme (formerly under section 80 CCA), and the Equity-Linked Savings Scheme (formerly under section 80 CCB). Within the overall ceiling of ₹ 60,000, a sub-ceiling of ₹ 10,000 was fixed in respect of investments in the Equity-Linked Savings Scheme in order to ensure continued viability of other saving schemes contained in Section 88.

Again, by the Finance Act, 1992, the scheme of tax credit under Section 88 was further liberalised in the case of authors, playwrights etc. to compensate them for the fluctuating nature of their income. As against the 20 percent tax rebate allowed normally, it was raised to 25 percent in their case. Also, the ceiling of the maximum rebate in their case was raised from ₹ 14,000 to ₹ 17,500. With a view to allowing this concession only to those persons having a significant portion of their income from the above mentioned professions, the enhanced rebate was allowed only to such persons whose income from their professions as authors, playwrights etc. was at least 25 percent of their total income.

Furthermore, the Finance Act, 1992, inserted a new Section 88B to provide for a special tax relief in the form of an additional rebate of 10 percent from the tax payable by resident individuals who had attained the age of 65 years and had a gross total income not exceeding ₹ 50,000. This special relief was designed to help senior citizens meet the increased expenses in their old age. The Finance Act, 1993, raised the tax rebate to 20 percent and further increased the income limit from ₹ 50,000 to ₹ 75,000. In 1994, the tax rebate admissible was raised from 20 percent to 40 percent and the benefit made available to senior citizens having an income up to ₹ 1,00,000. In 1996, the income limit was raised from ₹ 1,00,000 to ₹ 1,20,000. It is noteworthy that this rebate was admissible before computing any rebate under Section 88. By the Finance Act, 1997, the rate of rebate available to senior citizens was increased to 100 percent from the existing 40 percent subject to a limit of ₹ 10,000. Furthermore, the Finance Act, 1997 allowed tax rebate under section 88 on infrastructure bonds up to the value of ₹ 70,000. The scheme of rebate was modified a number of times after that and was finally withdrawn by the Finance Act, 2005.

9. Units of Assessment under Income Tax Act:

An Individual: An individual means only a natural person, i.e. a human being. An individual is taxed separately, though he may belong to any of the other units subject to tax.

A Hindu Undivided Family (HUF): HUF in India is a joint family recognised for all purposes, including taxation, as a separate and distinct legal unit. It is ordinarily headed by *Karta* who is either the father or some other senior member of the family. HUF consists of all persons lineally descended from a common ancestor and includes their wives and unmarried daughters.

The HUF enjoys a higher exemption limit for income tax purposes than for individuals. This is justified on the ground that the liabilities of HUF, in terms of the total membership of the HUF consisting of earners and their dependents, are, in general, larger than that of the individual income-earners. For income tax purposes HUF must satisfy two conditions: (a) that the family possesses common property, and (b) that there is a Hindu coparcenary.

A Company: Under Section 2(17), a company means: (i) any Indian company, or (ii) any body corporate incorporated under the laws of a foreign country, or (iii) any institution, association or a body which was assessed as a company for any assessment year up to and including the assessment year 1970-71 and (iv) any institution, association or a body which is declared by the Central Board of Direct Taxes to be a company for purposes of the income tax. Thus, the definition of the term 'company' under the Act is much wider than in the Companies Act, 1956.

Under Section 2(26) an Indian company means: (i) a company formed and registered in India under the Companies Act, 1956, (ii) a corporation established by or under a Central, State or Provincial Act, and (iii) any institution, association or a body which is declared by the Central Board of Direct Taxes to be an Indian Company. It is notable that in the foregoing cases, a company, corporation, institution, association or body will be treated as an Indian company only if its registered office is in India.

Domestic company is defined as an Indian company or any other company which in respect of its income liable to tax under the Act, has made prescribed arrangements for the declaration and payment of dividends within India. It has to meet the following three requirements before it could be called a domestic company: (a) The share register of the company for all shareholders should be regularly maintained at its principal place of business in India, (b) the general meeting for passing of accounts and for declaring dividends should be held only at a place within India, and (c) the dividends declared, if any, should be payable only within India to all shareholders.

Foreign company means a company which is not a domestic company.

Widely-held companies are companies in which the public are substantially interested [Section 2(18)]. The following types of companies are deemed to be widely-held companies: (i) A company owned by the Government or the Reserve Bank of India or in which not less than 40 percent of the shares are held by Government or the Reserve Bank of India or a corporation owned by that Bank; or (ii) a company registered under Section 25 of the Companies Act, 1956, viz. companies for promotion of commerce, art, culture etc. and prohibiting the payment of any dividends to its members; (iii) a company having no share capital and it is declared by the Central Board of Direct Taxes to be a company in which the public are substantially interested; or (iv) a company which carries on, as its principal business, the business of acceptance of deposits from its members and which is declared by the Central Government to be a *Nidhi* or a mutual benefit society; or (v) a company which is not a private company and its equity shares are listed in a recognised stock exchange in India; or (vi) a company which is not a private company and its shares carrying 50 percent of voting power have been allotted unconditionally to, or acquired unconditionally by: (a) the Government, or (b) a statutory corporation.

A company in which the public are not substantially interested is deemed to be a closely-held company (or private company).

An industrial company is a company which is mainly engaged in the business of generation or distribution of electricity or any other form of power or in the construction of ships or in the manufacture or processing of goods or in mining. A consultancy service company is an Indian company whose business consists wholly in the provision of technical know-how. An investment, company is one whose gross total income consists mainly of income chargeable under the heads 'income from house property', 'capital gains', and 'income from other sources'. Similarly, a trading company is one whose business consists mainly of dealing in goods or merchandise manufactured, produced or processed by a person other than that company.

A Firm: Persons who have entered into partnership with one another are individually called partners and collectively a firm. A firm is a taxable entity separate and distinct from its partners. For the purpose of assessment, a firm may be registered or unregistered. A registered firm means a firm registered under Sections 184 and 185 of the Act, and an unregistered firm means a firm which is not a registered firm. A registered firm gets the benefit of lower rates of tax than those which would otherwise apply to the income of a firm.

An Association of Persons or Body of Individuals: An association of persons may be an association of individuals, firms, Hindu Undivided Families or companies. It means, for income tax purposes, an association in which two or more persons join in a common purpose to produce income, profits or gains.

Local Authority: Local authority means a municipal committee, district board etc. and is a separate unit of assessment.

Every Artificial Juridical Person: It is a residuary classification covering deities and other artificial juridical persons like statutory corporations. It does not cover taxable units falling within any of the preceding classifications.

Under Section 2(19), a co-operative society means a society registered under the Co-operative Societies Act of 1912 or under any State law for the registration of co-operative societies. Such societies get favourable treatment under the Income-Tax Act in view of Government's policy to encourage co-operative activities.

10. Government of India, Ministry of Finance, *Speeches of Union Finance Ministers, 1947-48 to 1984-85*, p. 155.
11. Government of India, Ministry of Finance, *Final Report of Direct Taxes Enquiry Committee,* (Chairman: Justice K. N. Wanchoo) December 1971, para 2.52.
12. N.A. Palkhivala and B.A. Palkhivala, *The Law and Practice of Income Tax,* (Bombay: N.M. Tripathi Private Ltd., 1990), Vol. I, p. 9.
13. Government of India, Ministry of Finance, *Final Report of Direct Tax Laws Committee,* (Chairman: C.C. Chokshi), 1978, para 1-0, p. 10.

13

Wealth Tax

Following the recommendations of Professor Nicholas Kaldor, an 'integrated direct tax system' was introduced in India in the mid-1950s. Kaldor, a British economist, was invited by the Government of India in 1956 to examine the Indian tax system in the light of the revenue requirements of the Second Five Year Plan (1956-61) launched in the same year. Kaldor's review of Indian taxation was restricted to personal and business taxation and was widely debated. It may be recalled that an extensive review of the Indian tax system had already been undertaken by the Indian Taxation Enquiry Commission (Chairman: John Matthai), 1953-54.

In 1957 and 1958, three new taxes were introduced, viz. wealth tax, expenditure tax, and gift tax. Estate duty was already in operation since 1953. The basic philosophy underlying the introduction of the system of integrated direct taxes was to prevent evasion and avoidance of direct taxes and thereby to reduce inequalities of income and wealth. However, the yield from expenditure tax, gift tax, and estate duty was never of much significance in Central revenues. The meagre revenue collections from these taxes ultimately led to the abolition of expenditure tax in 1966, estate duty in 1985 and gift tax in 1998. Wealth tax continues to be in operation, though the revenue is negligible as compared to the total tax collections of the Central Government.

13.1 Rationale for Wealth Tax

Wealth tax is advocated on both benefit and ability-to-pay considerations. Protection of life and property has traditionally been the primary function of the government, and to perform it considerable cost is incurred on the law enforcement machinery and the judicial administration. The main beneficiaries of these services are people with fabulous wealth who as a rule should contribute towards the expenses on such services. Pavement sleepers hardly need the services of the state as a protector of property. Another dimension of the benefit argument is that public services like roads, street lighting, community centres, public parks etc. increase the value of real estates, conferring unearned benefits on the owners of such estates. It can, therefore, be argued that property owners should pay for these services.

In terms of ability-to-pay, possession of property is a measure of economic well-being and therefore of taxable capacity, quite apart from the income earned from that property. A tax on capital itself may seem undesirable when capital income is subject to income tax (as is generally the case). However, the coverage of capital income under the income tax is usually incomplete in view of liberal exemptions, tax avoidance, and evasion. Moreover, an income tax system does not include non-earning assets. Therefore, taxation of wealth is essentially a supplement to taxation of income. Hence, taxation of wealth is justified on equity criterion. It may be argued that wealth tax is unjust in cases where property does not yield money income directly. In this context Professor Kaldor has opined, "If a property does not yield money income, it must either yield an equivalent psychic income to the owner or it must be held in the expectation of a certain appreciation in value which makes it at least as attractive to the holder as other property on which a current money return is obtained". [1]

Yet another argument for taxation of wealth is social control over the most unjust and dangerous form of economic inequality. To quote Musgraves, "Alternatively, the taxation of wealth may be approached not as a matter of charging for benefits received or ability-to-pay, but as a form of social control. The social consequences of inequality in the distribution of wealth, as is easily seen, differ from those in the distribution of consumption, so that society may wish to deal with them separately. For this purpose, a progressive tax on wealth, rather than on income, is the proper instrument". [2] Situations may arise when certain taxpayers have taxable wealth but very low current incomes. One way to resolve this problem is to exempt from wealth tax liability all those taxpayers whose annual income from all sources does not exceed a specified limit.

In spite of being a potentially important source of revenue and economic control, the administration of wealth tax is difficult, particularly in developing countries. Imposition of wealth tax requires the preparation of an annual balance sheet of assets and liabilities of the taxpayer. For an honest exercise of this sort, an assessee should first declare, truthfully, all taxable assets with their proper current value. He must also make a genuine claim for deductible debts. Honesty of the sort required is an exception rather than the rule. Thus, tax officials for most of their part are busy detecting taxable assets, grappling with undervaluation of properties and verifying claims of deductible debts. Some of these problems (e.g. valuation of assets) are encountered also in connection with estate duty, capital gains tax, and local property tax. Valuation of assets for purposes of one tax is generally used as a basis for computing tax liability under another tax. However, the continuous rise in prices (leading to appreciation of real estates), the underdeveloped nature of money markets (causing difficulty in the valuation of shares), and the ingenuity of tax evaders leave the tax authorities groping in the dark without much success.

13.2 Wealth Tax Act, 1957: Main Provisions

An annual tax on net wealth was introduced in India with the enactment of the Wealth Tax Act, 1957, which came into force from April 1 of that year. The rationale behind the imposition of wealth tax lies essentially in furthering the equity objective of tax policy. Since ownership of wealth is the main source of economic inequalities in India, a tax on wealth is intended to reduce its concentration in a few hands to promote vertical equity.

Wealth Tax Act, 1957 (hereinafter called the Act), is amended from time to time by the annual Finance Act and other legislations pertaining to direct taxes. The law of wealth tax is stated here as applicable for the assessment year 1997-98. A set of Wealth Tax Rules also exists to enforce the provisions of the Act.

13.2.1 Persons Chargeable to Wealth Tax: Section 3 of the Act is the charging section. It provides for the levy of wealth tax for every assessment year in respect of net wealth, as on the valuation date, of individuals, Hindu undivided families, and all companies having net wealth exceeding ₹ 30 lakh. Wealth tax on companies was discontinued from the assessment year 1960-61. The Finance Act, 1983, however, revived the levy of wealth tax on closely-held companies from the assessment year 1984-85. The Finance Act, 1992, extended the scope of wealth tax to all companies.

13.2.2 Net Wealth and Residential Status: The wealth tax liability is affected by residence and citizenship of the assessee. In the case of an individual, the incidence of the tax depends upon his residential status and nationality. Thus, for an Indian citizen who is also 'resident' in India, the net wealth includes wealth in India as well as wealth outside India, but the foreign wealth is chargeable to wealth tax at half the average rate. However, if an Indian citizen is 'not ordinarily' resident, or is 'non-resident', the foreign wealth is completely exempt. In the case of an individual who is not a citizen of India, only his wealth in India is taxable. Furthermore, if the foreign national happens to be a non-resident, the wealth tax payable by him on his Indian wealth is reduced by 50 percent thereof (Section 6 of the Act). For the purpose of wealth tax, residential status is the same which an individual enjoys under the Income Tax Act.

13.2.3 Meaning of Net Wealth: Wealth tax in India is a levy made with reference to the net wealth which, as defined in Section 2(m) of the Act, broadly corresponds to the excess of assets over liabilities. It means provision is made for the deduction of debts from the assets owned by the assessee on the valuation date. All debts owned by the assessee, which have been incurred in relation to assets chargeable to tax, are deductible. As in the case of income tax, wealth tax is charged on a global basis, i.e. all pieces of wealth are pooled together and a flat rate tax is applied. In other words, all components of wealth tax are treated alike for the purpose of the tax.

Unlike income tax, there is no previous year for wealth tax. Wealth tax is imposed on net wealth possessed by an assessee on the valuation date and the value of his assets is determined as on that date. Valuation date means the last day of the previous year, i.e. March 31 [Section 2(q)]. For example, for the assessment year 2014-15, the valuation date will be March 31, 2014. Valuation of assets, for determining the net wealth of a taxpayer, is an important and difficult subject under the wealth tax law. Valuation is easy in the case of quoted shares and for assets like cash and bank balances. However, serious problems arise in most other cases partly because the value of assets changes from year to year. Under the Act, the value of an asset has been defined (Section 7) as the price it would fetch if sold in the open market on the valuation date. A wealth tax officer is empowered to make the estimate of market value subject to the various rules made in this regard. Since the tax is imposed on net wealth which represents the excess of assets over debts, it is necessary to understand the concepts of 'assets' and 'debts' as used in the Act.

13.2.4 Meaning of Assets: The term 'assets' has been described in Section 2(e) of the Act. The definition of 'assets' was drastically narrowed by the Finance Act, 1992. It means: (a) a guest house, (b) a residential (or commercial) house, (c) a farmhouse situated within 25 kilometres from the local municipal limits, (d) motor cars, (e) jewellery, bullion etc., (f) yachts, boats, and aircrafts, (g) urban land (of certain description), and (h) cash in hand in excess of ₹ 50,000.

It is noteworthy that the term 'assets' does not include, *inter alia*: (a) a house meant exclusively for residential purposes and allotted to a whole-time employee, (b) residential house, jewellery, bullion, motor cars used as stock-in-trade, and (c) yachts, boats, and aircrafts used for commercial purposes. In other words, assets held as stock-in-trade are not taxable.

From the assessment year 1997-98, commercial properties other than those occupied by the assessee for the purpose of any business or profession carried on by him have also been included in the term 'assets' and are consequently taxable.

13.2.5 Deemed Assets: As already noted, wealth tax is chargeable on the net wealth of an assessee. Ordinarily speaking, this would mean assets belonging to the assessee form part of his net wealth. However, the Act provides for the inclusion of certain assets in the net wealth of an individual though such assets do not legally belong to the individual on the valuation date. In other words, such assets are deemed to belong to the taxpayer. These provisions correspond to those contained in Section 64 of the Income Tax Act, 1961, which deals with the clubbing of income. The purpose of these provisions in both the cases is to check tax avoidance by the assessees. The following assets, *inter alia,* are included as belonging to the assessee while computing his net wealth (Section 4).

1. Assets held by the spouse of an individual where such assets have been transferred by the individual without adequate consideration.
2. Assets held by a minor child, not being a married daughter, of such individual. However, assets acquired by a minor child out of his income derived from manual work etc. are not included in the net wealth of his parent.
3. Assets held by a person to whom such assets have been transferred by the individual without adequate consideration for the immediate or deferred benefits of such individual, his or her spouse.
4. Assets held by a person to whom such assets have been transferred by an individual under a revocable transfer.
5. Assets held by an individual's son's wife to whom such assets have been transferred by such individual without adequate consideration.
6. Assets held by any person to whom such assets have been transferred by an individual for the benefit of his son's wife.
7. If an individual throws his self-acquired property into the common stock of the Hindu undivided family of which he is a member, the said property is included in his net wealth.
8. An individual, being a partner in a firm, may gift some money by crediting the amount in the account of the donee and by debiting his own account in the account books of the firm. In such cases, if the physical possession of the money is not given to the donee and the same continues to be invested in the business, and the gift is made only by making entries in the books of account without actually delivering the money to the donee, the value of such gift is included in the net wealth of the individual making the gift.

13.2.6 Assets Exempt from Wealth Tax: Section 5 of the Act provides for exemption of certain assets from the charge of wealth tax. Prior to the assessment year 1993-94, the list of exempted assets was quite lengthy and served to explain leakages in the base of wealth tax. The exempted assets were broadly divided into two categories: (a) assets which were totally exempt and therefore left out totally in computing the net wealth, and (b) assets which enjoyed only partial exemption. In the case of partial exemption, a ceiling was prescribed and the value of the assets in excess of the prescribed limit was included in the net wealth of the assessee for wealth tax purposes.

The Finance Act, 1992, drastically pruned the list of taxable assets for the purpose of wealth tax. Correspondingly, the list of exemptions/deductions allowable under Section 5 was also restricted. Thus, from the assessment year 1993-94, only the following assets are exempt from being included in the net wealth of an assessee:

1. Any property held by any assessee under trust for any public purpose of charitable or religious nature in India.
2. Interest of an assessee in the property of any Hindu undivided family of which he is a member. It may be noted that Hindu undivided family itself is liable to wealth tax.
3. Any one building in the occupation of an ex-ruler which is declared by the Government as his official residence.
4. Recognised heirloom jewellery of an ex-ruler.
5. Value of assets brought by persons of Indian origin.

13.2.7 Basic Exemption and Rate of Tax: Wealth tax liability is computed by applying the rate schedule to net wealth (i.e. taxable wealth). The rates of wealth tax are given in Schedule 1 of the Act. Till the financial year 2014-15, wealth tax was charged at the flat rate of 1 percent in the case of all assessees having taxable wealth exceeding ₹ 30 lakh.

13.3 Critical Comments

13.3.1 Shrinkage of Base: Prior to the enactment of the Finance Act, 1992, the term 'assets' as described in Section 2(e) included property of every description, movable and immovable, such as cash, bank balances, shares, jewellery, and other assets. The term 'assets' was of widest import and sufficiently comprehensive.

However, consequent upon the recommendations contained in the Interim Report of the Tax Reforms Committee, 1991, [3] the various provisions of the wealth tax law were drastically restructured by the Finance Act, 1992. The Committee had recommended that in order to encourage the taxpayers to invest in productive assets such as shares, securities, bonds, bank deposits, mutual funds etc., these financial assets should be exempted from wealth tax. Wealth tax should be levied on individuals, Hindu undivided families, and all companies only in respect of non-productive assets such as residential houses, jewellery, bullion, motor cars, yachts, and aircrafts which are not used for commercial purposes. Hence, the definition of the term 'assets' was significantly narrowed from the assessment year 1993-94. In short, the basis of taxation was shifted from wealth to unproductive assets. Following pressure that a residential house is a universal necessity and should not be subjected to tax, the Finance Act, 1993, exempted the value of one house from the levy of wealth tax.

13.3.2 Lowering of Top Marginal Rate: The maximum marginal rate of wealth tax, applicable to net wealth above ₹ 15 lakh, was quite high at 8 percent till the year 1975-76. It was drastically reduced to 2.5 percent the following year (1976-77). In a reversal of policy of low rates, it was increased to 3.5 percent in 1977-78, and further up to 5 percent in 1979-80. In 1985-86, it was again lowered to 2 percent and made applicable to net wealth over ₹ 20 lakh.

The Tax Reforms Committee, 1991, suggested that wealth tax should be charged at the flat rate of 1 percent with a basic exemption of ₹ 15 lakh instead of the then existing ₹ 5 lakh. These recommendations were accepted and incorporated in the Finance Act, 1992. The trends in the maximum marginal rate of wealth tax beginning with the year 1973-74 are given in Table 13.1.

Table 13.1: Trends in the Maximum Marginal Rate of Wealth Tax in India

Financial Year	Top Rate of Wealth Tax (percent)	Applicable to Net Wealth
1973-74 to 1975-76	8.0	Over ₹ 15 lakh
1976-77	2.5	Over ₹ 15 lakh
1977-78 and 1978-79	3.5	Over ₹ 15 lakh
1979-80 to 1984-85	5.0	Over ₹ 15 lakh
1985-86 to 1991-92	2.0	Over ₹ 20 lakh
1992-93 to 2008-09	Flat rate of 1 percent on wealth exceeding ₹ 15 lakh	
2009-10 to 2014-15	Flat rate of 1 percent on wealth exceeding ₹ 30 lakh	

Sources: Government of India, *Finance Acts* (various years).

In short, the scope of wealth tax, both in terms of base and rate, is very narrow. Presently, wealth tax has only decorative value for the statute book. In view of the meagre revenue and problems of administration and compliance, the Task Force on Direct Taxes (Chairman: Vijay Kelkar) recommended the abolition of wealth tax.

Wealth tax was abolished in the 2015-16 budget.

Endnotes

1. Nicholas Kaldor, *Indian Tax Reform: Report of a Survey* (Government of India, Ministry of Finance), 1956, p. 22.
2. Richard A. Musgrave and Peggy B. Musgrave, *Public Finance in Theory and Practice,* (McGraw-Hill, International Student Edition, 1980), p. 472.
3. Government of India, Ministry of Finance, *Interim Report of the Tax Reforms Committee,* (Chairman, Raja Chelliah), December, 1991, chapter 7.

14

Union Excise Duties

Excise duties [1] are an important source of indirect tax revenue for the Central Government. They are levied on a wide range of products of the industrial sector of the economy.

14.1 Constitutional Provisions

By virtue of powers vested in it under Entry 84 of List I (Union List) in the Seventh Schedule of the Constitution, the Central Government is authorised to impose, "duties of excise on tobacco and other goods manufactured or produced in India except: (a) alcoholic liquors for human consumption, and (b) opium, Indian-hemp and other narcotic drugs and narcotics, but including medicinal and toilet preparations containing alcohol or any substance included in sub-paragraph (b) of this entry". Excise duties on liquor and other narcotics are imposed by the State Governments under provisions of Entry 51 of List II (State List) in the Seventh Schedule. Duties of excise on medicinal and toilet preparations containing alcohol are levied by the Centre under Article 268 but they are collected and appropriated by the States within which they are leviable. These are levied by the Centre to ensure uniformity in their rate throughout the country.

Apart from allocating taxation powers, the Constitution also provides for the sharing of certain taxes between the Centre and the States. Prior to the Constitution (Eightieth Amendment) Act, 2000, excise duties belonged to the category of taxes which *may* be divided between the Centre and the States (Article 272) and the subject matter of this division fell within the purview of the Finance Commission [Article 280(3)(a)]. The sharing of excise duties was permissive and therefore the States did not enjoy a constitutional right to claim a share out of the revenues from Central excises. However, successive Finance Commissions took the view that permissive sharing, contemplated under Article 272 was not only justified but even necessary in view of the growing financial needs of the States. Therefore, ever since April 1, 1952, the States got a share of the proceeds of Central excises. The Tenth Finance Commission fixed this share at 47.5 percent for the quinquennium 1995-2000. However, the Constitution (Eightieth Amendment) Act, 2000 substituted a new Article for Article 270 under which States are now given a percentage share of all Central taxes and duties.

However, the surcharge levied for purposes of the Union under Article 271 is excluded from the divisible pool. Moreover, Article 272 of the Constitution was omitted by the same amendment.

14.2 Various Types of Excise Duties

In accordance with the provisions of the Constitution, various types of excise duties and cesses are imposed by the Union Government on commodities covered by the Central Excise Act, 1944 and other Acts. The important duties currently in operation are the following.

14.2.1 Basic Excise Duty: Levied under Section 3 of the Central Excise Act, 1944, this is the main duty commonly known as basic excise duty. This duty may be fixed with reference to the value, weight, volume, unit, length or area of the excisable goods. These details are given in the Schedule of the Central Excise Tariff Act, 1985.

14.2.2 Additional Duties in Lieu of Sales Tax: These duties are imposed under the Additional Duties of Excise (Goods of Special Importance) Act, 1957, which provides for the levy and collection of additional duties on sugar, tobacco, cotton fabrics, rayon or artificial silk fabrics and woollen fabrics produced or manufactured in India. These duties are in addition to the duties payable under the Central Excises and Salt Act, 1944, and replace, by agreement with State Governments, the sales tax levied by them on these commodities. The net proceeds from additional excise duties are distributable among the States in accordance with the principles of distribution formulated and the recommendations made by the Finance Commissions from time to time.

14.2.3 Cesses: These are levied under separate enactments on certain commodities and the revenue is earmarked for specific purposes. For example, handloom cess is levied on fabrics to raise funds for developing *khadi* and other handloom industries and for promoting the sale of *khadi* and other handloom cloth. Cesses are also levied under various Acts on tea, jute, indigenous crude oil, paper, sugar, *bidis*, automobiles, vegetable oils, and television sets.

The Central Excise Act, 1944, is the main enactment under which duties are levied on different commodities. Under Section 37 of this Act, a set of rules known as the Central Excise Rules, 1944, has been framed to implement the provisions of the Act. Another set of rules under the same section deals exclusively with the valuation of the excisable commodities and is known as Central Excise (Valuation) Rules, 1975. The Act and the Rules are amended from time to time. Broadly speaking, the Act embodies substantive law, and the Rules contain both substantive law and procedural matters.

Although the Central Government is empowered to levy duties on agricultural products also, it has refrained to do so in view of the administrative difficulties involved. Therefore, the excise system has remained confined mostly to the products of the industrial sector with the notable exceptions of tea and coffee.

14.3 Different Procedures to Collect Excises

Central excise duties are assessed and collected through a vast network of offices scattered all over the country. There are various procedures to assess and collect excise duties.

14.3.1 Physical Control System: This procedure, based on personal verification of production by excise officers, was the chief procedure to realise excise duties till it was replaced by a new system called self-removal procedure from June 1, 1968. Under the physical control method, excise control was exercised by the officers of the Excise Department who were posted at the factory to keep watch over the operations in the various departments of the factory to prevent illegal disposal of the manufactured articles. The physical control procedure was based on personal verification of production, storage, and clearance of excisable goods.

The manufacturers, however, were unhappy with this direct interference in the manufacturing process. Therefore, ever since Independence they had been demanding abolition of the physical control scheme and its replacement by a system based on audited accounts. The Taxation Enquiry Commission, 1953-54, favoured the retention of the physical control system. It observed, "It seems to us reasonable for the Government to ensure that for the period intervening between production and clearance the goods should be kept in a proper place and under adequate supervision. The procedure followed in India in this regard is also practically the same as that obtaining elsewhere. Physical supervision is considered to be necessary in such cases in almost every country". [2]. The organised sector, however, continued to build up pressure for the replacement of the physical control system and ultimately the self-removal procedure was introduced with effect from June 1, 1968. A few commodities are still subject to the physical control system including sugar, chewing tobacco, and matches.

14.3.2 Self-Removal Procedure (SRP): Under this liberal system, introduced in place of the physical control system, an assessee is allowed to take clearances on his own assessment of the duty liability without prior permission of physical checks by excise officers. This procedure is applicable to most of the commodities under the excise net. An assessee is, however, required to get his classification list approved by the excise authorities before effecting any removal. In the classification list the assessee details the description of the goods produced so that they may be categorised in terms of the rate of duty applicable to them. In case of *ad valorem* duties, the assessee is further required to submit a price list showing the prices charged along with discounts and deductions, if any. In essence, the SRP is a record-based system of duty collection relying on mutual trust and belief. Unfortunately, heavy evasion of excise duty has taken place under this scheme. Excise evasion under this liberal scheme is generally resorted to by following such malpractices as incorrect accounting of goods, undervaluation of goods, and flouting the conditions subject to which any goods may be exempted from duty.

14.3.3 Compounded Levy Scheme: This is another procedure for the benefit of small-scale sector and for administrative convenience. Levying of excise duties on small-scale sector has always remained a major problem of the Indian excise system. In many cases, small-scale sector accounts for a significant portion of the output of an industry and it becomes necessary to subject it to excise taxation. However, the procedures adopted for collection of excise from big firms have often been found expensive and time-consuming when applied to small firms. This has necessitated the adoption of special procedures suitable for small-scale sector.

Under the compounded levy scheme introduced in 1954, a lump sum payment is made on the basis of some installations, e.g. the number of looms in case of textile units. Once the compounded levy has been paid, the producer becomes free from all excise formalities except to maintain a record of looms in operation. The scheme is applicable at present to small units producing *khandasari* and cotton fabrics produced on powerlooms. This system affords considerable advantages to the small producers insofar as they are saved from the cumbersome normal excise procedures and also by the fact that the fiscal burden under compounded levy is generally lower than the burden under normal procedures.

14.4 New Excise Tariff Nomenclature

The year 1986 was a landmark in the evolution of excise taxation in India. In that year a new internationally accepted harmonised system of commodity classification was introduced in place of the then existing antiquated system introduced by the British. The history of excise tariff classification dates back to the year 1944 when the Central Excises and Salt Act was passed, consolidating separate enactments for different goods. This Act of 1944 covered 11 tariff items which were arranged in alphabetical order.

In 1960, the tariff items, the number of which had soared to 30, were rearranged in accordance with the sections of the Standard International Trade Classification (SITC). By 1986, the excise tariff schedule covered 137 tariff items and if account is taken of the sub-items, the number was well over 355 main classifications. The description of tariff commodities was based on the definitions of the Indian Standard Institution, and the descriptions and explanatory notes of the Customs Co-operation Council Nomenclature (CCCN). The domestic trade parlance was also relied upon.

On September 22, 1984, the Government set up a Technical Study Group to undertake a comprehensive review of the then existing tariff nomenclature. The Group drafted a comprehensive and elaborate tariff nomenclature broadly patterned on Harmonised System Nomenclature (HSN), fully corresponding up to 2-digit level (i.e. Chapter level) in respect of 82 of the effective 96 chapters in the HSN. It also suggested that the new tariff should be provided for by a separate Act to be called the Central Excise Tariff Act in place of the then existing system of tariff being governed by the First Schedule of the Central Excises and Salt Act, 1944.

The recommendation of the Technical Study Group as regards the new tariff nomenclature was accepted by the Government and a new Central Excise Tariff Act, 1985, was passed for the purpose. The excise tariff based on the internationally accepted harmonised commodity description and coding system came into effect from February 28, 1986, ushering a new era in excise taxation. The Schedule of the Central Excise Tariff Act, 1985, describes the excisable commodities and the rate of duty leviable on them. The new tariff is spread over 91 chapters and covers around 700 four-digit headings and 1,400 six-digit headings.

14.5 Administration of Excise Taxation

There is an elaborate administrative machinery for the collection of excise duties. At the apex level is the Central Board of Excise and Customs which is a statutory Board forming part of the Department of Revenue in the Ministry of Finance. The Board, consisting of a chairman and five members, is responsible for the proper collection of customs and Central excise duties, and framing and implementation of related fiscal policies under the control and direction of the Union Finance Minister.

At the field level, under the Central Board of Excise and Customs there are 34 Commissionerates of Central excise entrusted with the task of collecting Central excise duties. Each of the Commissionerates is headed by a Commissioner of Central Excise who is aided by a number of Additional Commissioners and Deputy Commissioners. A group of Commissionerates is headed by a Chief Commissioner.

For administrative convenience, each Commissionerate is divided into a number of divisions, each such division headed by an Assistant Commissioner. A division is further sub-divided into a number of ranges. Each range is headed by a Superintendent of Central Excise who in turn is assisted by a number of Inspectors.

In fact, the range is the basic unit in the administrative set up responsible for the proper assessment of Central excise duties and generation of the statistical information relating to revenue collection. The range is the primary unit which is in contact with the assessees and tries to ensure that the laws and procedures are properly followed by the production units.

To ensure that the goods are properly classified, assessable value correctly determined, and the duties correctly paid, each Commissionerate has an internal audit wing which is headed by an Additional Commissioner directly responsible to the Commissioner of Central Excise. The internal audit is in addition to the statutory audit conducted by the Comptroller and Auditor-General of India.

Each Commissionerate has an anti-evasion wing headed by an Additional Commissioner directly responsible to the Commissioner of Central Excise. The anti-evasion wing makes checks on the basis of intelligence and information to ensure that proper duties are paid and there is no evasion of duties or leakage of revenue. In some Commissionerates, there is a separate Commissioner to look after the judicial and adjudication work. There are Commissioners who attend to appeals against orders passed by officers lower in rank to them.

Moreover, a number of supportive organisations under the Central Board of Excise and Customs undertake work of a specialised nature. Thus, there is the Directorate of Inspection headed by a Chief Commissioner which undertakes the inspection of Central excise formations. The Directorate of Anti-Evasion has the responsibility to ensure all-India co-ordination of anti-evasion work. The National Academy of Customs, Excise and Narcotics is entrusted with the task of training officers. The Directorate of Publicity and Public Relations is responsible for printing and publicity. The Directorate of Statistics and Intelligence is responsible for compiling and updating statistical information.

14.6 Revenue Significance

In the post-Independence period, the relative share of excise duties in Central Government's tax collections has increased precipitously. In 1950-51, excise duties accounted for a modest 16.8 percent of the total Central tax collections: ₹ 68 crore out of ₹ 404 crore. Within a span of 20 years, the proportionate share shot up to 54.9 percent in 1970-71. It declined to 49.3 percent in 1980-81 and further down to 42.6 percent in 1990-91. It stood at 36.3 percent in 2000-01 and 17.4 percent in 2010-11. It was estimated at 15.9 percent in the budget for 2015-16 (Table 14.1). A Government document noted the following reasons for this downward trend, "The buoyancy of excise has suffered because of a variety of factors including numerous exemptions and concessions which have given rise to substantial administrative and legal complexities. Recent years have witnessed an unprecedented increase in litigation". [3]

Table 14.1: Trends in the Relative Significance of Union Excise Duties in Gross Tax Revenues* of the Central Government: Selected Years

(₹ crore)

Central taxes	1950-51	1960-61	1970-71	1980-81	1990-91	2000-01	2010-11	2015-16
A+B Gross tax revenues	404 (100.0)	888 (100.0)	3,206 (100.0)	13,179 (100.0)	57,576 (100.0)	1,88,603 (100.0)	7,93,072 (100.0)	14,49,490 (100.0)
A. Direct Taxes	174 (43.1)	290 (32.6)	870 (27.1)	3,004 (22.8)	11,025 (19.1)	68,306 (36.2)	4,45,962 (56.2)	7,97,995 (55.1)
B. Indirect taxes of which	229 (56.7)	599 (67.5)	2,337 (72.9)	10,175 (77.2)	46,552 (80.9)	1,20,297 (63.8)	3,47,110 (43.8)	6,51,495 (44.9)
Union excise duties	68 (16.8)	414 (46.6)	1,759 (54.9)	6,500 (49.3)	24,514 (42.6)	68,526 (36.3)	1,38,299 (17.4)	2,29,808 (15.9)

* Before transferring States' share in Central taxes; 2015-16 Budget estimates

Figures in parentheses are corresponding percentages of gross tax revenues.

Sources: Government of India, Ministry of Finance, *Explanatory Memorandum on the Budget of the Central Government* (various years); *Receipts Budget* (various years); and *Budget at a Glance*, 2015-16.

Although excise duties are imposed on a large number of commodities, a substantial proportion of revenue is derived from a limited number of items. These high revenue yielding commodities include iron and steel, motor spirit, tyres and tubes, cigarettes, cement, plastics and refined diesel oil. It is noteworthy that many of the high revenue yielding items are commodities of mass consumption and therefore the burden of excise duties falls on all sections of society.

14.7 Commodity Coverage

As already noted, excise taxation in India was fairly selective in terms of commodity coverage during the pre-Independence period. However, the need for resources required for planned economic development made it necessary to rely on excise taxation for additional funds. This was particularly so in view of the extremely narrow base for direct taxation and the dwindling relative revenue significance of customs duties owing to euphoria for import restrictions and substitution. The scope for extension of excise coverage improved considerably as development efforts were intensified for the production of industrial goods that enjoyed a relatively large and stable domestic market.

The Taxation Enquiry Commission (TEC), 1953-54, after having studied the then existing excise system, made important recommendations in terms of commodity coverage. It recommended the extension of excise coverage to sewing machines, vegetable oils, woollen textiles, biscuits, paper, dry batteries, electric lamps, aerated waters, electric fans, glass and glassware, paints and varnishes, and ceramics. In the opinion of the TEC these industries had developed sufficiently as a result of protection and it was necessary to impose excises on them to raise the much needed revenue for financing development programmes.

Consequent upon the recommendations of the TEC, the history of excise taxation in India since 1954 is one of increasing commodity coverage. Cement, footwear, rayon or artificial silk fabrics, and soap were added to the excise system in 1954. In 1955, excise duties were imposed on paints and varnishes, paper, woollen fabrics, electric batteries, electric light bulbs, and electric fans. In 1956, the excise net was extended to vegetable non-essential oils, rayon or synthetic fibres and yarn, and motor cars.

With the start of production of diesel oil and other fuel oils at the new refineries in Bombay, excise duty was imposed on a variety of petroleum products for the first time in 1956. These included refined diesel oil, diesel oil, and furnace oil. In 1959, excise duties were imposed on asphalt, bitumen, and tar.

The early 1960s witnessed another big expansion in the coverage of excise taxation in India. In 1960, eleven additional goods were subjected to excise duties including aluminium, pig iron, silk fabrics, and motor vehicles. In 1962, the number of additional products brought under the excise system was sixteen and included, *inter alia*, soda ash, caustic soda, cosmetics and toilet preparations, glass and glassware, copper and copper alloys etc. In 1962, ten more products including gases, rubber products, plywood, jute manufactures, and iron and steel products were covered under the excise net.

In 1968, duties were imposed on radio-parts, steel furniture, leather cloth, and chocolates. The biggest expansion was witnessed in 1971 when 25 additional products including linoleum, ready-made garments, vacuum flasks, and pressure cookers were brought under the excise net. The process of covering more and more items under the excise system reached its pinnacle when Tariff Item No. 68 was introduced in 1975. Tariff Item No. 68 was a catch-all item which encompassed all goods not elsewhere specified in the excise tariff. This residual tariff item was abolished with the introduction of a harmonised system of commodity classification introduced from February 28, 1986. The large assortment of commodities under this head got scattered under proper heads in the new nomenclature of excise tariff.

The Tax Reforms Committee, 1991, identified many items which are currently outside the excise net but which could be considered for levying excise duty. Some of the identified items are: butter and cheese, skimmed milk powder, spices, fertilisers, feature films, wood pulp, umbrellas, bicycles, toys and sports goods, buttons, and vacuum flasks.

14.8 Excise Tariff Structure

Once the commodities for excise taxation are identified, the next step is to formulate a tariff structure for various commodities. The nature of excise tariff and the issues related to its rationalisation are now described.

14.8.1 Statutory versus Effective Rates: Rates of excise duty approved by the Parliament are termed as statutory or tariff rates. However, the Government enjoys the power to exempt, by notification, any excisable goods from the whole or any part of duty leviable on such goods. In exercise of this power, the Government determines and notifies from time to time the effective rates of duty. The rationale for granting such powers to the executive is that during the period intervening two consecutive budgets, necessary adjustments might be made to regulate exports, consumption, and prices of different commodities. However, the delegation of this power to the executive has led to frequent changes in excise rates, creating an unsettling atmosphere for trade and industry and problems for the administration.

Moreover, since the notifications are technically not rules, there is no obligation to place them on the table of the House. Consequently, the Parliament does not always have the information on the variations made in the rates approved by it. The determination of the operative or effective rates of duty by executive decisions leads to abridgement of Parliamentary control over the excise system. Duty changes should be discussed and legislated in sessions of Parliament which are held regularly at short intervals.

Under the Central Excise Tariff Act, 1985, the Government is empowered to enhance the rates of duty specified in the Schedule of the Act through notifications. The increase of duty is subject to certain limits and such powers are exercised only in emergent circumstances. The notifications bringing into force such increases are subject to approval by the Parliament. The said limits are: (a) in case where the rate of duty immediately before the issue of notification is nil, a rate of duty not exceeding 50 percent *ad valorem* may be specified, and (b) in any other case, the increase in the rate of duty shall not be more than twice the rate of duty in force immediately before the issue of notification.

14.8.2 Specific versus *Ad Valorem* Duties [4]: In the early days of the excise system of independent India, the emphasis was on specific rates due to administrative reasons. However, the emphasis shifted to *ad valorem* rates when the economy started experiencing frequent spells of inflation. The 1970s saw a big shift from specific rates of duty to *ad valorem* rates. While introducing the change in the 1969-70 budget, the Finance Minister observed, "...*ad valorem* duties are more rational than specific duties whose incidence declines during periods of rising prices and increases when prices fall. *Ad valorem* duties can also act as a spur to reduction in costs and prices". [5] He converted the then existing specific rates into *ad valorem* rates on cement, vegetable products, electric fans, lighting tubes and bulbs, soaps, soda, and sodium silicate. The change of duties on paper and cotton fabrics into *ad valorem* tax was effected in 1976 and on paints, varnishes, radios, and tape recorders in 1977.

However, beginning with the 1980s, the tendency to shift to *ad valorem* rates was not only halted but reversed in view of an unprecedented spurt in litigation which mainly pertained to disputes over classification and valuation of goods for purposes of excise levies. As a measure to combat tax avoidance and evasion, the basis of duty was changed from *ad valorem* to *ad valorem*-cum-specific rate or specific rate on a number of commodities. Important commodities where the shift took place (with year of change given in brackets) were: flat glass, aluminium metal (1982), paper, aerated waters, motor cars, cigarettes, sugar (1983), paper boards, tyres for buses and trucks (1984), gases, tubes and flaps of tyres, and colour television sets (1985).

The Technical Study Group on Central Excise Tariff, 1985, made estimates of the relative revenue significance of various forms of excise duty. The share of specific duties (including the specific component of *ad valorem*-cum-specific duties) was estimated at ₹ 8,242.91 crore or 66.7 percent of the total estimated excise revenue of ₹ 12,361.35 crore for the year 1985-86. The rest of the revenue was attributable to *ad valorem* duties. Broadly speaking, specific duties accounted for two-thirds of the revenue and the *ad valorem* duties for the remaining one-third. [6]

The balance further tilted in favour of specific duties as the policy of conversion from *ad valorem* rates to specific rates continued right up to 1990-91. In this connection, the Tax Reforms Committee, 1991, observed, "As a result of this gradual shift to more and more specific rates over the years, the share of revenue from specific-rated items has increased from a level of about 46 percent of the total revenue in 1981-82 to 65 percent in 1986-87 and has currently (presumably 1990-91) reached a level of about 70 percent". [7] The Committee examined the advantages and disadvantages of *ad valorem* and specific rates of duty and concluded, "the advantages of having *ad valorem* duties far outweigh the administrative benefits derived by switching over to specific duties. In a system of comprehensive taxation with a wide coverage of Modvat, it would be necessary to have by and large only *ad valorem* duties in order to ensure a rational system of taxation". [8] Following the recommendations of the Committee, a modest switch over to *ad valorem* rates was made in the 1992-93 budget.

At present, important commodities which bear wholly specific rates of duty are cigarettes, coffee, tea, sugar, beverages, mineral fuels, mineral oils, silk, man-made staple fibres, and iron and steel. *Ad valorem* rates of duty predominate for commodities including organic chemicals, pharmaceutical products, leather, footwear, ceramic products, tools and implements, machinery and mechanical appliances, electrical machinery and equipment, and miscellaneous manufactured articles. A few commodities, viz. cotton fabrics, paper and paper boards, are subject to *ad valorem*-cum-specific rates of duty.

14.8.3 Multiplicity of Excise Tariff: The excise rate structure is provided by the Schedule of the Central Excise Tariff Act, 1985, which includes goods ranging from toys to nuclear reactors. The Schedule is divided into 20 sections covering 96 chapters. Goods falling under each chapter are divided and sub-divided into numerous headings and sub-headings. The statutory rate of duty applicable in respect of each item is shown against the appropriate commodity heading/sub-heading. These statutory rates are modified, if necessary, by Government notifications to determine effective rates of duty.

Prior to tax reforms initiated in 1991, excise taxation in India was an interesting example of the multitude of rates which were subject to frequent revisions. Numerous considerations contributed to the complexity of excise rates. The labyrinthine intricacies of the tariff often led to confusion and litigation amongst the taxpayers and revenue authorities.

Commodities such as sewing machines, water coolers, and bicycles, though on the tariff list, were completely exempt from the payment of duty. However, a host of other commodities were subject to a wide amplitude of excise rates. The rate of duty on necessities of life like food products (cheese, butter, vegetable oils), pharmaceutical products, and footwear ranged from 10 to 15 percent *ad valorem*. Rates of excise duty on semi-luxuries like washing machines, tape recorders, refrigerators, and colour televisions ranged from 25 percent to 40 percent *ad valorem*. Luxury items like cosmetics and air-conditioners suffered a high rate of duty ranging from 100 to 110 percent.

Most capital goods, classified under chapter 84 of excise tariff, were subject to duty ranging from 15 to 20 percent *ad* valorem. Some important items under this category were machine tools, cranes, agricultural machinery, textile machinery, printing machinery, calculating machines, automatic data processing machines, and other office machines.

Tobacco items were, and continue to be, conspicuous by high rates of duty. Successive upward revision of excise duty on cigarettes has all along remained a notable feature of tobacco tariff in India. Upward revision of excise duty on cigarettes is almost an annual feature. No surprise that the commodity has earned such nicknames as *annual hardy, old faithful* etc. In the 1997-98 budget, excise duty on various categories of cigarettes was increased ranging from ₹ 20 to ₹ 70 per thousand.

Broadly speaking, necessities of life were either exempt or paid a low rate of duty, semi-luxuries were moderately taxed, and luxuries and tobacco products stood out distinctly as high-rated tariff items. Capital goods were subject to a relatively low rate of duty.

14.8.4 Committee on Rationalisation and Simplification of Tax Structure (Chairman: S. Bhoothalingam), 1968: In 1968, the Government of India appointed Mr. S. Bhoothalingam to examine the structure of direct and indirect taxes in India. In his report he recommended, *inter alia*, a general excise duty at the rate of 10 percent *ad valorem* on all manufactured products. [9] However, this recommendation was not accepted by the Government.

14.8.5 Indirect Taxation Enquiry Committee (Chairman: L.K. Jha), 1978: The problem of multiplicity of rates was also considered by the Indirect Taxation Enquiry Committee, 1978 which recommended a set of four excise rates. The Committee observed, "Instead of a pattern of which some product groups are very heavily taxed while others have remained either totally exempt or have been taxed at very low rates, the attempt should be to tax all consumer products, including those now falling under Tariff Item No. 68, at rates of 10, 20, 30 or 40 percent (cumulative), though some exceptional products may need to be taxed at lower or higher rates on special consideration". [10]

By suggesting a 10 to 40 percent range, the Committee virtually favoured a ceiling on excise rates. The Government disfavoured any drastic regrouping of the then existing rates. In his 1979-80 budget speech the Finance Minister observed, "A major restructuring of the excise tariff has to be ruled out in view of the need for resources and on other pragmatic considerations. Also, there is reason to apprehend that a major departure from the present pattern of excise taxation may upset the balance between different sectors of production". [11]

14.8.6 Technical Study Group on Excise Tariff (Chairman: J. Dutta), 1985: The Technical Study Group on Central Excise Tariff, 1985, also favoured a drastic reduction in the number of duty rates to simply duty collection and compliance. The group recommended a band of five duty rates: middle rate, two rates below it and two above. Besides this, it also suggested a *zero rate* category. The middle rate (M) was defined to represent overall average incidence of excise duties. The two rates below this middle rate (L1 and L2) were suggested for adoption for inputs and important items of real mass consumption. The two rates in the upper scale (H1 and H2) could be applied to a few inputs, consumer durables and items consumed largely by the rich. The *zero rate* was recommended for products which deserve exceptional treatment on economic or social or administrative considerations.

The Group attempted only a broad and vague exercise of rate levels in terms of middle, below the middle, and above the middle rates of duty without specifying, even on a tentative basis, the duty rates in numerical terms. By leaving the actual fixation of rates to fiscal authorities, the Group left the exercise wide open.

The Finance Minister announced, in his 1997-98 budget speech, three new rates of excise duty, namely 8 percent, 13 percent and 18 percent. He was of the view that eventually the excise rate should gravitate towards a mean rate of 18 percent.

14.8.7 Triple Rate Excise Structure: Multiple rates of commodity taxes have long been considered a weakness of the indirect tax system of India. Admitting the problems created by the multiplicity of rates, the Finance Minister in his 1999-2000 budget speech observed, "The multiple rates of indirect tax are generally recognised to be a major source of misclassification, tax evasion and avoidance and cumbersome litigation. The multiplicity also encourages inefficient allocation of resources. Over a 100 countries in the world now enjoy the benefits of a value added tax (VAT) with very small number of rates in each case". [12]

Thus, in a landmark move, the Finance Minister announced in his 1999-2000 budget a triple rate excise structure. In other words, the then existing 11 major ad valorem rates were reduced to 3, viz. a central rate of 16 percent, a merit rate of 8 percent and a demerit rate of 24 percent. This was done by: (a) merging the existing rates of 5 percent, 10 percent and 12 percent into the existing 8 percent rate, (b) creating a new rate of 16 percent by merging the existing 13 percent, 15 percent and 18 percent rates into it, and (c) fixing a new rate of 24 percent in substitution of the existing rate of 25 percent. The initiative of the Finance Minister to rationalise the rate structure of excise system was widely appreciated.

The standard rate of excise duty (CENVAT) which was brought down to 8 percent after two successive reductions in December 2008 and February 2009 was increased to 10 percent in the Budget for 2010-11. It was further increased to 12 percent in the Budget for 2012-13 and remained the same for the financial year 2013-14 and 2014-15. As part of the movement towards Goods and Services Tax (GST), the Finance Minister in his 2015-16 budget subsumed the education cess and the secondary and higher education cess in central excise duty. Thus, the general rate of excise duty became 12.5 percent.

14.8.8 Task Force on Indirect Taxes (Chairman: Vijay Kelkar), 2002: The Task Force on Indirect Taxes recommended the following excise duty structure (Table 14.2).

As regards duty exemption for the small scale sector, the Task Force on Indirect Taxes recommended as under:

- Duty exemption should be extended to only small units with a turnover of ₹ 50 lakh.
- Duty exemption limit for the larger SSI units should be gradually brought down to ₹ 50 lakh as per the following time frame: from ₹ 100 lakh to ₹ 75 lakh by the year 2004-05 and from ₹ 75 lakh to ₹ 50 lakh by the year 2005-06.

Table 14.2: Central Excise Duty Structure Recommended by the Task Force on Indirect Taxes

0 percent	For life-saving drugs and equipments, security items, food items, necessities and the like, and agricultural products.
6 percent	For processed food products and matches.
14 percent	Standard rate for all items not mentioned against other rates.
20 percent	For motor vehicles, air-conditioners and aerated water.
Separate rates for tobacco products and their substitutes (like pan masala)	

Source: Government of India, Ministry of Finance and Company Affairs, *Report of the Task Force on Indirect Taxes*, December 2002, p. 181.

14.9 Excises on Inputs

One perennial problem of the Indian excise system has been the taxation of inputs (raw materials, components, and other intermediates) and the resulting cascading effect on the prices of final products. Prior to the Second Five Year Plan (1956-61), excise coverage was limited to consumer goods with the notable exception of steel ingots. However, the need for additional resources for successive Plans necessitated extension of the excise net to capital goods and raw materials. Various inputs like internal combustion engines, aluminium, cotton yarn, woollen yarn, fertilisers, chemicals, were, and continue to be, within the excise ambit. The disadvantages of input excises are well-known. [13] However, levies on inputs form an integral part of the excise system in India for reasons of sheer administrative convenience.

14.9.1 Pre-MODVAT Arrangements: Prior to the introduction of MODVAT in 1986, there were provisions in the Central Excises and Salt Rules, 1944, under which certain inputs were exempted from taxation to minimise the cumulative effect of excise levies. Thus, Rule 56-A of the said Rules, introduced in 1962, allowed the manufacturers of certain notified finished excisable goods to bring excise-paid components (for example compressors for refrigerators) to take credit for the said duty in the Proforma Credit Account to get adjustment of duty on the final excisable good.

The Indirect Taxation Enquiry Committee, 1978, which made an in-depth study of the cascading effect of input excises, recommended a wider extension of Rule 56-A to products falling under different tariff items. The same Committee recommended also the introduction of value added tax (VAT) at the manufacturing stage, called MANVAT, to tackle the problem of cascading effect of excise taxation.

The Long Term Fiscal Policy (December 1985) also envisaged the extension of the Proforma Credit Scheme and observed, "The basic approach will be to move towards an extension of the present system of proforma credit to all excisable commodities with the exception of a few like petroleum, tobacco, and textile products. This programme would amount to a modified system of VAT or MODVAT for short. The programme will be implemented in a phased manner over a period of years, taking due account of the revenue implications, the need to revise administrative procedures and the lessons from experience gained in the early stages of the reform". [14] In pursuance of the proposal made in the Long Term Fiscal Policy Statement, the Government introduced a modified system of value added tax or MODVAT with effect from March 1, 1986.

14.9.2 MODVAT Scheme: The features and advantages of MODVAT scheme are explained below.

A. Features: MODVAT scheme provides for instant and complete reimbursement of excise duty and additional duty of customs (countervailing duty) paid on the components and raw materials when used in the manufacture of the final products. Articles which are not used as inputs in the manufacturing process are not eligible for credit under this scheme.

Initially, the MODVAT scheme covered 38 chapters of the schedule to the Central Excise Tariff Act, 1985. These chapters pertained to the products of chemical and allied industries, paints and packaging materials, plastics, glass and glassware, rubber products, base metals and articles of base metals, machinery and mechanical appliances including electrical equipment, motor vehicles, and certain miscellaneous manufactured products. The scheme was extended to all the remaining chapters (except those relating to textiles, tobacco, and the petroleum sector) in 1987. The extension covered food products, mineral products, leather and travel goods, footwear, paper and paper-board, wood and cork products, asbestos cement products, and precious metals. As long as the inputs and the final products are covered by the specified chapters, credit of duty on inputs is available. In 1994, MODVAT scheme was extended to tobacco, fibres, yarn and fabrics, and petroleum products (excluding motor spirit and high speed diesel oil) used as input. The features of the MODVAT scheme are as follows.

1. The credit under MODVAT is available to a manufacturer of a final product only if the final product is dutiable. Where the final product manufactured by

a manufacturer is exempt from excise duty then no credit of the duty paid on the inputs is available. Credit is allowed only after the evidence of payment of duty has been received by the Department.

2. Where the same input is used for different finished products, some of which are not dutiable, the credit of duty is allowed only for that part attributable to inputs which are used for the manufacture of dutiable finished products.
3. The credit of the duty paid on the inputs under the MODVAT scheme may be utilised for payment of duty on the final products in which the inputs are used.
4. Under the MODVAT scheme, credit of duty is not restricted to raw materials and components only but covers all specified inputs which are used in the manufacture of final products.
5. Machines, plant, equipments, apparatus, tools or appliances used in the manufacture of the final products are not covered by the term 'inputs' for the purpose of MODVAT benefits.
6. Under the MODVAT scheme, inputs may be either procured from outside or manufactured within the factory. In either case, the duty credit would be available to the extent of duty actually paid.

The Government had made it clear in its Long Term Fiscal Policy that the proposed MODVAT scheme was to be broadly revenue-neutral. Thus, along with the introduction of MODVAT which considerably reduced the cost of final products, the rates of duty on final products were suitably revised upwards by the Finance Act, 1986, to retain the collection of excise duties at the earlier level. This was justified on grounds of resource mobilisation for the Plans.

B. Advantages: MODVAT scheme is claimed to have the following advantages:

1. It aims at making excise levies transparent so that the effective rate of taxation on a particular commodity can be known. This information will be helpful in undertaking meaningful studies of excise incidence. The results of these studies may be used to control excise burden on different commodities to ensure the desired degree of progressivity in the excise levies.
2. It seeks to avoid cascading effects associated with a traditional turnover tax. In particular, it will work as a cost-saving device through the availability of instant credit of the duties paid on the inputs and the consequent reduction of the interest costs.
3. MODVAT scheme will improve the competitive strength of the small-scale sector by allowing credit of duty which may be in excess of the duty actually paid on the inputs made by the small-scale units.
4. MODVAT scheme is claimed to encourage indigenisation because full set off

is available when indigenous inputs are used. However, no credit of basic and auxiliary customs duties is permissible on imported materials and components. Although MODVAT scheme provides for set off of countervailing duty [15], this element of import duty is not very significant in comparison with other elements of import duty viz. basic and auxiliary duties. As the scope of MODVAT is widened, the process of indigenisation would gather momentum.

5. MODVAT scheme is designed to encourage exports by making them more competitive in the international market. Since MODVAT allows set off through different stages of production, the final duty becomes clear on final goods which can be exported without payment of duty under bond. The payment of duty drawback will be swifter in view of the transparency of excise duty.
6. It is claimed that MODVAT will check excise evasion because credit of input duty cannot be claimed unless actual production is declared to the excise authorities.
7. MODVAT scheme will also help reduce the number of disputes, arising on account of classifications requiring lower or higher rates of duty, because the duty element on a large number of components will become irrelevant for manufacturers in view of set off. Previously, a selective set off triggered disputes as regards the eligibility of an input for set off. The introduction of Harmonised System Nomenclature will further reduce the scope for ambiguities.

Some experts feel that MODVAT is old wine in a new bottle because the facility under it is practically the same as was and is still available under Rule 56-A. In other words, MODVAT scheme is only an extension and liberalisation of the proforma credit facility in operation for the last three decades. Though some degree of similarity does exist, the two schemes cannot be termed identical. Rule 56-A scheme was restrictive and had several procedural formalities, e.g. a manufacturer had to intimate the Excise Department about the arrival of input materials for verification by the excise officials. Moreover, it was applicable on a commodity-to-commodity basis and involved discretion in taking decisions. MODVAT scheme is more comprehensive and rule-based and therefore curtails the discretionary powers of the Excise Department. MODVAT credit on inputs can be availed on the basis of a duplicate copy of the invoice.

The Tax Reforms Committee, 1991, examined, *inter alia,* the scope of extending the MODVAT scheme and observed, "there is no alternative to gradually transforming the present excise tax system, consisting of two parts, namely: (a) MODVAT, and (b) excise on gross value basis with no set off for some sectors, into a genuine VAT at the manufacturing level. Manufacturing and such a VAT should include also the 'manufacture' of services although some services may be exempted on practical considerations". [16]

14.9.3 Introduction of CENVAT: In his 1999-2000 budget, the Finance Minister had introduced three ad valorem rates of basic excise duty, namely 8 percent, 16 percent and 24 percent. Furthering the reform of excise taxation, the 2000-01 budget introduced a single rate Central Value Added Tax (CENVAT) by converging the three ad valorem rates to a single rate of 16 percent. The 8 percent excise rate was abolished and most of the items under it were moved to 16 percent rate. Similarly, items that were mainly in the nature of raw materials or intermediates were moved from the 24 percent rate to 16 percent CENVAT.

However, in addition to the 16 percent CENVAT rate, three rates of special excise, viz. 8 percent, 16 percent, and 24 percent were introduced. While the CENVAT rate is modvatable, the special excise duties are not, i.e. users cannot avail of MODVAT credit of these duties. Some of the commodities on which special excise duties apply include white cement, glazed tiles, cosmetics, air conditioners, aerated water and chewing tobacco. Since these commodities are not in the nature of inputs therefore they are not modvatable.

MODVAT scheme (rechristened as CENVAT scheme) was further expanded and rationalised in the sense that now all inputs (excepting high speed diesel oil and petrol) and all capital goods are included in the eligible list of MODVAT scheme. However, the availability of MODVAT credit on capital goods is spread over a period of two years.

Underlining the significance of CENVAT, the Finance Minister observed that it would eliminate disputes pertaining to classification of goods and remove uncertainties in the minds of producers. He hoped that the establishment of CENVAT would encourage the State Governments to implement their agreed programme for converting their sales tax into VAT by April 1, 2001.

It is noteworthy that under the Constitution, the Central Government is empowered to impose excise duty on goods produced or manufactured. It has no power to carry forward the tax up to the retail stage. Thus, CENVAT is a kind of VAT at the manufacturing stage. In any case, it has paved the way for a national VAT.

14.9.4 Further Simplification: In his 2001-02 budget, the Finance Minister reduced the three rates of special excise duty to a single rate of 16 percent. In other words, the 8 percent and 24 percent rates of special excise duty were abolished. Some of the items which bear 16 percent basic rate of CENVAT plus 16 percent special duty (32 percent total duty) include aerated soft drinks, soft drink concentrates and motor cars).

Following these measures, about 80 percent of the revenue in respect of ad valorem duties comes from the single rate of 16 percent and about 17 percent from the combined rate of 32 percent. [17] Feeling satisfied after completing the task of excise rate rationalisation, the Finance Minister remarked, "...in the matter of rates of duties of excise, I have almost achieved the ultimate with only one basic rate of CENVAT and one rate of special excise duty". [18] Undoubtedly, the Government has provided a stable excise system to create confidence among the entrepreneurs, particularly the prospective ones, so that they may plan their investment and production without the Damocles sword of excise changes hanging over their heads.

14.10 Exemptions and Concessions

14.10.1 Rationale: As in other countries, exemptions and concessions are an integral part of the Indian excise system. Excise preferences and reliefs are given to promote a wide spectrum of socio-economic objectives. If judiciously used, such tax preferences can become an effective tool of economic change on desired lines. The rationale for excise preferences is as follows.

1. Exemptions and concessions are necessary to ensure progressivity in the structure of commodity taxation.
2. Excise preferences are justified to induce entrepreneurs to undertake activities which they would otherwise shirk, e.g. adopting labour-intensive techniques of production. Concessions are designed to promote enterprises deemed *vital* by society though it is controversial as to which activities are *vital* and require governmental support.
3. Exemptions/concessions provide the desired flexibility to the tax system to deal with changing market situation. They are used as a corrective mechanism to stabilise demand, production, and profits of different industries. Due to continuous diversification of the economy and inflation, markets for various commodities have not remained stable in India after Independence. Because of the changing market conditions, the levels of profit in different industries have also been fluctuating and on balance have shown a rising trend. Excise rates, it may be argued, should be modified upward to mop up excess profits and downward to boost sluggish demand for idle-capacity industries.
4. Exemptions may be granted on administrative considerations. The duty on unmanufactured tobacco was abolished in 1979 mainly on account of the administrative difficulty of assessing and collecting duty from a large number of growers, and curers. Similarly, exemption of smaller of the small industries is also due to administrative problems. Agricultural products are also exempt owing to the same reason.

14.10.2 Problems Created by Concessions: The desirability of excise preferences is to be viewed against problems created by them.

1. Excise concessions narrow the tax base and therefore shrink governmental revenues.
2. Excise concessions interfere with the designing of the excise system and lead to complexities in the excise law which in turn may lead to tax evasion and litigation.
3. They also obscure the evaluation of excise system, particularly from equity angle.
4. Excise concession to a particular industry may lead to a chain reaction, i.e. similar demands by other industries, causing unsettling effects on producers, consumers, and the administration. Exemptions/concessions are often the result of persistent representations and pressure tactics by industry and trade than any economic justification.
5. It is not always possible to segregate the effects of duty reduction on production, costs, prices, and consumption because duty concessions operate in conjunction with other non-tax policy measures to affect the production process.

14.10.3 General Exemptions: There are various general exemptions which purport to serve a wide variety of socio-economic objectives. Thus, goods of the following description are exempt from the whole of the duty of excise leviable thereon.

1. All excisable goods, produced in a technical, educational and research institute during the course of imparting technical training of an academic or vocational nature.
2. All excisable goods donated for the welfare of defence personnel.
3. All excisable goods donated to the National Defence Fund or to the Ministry of Defence.
4. Excisable goods, supplied as stores for consumption on board a vessel of the Indian navy.
5. All excisable goods sent abroad as exhibits in any international trade fair or exhibition.

Apart from these general exemptions, excise tariff is extensively used to serve a host of other objectives including export promotion, industrial development, and mopping up a part of high profits earned by certain industries. Excise exemptions and concessions are particularly important in promoting labour-intensive technology and small-scale industries. Central excise law contains provisions the sole objective of which is employment generation. Products of a number of industries are exempt from excise duty if they are manufactured without the aid of power. Duty differentials have been used to discourage mechanisation in certain industries.

Similarly, concessions are available to the handloom sector of the textile industry. Processed *khadi* cloth woven on handloom wholly from hand spun cotton yarn or in admixture with similar silk and/or woollen yarn enjoys full exemption since 1969. Cotton fabrics manufactured on handlooms and processed by a factory owned by a registered handloom co-operative society enjoy full exemption from duty.

The Expert Committee on Tax Measures to Promote Employment, 1980, made estimates of the annual cost of protecting or subsidising employment through concessions in excise duties. It found that the annual cost of protecting or subsidising employment through concessions in excise duties was ₹ 523 per full-time worker in the handloom industry, ₹ 881 in *khandasari*, and ₹ 2,669 in the cottage sector of the match industry. [19]

14.10.4 Concessions to Small Industries: In line with Government's policy of encouraging small-scale industries, a wide range of concessions and exemptions from excise duty is available to small producers to enable them to stand in competition with large-scale manufacturers. Also, relatively simple and concessional procedures are followed for the assessment and collection of excises from the small-scale sector. As a part of the Comprehensive Policy Package on SSI and Tiny Sector announced by the Prime Minister on August 30, 2000, the excise exemption limit for SSI was raised from ₹ 50 lakh to ₹ 1 crore with effect from September 1, 2000.

14.10.5 Misuse of Concessions: Though preferential treatment to small units and labour-intensive methods of production is desirable, the misuse of these concessions has created doubts as regards the ultimate beneficiaries of such facilities. Concerned about the misuse of excise concessions, the Finance Minister in his 2001-2002 budget speech announced the withdrawal of exemption on certain items and observed, "Products of SSI are exempt from excise duty up to ₹ 1 crore. This exemption is intended to provide fiscal support to the genuinely small producers. I propose to withdraw this exemption in respect of the following items, in which misuse of the exemption is more than likely: (a) cotton yarn, (b) ball or roller bearings, and (c) arms and ammunition for private use". [20]

It has now been well-established that certain products, particularly footwear, domestic electrical appliances, electronic goods, and wires and cables are purchased on a fairly large scale by established concerns from the exempted sector and marketed in the brand names of such concerns. However, under the present scheme introduced in 1986, a small-scale manufacturer of excisable goods is allowed to clear his goods with the brand name of another manufacturer and is eligible for exemption for such clearances. It is clear that small producers depend heavily on private marketing organisations to sell their products and this dependence needs to be reduced by strengthening and building up co-operatives and other officially sponsored marketing organisations to market the products of small sector. This seems to be one way out of the existing dilemma.

Endnotes

1. For historical evolution of excise duties in India, see section 2.3 of chapter 2 of this book.
2. Government of India, Ministry of Finance, *Report of the Taxation Enquiry Commission,* (Chairman: John Matthai), 1953-54, Vol. II, p. 323.
3. Government of India, *Long Term Fiscal Policy*, 1985, p. 25.
4. Excises are levied in specific and/or *ad valorem* forms. A specific or volumetric duty represents a fixed amount of tax on a unit of the physical quantity of the product. This type of duty is generally preferred for commodities the classifications and sub-classifications of which are not numerous, i.e. the commodity is standardised, e.g. sugar. Specific duties are easy to apply and have the political and psychological advantages of obscuring the actual ratio of the tax to the selling price. They are, however, price-neutral, i.e. price changes, if any, in the product do not affect the revenue yield. Specific duties are quality-neutral also unless differential rates are prescribed with reference to the quality of the product.
   Ad valorem duties are imposed as a fixed percentage of the price of the product taxed. They are preferred when a commodity has many classifications and sub-classifications, e.g. textiles. *Ad valorem* duties are responsive to price changes and thus help maintain the proportion of taxes in national income. The main problem in applying *ad valorem* rates is the determination of the tax base, i.e. valuation of production.
5. Government of India, Ministry of Finance, *Speeches of Union Finance Ministers, 1947-48 to 1984-85*, p. 313.
6. Government of India, Ministry of Finance, *Report of the Technical Study Group on Central Excise Tariff,* Part I, 1985, Table 6, p. 7.
7. Government of India, Ministry of Finance, *Interim Report of the Tax Reforms Committee,* (Chairman: Raja Chelliah), 1991, p. 113.
8. *Ibid.,* p.114.
9. Government of India, Ministry of Finance, *Final Report on Rationalisation and Simplification of Tax Structure,* (Chairman: S. Bhoothalingam), 1968, p. 8.
10. Government of India, Ministry of Finance, *Report of the Indirect Taxation Enquiry Committee,* (Chairman: L.K. Jha), Part II, 1978, p. 174.
11. *Speeches of Union Finance Ministers,* op. cit., p. 459.
12. Government of India, Ministry of Finance, *Budget Speech of the Finance Minister*, 1999-2000, Part B, p. 21.
13. Excises on inputs enhance costs and profits and therefore increase the prices of goods much more than the amount of excise collected. The cost of production increases because producers and middlemen require larger amounts of working capital to maintain the necessary stocks of inputs. Prices of finished products tend to reflect taxes imposed on inputs used. If the middlemen apply fixed percentage mark ups to purchase prices as their profit and if the purchase prices include taxes, the mark ups will be applicable to the tax component of the purchase price as well. In other words, increase in the price of the manufactures is in excess of the excise revenue accruing from input taxes.

Further still, excises on inputs may promote vertical integration in an industry, a trend which is harmful to the growth of small-scale sector. Lastly, input excises impose an inequitable burden on different economic classes by not discriminating between essential and non-essential uses of a product. For example, an excise on aluminium hits indiscriminately the use of the product for decoration purpose as well as for making utensils (generally used by the poor).

Notwithstanding the various disadvantages of input excises, governments in many countries impose duties on inputs due to administrative convenience. Many items of inputs are the end-product of one manufacturer but merely a component for another (e.g. tyres and tubes) and are also used as replacement items. Exemption of such items will be discrimination in favour of replacement consumption and certain commodities (say motor cars) may be sold with avoidable components and accessories stripped off. Moreover, provisions can be made in tax laws to minimise the cascading effects of input excises.

14. *Long Term Fiscal Policy,* op. cit., p. 38.
15. It is an element of import duty equivalent to excise duty on domestically produced goods.
16. Government of India, Ministry of Finance, *Final Report of the Tax Reforms Committee,* (Chairman: Raja Chelliah), Part I, 1992, p. 36.
17. Government of India, Ministry of Finance, *Budget Speech of the Finance Minister, 2001-2002, Part B*, p. 26.
18. Government of India, *Long Term Fiscal Policy*, 1985, p. 38.
19. Government of India, Ministry of Finance, *Report of the Expert Committee on Tax Measures to Promote Employment* (Chairman: V.M. Dandekar), 1980, pp. 91, 113 and 117.
20. Government of India, Ministry of Finance, *Budget Speech of the Finance Minister, 2001-2002, Part B*, p. 27.

15

Taxation of Services

Service sector is very wide in its range. It includes, *inter alia*, health care, education, social security, leasing, entertainment, credit rating agencies, telecommunications, transport, publicity and advertising, insurance, banking, legal and financial services.

15.1 Justification for Taxing Services

From equity point of view, services should be taxed in the same way as goods. Taxation of goods and exclusion of services distorts the relative prices of goods vis-à-vis services, encouraging artificially the demand for services. In the process, the allocation of resources is also distorted. If tax is imposed on goods and not on services, a relatively high rate of tax would be required on goods to generate a given amount of revenue. If tax is imposed both on goods and services, a moderate tax rate can yield the given revenue. Administratively, taxation of both goods and services is desirable because it would reduce disputes pertaining to distinction between goods and services.

Like goods, services can also be classified into two broad categories: essential services (e.g. health and education) and luxury services (e.g. entertainment and tourism). The rationale for exemption/lenient tax treatment of essential services is the same as for essential goods. Similarly, luxury services should be taxed at a high rate like luxury goods.

15.2 Constitutional Provisions

A scrutiny of List II (State List) in the Seventh Schedule of the Constitution of India shows that State Governments are empowered to tax entertainment and professional services (Entries 16 and 18 of List II). The Central Government had no specific powers to tax services when it introduced service tax on select services in 1994. It was done under its residual powers of taxation vide entry 97 of List I (Union List) in the Seventh Schedule. The collection of service tax was entrusted to the excise department.

However, the Constitution (Eighty-eighth Amendment) Act, 2003 put service tax in the Union List by inserting Entry 92C in that List. Furthermore, service tax was put under Article 268A of the Constitution which specifies that the principles of collection and appropriation of taxes on services will be determined by Parliament. In other words, revenue from service tax is outside the purview of the Finance Commission.

15.3 Growth of Service Sector in India

The composition of national income has changed steadily over the planning era. While the share of agriculture and allied activities in the gross domestic product (GDP) has declined, that of the tertiary sector has increased. The expansion of services has not only been conducive for employment generation but also for better efficiency of the system and better quality of life. As a result of significant fall in the share of agriculture in GDP, the aggregate GDP has become relatively less sensitive to fluctuations in agricultural performance. Highlighting the changes in the sectoral composition of GDP over the years, the *Economic Survey*, 2011-12 observed, "The structure of the economy has also undergone significant changes over time. Between 1950-51 and 1980-81, the industrial sector registered a higher growth rate than the services sector. The converse has been the case since then. This resulted in the share of the industry sector in GDP increasing by around 9 percentage points from 16.6 percent to 25.9 percent during the period from 1950-51 to 1980-81. The share of the services sector increased from 30.3 percent in 1950-51 to 38 percent in 1980-81. It started growing rapidly thereafter and this phenomenon became more pronounced in the 1990s. Consequently, since 1980-81, the share of the industry sector has remained in the range of 26 to 28 percent of GDP, while the entire decline in share of agriculture has been balanced by an increase in share of the services sector. Thus, the resilience of the economy to shocks owes to the services sector which has the largest share and most consistent growth performance". [1]

The Document further noted, "Notwithstanding the declining trend in agriculture's share in GDP, the importance of the sector to the economy is best understood with reference to its share in employment and in terms of its criticality for macroeconomic stability. While the former was well known, the latter became manifest with rising growth in incomes since the mid-2000s. Hence, growth in agriculture and allied sectors remains an important objective and a 'necessary condition' for inclusive growth". [2] The changes in relative shares of various sectors in GDP are shown in the Table 15.1.

The compositional shift in favour of the service sector, brought about by the rapid expansion of the service sector, is in line with the development experience of a number of countries. It is well-known that as an economy develops, the shares of industrial and service sectors in GDP increase at the cost of the agricultural sector.

Table 15.1: Changes in the Sectoral Composition of GDP

Year	Agriculture	Industry	Services
1950-51	53.1	16.6	30.3
1960-61	48.7	20.5	30.8
1970-71	42.3	24.0	33.8
1980-81	36.1	25.9	38.0
1990-91	29.6	27.7	42.7
2000-01	22.3	27.3	50.4
2012-13	13.9	27.3	58.8
2013-14*	13.9	26.1	59.9

* Provisional.
Source: Government of India, *Economic Survey*, 2013-14, p. 6.

The need to tax service sector is well recognised by the Government. To quote, "The tax revenue from the agricultural sector being negligible, the industrial sector continues to constitute the only principal tax base though it has suffered a reduction in the share of GDP over the period.

Despite the fact that the services sector has shown substantial buoyancy, its contribution to the exchequer is not significant in relation to its sizeable share in GDP.

Thus, in order to impart buoyancy to the revenue receipts and to provide consistency and equity in the tax structure via-a-via the composition of income, it is imperative to bring a major part of the services sector under the tax net". [3]

Although the contribution of service sector to GDP has increased over the years, the tax system has remained confined mainly to commodity production. In this connection, the Finance Minister observed in his 1994-95 budget speech, "There is no sound reason for exempting services from taxation when goods are taxed and many countries treat goods and services alike for tax purpose". [4] The Tax Reforms Committee (TRC) [Chairman: Raja Chelliah], 1991 also recommended imposition of tax on certain select services, viz. advertising, non-life insurance and telephone services and services of stock brokers.

15.4 Present Structure of Service Tax

In view of the need for additional resources, rising contribution of service sector to GDP and the recommendations of TRC, a modest effort was made in the 1994-95 budget when a 5 percent tax was imposed on telephone and non-life insurance services and services of stock brokers with effect from July 1, 1994. The coverage of service tax was extended to advertising, courier and radio paging services from November 1, 1996.

In his 1997-98 budget speech, the Finance Minister maintained that services are products as much as manufactured goods and hence both must bear taxes. With these considerations in view he extended the service tax to the services provided by the following: transporters of goods by road, consulting engineers, custom house, steamer and clearing and forwarding agents, air travel agents, tour operators and car rental agencies, outdoor caterers, *pandal* contractors and *mandap* keepers, and manpower recruitment agencies.

In the 1998-99 budget, service tax on the transportation of goods by road, outdoor caterers, and *pandal* contractors was abolished. However, its net was extended to services provided by architects, interior decorators, management consultants, chartered accountants, cost accountants, company secretaries, private security services, real estate agents and real estate consultants, market research agencies, credit rating agencies, underwriting agencies, and slaughter houses using mechanised means for large animals.

Acknowledging the potential of service tax, the Finance Minister in his 2000-2001 budget speech announced the setting up of an Expert Group to go into all its aspects and make suitable recommendations. The net of service tax was greatly expanded when the following 15 services were added to the list of taxable services in the 2001-02 budget.

1. Specified banking and financial services.
2. Authorised service stations for servicing of vehicles including two wheelers.
3. Port services.
4. Broadcasting services.
5. Photographic services.
6. Convention services.
7. Sound recording services.
8. Scientific and technical consulting services.
9. Telex services.
10. Telegraph services.
11. Facsimile services.
12. Online information and data base retrieval services.
13. Video tape production services.
14. Services auxiliary to insurance.
15. Services provided to lease circuit line holders.

In his 2004-05 budget speech, the Finance Minister announced the inclusion of some more services under the service tax ambit. These were the following.

1. Business exhibition services.
2. Airport services.
3. Services provided by transport booking agents.

4. Transport of goods by air.
5. Survey and exploration services.
6. Opinion poll services.
7. Intellectual property services other than copyright.
8. Brokers of forward contracts.
9. *Pandal* and *shamiana* contractors.
10. Outdoor caterers.
11. Independent TV/radio programme producers.
12. Construction services in respect of commercial or industrial constructions.
13. Life insurance services to the extent of the risk premium.

In the 2005-06 Budget, the following 9 items were added to the list of taxable services.

1. Transport of goods through pipeline or other conduit.
2. Site preparation and clearance, excavation, earth moving and demolition services, other than those provided to agriculture, irrigation and watershed development.
3. Dredging services of rivers, ports, harbours, backwaters and estuaries.
4. Survey and map making other than by Government Departments.
5. Cleaning services other than in relation to agriculture, horticulture, animal husbandry or dairying.
6. Membership of clubs or associations.
7. Packaging services.
8. Mailing list compilation and mailing.
9. Construction of residential complexes having more than twelve residential units of apartments together with common areas and other appurtenances.

The 2005-06 Budget also expanded the scope of certain existing services in the following manner.

1. Commercial or industrial construction service to include renovation of such building or civil structure, post construction completion and finishing services for such building or civil structure, construction, repair, alteration, renovation or restoration of pipeline or conduits.
2. Erection, commissioning or installation services to include specified installation services.
3. Maintenance or repair services to include maintenance or management of immovable properties, maintenance or repair including reconditioning or restoration undertaken as part of any contract or agreement.
4. Broadcasting services to include charges recovered by broadcasting agencies from multi-system operator and provision of direct to home signals to the customers.

5. Sound recording to include recording of sound on any media and includes post-production services such as sound mixing or re-mixing.
6. Videotape production to include recording of any programme, event or function on any media and includes post production services.
7. Taxable services provided by authorised service station to include reconditioning or restoration of motor cars, two wheeled and light motor vehicles.
8. Beauty parlour services to include all services provided by beauty parlours.
9. Manpower recruitment service to include supply of manpower, temporary or otherwise.
10. Franchisee service to cover all agreements by which, the franchisor grants representational rights to franchise to sell or manufacture goods or provide services identified with the franchisor.
11. Business auxiliary service to include production or processing of goods for or on behalf of the client.
12. Outdoor catering service to include catering from a place or premises provided, by way of tenancy or otherwise by the person receiving such services.

The Budget for 2006-07 added the following new services under the service tax net.

1. Service provided by a registrar to an issue.
2. Service provided by share transfer agent.
3. Automated teller machine operations, maintenance or management.
4. Service provided by recovery agent.
5. Sale of space or time for advertisement, other than in print media.
6. Sponsorship services provided to anybody, corporate or firm, other than sponsorship of sports events.
7. Transport of passengers, other than economy class passengers, embarking on international journey by air.
8. Transport of goods in containers by rail by any person, other than Government railway.
9. Business support services.
10. Auctioneers' service, other than auction of property under directions or orders of a court of law or auction by the Central Government.
11. Public relation service.
12. Ship management service.
13. Internet telephony service.
14. Transport of persons by cruise ship.
15. Credit card, debit card, charge card or other payment card related services.

In the 2007-08 Budget, service tax net was extended to the following services.

1. Services outsourced for mining of mineral, oil or gas.
2. Renting of immovable property for use in commerce or business; however, residential properties, vacant land used for agriculture and similar purposes, land for sports, entertainment and parking purposes, and immovable property for educational or religious purposes will be excluded.
3. Development and supply of content for use in telecom and advertising purposes.
4. Asset management services provided by individuals.
5. Design services.

The Budget for 2011-12 retained the service tax rate at 10 percent (increased to 12 percent in Budget 2012-13) and focused on achieving a closer fit between the present service tax regime and the proposed GST. This was sought to be done by: (a) adding a few new services on the ability to pay principle, (b) expanding or rationalizing the scope of existing services, (c) rationalizing certain provisions relating to important services and valuation, and (d) modifying provisions of the Cenvat credit scheme seeking to effect the right balance between input credits and output tax, and harmonizing the provisions of the scheme across goods and services, incentivizing honesty and penalizing dishonesty in compliance, and adoption of point of taxation rules to facilitate accrual basis of the collection.

Detailed below are the major initiatives of Budget 2011-12 in respect of service tax:

Service tax was imposed on the following services:

1. Services provided by air-conditioned restaurants having a licence to serve alcoholic beverages in relation to serving of food and/or beverages.
2. Short-term accommodation provided by a hotel, inn, guesthouse, club or campsite, or any other similar establishment for a continuous period of less than three months.

Scope of certain existing services was expanded or altered as under:

1. Scope of 'life insurance service' widened to cover all services provided to a policy holder or any person, by an insurer, including re-insurer carrying on life insurance business. Tax to be charged on the portion of the premium other than what is allocated for investment, when the break-up of premium is shown separately in any document given to the policy holder. The rate of composition increased from 1 percent to 1.5 percent.
2. Scope of 'club or association service' expanded to include service provided to non-members within its ambit.
3. Scope of the service of 'authorized service station' expanded to: (a) include services provided by any person; (b) cover all motor vehicles other than those

meant for goods carriage and three-wheeler scooter auto-rickshaws; and (c) cover decoration and other similar services in respect of vehicles along with the services already covered.

4. Definition of 'business support services' amended so as to include services provided by way of operational or administrative assistance in any manner.
5. Scope of legal consultancy services expanded by bringing within their ambit: (a) service provided by a business entity to individuals in relation to advice, consultancy, or assistance in any branch of law, in any manner; (b) representational service provided by any person to any business entity (representational services provided to individuals to continue to be exempt); and (c) 'arbitration' service provided by an arbitral tribunal to any business entity.
6. In commercial training or coaching services, the definition of 'commercial training or coaching centre' amended so as to bring all unrecognized courses within the tax net, irrespective of the fact that such courses are conducted by an institute which also conducts courses that may lead to grant of a degree or diploma.

Certain exemptions were extended as follows:

1. Exemption provided to services rendered in relation to business exhibitions held abroad.
2. An abatement of 25 percent from the taxable value provided for the purpose of levy of service tax under 'transport of goods through coastal and inland shipping'.
3. Exemption provided to 'works contract' service rendered for construction or finishing of new residential complexes under the Jawaharlal Nehru National Urban Renewal Mission and Rajiv Awaas Yojana.
4. Exemption provided to services rendered within a port or other port or an airport under 'works contract' service for specified areas.
5. Exemption provided to the Rashtriya Swasthya Bima Yojana under general insurance service.
6. Value of air freight included in the assessable value of goods for charging customs duties excluded from taxable value for the purpose of levy of service tax under 'transport of goods by air' service.
7. Services related to transportation of goods by road, rail, or air when origin and destination are located outside India exempted from service tax.
8. A modified scheme introduced to refund service tax to SEZ units and developers.
9. Some existing exemptions on domestic and international travel and club or association services were withdrawn.

For the financial year 2015-16, the standard rate of service tax is 14 percent.

Keeping in view the social objectives of state policy, the Government of India has refrained from taxing services in the field of health and education. [5] Table 15.2 records the growth in revenue from service tax in India.

Table 15.2: Trends in the Relative Significance of Service Tax in Gross Tax Revenues* of the Central Government: 1994-95 to 2015-16

(₹ crore)

Year	Gross Central Taxes	Revenue from Service Tax	Col. 3 as % of Col. 2
1	2	3	4
1994-95	92,297	407	0.4
1995-96	1,11,224	862	0.8
1996-97	1,29,762	1,059	0.8
1997-98	1,39,220	1,586	1.1
1998-99	1,43,797	1,957	1.4
1999-00	1,71,752	2,128	1.2
2000-01	1,88,603	2,613	1.4
2001-02	1,87,060	3,302	1.8
2002-03	2,15,905	4,122	1.9
2003-04	2,54,348	7,891	3.1
2004-05	3,04,957	14,200	4.7
2005-06	3,66,151	23,055	6.3
2006-07	4,73,513	37,598	7.9
2007-08	5,93,147	51,301	8.6
2008-09	6,05,298	60,941	10.1
2009-10	6,24,527	58,422	9.4
2010-11	7,93,072	71,016	9.0
2011-12	8,89,176	97,509	11.0
2012-13	10,36,235	1,32,601	12.8
2013-14	11,38,734	1,54,778	13.6
2014-15	12,51,391	1,68,132	13.4
2015-16	14,49,490	2,09,774	14.4

* Before transferring States' share in Central taxes.
2014-15 = Revised estimates; 2015-16 = Budget estimates.
Sources: Government of India, Ministry of Finance, *Explanatory Memorandum on the Budget of the Central Government* (various years); *Receipts Budget* (various years); and *Budget at a Glance*, 2015-16.

To sum up, the Indian tax system has traditionally relied on commodity taxation for generating revenue for the Central and State Governments. The two major commodity taxes of the Central Government are excise duties and customs duties while at the level of the States, sales tax/value added tax (VAT) is the main commodity tax of States' own tax revenues.

The extension of excise duties to more and more commodities of the industrial/manufacturing sector has now reached a saturation point. However, the service sector remained outside the tax net till 1994. This pattern of tax structure development in India was contrary to the experience of most other countries where taxation of commodities and services grew hand in hand.

The introduction of service tax in 1994-95 ushered in a major structural change in indirect taxes in the form of a wider tax base and facilitated the process of rationalization of excise duties, resulting in lower tax burden on productive sectors. Over the years, there has been an increase in the number of services and the rate of service tax leviable.

The expanding base of service tax has provided a promising source of revenue, but there are some caveats which have to be kept in mind. First, the scope for expanding the service tax net to more and more services gets narrower as the net is widened. The contribution of the expanding net will, therefore, reduce over time. Second, the preponderance of small service providers below the taxable limit of turnover constrains the scope of revenue mobilization beyond a certain level.

Presently, service tax is levied on as diverse services as credit rating on the one hand and mechanised slaughter houses on the other. It is clear that service sector in India constitutes a tax base with vast potential which has not been exploited as yet.

To quote in conclusion, "Central Service tax reform and extension must be designed to integrate it with the CENVAT by the end of the 10th Plan, keeping in mind the ultimate objective of a National VAT. All services, particularly modern production services such as transport, communication and financial services, under the tax authority of the centre should be subject to the same basic CENVAT rate. Similarly the tax paid on any services used as input into the production of excisable services or goods should be given set-off. Any comprehensive Service Tax law must keep these objectives in view". [6]

Endnotes

1. Government of India, *Economic Survey,* 2011-12, p. 8.
2. *Ibid.*, p. 9.
3. Reserve Bank of India, *Report on Currency and Finance*, 1998-99, p. V-6.
4. Government of India, Ministry of Finance, *Budget Speech of the Finance Minister, 1994-95, Part B*, p. 24.
5. In the case of excise and sales tax also, commodities such as medicines and books are either exempt or taxed at very low rates.
6. D.K. Srivastava, *Issues in Indian Public Finance,* (New Century Publications: New Delhi), 2005, p. 78.

16

Customs Duties

16.1 Introduction

Customs duties [1] are probably the most ancient form of taxation. They are as old as international trade itself. Just as domestic production flows provide the base for excise taxation so also international trade flows are the basis for customs duties. Customs duties are payable on goods exported from or imported into a country. Import duties are usually levied with *ad valorem* rates and their base is determined by the domestic value of the imported goods calculated at the official exchange rate. Similarly, export duties are imposed on export values expressed in domestic currency. Customs duties are imposed to raise revenue for the government. Apart from the revenue function, import duties provide a protective barrier for domestic industries. Other measures to protect indigenous industries from foreign competition include import licensing, import quotas, and outright import ban.

16.2 Legal Framework

The Constitution of India grants exclusive powers to the Central Government to impose duties of customs. By virtue of entry 83 of List I in the Seventh Schedule of the Constitution of India, the Central Government is empowered to impose 'duties of customs including export duties'.

During the British rule, various customs and tariff enactments were passed from time to time, the following two being the main: (a) The Sea Customs Act, 1878, and (b) The Tariff Act, 1934. After Independence, the Sea Customs Act and other allied enactments were repealed by a consolidating and amending legislation entitled the Customs Act, 1962. Similarly, the Act of 1934 was repealed by the Customs Tariff Act, 1975.

16.2.1 Various Types of Customs Duties: In accordance with the provisions of the Constitution, various types of customs duties are imposed by the Government under different Acts of Parliament. Following are the important customs duties levied on goods imported into or exported from India.

A. Basic Customs Duty: Under Section 12 of the Customs Act, 1962 (the main enactment), all goods imported into India are chargeable to a duty. The rates of this duty, popularly known as basic customs duty, are indicated in the First Schedule of the Customs Tariff Act, 1975. The duty may be a percentage of the value of the goods or at a specific rate. The Central Government has the power to reduce or exempt any goods from these duties.

B. Additional (Countervailing) Duty of Customs: Under Section 3(1) of the Customs Tariff Act, 1975, an additional duty on goods imported into the country is leviable. The rate of this duty, popularly known as countervailing duty, is equal to the excise duty on like articles if produced or manufactured in India. If the rate of this duty is on *ad valorem* basis, the value for this purpose will be the total of the value of the imported article and the customs duty on it (both basic and auxiliary). The underlying philosophy of a countervailing duty is to ensure that the protection provided by the import duty to domestic industry is not reduced. Till the early 1960s, countervailing duty was levied on a select basis on products which were considered to erode the margin of protection to the domestic industry on account of the excise duty. In course of time when the number of excisable goods increased, the selective use of countervailing duty was found to be inadequate and complicated. Therefore, the Indian Tariff Act, 1934, was amended in 1963 to insert a new Section 2A to provide for the levy of countervailing duty in all cases where excise duty was leviable on a similar indigenous commodity.

C. Export Duty: Under Section 12 of the Customs Act, 1962, goods exported from India are chargeable to an export duty. The items on which export duty is chargeable and the rate at which the duty is levied are given in the Second Schedule of the Customs Tariff Act, 1975. Under Section 8 of this Act, the Government enjoys emergency powers to increase the existing rate or to levy fresh export duty depending on the circumstances.

D. Cesses on Exports: Certain cesses are leviable on specified articles of export under various enactments of the Government of India. These cesses are collected as duties of customs and handed over to the agencies in-charge of the administration of the commodity concerned. Presently, cesses are imposed on exports of coffee, coir, lac, mica, tobacco (unmanufactured), oil cakes and meal, marine products, cashew kernels, black pepper, cardamom, iron ore, animal feed and turmeric.

16.3 New Customs Tariff Nomenclature

As in the case of excise duties, a major problem in the administration of customs duties pertains to disputes and delays relating to interpretation of definitions of dutiable goods. The enactment of the new Customs Tariff Act, 1975, was a landmark in the history of customs tariff in India. The revised nomenclature for customs tariff was recommended by the Tariff Revision Committee set up in 1964. Though the Government accepted the recommendations of the Committee, the Bill to implement the revised nomenclature could only be passed in 1975 and came into effect from

August 2, 1976. The Act of 1975, which replaced the Indian Tariff Act, 1934, is based on the Customs Co-operation Council Nomenclature (originally known as Brussels Tariff Nomenclature). The First Schedule of the Act contains import tariff while the Second Schedule deals with export tariff. As a further measure to rationalise and modernise customs administration, the Parliament passed the Customs Tariff Amendment Act, 1985, to adopt the Harmonised Commodity Description and Coding System. The new commodity classification became operative from February 28, 1986. Similarly, India adopted the GATT Valuation Agreement (Valuation Code) on August 16, 1988. The GATT Valuation Code lays down broad principles for valuation of goods for levy of customs duty.

16.4 Revenue Significance

The relative contribution of customs revenue in the total tax yield of the Central Government has shown fluctuations due to changes in the foreign exchange situation, domestic production levels, and trends in international trade. For example, in the late 1950s, several restrictions and bans were imposed on imports in view of the difficult foreign exchange position, resulting in fall in revenue from import duties.

During pre-Independence days and even during early post-Independence period, customs duties formed the mainstay of Central tax revenues. However, the relative share of customs duties started declining from early 1950s in view of protective trade policy and dwindling foreign exchange reserves. The share of customs revenue in Centre's total tax collections dropped from 38.9 percent in 1950-51 to as low as 16.3 percent in 1970-71. Since then, customs revenue has maintained an upward swing, accounting for 25.8 percent in 1980-81, and 35.8 percent in 1990-91 (Table 16.1). This upward trend was attributable to the changed emphasis from physical to fiscal controls to regulate imports. As the Long Term Fiscal Policy, 1985, maintained, "The basic thrust of customs tariff reforms will be to place increasing reliance on tariffs to regulate imports and progressively reduce the role of quantitative restrictions in this regard. The move in this direction should increase revenues, encourage less import-intensive forms of production, moderate the unjustifiably high protection granted by quantitative restrictions to certain industries and reduce the delays and uncertainties associated with the administration of import licensing". [2]

Of late, there has been a decline in the relative importance of customs as a source of revenue. In 2000-01, the share of customs revenue in the total Central tax collections stood at 25.2 percent which further declined to 17.1 percent in 2010-11. It was estimated at 14.4 percent in the budget for 2015-16 (Table 16.1). This reversal of trend is due to opening up of the economy and the policy of progressively reducing import duties.

Table 16.1: Trends in the Relative Significance of Customs Duties in Gross Tax Revenues* of the Central Government: Selected Years

(₹ crore)

Central taxes	1950-51	1960-61	1970-71	1980-81	1990-91	2000-01	2010-11	2015-16
A+B Gross tax revenues	404 (100.0)	888 (100.0)	3,206 (100.0)	13,179 (100.0)	57,576 (100.0)	1,88,603 (100.0)	7,93,072 (100.0)	14,49,490 (100.0)
A. Direct taxes	174 (43.1)	290 (32.6)	870 (27.1)	3,004 (22.8)	11,025 (19.1)	68,306 (36.2)	4,45,962 (56.2)	7,97,995 (55.1)
B. Indirect taxes of which	229 (56.7)	599 (67.5)	2,337 (72.9)	10,175 (77.2)	46,552 (80.9)	1,20,297 (63.8)	3,47,110 (43.8)	6,51,495 (44.9)
Customs duties	157 (38.9)	170 (19.1)	524 (16.3)	3,409 (25.8)	20,644 (35.8)	47,542 (25.2)	1,35,813 (17.1)	2,08,336 (14.4)

* Before transferring States' share in Central taxes; 2015-16 Budget estimates.
Figures in parentheses are corresponding percentages of gross tax revenues.
Sources: Government of India, Ministry of Finance, *Explanatory Memorandum on the Budget of the Central Government* (various years); *Receipts Budget* (various years); and *Budget at a Glance*, 2015-16.

Presently, customs revenue is mainly composed of import duties levied on a wide range of commodities. In the budget estimates for 2015-16, import duties accounted for ₹ 2,01,397 crore (96.7 percent) of total customs revenue of ₹ 2,08,336 crore (Table 16.2). Apart from revenue function, import duties act as policy instrument to provide protection to domestic industry, conserve and ration scarce foreign exchange, and frame general international trade policy.

Although at present the share of export duties in customs revenue is very low (3.3 percent in the 2015-16 budget), it was not always so. In the early 1950s, export duties formed a significant proportion of customs revenue, though this situation could not be maintained for long. The yield from export duties reached a peak figure when it formed 29.9 percent of total customs revenue in 1950-51. By 1960-61, export duty revenue had been reduced to 8.2 percent of total customs revenue.

Another upsurge in the relative share of export duties is observed in 1970-71 when they formed 12.0 percent of customs revenue. Since then, the revenue importance of export duties has decreased (Table 16.2).

Like excise levies, the revenue from import duties is also concentrated in a select few commodities including petroleum oils and crude, electrical machinery, organic chemicals, project imports, plastics etc. These are the items which form the bulk of India's imports and hence customs revenue.

Table 16.2: Trends in the Relative Shares of Import and Export Duties in Total Customs Duties: Selected Years

(₹ crore)

Year	Customs Duties	Import Duties	Export Duties	As Percent	
				Col.3 of Col. 2	Col. 4 of Col. 2
1	2	3	4	5	6
1950-51	157	110	47	70.1	29.9
1955-56	166	128	38	77.1	22.9
1960-61	170	156	14	91.8	8.2
1965-66	539	537	2	99.6	0.4
1970-71	524	461	63	88.0	12.0
1975-76	1,419	1,336	83	94.1	5.9
1980-81	3,409	3,292	117	96.6	3.4
1985-86	9,526	9,443	83	99.1	0.9
1990-91	20,644	20,532	36	99.5	0.5
1995-96	35,757	35,647	110	99.7	0.3
2000-01	47,542	47,400	142	99.7	0.3
2005-06	81,800	81,015	795	99.1	0.9
2010-11	1,35,813	1,32,541	3,272	97.6	2.4
2011-12	1,49,328	1,42,849	6,479	95.7	4.3
2012-13	1,65,346	1,62,496	2,850	98.3	1.7
2013-14	1,72,085	1,64,337	7,748	95.5	4.5
2014-15	1,88,713	1,82,173	6,540	96.5	3.5
2015-16	2,08,336	2,01,397	6,939	96.7	3.3

2014-15 Revised estimates; 2015-16 Budget estimates.

Sources: Government of India, Ministry of Finance, *Explanatory Memorandum on the Budget of the Central Government* (various years); *Receipts Budget* (various years).

16.5 Import Tariff Policy

16.5.1 Early Post-Independence Period: Soon after Independence, the Government decided to follow a restrictive import policy, particularly in view of the rapid depletion of sterling balances. In his very first budget (1947-48) of independent India, the Finance Minister outlined the salient features of this restrictive policy in the following words:

"Broadly speaking, that policy consists of dividing imports into three categories: free, restricted, and prohibited. Imports of food, capital goods, the raw material of industry and certain essential consumer goods are free and no exchange restrictions are placed upon their imports. Consumer goods which are not absolutely essential are licensed on a quota basis, while others which in the context of the economy of this country must be regarded as totally unessential and luxury imports have been altogether prohibited". [3]

During the early post-Independence period, customs policy remained in turmoil owing to a series of domestic and international happenings. India's commitments under the General Agreement on Tariffs and Trade (GATT) were given effect to in 1948, the rupee was devalued in September 1949, and the Korean War broke out in 1950. Being a signatory to GATT, India could not raise, above a certain level, import duties on a wide variety of goods, but enjoyed reciprocal concessions from its trade partners. Imports of articles which enjoyed concessions under GATT constituted 19 percent of the value of total imports while the value of exports which received concessions was 79.6 percent of our total exports in 1952-53. The concessions obtained included items like mica, cashewnut, and various jute goods. The concessions granted pertained mainly to consumer goods and machinery. Since the actual rates of import duty on machinery, which formed the bulk of imports, were already low than the rates fixed by the Agreement, the effective concessions were chiefly on consumer goods. Although the Fiscal Commission, 1949-50, supported India's adherence to GATT in view of the need for international co-operation, the country later on felt the need to withdraw from GATT 'bindings' when the domestic production base was strengthened and diversified. Following re-negotiations in 1971 and 1973, a host of items 'bound' under GATT were freed to provide protection to domestic industries.

After the outbreak of the Korean War, important changes were introduced in the tariff structure under the Finance Act, 1951. The general surcharge of one-fifth on import duties (levied in 1942) was increased to one-fourth. The rate of surcharge on liquors which was fixed at 100 percent in 1948 was raised to 155 percent.

In pursuance of its general policy of gradually replacing quantitative restrictions by higher import duties, the Government raised import duties on a number of items including articles made of paper, cutlery etc., in the 1955-56 budget. Simultaneously, import quotas were liberalised. The already high level of import duties, particularly on luxury articles, did not leave much scope for raising additional revenue from this source, a fact lamented by the Finance Minister in his 1957-58 budget (final) speech.

16.5.2 Customs Reorganisation Committee (Chairman: F.C. Badhwar), 1957-58: In January 1957, the Government of India appointed the Customs Reorganisation Committee under the chairmanship of F.C. Badhwar. The Committee was asked "to conduct a comprehensive enquiry into customs procedures and organisation and to make recommendations for their improvement". The Committee found that a major cause of disputes and delays in the clearance of imported goods was the faulty and inadequate classification system for determining customs tariff. It observed, "The complexity of the Customs Tariff will be evident from the fact that the whole range of goods constituting the country's foreign trade are grouped under 576 tariff items only as compared with 4850 classification heads in the 'Statistical Indian Trade Classification' which has recently been adopted for purposes of recording the country's trade statistics. Whilst the range and variety of imported goods have been continuously expanding in the post-war period, there has been little or no corresponding revision or elaboration of the customs tariff schedule". [4]

The Committee was also critical of too many rates of duty. It commented, "we should similarly point out the existence in the Indian Customs Tariff of too wide a range of *ad valorem* rates of duty which must inevitably add to the difficulties in the day to day application of the tariff, particularly when tariff descriptions carrying different rates could apply to the same article. Almost all multiples of 5 up to 100 are to be found in these rates". [5].

The Committee recommended, *inter alia*: (a) thorough revision of the Customs Tariff by aligning it closely with the Import Trade Control Licensing Schedule, and (b) removal of anomalies in rates of duty for similar categories of goods.

The worsening foreign exchange crisis reached its climax when in 1965 foreign exchange reserves touched the critically low level of less than ₹ 100 crore. Moreover, the Customs Reorganisation Committee, 1957-58, had criticised the multiplicity of tariff rates. Consequently, a drastic rationalisation of the import duty structure was undertaken in 1965, resulting in the introduction of a set of three rates of import duty: 40 percent on basic raw materials, 60 percent on semi-processed and intermediate goods, and 100 percent on finished consumer goods. The Committee on Rationalisation and Simplification of Tax Structure, 1968, also favoured few rates of import tariff. It opined, "Except for a few 'luxury' items like watches, jewellery, alcoholic beverages and perfumes, there is need only for three or four rates of duty". [6]. In spite of the rationalisation exercise of 1965, duty changes were made frequently depending upon the emerging situation. The three rates of import duty were scaled down following devaluation of the rupee in June 1966 to prevent the cost of imports going up to the full extent of the devaluation. However, in view of the difficult balance of payments position, the rates of import duty were gradually restored in due course to pre-devaluation levels. Rationalisation of import tariff was again attempted in 1971 when the following four rates of import duty were introduced: 30 percent, 40 percent, 60 percent, and 100 percent.

16.5.3 Indirect Taxation Enquiry Committee (Chairman: L.K. Jha), 1978: The Indirect Taxation Enquiry Committee, 1978, examined at length the structure of import duties and recommended its rationalisation on the following lines: "(a) a levy adequate to give the degree of protection deemed necessary for particular products, (b) a revenue element, which would generally be the countervailing duty, being equal to the excise duty leviable on the same or similar domestic product, and (c) a regulator element which will be used on such factors as reinforcing import restrictions, preventing excess profits on account of scarcity of products in domestic market, and generally to regulate imports from the angle of conserving foreign exchange". [7]

16.5.4 Long-Term Fiscal Policy, 1985: The need for import tariff rationalisation was underlined in the Long Term Fiscal Policy (LTFP), 1985, also. The official document noted that the prevailing tariff rates were high and the tariff system was very complicated. Therefore, it stressed the need to reduce the rates and simplify the system. For carrying out these reforms, the LTFP distinguished between the following broad categories of imports:

1. Capital goods.
2. Raw materials.
3. Other intermediate goods including components.
4. Essential consumer goods like foodgrains, edible oils, and life saving drugs.
5. Non-essential consumer goods.

Understandably, essential goods were preferred to either remain exempt or bear low rates of import duties while non-essential items were singled out to either remain banned or subjected to high import tariff. Regarding the first three categories of goods the LTFP observed, "Ideally, in the long-run, there is a strong case for subjecting all capital goods, raw materials, components and other intermediate products to the same rate of nominal tariff. This system, if it could be implemented, would have several important advantages. First, the substitution of the present multiplicity of nominal tariff rates by a single rate would constitute an enormous simplification for both trade and industry as well as for the customs administration. Second, this would vastly reduce incentives for misclassification of imports to evade taxes. Third, a single nominal rate of import duty would assure a uniform rate of effective protection (that is, protection of value added) at different stages of production of intermediate and capital goods. This would encourage the economy to specialise in those activities in which it has competitive strength". [8]

However, the LTFP cautioned that a major deviation from the present pattern of import tariff is not immediately feasible. Domestic industries have grown under different levels of protection and are in different stages of maturity. The rationalisation of import tariff has to be phased over a long period providing some differentials in import tariff short of a uniform system of duties.

Consequent upon the rationalisation of import tariff on capital goods by the

Finance Act, 1987, the rate of import duty on general machinery was reduced to 85 percent *ad valorem*. Import duty on components for machinery was fixed at 15 percent below the applicable rate on complete machines. This differential, in line with the recommendations of the LTFP, was intended to encourage the domestic production of capital machines instead of their total imports. Imports of capital goods for certain preferred sectors were allowed at relatively low rates of duty. For example, duty on equipment for fertiliser plants was 15 percent *ad valorem* and on machines, equipment, and tools for gem and jewellery 25 percent *ad valorem*. Electronics industry emerged as a preferred sector for fiscal incentives. The Finance Act, 1988, fixed a uniform concessional import duty of 60 percent *ad valorem* in respect of 280 items of machinery for the electronics sector. By the same Act, the duty on moulds, tools, and dies required by the electronics industry was reduced from 60 percent to 30 percent *ad valorem* with the underlying purpose of indigenisation and development of electronics and computers.

In short, guidelines suggested by the LTFP for reform of import tariff were never implemented comprehensively. In a half-hearted manner, some rationalisation of rates was effected in the case of components of capital goods, drug intermediates, and electronic goods.

In mid-l991 when the new Government assumed office at the Centre, it began the process of reducing import duties. The Finance Act (No. 2), 1991, reduced the *ad valorem* rate of basic plus auxiliary duties of customs to a maximum of 150 percent where it was more than that. Thus, tariff peaks above 150 percent were eliminated with the exceptions of duty on imported alcoholic beverages and passenger baggage. The then prevailing rates of import duty on capital goods for general projects and machinery were reduced from 85 percent to 80 percent. The rate of duty on their components was also reduced by 5 percentage points from the existing level of 65 percent.

16.5.5 Tax Reforms Committee (Chairman: Raja Chelliah), 1991: Reform of the customs tariff was high on the agenda of the Tax Reforms Committee constituted by the Government in August 1991. Its terms of reference enjoined it to examine and make recommendations, *inter alia*, on "simplification and rationalisation of customs tariffs with a view to reducing the multiplicity and dispersion of rates and to eliminate exemptions which have become unnecessary; (and) reducing the level of tariff rates, keeping in view the need for mobilising resources to facilitate fiscal adjustment and the objective of promoting international competitiveness". [9]

In its Interim Report submitted to the Government in December 1991, the Committee suggested the following as elements of the programme of import tariff reform: "(a) reduction of the general level of tariff, (b) reduction of the spread or dispersion of tariff rates, (c) simplification of the tariff system, (d) rationalisation of tariff rates, along with the abolition of numerous exemptions and concessions, and (e) abolition of the practice of making changes in effective rates through notifications". [10]. Stressing the need for time-bound action, the Committee observed, "By 1995-96, the average tariff rate should be brought down to about 50 percent and the peak rate to about 80 percent. In the years 1996-97 to 1998-99, tariff rates should be reduced further to bring down the average rate to around 25 percent and the maximum rate to 50 percent by 1998-99". [11]

16.6 Post-liberalisation Reduction and Rationalisation of Import Tariff

Following the recommendations of the Tax Reforms Committee, 1991, the Finance Act, 1992, lowered the peak level of import duties to 110 percent with the exception of passenger baggage and alcoholic beverages. With a view to reduce the cost of new investment, the duty on project imports was lowered from 80 percent to 55 percent and in the case of electronic industry to 50 percent. A deeper reduction to 30 percent was granted for capital goods for projects of coal mining and crude petroleum refining. For power projects, a uniform duty of 30 percent was fixed.

The underlying philosophy of reduction in tariffs was to promote competitiveness in the Indian industry. There was a feeling in Government circles that high tariff rates had the effect of creating a high cost industrial structure.

The Finance Act, 1993, made a significant simplification in the import tariff by merging auxiliary duty with basic duty, and also by reducing the maximum rate of import duty from 110 percent to 85 percent. The peak rate of import duty was further reduced from 85 percent to 65 percent by the Finance Act, 1994.

Continuing the process of reducing the high level of protection to domestic industry is continuing so as to foster competition and promote efficiency. The peak rate of import duty was reduced from 65 percent to 50 percent in 1995, and further down to 40 percent in the 1997-98 budget.

A special customs duty of 2 percent was imposed in the 1996-97 budget and a further special customs duty of 3 percent was imposed on certain items in 1997-98. In other words, special customs duty of 5 percent was in force for a period valid till 31.3.1999. However, the Finance Minister announced in his 1999-2000 budget speech the discontinuance of the 5 percent special customs duty with effect from 28.2.1999.

In another significant move, the Finance Minister reduced the then existing 7 major ad valorem rates of customs duty to the following 5 basic rates.

- 5 percent (the existing one).

- 15 percent (by substituting the existing 10 percent rate).
- 25 percent (by merging the 20 percent and 25 percent rates).
- 35 percent (by merging the 30 percent and 35 percent rates).
- 40 percent (the existing one).

However, in another move the Finance Minister imposed a uniform surcharge of 10 percent on all commodities excluding the following categories: (a) crude oil and petroleum products, (b) items attracting 40 percent rate of basic duty, (c) certain GATT-bound items, and (d) gold and silver.

In other words, the imposition of surcharge raised the basic rate by 10 percent. For example, basic rate of 5 percent became 5.5 percent and 15 percent became 16.5 percent.

Still further, the Finance Minister reduced the peak rate of basic customs duty from 40 percent to 35 percent in his 2000-2001 budget, thereby reducing the total number of customs duty rates from 5 to 4, i.e. 35 percent, 25 percent, 15 percent and 5 percent. The surcharge of 10 percent imposed in the 1999-2000 budget became applicable to new peak rate of 35 percent. However, in the 2001-2002 budget, the surcharge of 10 percent was discontinued, making the peak level of customs duty decline from 38.5 percent to 35 percent. As regards further reduction in the peak rate of duty, the Finance Minister observed, "I have already promised that our customs tariff would be brought down to East Asian levels. I will like to move progressively within three years to reduce the number of rates to the minimum with a peak rate of 20 percent". [12]

The Government reduced the peak customs duty from 30 percent to 25 percent in the 2003-04 budget.

16.6.1 Off-budget Package of Tax Concessions, January 2004: The Finance Minister Jaswant Singh announced on January 8, 2004 an off-budget package of tax concessions which mainly pertained to indirect taxes (excise and customs). The most notable of these was the reduction in the peak rate of import duty across the board (except for agricultural goods) from 25 percent to 20 percent. Simultaneously, he abolished the 4 percent special additional customs duty (SACD). Both these changes became effective from January 9, 2004. These measures considerably lowered the protection levels for the domestic industry. However, the two measures are expected to bring down input costs of the manufacturing sector, enabling it to make Indian products globally competitive.

It may be recalled that former Finance Minister Yashwant Sinha announced an 8 percent SACD in 1998-99 and rolled it back to 4 percent in the official amendments. SACD was meant to offset the burden of local taxes borne by the domestic industry.

In the 2005-06 Union budget, the peak rate of import duty on non-agricultural products was reduced from 20 percent to 15 percent. It was further reduced to 12.5 percent and 10 percent in the 2006-07 and 2007-08 budgets respectively. The 10 percent rate continues for the financial year 2015-16. Table 16.3 records the progressive reductions in the peak rate of import duty. In this context, *Economic Survey*, 2009-10 observed, "India has been progressively lowering peak customs duty. Contrary to popular belief, the fall in peak duty has neither led to a fall in revenue collections, nor a wiping out of the domestic manufacturing sector. In fact, peak duty falls have been accompanied by rise in customs duty collections. The trend follows the Laffer Curve Effect which indicates that lowering of taxes produces higher economic activity and higher revenue realization". [13]

Table 16.3: Progressive Reductions in Peak Rate of Import Duty

(percent)

Year	Rate of Peak Duty.
1999-00	40
2000-01	38.5
2001-02	35
2002-03	30
2003-04	25
2004-05	20
2005-06	15
2006-07	12.5
2007-08 to 2015-16	10

Source: Government of India, *Budget Papers* (various years).

16.7 Recent Thinking on Customs Tariff

16.7.1 Customs Tariff Report (Chairman: Arvind Virmani), 2002: This Report was submitted to the Government by the Inter-ministerial Group in January 2002.

The Report made the following main recommendations to the Government.

- Introduction of a single customs duty (20 percent) on all products by 2004-05. Tariff rates below 20 percent on some products be brought to 20 percent while peak tariff rate be brought down to 20 percent. According to the Report, a single uniform import tariff implies that the effective protection for all producers is also equal to this single uniform tariff.
- Phasing out all exemptions, barring those on security considerations, by 2004-05.
- Removal of all anomalies in the levy of customs duty by reclassifying all goods

and services into two broad categories, viz. producer goods and consumer goods instead of raw materials, components and parts, and final goods.

The Group made out a case for reducing import duties to a near-uniform basic rate of 10 percent by the end of 2005-06 and 5 percent by the end of 2011-12. The ASEAN free trade agreement proposes to bring down ASEAN rates to the 0-5 percent range by 2010 even for highly sensitive agricultural goods.

It is noteworthy that producers seek a low import tariff on raw materials and intermediate goods, and high tariff on finished goods.

16.7.2 Import Duty Structure Recommended by Task Force on Indirect Taxes (Chairman: Vijay Kelkar), 2002: The Task Force laid down a broad approach to customs tariff reforms in India. It envisages a zero duty for essential items, 10 percent duty for raw materials, inputs and intermediate goods and 20 percent for final goods by 2004-05. Following introduction of States' Value Added Tax (VAT), these duties are proposed to be further reduced to 5 percent for basic raw materials, 8 percent for intermediate goods, 10 percent for finished goods and 20 percent for consumer durables by 2006-07. However, in order to reap efficiency gains from further opening up of the economy, systemic changes in customs procedures and trade facilitation based on modern best practices, which rely on self compliance, may be necessary.

As regards customs exemptions, the Task Force recommended removal of all exemptions except in case of: (a) life-saving goods, (b) goods of security and strategic interest, (c) goods for relief and charitable purposes, and (d) international obligations including contracts. The Task Force recommended the following pattern of import duty (Table 16.4).

Table 16.4: Import Duty Structure Recommended by the Task Force on Indirect Taxes

0 percent	For items like life-saving drugs and equipments, sovereign imports (defence and security related goods) and imports by RBI.
For other goods by 2004-05	10 percent for raw materials, inputs and intermediate goods. 20 percent for consumer durables.
By 2006-07	5 percent for basic raw materials like coal, ores and concentrates, xylenes etc. 8 percent for intermediate goods which will be used for future manufacture (capital goods, basic chemicals, metals etc.) 10 percent for finished goods other than consumer durables. 20 percent for consumer durables.

Source: Government of India, Ministry of Finance and Company Affairs, *Report of the Task Force on Indirect Taxes*, December 2002, p. 169.

To recapitulate, prior to tax reforms initiated in 1991, import tariff had a variety of rates for different items, and even for the same item depending on its end use. Such a cumbersome system led to legal disputes pertaining to import classifications and encouraged corruption in the administration of customs tariff.

Radical reforms have been introduced in the import tariff since 1991. These reforms were necessary because the customs tariff had become, over the years, very complicated in terms of multiple rates, innumerable exemptions, excessive controls, and elaborate procedures. These infirmities of the customs tariff often led to delays, harassment, corruption, and litigation. Moreover, rationalisation and simplification of the customs duties was needed to move towards a market economy, freedom of trade, and opening up the Indian economy to the outside world. The country has moved towards moderate rates of taxation with a view to improve compliance and reduce litigation.

16.8 Export Tariff Policy

Export duties can become an important source of revenue when a country enjoys monopoly or near-monopoly in certain products in the international market. In the early 1950s, India had foreign market dominance in commodities such as jute, tea, and textiles. Hence, export duties fetched sizeable revenues. As this dominance grew weaker over the years, the rates of export duty had to be reduced.

The devaluation of rupee, along with the sterling, against the dollar in September 1949, and the Korean boom considerably increased the demand for India's exports. The comparatively strong position in respect of certain commodities in the world market led to wide profit margins, encouraging the Government to impose or enhance export duty on a number of items including jute manufactures, cotton textiles, and black pepper. Apart from raising revenue, export duties also served to stabilise domestic prices. However, the need to promote India's exports led to a gradual scaling down of export duties. Following the devaluation of the rupee in 1966, export duties were re-imposed on a number of goods including jute manufactures, tea, raw cotton, groundnuts, hides and skins, and mineral ores. The objective was to mop up a part of the windfall gain accruing to the exporters as a result of devaluation. However, they had to be withdrawn in course of time to ensure competitiveness of our exports in the world market. Exports are encouraged, in certain cases through subsidies, to narrow the ever-widening deficit in the balance of payments.

Despite the fact that export duties have lost their importance from revenue angle (Table 16.2), they have not been completely dispensed with. Occasions do arise when there is considerable disparity between the domestic and international prices of certain goods enjoying a comparatively stronger position in the export market, and levying of export duties may be justified to mop up a part of the profits of the exporters. At present, export duties are levied on a few commodities such as coffee, mica, black pepper, hides and skins and leather. Export duty on an item is levied after considering such factors as domestic production and likely exportable surpluses, demand for the item in the foreign markets, changes in exchange rates, and the prices prevailing in the international market. It is noteworthy that the Government can impose/enhance export duties without prior approval of the Parliament because such duties do not fall on the Indian consumers.

Endnotes

1. For historical evolution of customs duties in India, see section 2.4 of chapter 2 of this book.
2. Government of India, *Long Term Fiscal Policy,* 1985, p. 40.
3. Government of India, Ministry of Finance, *Speeches of Union Finance Ministers: 1947-48 to 1984-85,* p. 8.
4. Government of India, *Report of the Customs Reorganisation Committee,* (Chairman: F.C. Budhwar), 1957-58, p. 12.
5. *Ibid.*, p. 13.
6. Government of India, *Final Report on Rationalisation and Simplification of Tax Structure,* (Chairman: S. Bhoothalingam), 1968, p. 14.
7. Government of India, Ministry of Finance, *Report of the Indirect Taxation Enquiry Committee,* (Chairman: L.K. Jha), Part II, 1978, p. 139.
8. *Long Term Fiscal Policy,* op. cit., p. 41.
9. Government of India, Ministry of Finance, *Interim Report of the Tax Reforms Committee,* (Chairman: Raja Chelliah), December 1991, p. l.
10. *Ibid.,* p. 97.
11. *Ibid.*, pp. 143-144.
12. Government of India,. Ministry of Finance, *Budget Speech of the Finance Minister, 2001-2002, Part B*, p. 31.
13. Government of India, *Economic Survey*, 2009-10, p. 172.

17

Direct Taxes Code (DTC)

17.1 Need for DTC

In the Central Government Budget for 2009-10, the importance of continuing the process of structural changes in direct taxes was reiterated and a comprehensive code to this effect was envisaged. The Government signalled its intention to consolidate and comprehensively amend the existing Income Tax Act 1961 and Wealth Tax Act 1957 through a single legislation, by releasing a draft Direct Taxes Code (DTC) and a Discussion Paper for public comments in August 2009. Based on analysis of the numerous inputs received from stakeholders, a Revised Discussion Paper was released in June 2010 followed by the introduction of the Direct Taxes Code Bill, 2010 in Parliament in August 2010. It was proposed to make it effective from April 1, 2012.

However, the Union Finance Minister informed the Parliament in his budget speech for 2012-13 that the Government received the Report of the Parliamentary Standing Committee on March 9, 2012. Enactment of DTC would take place after the report is examined.

In his Budget Speech for 2013-14, the Finance Minister observed, "The Direct Taxes Code (DTC) work is in progress. The DTC is not intended to be an amended version of the Income-tax Act, 1961 but a new code based on the best international practices that will be compatible with the needs of a fast developing economy. The Standing Committee on Finance has submitted its report and we attach great weight to its recommendations. My team in the Ministry of Finance is examining the recommendations and I intend to work with the Standing Committee and its Chairman in order to finalise the official amendments. I shall endeavour to bring the Bill back to this House before the end of the Budget Session". [1]

17.2 Objectives and Salient Features of DTC

17.2.1 Objectives: DTC seeks to consolidate and amend the law relating to all direct taxes, namely income tax, dividend distribution tax and wealth tax so as to establish an economically efficient, effective and equitable direct tax system which will facilitate voluntary compliance and help increase the tax-GDP ratio.

All the direct taxes have been brought under a single code and compliance procedures unified, which will eventually pave the way for a single unified taxpayer reporting system. The need for DTC arose from concerns about the complex structure of half a century old Income Tax Act, 1961, which has been amended a large number of times, making it incomprehensible to the average taxpayer.

As the marginal tax rates have been steadily lowered and the rate structure rationalized to reflect best international practices, any further rationalization of the tax rates may not be feasible without corresponding increase in the tax base to enhance revenue productivity of the tax system and improve its horizontal equity. Hence, a three-fold strategy for broadening the base has been articulated in the DTC.

The first element of the strategy is to minimize exemptions that have eroded the tax base. The removal of these exemptions would: (a) increase tax-GDP ratio, (b) enhance GDP growth, (c) improve equity (both horizontal and vertical), (d) reduce compliance costs, (e) lower administrative burdens, and (f) discourage corruption.

The second element of the strategy seeks to address the problem of ambiguity in the law which facilitates tax avoidance.

The third element of the strategy relates to checking of erosion of the tax base through tax evasion.

17.2.2 Salient Features: The salient features of DTC are as under:

1. It consolidates and integrates all direct tax laws and replaces both the Income Tax Act 1961 and the Wealth Tax Act 1957 with a single legislation.
2. It simplifies the language of the legislation. The use of direct, active speech, expressing only a single point through one sub-section and rearranging the provisions into a rational structure will assist a layperson to understand the provisions of the DTC.
3. It indicates stability in direct tax rates. Currently, the rates of tax for a particular year are stipulated in the Finance Act for that relevant year. Therefore, even if there is no change proposed in the rates of tax, the Finance Bill has still to be passed indicating the same rates of tax. Under DTC, all rates of taxes are proposed to be prescribed in Schedules to DTC, thereby obviating the need for an annual Finance Bill, if no change in the tax rate is proposed. DTC proposes a corporate tax rate of 30 percent against the current effective rate of 33.2 percent and raises the exemption limit as well as broadens the tax slabs for personal income tax.
4. It strengthens taxation provisions for international transactions. In the context of a globalized economy, it has become necessary to provide a stable framework for taxation of international transactions and global capital. This has been reflected in the new provisions. The new provisions with regard to international taxation are the following:

- Advance pricing agreements for international transactions: This will bring in certainty in transfer-pricing issues as any taxpayer can enter into an agreement with the tax administration, which will be valid for a period up to five years, regarding the manner in which the taxpayer would compute arm's length price in respect of the taxpayer's international transactions.

- Alignment of concept of residence (of a company) with India's tax treaties by introduction of concept of *place of effective management* instead of *wholly controlled* in India.
- Controlled foreign company regulations: This is a provision which will assist in taxation of profits of a foreign company in the hands of resident share-holders who may have incorporated such a company in low tax jurisdictions and are accumulating passive income (i.e. interest, dividends, capital gains etc.) in the company without repatriating the income to India.
- Branch profit tax on foreign companies: Currently, foreign companies are taxed at the rate of 42.2 percent (inclusive of surcharge and cess) while domestic companies are taxed at the rate of 33.2 percent (inclusive of surcharge and cess) plus a dividend distribution tax at the rate of 16.6 percent when they distribute dividend from accumulated profits. It is proposed to equate the tax rate of foreign companies with that of domestic companies by prescribing the rate at 30 percent and levying a branch profit tax (in lieu of dividend distribution tax) at the rate of 15 percent. This will provide tax neutrality between a branch and a subsidiary of a foreign company in India.
- Taxation of assets held abroad under wealth tax: It is proposed to include certain assets of residents which are held abroad, such as deposits in bank accounts in the case of individuals and interest in a foreign trust or in a controlled foreign corporation. This will create a reporting requirement mechanism for assets held abroad.

5. Phasing out profit-linked tax incentives and replacing them by investment-linked incentives: It has been observed that profit-linked deductions are inherently discriminatory, prone to misuse by shifting of profits from non-exempt to exempt entity or by reporting higher profits in exempt income entity, and also lead to high level of litigation and revenue foregone. They also impede the Government's efforts to give a moderate tax rate to other taxpayers as the higher taxes paid by others by implication cross-subsidize the lower tax rates of the profit-linked deduction sectors. Such profit-linked deductions are being phased out of the Income Tax Act and have also been dropped in the DTC. They are being replaced by investment-linked deductions for specified sectors. Investment-linked incentives are calibrated to the levels of creation of productive capacity and therefore are superior

instruments. Profit-linked deductions currently being availed of have been protected for the unexpired period in the DTC.

6. Rationalization of tax incentives for savings: In order to focus savings incentives on long-term savings for social security of the taxpayer during his non-working life, deduction of up to ₹ 1 lakh has been provided for investments in approved provident funds, superannuation funds, and pension funds.
7. DTC proposes to rationalise the tax incentives for savings through the introduction of the exempt-exempt-taxation (EET) method of taxation of savings. Under this method, the contributions are exempt from tax (this represents the first E under the EET method), the accumulations/accretions are exempt (free from any tax incidence) till such time as they remain invested (this represents the second E) and all withdrawals at any time would be subject to tax at the applicable personal marginal rate of tax (this represents the T under the EET method).
8. General anti-avoidance rule to curb aggressive tax planning: Direct tax rates have been moderated over the last decade and are in line with international norms. A general anti-avoidance rule assists the tax administration in deterring aggressive tax avoidance in a globalized economy. Such general anti-avoidance rules already form a part of the tax legislation in a number of G-20 countries.
9. Taxation of non-profit organizations: It is proposed to tax non-profit organizations set up for charitable purposes on their surplus (at the rate of 15 percent), after allowing for accumulation of a specified proportion for creation of assets or for long-term projects, a further carry forward for receipts of the last month of the year, and also after a basic exemption limit of ₹ 1 lakh. Donations to these non-profit organizations will be eligible for tax deduction in the hands of the donor.
10. DTC argues against area-based exemptions which allocate/divert resources to areas where there is no comparative advantage. Such exemptions also lead to tax evasion and avoidance. It proposes that area-based exemptions that are available under the Income Tax Act, 1961 will be grandfathered.
11. Under DTC, residence-based taxation is applied to residents and source-based to non-residents. A resident of India will be liable to tax in India on his worldwide income. However, a non-resident will be liable to tax in India only in respect of accruals and receipts in India (including deemed accruals and receipts).
12. The draft Code simplifies the dualistic concepts of *previous year* and *assessment year* used in the Act and replaces them with the unified concept of *financial year* and decrees that all rights and obligations of the taxpayer and the tax administration will be made with reference to the *financial year*.

13. DTC also seeks to eliminate the present distinction between short-term investment asset and long-term investment asset on the basis of the length of holding period of the asset. [2]

In short, DTC, as and when implemented, would yield gains by removing distortions of individual and corporate decision-making, reducing compliance cost and litigation, and improving tax collections. DTC is required as a modern replacement for the existing income tax law. The key objective must be a simplification with unambiguous conceptual core, and the removal of a large number of special cesses and exemptions that favour special interest groups.

In his Budget Speech to the Parliament on February 28, 2015, the Finance Minister observed on DTC as follows, "Enactment of a Direct Taxes Code (DTC) has been under discussion for quite some time. Most of the provisions of the DTC have already been included in the Income-tax Act. Among the very few aspects of DTC which were left out, we have addressed some of the issues in the present Budget. Further, the jurisprudence under the Income-tax Act is well evolved. Considering all these aspects, there is no great merit in going ahead with the Direct Tax Code as it exists today". [3]

Endnotes

1. Government of India, Ministry of Finance, *Budget Speech of the Finance Minister, 2013-2014,* para 154.
2. It may be noted that the Discussion Paper released by the Government argued for special treatment of capital gains under an income tax regime for two reasons. Firstly, taxing gains each year, as they accrue, would strain the finances of an individual who is yet to receive these gains in hand. Secondly, the capital gain realized when a capital asset is sold is usually the accumulated appreciation in the value of the asset over a number of years. The *bunching* of such appreciation in the year in which the asset is sold pushes the seller into a higher marginal tax bracket, if the value of the asset is sufficiently high. As such, if no special treatment is accorded to capital gains, a progressive income tax would discriminate against those whose income from capital assets is in the form of capital gains as compared to those whose income is derived from interest or dividends.
3. Government of India, Ministry of Finance, *Budget Speech of the Finance Minister, 2015-2016,* para 129.

18

National Level Goods and Services Tax (GST)

18.1 What is GST?

The strategy of the Government in respect of indirect taxes is to continue the tariff reform process towards mean ASEAN levels of customs tariff, convergence towards CENVAT rate for excise duty, widening of service tax base and phased move towards a fully integrated goods and services tax by April 1, 2010. In his 2006-07 budget speech, the Union Finance Minister observed, "It is my sense that there is a large consensus that the country should move towards a national level Goods and Services Tax (GST) that should be shared between the Centre and the States. I propose that we set April 1, 2010 as the date for introducing GST. World over, goods and services attract the same rate of tax. That is the foundation of a GST. People must get used to the idea of a GST". [1] GST was first recommended by the Kelkar Task Force on Implementation of the Fiscal Responsibility and Budget Management FRBM Act, 2003.

Thus, GST is a part of the proposed tax reforms to evolve an efficient and harmonized consumption tax system in the country. Presently, there are parallel systems of indirect taxation at the Central and State levels. Each of the systems needs to be reformed to eventually harmonize them.

GST is proposed to be a comprehensive indirect tax levy on manufacture, sale and consumption of goods as well as services at the national level. GST would give India a world class tax system and improve tax collections. It would end the long standing distortions of differential treatment of manufacturing and service sector. The introduction of GST will lead to the abolition of various Central and State indirect taxes and eliminate the cascading effects of multiple layers of taxation. It is claimed that GST will facilitate seamless credit across the entire supply chain and across all states under a common tax base.

The changeover to GST will be a game-changing tax reform measure which will significantly contribute to the buoyancy of tax revenues, acceleration of growth, and generation of many positive externalities.

While presenting the budget for 2010-11 to the Parliament on February 26, 2010, Minister of Finance Shri Pranab Mukherjee, rescheduled the time limit for the implementation of GST and expressed the hope that GST, along with the Direct Tax

Code (DTC), would be introduced from April 1, 2011.

18.2 Salient Features of GST

The introduction of the GST would be a significant step in the field of indirect tax reforms in India. By subsuming a large number of central and state taxes into a single tax, it would mitigate cascading or double taxation in a major way and pave the way for a common national market. Introduction of the GST is also expected to make Indian products competitive in domestic and international markets.

The broad features of the proposed GST model are as follows:

1. GST would be applicable on supply of goods or services as against the present concept of tax on the manufacture or on sale of goods or on provision of services.
2. GST would be a destination-based tax as against the present concept of origin-based tax.
3. It would be a dual GST with the centre and the states simultaneously levying it on a common base. The GST to be levied by the centre would be called central GST (CGST) and that to be levied by the states would be called state GST (SGST).
4. An integrated GST (IGST) would be levied on inter-state supply (including stock transfers) of goods or services. This would be collected by the centre so that the credit chain is not disrupted.
5. Import of goods or services would be treated as inter-state supplies and would be subject to IGST in addition to the applicable customs duties.
6. CGST, SGST, and IGST would be levied at rates to be recommended by the Goods and Services Tax Council (GSTC) which will be chaired by the Union Finance Minister and will have Finance Ministers of states as its members.
7. GST would apply to all goods and services except alcohol for human consumption.

Implementation of a comprehensive GST in India is expected to lead to efficient allocation of factors of production thus bringing about gains in national income and exports.

18.3 Roadmap for GST

While declaring its intention to introduce GST from April 1, 2010, the Central Government had indicated that the Empowered Committee of State Finance Ministers would work with the Central Government to prepare a road map for introduction of GST. The Empowered Committee of State Finance Ministers prepared a report on a model and road map for GST.

In November 2007, a Joint Working Group consisting of representatives of the Empowered Committee and the Government of India prepared a report on the changeover to GST. This report was discussed by the Empowered Committee, which then prepared *A Model and Road Map for Goods and Service Tax in India* (April 2008). The model and roadmap, while recommending that a dual GST be put in place, also provided preliminary views on the Central and State taxes to be subsumed within the GST.

The model detailed the operational issues which needed to be addressed, including the number of rates, exemptions and exclusions from GST, as well as the treatment of inter-state transactions.

The roadmap outlined the legal and administrative steps which needed to be taken in order to comply with the April 1, 2010 deadline.

The comments of Government of India on the proposed design of GST were sent to the Empowered Committee in January 2010. A joint group of officers was constituted to prepare draft Constitutional Bill, Central GST legislation, model State GST legislation and rules required to introduce GST.

To operationalize the GST, the Constitution (115th Amendment) Bill was introduced in the Lok Sabha in March 2011 to enable Parliament and State Legislatures to make laws for levying GST on every transaction of supply of goods or services or both. Some goods, namely crude petroleum, diesel, petrol, aviation turbine fuel, natural gas and alcohol are not to come under the purview of the GST.

18.4 GST Council

The Constitutional Amendment Bill also seeks to empower the President to set up within 60 days of the passage of the legislation, a GST Council with the Union Finance Minister as chairperson and Union Minister of State for Revenue and Finance Ministers of all the states as members. The GST Council is to work on the basis of consensus and make recommendations on issues like GST rates, exemption lists, and threshold limits.

Further, the Bill provides for setting up of a GST dispute settlement authority, comprising a chairperson and two members to resolve disputes arising out of deviations from the recommendations of the GST Council either by the Central or State Governments. The draft Bill has since been referred to the Parliamentary Committee on Finance for examination.

18.5 GST Network

Among the other steps that are being taken for the introduction of GST is the establishment of a strong information technology (IT) infrastructure. For this purpose the Government has set up an Empowered Group (Chairman: Nandan Nilekani). Significant progress has been made in the conceptualization and design of the GST Network (GSTN)—a common portal for the Centre and States that will enable electronic processing of the key business processes of registration, returns, and payments. For this purpose, the structure of these processes is in advanced stages of finalization.

The National Securities Depository Limited (NSDL) has been selected as technology partner for incubating the National Information Utility that will establish and operate the IT backbone for the GST. In this regard the NSDL has set up a pilot project in collaboration with 11 States prior to its roll-out across the country. 3 Joint Working Groups of officials have also been constituted comprising officials from the Central Government, State Governments, and an Empowered Committee of State Finance Ministers to work on legislation, business procedures and IT infrastructure respectively.

The structure of GST Network (GSTN) has been approved by the Empowered Committee of State Finance Ministers. GSTN will be set up as a National Information Utility and will become operational by August 2012. The GSTN will implement common PAN-based registration, returns filing and payments processing for all States on a shared platform. The use of PAN as a common identifier in both direct and indirect taxes, will enhance transparency and check tax evasion.

To prepare for the implementation of GST, Central Government has also begun a phased reduction of Central Sales Tax (CST). The Central Government has brought down the level of CST over the last few years from 4 percent to 2 percent as a precursor to rolling out GST. This is because CST, which is an origin-based tax, is inconsistent with value added taxes, which are destination based—the two should not co-exist. As revenue from CST was transferred to the States, they are to be compensated by being given the right to levy service tax on certain commodities. A Group of State Finance Ministers has been constituted to work on the modalities for the introduction of GST on lines similar to the Group that had been set up for the introduction of State VAT.

Once the integrated GST across the country is introduced, it will simplify tax administration and eliminate cascading of taxes. It will lead to reduction in the distortions in the structure of production, consumption and exports and further to a more efficient allocation of resources. The demand for manufactured goods can be expected to grow significantly. In this connection, the Twelfth Five Year Plan (2012-17) remarked, "The Centre must persevere with reforms of the tax structure, notably the introduction of Good and Services Tax (GST), which will represent a major modernisation of the indirect tax system. GST will greatly simplify the system and improve revenue mobilisation, primarily by plugging loopholes. Since introduction of GST requires a Constitutional amendment, it needs a broad political support which has taken time to build. However, if it can be introduced soon, it will give a boost to efficiency and to revenue mobilisation without raising rates". [2]

Hoping for the early implementation of the GST, the Finance Minister in his 2013-14 Budget Speech observed, "Hon'ble Members will recall that I had first mentioned the Goods and Services Tax (GST) in the Budget speech for 2007-08. At that time, it was thought that GST could be brought into effect from 1.4.2010. Alas, that was not to be, although all States swear by the benefit of GST. However, my recent meetings with the Empowered Committee of State Finance Ministers has led me to believe that the State Governments—or, at least, the overwhelming majority—are agreed that there is need for a Constitutional amendment; there is need for State Governments and the Central Government to pass a GST law that will be drafted by the State Finance Ministers and the GST Council; and there is need for the Centre to compensate the States for loss due to the reduction in the CST rate. I hope we can take this consensus forward in the next few months and bring to this House a draft Bill on the Constitutional amendment and a draft Bill on GST. Hope inspires courage. I propose to take the first decisive step by setting apart, in the Budget, a sum of ₹ 9,000 crore towards the first instalment of the balance of CST compensation. I appeal to the State Finance Ministers to realise the serious intent of the Government to introduce GST and come forward to work with the Government and bring about a transformational change in the tax structure of the country". [3]

GST, if approved, would replace a number of Central and State taxes, make India more of a national integrated market, and bring more producers into the tax net. By improving efficiency as well as revenues, it can add substantially to growth as well as helping government finances.

Indirect tax system of India is currently mired in multi-layered taxes levied by the Central and State Governments at different stages of the supply chain, viz. excise duty, value added tax (VAT), octroi and others. GST, when implemented, will subsume all these taxes under a single regime.

GST is India's most ambitious indirect tax reform plan. Its objective is to levy a single national uniform tax across India on all goods and services.

GST can be rolled out only when Parliament passes the Constitution Amendment Bill, which has been pending in Parliament since March 2011. That requires votes of at least two-thirds of the members in its favour. In addition, at least half of the State Assemblies will have to pass the Bill.

Parliament's Standing Committee on Finance has not yet submitted its report on the Bill. In addition to the passage of the Bill, it is also necessary to have a robust country-wide IT network and infrastructure to make the implementation seamless.

The IT network is still in progress.

In his Budget Speech to the Parliament on June 10, 2014, the Finance Minister made the following observations regarding GST, "The debate whether to introduce a Goods and Services Tax (GST) must now come to an end. We have discussed the issue for the past many years. Some States have been apprehensive about surrendering their taxation jurisdiction; others want to be adequately compensated. I have discussed the matter with the States both individually and collectively. I do hope we are able to find a solution in the course of this year and approve the legislative scheme which enables the introduction of GST. This will streamline the tax administration, avoid harassment of the business and result in higher revenue collection both for the Centre and the States. I assure all States that government will be more than fair in dealing with them". [4]

In his Budget Speech to the Parliament on February 28, 2015, the Finance Minister observed on GST as follows, "We need to revive growth and investment to ensure that more jobs are created for our youth and benefits of development reach millions of our poor. We need an enabling tax policy for this. I have already introduced the Bill to amend the Constitution of India for Goods and Services Tax (GST) in the last Session of this august House. GST is expected to play a transformative role in the way our economy functions. It will add buoyancy to our economy by developing a common Indian market and reducing the cascading effect on the cost of goods and services. We are moving in various fronts to implement GST from the next year". [5] Lok Sabha passed the 122nd Constitutional Amendment—Goods and Services Tax Bill on May 6, 2015.

To sum up, GST, as and when implemented, would be a major milestone in reforming India's indirect tax system. Replacing all existing indirect taxes by the GST would: (a) eliminate cascading effects of commodity taxes, (b) create a national market, and (c) align taxation of imports and exports correctly. It would also improve the competitiveness of production and export from India. Implementation of a Central GST (CenGST) could be the first step towards the GST. Once the CenGST is implemented, it would be easier for the Central and State Governments to switch over to GST.

Endnotes

1. Government of India, Ministry of Finance, *Budget Speech of the Finance Minister,* 2006-07, Part B, p. 26.
2. Government of India, Planning Commission, *Twelfth Five Year Plan (2012-17)*, Vol. I, Chapter 1, para 1.144.
3. Government of India, Ministry of Finance, *Budget Speech of the Finance Minister, 2013-14.*
4. Government of India, Ministry of Finance, *Budget Speech of the Finance Minister, 2014-15.*
5. Government of India, Ministry of Finance, *Budget Speech of the Finance Minister, 2015-16,* para *96.*

Part V: Structure of State Taxes

19

Trends in the Level and Composition of State Taxes

From a modest amount of ₹ 222 crore in 1950-51, revenue from States' taxes has grown consistently over the years and was estimated at ₹ 7,96,619 crore in the 2013-14 budgets of the State Governments. The relative significance of State taxes has changed over the years since Independence in 1947. Land revenue, which contributed 22.1 percent to State taxes in 1950-51, has almost disappeared. In the 2013-14 budgets of the State Governments, the share of land revenue was estimated at 1.5 percent. Conversely, sales tax, which contributed 26.1 percent to State taxes in 1950-51, has become the mainstay of State finances. In the 2013-14 budgets of the State Governments, the share of sales tax in State taxes was estimated at 60.8 percent (Table 19.3). Apart from sales taxes, other important state level taxes are state excise duties, motor vehicle tax, stamp duties and registration fees, entertainment tax, and electricity duties.

19.1 State Taxes as Percent of GDP

In 1950-51, state taxes accounted for 2.13 percent of GDP. This percentage started increasing with every passing decade with the growth of tax bases allocated to the states under the Constitution. The percentage increased to 2.54 in 1960-61, to 3.09 in 1970-71 and to 4.45 in 1980-81.

On the eve of initiation of economic reforms, state taxes accounted for 5.14 percent of GDP in 1990-91. The percentage rose to 5.38 in 2000-01 and to 6.14 in 2010-11. For the year 2013-14, it was estimated at 7.01 (Table 19.1). This improvement is chiefly attributed to agreement among the States to implement floor rates of sales tax and to reduce and rationalize various exemptions and concessions.

19.2 Direct and Indirect Taxes

States' own tax revenue has increasingly relied upon indirect taxes during the post-Independence period. The ratio between direct and indirect taxes at the State level dropped from 24.7:75.3 in 1950-51 to 24.2:75.8 in 1960-61, to 9.1:90.9 in 1970-71 and further down to 4.1:95.9 in 1980-81.

During the post-reforms period, the ratio between direct and indirect taxes worsened further. It declined from 4.1:95.9 in 1990-91 to 2.9:97.1 in 2000-01 and to 2.6:97.4 in 2010-11. It was estimated at 2.2:97.8 for the year 2013-14 (Table

19.2). Presently, there is no direct tax of revenue significance at the level of States. This highly unbalanced tax structure is a cause for concern.

Table 19.1: States' Own Tax Revenue as Percent of GDP: Selected Years

(₹ crore)

Year	States' own taxes	Col. 2 as % of GDP	Year	States' own taxes	Col. 5 as % of GDP
1	2	3	4	5	6
1950-51	222	2.13	1990-91	30,145	5.14
1955-56	283	2.49	1995-96	64,034	5.22
1960-61	455	2.54	2000-01	1,16,717	5.38
1965-66	861	2.98	2005-06	2,21,537	6.00
1970-71	1,546	3.09	2010-11	4,78,594	6.14
1975-76	3,573	4.12	2011-12	5,78,993	6.43
1980-81	6,665	4.45	2012-13	6,88,512	6.87
1985-86	14,597	5.04	2013-14	7,96,619	7.01

2012-13 = Revised estimates; 2013-14 = Budget estimates.

Note: The ratios to GDP at market prices are based on CSO's National Accounts 2004-05 series.

Source: Rearranged data from Government of India, Ministry of Finance, *Indian Public Finance Statistics, 2013-2014*, Tables 1.7 and 1.8. For full time series data from 1950-51 to 2013-14, see Table 5 in Part VIII of this Book.

19.3 Composition of Direct Taxes

There is no direct tax which can claim a prominent place in the tax systems of the States. However, the following are noteworthy.

19.3.1 Land Revenue: Land revenue (Entry 45 in List II in the Seventh Schedule of the Constitution) which formed the bulwark of States' tax revenue during the pre-Independence period and even in the early post-Independence years has declined in importance over the years (Table 19.3). In some States, land revenue has been abolished altogether.

19.3.2 Agricultural Income Tax: Agricultural income tax (Entry 46 of List II in the Seventh Schedule of the Constitution) which could have been an important source of revenue for the States has remained negligible till date. This tax is discussed separately in chapter 20 of this book.

19.3.3 Professions Tax: A tax on professions (Entry 60 of List II in the Seventh Schedule of the Constitution) is levied as a fixed amount per person per year on professions. It is a kind of licence fee to practice a profession. The tax is levied irrespective of the income derived by a person from the profession practiced by him. The scope of this tax is spelt out in Article 276, the clause (2) of which fixes the amount payable by a person on account of this tax. Presently, the total amount payable in respect of any one person to the State by way of such tax is not to exceed ₹ 2,500 per annum.

Table 19.2: States' Own Tax Revenue, Breakdown between Direct and Indirect Taxes with Percentage Shares: Selected Years

(₹ crore)

Year	States' Own Taxes (3+4)	Direct Taxes	Indirect Taxes	Col. 3 as % of Col. 2	Col. 4 as % of Col. 2
1	2	3	4	5	6
1950-51	222	55	167	24.7	75.3
1955-56	283	88	195	31.1	68.9
1960-61	455	110	345	24.2	75.8
1965-66	861	136	725	15.8	84.2
1970-71	1,546	140	1,406	9.1	90.9
1975-76	3,573	288	3,285	8.1	91.9
1980-81	6,665	271	6,394	4.1	95.9
1985-86	14,597	632	13,965	4.3	95.7
1990-91	30,145	1,230	28,915	4.1	95.9
1995-96	64,034	2,213	61,822	3.5	96.5
2000-01	1,16,717	3,457	1,13,260	2.9	97.1
2005-06	2,21,537	5,298	2,16,239	2.4	97.6
2010-11	4,78,594	12,307	4,66,287	2.4	97.6
2011-12	5,78,993	13,235	5,65,758	2.3	97.7
2012-13	6,88,512	15,004	6,73,508	2.2	97.8
2013-14	7,96,619	17,902	7,78,717	2.2	97.8

2012-13 = Revised estimates; 2013-14 = Budget estimates.

Note: The ratios to GDP at market prices are based on CSO's National Accounts 2004-05 series.

Source: Rearranged data from Government of India, Ministry of Finance, *Indian Public Finance Statistics, 2013-2014*, Tables 1.7 and 1.8. Columns 5 and 6 calculations own. For full time series data from 1950-51 to 2013-14, see Table 5 in Part VIII of this Book.

19.4 Composition of Indirect Taxes

19.4.1 Sales Tax: An outstanding development in the sphere of State finances since Independence has been the precipitous growth in the relative revenue significance of sales tax levied under Entry 54 of List II in the Seventh Schedule of the Constitution. It has grown considerably in depth and coverage, and forms the mainstay of States' tax revenue. It is levied not only on consumer goods but also on raw materials and capital goods. In 1950-51, the relative share of sales tax was 26.1 percent: ₹ 58 crore out of a total collection of ₹ 222 crore from States' taxes. In the budget estimates for 2013-14, this share stood at 60.8 percent (Table 19.3).

Prior to tax reforms initiated in early 1990s, sales tax was characterised by a multiplicity of tax rates and exemptions, lack of uniformity across States, large number of exemptions and concessions, and differing procedures for tax collection. In mid-1990s, most states had agreed to phase out the incentive-related exemptions and implement floor rates of sales tax. As part of the nation wide efforts to redesign commodity taxation and the implementation of CENVAT at the level of the Centre, many States have modified their sales tax regimes to launch a state level VAT under the scheme prepared by the Empowered Committee for this purpose. Sales tax is examined separately in chapter 21 of this book.

Table 19.3: Trends in the Level and Composition of Revenue from States' Own Taxes: Selected Years

(₹ crore)

State taxes	1950-51	1960-61	1970-71	1980-81	1990-91	2000-01	2010-11	2013-14
A+B Revenue from States' taxes	222 (100.0)	455 (100.0)	1,546 (100.0)	6,665 (100.0)	30,145 (100.0)	1,16,717 (100.0)	4,78,594 (100.0)	7,96,919 (100.0)
A. Direct taxes of which	55 (24.7)	110 (24.2)	140 (9.1)	271 (4.1)	1,230 (4.1)	3,457 (2.9)	12,307 (2.6)	17,902 (2.2)
1. Land Revenue	49 (22.1)	97 (21.3)	113 (7.3)	145 (2.2)	603 (2.0)	1,377 (1.2)	7,537 (1.6)	11,740 (1.5)
2. Agricultural Income tax	3 (1.3)	10 (2.2)	10 (0.6)	46 (0.7)	169 (0.6)	76 (0.0)	173 (0.0)	135 (0.0)
3. Other taxes*	3 (1.3)	3 (0.6)	17 (1.1)	80 (1.2)	457 (1.5)	1,993 (1.7)	4,597 (1.0)	6,027 (0.7)
B. Indirect taxes of which	167 (75.3)	345 (75.8)	1,406 (90.9)	6,394 (95.9)	28,915 (95.9)	1,13,260 (97.1)	4,66,287 (97.4)	7,78,717 (97.8)
1. Sales tax	58 (26.1)	158 (34.7)	755 (48.8)	3,887 (58.3)	16,476 (54.6)	68,386 (58.6)	2,90,682 (60.7)	4,84,385 (60.8)
2. State Excises	48 (21.6)	53 (11.6)	194 (12.5)	824 (12.4)	4,798 (15.9)	15,825 (13.6)	61,407 (12.8)	98,368 (12.3)
3. Taxes on Vehicles	7 (3.2)	33 (7.2)	104 (6.7)	415 (6.2)	1,535 (5.1)	6,506 (5.6)	25,023 (5.2)	40,534 (5.1)
4. Stamps and registration fees	26 (11.7)	43 (9.4)	122 (7.9)	425 (6.4)	2,089 (6.9)	9,343 (8.0)	54,086 (11.3)	92,021 (11.5)
5. Other taxes**	28 (12.6)	58 (12.7)	231 (14.9)	843 (12.6)	4,017 (13.3)	13,200 (11.3)	35,089 (7.3)	63,409 (8.1)

2013-14 Budget estimates

*Profession tax, surcharge on cash crops and urban immovable property tax.

**Taxes on passengers and goods, electricity duty, entertainment tax and cess on sugarcane etc.

Figures in parentheses indicate corresponding percentages of the total revenue from States' own taxes.

Sources: Reserve Bank of India, *Report on Currency and Finance,* Volume II, (various years); and Government of India, Ministry of Finance, *Indian Public Finance Statistics, 2013-2014,* Tables 1.7 and 3.2.

19.4.2 State Excises: Under Entry 51 of List II in the Seventh Schedule of the Constitution, the States are empowered to levy, "duties of excise on: (a) alcoholic liquors for human consumption; (b) opium, Indian hemp and other narcotic drugs and narcotics; but not including medicinal and toilet preparations containing alcohol or any substance included in sub-paragraph (b) of this entry". The revenues accrue to the states in the form of licence duties from the vendors as well as the tax, which can be specific or ad valorem.

After sales tax, State excise duties (on liquors and other narcotics) are the most important source of States' own tax revenues. Though second in importance, their relative revenue significance has declined over the years from 21.6 percent in 1950-51 to 12.3 percent in 2013-14 (Table 19.3). This has happened mainly because of the policy of prohibition adopted in some States from time to time. However, it is difficult to totally prohibit the consumption of alcohol in the states. Attempts at full prohibition lead to illegal production and export of the tax base to the neighbouring states.

It is noteworthy that while in Western countries the main objective of duties on intoxicants is revenue collection, in India the overriding consideration in imposing these duties is to discourage consumption of intoxicants as a matter of public policy. Since demand for alcoholic beverages is generally price-inelastic, this tax provides a case for keeping high tax rates for controlling the level of consumption. In fact, high tax rates yield both high revenues and greater control on consumption.

19.4.3 Taxes on Motor Vehicles: Under Entry 57 of List II in the Seventh Schedule, State Governments enjoy the power to levy taxes on vehicles suitable for use on roads. These are levied for registration, permits, driving licences etc. and are based on the type of vehicle (truck, bus, car, scooter etc.). In 2013-14, taxes on vehicles accounted for 5.1 percent of tax revenue from States' own taxes (Table 19.3). In most states a compounded system of motor vehicle tax exists, where a one time levy is paid for the life of the vehicle. This arrangement has saved the taxpayers from the hassle of interacting with the tax department every year.

19.4.4 Entertainment Tax: Under Entry 62 of List II in the Seventh Schedule of the Constitution, States are empowered to levy taxes on entertainment. Such taxes are levied on the price charged for admission to any place of entertainment such as a circus, cinema, theatre, exhibition, variety show, etc. The bulk of revenue from this tax is provided by the cinema shows. Though the tax is collected from the exhibitors, the ultimate burden is borne by the cinegoers. According to Tenth Five Year Plan (2002-07), "The tax rates in the entertainment industry are among the highest in the world. Though some State Governments are waiving entertainment tax on multiplex theatres for periods ranging from three to ten years, on the whole tax on film theatres continues to be high. Lowering of these rates will not only benefit the entertainment industry, which has an annual turnover of ₹ 400 crore, but will also promote real estate development in the form of theatres in cities, towns and even villages". [1]

In recent times, entertainment tax has lost its importance due to proliferation of means of home-based entertainments.

19.4.5 Stamp Duty and Registration Fees: Under Entry 63 of List II in the Seventh Schedule of the Constitution, Stamp duty is levied on the registration of property or other conveyances. In 2013-14 budgets of the State Governments, the share of stamp duty and registration fees in revenue from own taxes of the States was estimated at 11.5 percent (Table 19.3).

Till recently, the stamp duty rates were quite high in most states and the procedures for evaluating the conveyances were also complicated. In this context, the Tenth Five Year Plan (2002-07) remarked, "Stamp duty needs to be paid on all documents which are registered and the rate varies from state to state. With stamp duty rates of 13 percent in Delhi, 14.5 percent in Uttar Pradesh and 12.5 percent in Haryana, India has perhaps one of the highest levels of stamp duty. Some states even have double stamp incidence, first on land and then on its development. In contrast the maximum rate levied in most developed markets whether in Singapore or Europe is in the range of 1-2 percent. Even the National Housing and Habitat Policy, 1998, recommended a stamp duty rate of 2-3 percent. Most of the methods to avoid registration are basically to avoid payment of high stamp duty.

Another fall out of high stamp duty rates is the understatement of the proceeds of a sale. This is also linked to payment of income tax and capital gains tax. When registration has not been effected, a transfer is not deemed to have taken place and hence capital gains tax can be totally avoided. Thus, the present provisions in various laws and their poor implementation have led to a situation where there is considerable financial loss to the exchequer on account of understatement of sale proceeds, non-registration and consequent non-payment of stamp duty and avoidance of capital gains tax". [2]

Of late, states have undertaken reforms by reducing the duty rates and streamlining procedures for evaluation of property. After the reduction of rates, the general experience has been revenue-augmenting due to improved compliance of law.

19.4.6 Electricity Duty: Under Entry 53 of List II in the Seventh Schedule of the Constitution, the electricity duty is charged to consumers along with the electricity consumption rates. The rates are meant for the providers of electricity (electricity boards) while the electricity duty is meant for the state treasury.

19.4.7 Octroi: Octroi, an important source of revenue for local bodies, is a tax on the entry of goods into a local area from other areas for the purpose of consumption or sale. It is mentioned in Entry 52 of List II (State List) in the Seventh Schedule. Industry and trade circles have criticised the continuation of octroi and termed it as a retarding factor in the growth of business and commerce in the country. By obstructing the free movement of vehicles carrying goods, the levy of octroi causes delays and thus hampers industrial progress. Therefore, it is suggested that octroi should be replaced by some other form of taxation, e.g. surcharge on sales tax. Unfortunately, State Governments are not favourably disposed to these suggestions and prefer to continue with the controversial levy.

19.4.8 Land and Buildings: Under Entry 49 of List II in the Seventh Schedule of the Constitution, States are empowered to impose taxes on land and buildings, popularly known as property tax or house tax. State Governments generally assign this tax to municipal bodies.

Property tax is charged by the municipal authorities for the upkeep of basic civic services in the city. Generally, the property tax is levied on the basis of reasonable rent at which the property might be let from year to year. The reasonable rent can be actual rent if it is found to be fair and reasonable. In the case of un-let properties, the rental value is to be estimated on the basis of letting rates in the locality.

19.5 Local Finance

The Constitution does not reserve any taxes for the local bodies. Since local government is a State subject (Entry 5 of List II), State Governments may assign any of the taxes in the State List, wholly or partially, to urban local bodies. Taxes usually assigned to local bodies are property taxes, octroi and taxes on professions. Property tax (house tax) is an important source of revenue for local bodies.

Assigning taxes enables State Governments to exercise a degree of supervision and control over the affairs of city corporations, municipalities, district boards, and other local bodies. These local bodies provide certain public services like basic health and education, construction and maintenance of local roads, sanitation, street lighting, and parks. Local governments also receive grants-in-aid from State Governments and earn non-tax revenue from enterprises operated by them. Local finance is discussed separately in chapter 23 of this book.

Endnotes

1. Government of India, Planning Commission, *Tenth Five Year Plan* (2002-07), Vol. II, p. 835.
2. *Ibid.*, pp. 833-834.

20

Taxation of Agricultural Income

When income tax was introduced in India in 1860, agricultural income was also subject to taxation. However, the Income Tax Act, 1886, defined agricultural income and exempted it from the purview of income tax law and this arrangement continued till the enactment of the Government of India Act, 1935. The Act of 1935, segregated agricultural and non-agricultural incomes and provided, for the first time, a separate provincial levy on agricultural incomes.

20.1 Constitutional Provisions

The Constitution retained the distinction between the two types of income and allocated the power to tax agricultural incomes to the States. [1] Entry 82 of List I (Union List) in the Seventh Schedule of the Constitution empowers the Parliament to levy 'taxes on income other than agricultural income'. The State Governments enjoy exclusive powers to make laws with respect to taxes on agricultural incomes vide Entry 46 of List II (State List) in the Seventh Schedule. Although exempt from Central income tax, agricultural incomes are taken into account for the limited purpose of determining the rate of tax on non-agricultural incomes in certain cases from the assessment year 1974-75.

Presently, about half a dozen States levy agricultural income tax, in three of them it is confined to plantation crops, and in all cases the revenue is meagre. The share of this tax in the total revenue from States' taxes is negligible (Table 20.1). Thus, agricultural income tax, which could have been a dependable source of revenue for the States, has remained largely untapped so far. Moreover, land revenue which formed the mainstay of States' tax revenue during pre-Independence years and even in the early post-Independence period, has receded into insignificance over the years (Table 20.1).

20.2 Committee on Taxation of Agricultural Wealth and Income, 1972

The Taxation Enquiry Commission, 1953-54, had suggested the taxation of agricultural income by all States on equity considerations. A more comprehensive examination of the question of direct taxation of agriculture was undertaken by the Committee on Taxation of Agricultural Wealth and Income (Chairman: K.N. Raj). [2] Appointed in February 1972 by the Government of India, the Committee was required, under the terms of reference, to suggest methods by which direct taxation of agricultural wealth and income could be used more effectively for raising additional resources for development. It was further asked to recommend specifically ways and means by which taxation of agricultural wealth and income could be used to reduce economic disparities and promote more efficient utilisation of the available land and labour resources. The Committee submitted its report in October 1972.

Table 20.1: Trends in the Relative Shares of Land Revenue and Agricultural Income Tax in States' Own Taxes: Selected Years

(₹ crore)

State taxes	1950-51	1960-61	1970-71	1980-81	1990-91	2000-01	2010-11	2013-14
A+B Revenue from States' own taxes	222 (100.0)	455 (100.0)	1,546 (100.0)	6,665 (100.0)	30,145 (100.0)	1,16,717 (100.0)	4,78,594 (100.0)	7,96,619 (100.0)
A. Direct taxes of which	55 (24.8)	110 (24.2)	140 (9.0)	271 (4.1)	1,230 (4.1)	3,457 (2.9)	12,307 (2.6)	17,902 (2.2)
Land Revenue	49 (22.1)	97 (21.3)	113 (7.3)	145 (2.2)	603 (2.0)	1,377 (1.2)	7,537 (1.6)	11,740 (1.5)
Agricultural income tax	3 (1.3)	10 (2.2)	10 (0.6)	46 (0.7)	169 (0.6)	76 (0.0)	173 (0.0)	135 (0.0)
B. Indirect Taxes	167 (75.2)	345 (75.8)	1,406 (90.9)	6,394 (95.9)	28,915 (95.9)	1,13,260 (97.1)	4,66,287 (97.4)	7,78,717 (97.8)

2013-14 Budget estimates

Figures in parentheses indicate corresponding percentages of the total revenue from States' own taxes.

Sources: Reserve Bank of India, *Report on Currency and Finance,* Volume II, (various years); and Government of India, Ministry of Finance, *Indian Public Finance Statistics, 2013-2014,* Tables 1.7 and 3.2.

The Committee disfavoured, on practical considerations, a full-scale coverage of agricultural incomes under the Central income tax. However, it suggested partial integration of agricultural incomes with non-agricultural incomes for the limited purpose of determining the rates of taxation. It also maintained that the additional revenue realised as a result of the partial integration of agricultural with non-agricultural income in the above manner, should go entirely to the State of origin of the agricultural income so aggregated. Consequently, from the assessment year 1974-75, Central income tax takes into account the income of an assessee from agriculture for the limited purpose of determining the rate of tax on non-agricultural incomes in certain cases.

Although averse to the idea of full integration of agricultural and non-agricultural incomes for income tax purposes, the Committee favoured the possibility, with certain cautions, of integrated taxation of agricultural and non-agricultural wealth. While the power to tax agricultural income belongs exclusively to the States, there is no constitutional impediment to an integrated taxation of agricultural and non-agricultural wealth by the Centre.

As its main recommendation, the Committee suggested the imposition of agricultural holding tax (AHT) which in its view would secure for the States an additional revenue from well-off sections of agriculturists with much less harassment of the assessees than is likely if Central income tax is extended to the farm sector. The Committee accepted the view that the incidence of direct taxation should broadly be the same on comparable income and wealth groups irrespective of the sources and the forms in which wealth is held. In devising a system of direct taxation of agriculture, it is necessary to ensure progressivity, a principle that has not governed the land revenue. The Committee emphasised that for purposes of direct taxation, the family should be the basic unit of assessment so as to prevent large-scale avoidance.

For a rational system of direct taxation of agriculture, the Committee laid down the following criteria:

1. It should take account of the difference in productivity of land depending upon the particular crops grown in a region.
2. Its incidence should be uniform in different parts of the country.
3. It should reflect changes in productivity and prices over a period of time.
4. It should be possible to build into the tax an element of progression. As for differences in productivity of land, the Committee pinpointed the following factors: (a) soil-climatic differences, (b) conditions of water supply, and (c) crops grown.

Taking into account various factors which cause variations in the productivity of land, the Committee recommended a scheme of agricultural holding tax (AHT) with the following salient features.

1. The country should be divided into a sufficiently large number of soil-climatically homogenous districts/tracts so that differences having any significant influence on productivity are taken into account.
2. For each such district/tract norms of output of different crops per hectare for each year should be worked out on the basis of estimates of yield for the previous 10 years and these should be valued at the relevant average harvest prices of the preceding three years.
3. From the value of the gross output of the crops arrived at in the above manner, allowance should be made for the paid out costs of cultivation (40 to 50 percent of the value of gross output) and also for depreciation of assets.
4. The norms arrived at in the above manner would form the rateable value of a hectare of land growing different crops in different districts/tracts.

5. To provide for the costs of development, the Committee suggested granting of development allowance to all agricultural holdings at the rate of 20 percent of the rateable value subject to a maximum of ₹ 1,000.
6. To determine the actual tax liability under AHT, the Committee devised a simple formula to be applied to the rateable value of the holdings minus the development allowance. If the rateable value of a holding (minus the development allowance) is 'X' thousand rupees, the AHT should form X/2 percent of this amount. For example, if the rateable value of a holding is ₹ 10,000, the AHT would be 9/2 or 4.5 percent of ₹ 9,000 (i.e. ₹ 10,000 minus ₹ 1,000 deductible as development allowance) which is equal to ₹ 405.
7. As the incidence of AHT decreases progressively on small holdings, the Committee favoured the application of the formula to rateable value up to ₹ 600. For holdings of rateable value below ₹ 600, the AHT may be fixed at a flat rate of ₹ 1 per holding.

Although the recommendations of the Committee were widely welcomed, it is unfortunate that the State Governments have generally remained lukewarm in taxing agriculture directly. Exemption of agricultural income from taxation deprives the States of a potential source of revenue. Emphasising the need for taxing agricultural sector, the Sixth Five Year Plan noted, "Direct taxes on agriculture at present constitute less than 1 percent of the total agricultural income. Land revenue, which is the principal direct tax on agriculture, is generally a flat rate levy and, consequently, regressive in character. Fixation of minimum support and procurement prices for major agricultural crops and provision of various inputs such as fertilisers, irrigation, and electricity at subsidised or concessional rates have helped raise agricultural incomes particularly of large farmers. It is, therefore, necessary to consider measures for raising additional resources from the agricultural sector and introducing a measure of progressivity in agricultural taxation". [3]

20.3 Views of the State Governments

The States, on their part, have highlighted serious problems in the assessment of agricultural incomes. These include shrinkage of the tax base due to the ceiling on holdings, widely dispersed potential assessees, fluctuations in production due to uncertain weather conditions, and lack of accounting practices in the agricultural sector. Although disinterested in levying tax on agricultural incomes, States have also expressed themselves against any move to transfer the tax to the Union List. More interestingly, the Centre too is not enthusiastic to adopt the tax as was made clear in the Long Term Fiscal Policy, "It is often stated that exclusion of agricultural income is a major shortcoming of the personal income tax base in India and constitutes an important explanation for the weak revenue-raising capacity of the personal income tax. Taxing agricultural income presents many conceptual and administrative problems. Land revenue and taxation of agricultural income are State subjects under the Constitution. The Centre has no intention of seeking any change in this position". [4] For proper assessment of agricultural incomes, some knowledge of local conditions is required and so the primary responsibility of administering agricultural income tax should preferably be left to the States. Therefore, the taxation of agricultural incomes continues to remain a doubly neglected child of the Indian tax system.

It is well-known that since Independence, agriculture has remained the focus of developmental efforts in terms of irrigation facilities, availability of better quality seeds, subsidised fertilisers and electricity, credit and marketing facilities, and support prices for the main crops. The success of green revolution in many parts of the country is reflected in the increased productivity per hectare of various crops, and in the total production of foodgrains.

It is also a known fact that the benefits of green revolution are unevenly distributed, creating an affluent elite group in rural areas. It is this class which must pay its due to the national exchequer, and revenue so raised may be earmarked for ameliorating the economic conditions of the downtrodden in villages. The States must exercise their constitutional power and tax the upper income agriculturists.

20.4 Tax Reforms Committee, 1991

The Tax Reforms Committee (Chairman: Raja Chelliah), 1991, recommended that agricultural income above ₹ 25,000 accruing to non-agriculturist assessees should be brought under the tax net. To quote, "the provisions for the taxation of agricultural income by the Central Government that we have recommended would not affect those agriculturists who: (a) have agricultural income not exceeding ₹ 25,000 per year; or (b) have non-agricultural income not exceeding ₹ 28,000. This means that agriculturists who have only agricultural income or who have also non-agricultural income but have agricultural income not exceeding ₹ 25,000 will be left out. Thus, the tax will fall mainly on the larger non-agricultural assessees whose agricultural incomes exceed ₹ 25,000". [5] The Committee suggested that the tax proceeds attributable to the agricultural component of income should be distributed in their entirety among the States on the basis of origin.

In terms of the recommendations of the Committee, a person having agricultural income say of ₹ 26,000 and non-agricultural income of ₹ 36,000 (above the then existing exemption limit of ₹ 35,000) pays tax on both the incomes while another person having agricultural income of say ₹ 3 lakh (or even more) and non-agricultural income of ₹ 34,000 has no tax liability on any of his income. Such an arrangement will hardly stand the test of equity. True, the entire tax yield attributable to the agricultural component of income is to be distributed among the States on the basis of origin, there is the need for obtaining the consent of State Governments for making a Central provision for such a tax. It can be a lengthy and uncertain process.

20.5 Task Force on Direct Taxes, 2002

The Task Force on Direct Taxes (Chairman: Vijay Kelkar) suggested the taxation of agricultural income in its report presented to the Government. [6] It recommended a tax rental arrangement between the Centre and the States (under Article 252 of the Constitution) authorising the Centre to impose a tax on agricultural incomes, the proceeds of which will be assigned to the States. The main argument for the proposal is the shifting of non-agricultural income to agricultural income by some unscrupulous assessees.

20.5.1 Critical Comments: The proposal needs to be examined from the following three different, though related, angles: economic logic, administrative feasibility, and political expediency. The case for taxing agricultural income is weak on all the three counts.

From the economic viewpoint, agriculture in India, for most farmers, is not a business as is the case in the United States, Canada, Australia, New Zealand and some other developed Western countries. It is essentially subsistence farming for the large majority of Indian farmers. This is borne out by the niggardly land-man ratio (0.33 hectare) and the utterly small average size of farms (1.6 hectares). With land availability remaining the same, the two ratios are expected to fall further in view of the increasing population. There is hardly any surplus for the tax collector.

Also, agriculture is gradually losing its shine as the leading sector of the Indian economy. A quarter of a century ago, it contributed around 50 percent to India's national income. Presently, the figure stands at around 14 percent. Hence, agriculture is a receding economic activity, at least in relative terms. Conversely, the services sector has emerged as the dominant field of activity, accounting for 47 percent share in national income. Tax collectors would do well if they concentrate on sunrise rather than sunset sectors.

The Kelkar Committee has taken the view that tax exemption of agricultural income violates the principle of horizontal equity (equal treatment of equals). This view is based on the erroneous assumption that incomes from various sources are alike. In fact, the amount of toil and suffering associated with an earning differs from case to case. Thus, it would be imprudent to treat alike ₹ 1 lakh earned by a property dealer in one transaction and ₹ 1 lakh earned by a farmer through year-long exertion and uncertainty. Income tax laws of various countries recognise this fact and accordingly treat different sources of income differently for tax purposes (called the schedular system of taxation). For example, in the United States the law distinguishes between earned and unearned incomes to provide tax credit (rebate) to earned income. Even in India, the distinction between earned and unearned incomes, introduced in 1945, continued for a long time before it was abolished from April 1, 1968. The present law of income tax does recognise and tax different sources of income differently, though to a limited extent. Thus, long-term capital gains enjoy special concessions including inflation indexing and a flat rate tax of 20 percent. Till 1990-91, the differentiation principle was followed in the case of company taxation when trading and investment companies were subject to a higher flat rate tax (50 percent) than industrial and other companies (45 percent).

It is true, as pointed out by the Kelkar Committee, that some dishonest assessees do report their non-agricultural income as agricultural income to evade taxation. However, this is by no means a general practice and it would be unwise to punish the Indian farming community at large for the misdeeds of a few tax dodgers. Moreover, if such cases of fraud come to the notice of assessing officers, the culprits can be proceeded against under the existing anti-evasion laws. Showing non-agricultural income as agricultural income is simply a case of wrong-reporting of income and should be dealt with in the same manner as non-reporting and under-reporting of income.

Still further, Government concessions to the agricultural sector (fertiliser subsidy, minimum support price) are under review for possible reduction/withdrawal in the near future. To burden the agricultural sector with additional taxation at this juncture would be a retrograde step.

Administratively, taxing agricultural income is nothing short of a nightmare for tax authorities. There are serious conceptual and administrative problems in the assessment of agricultural incomes. These include widely dispersed potential assessees, fluctuations in production due to uncertain weather conditions, and lack of accounting practices in the agricultural sector. Furthermore, for proper assessment of agricultural incomes, some knowledge of local conditions is required and in the absence of it, the Central Government staff would be hard-pressed to administer agricultural income tax.

Taxing agricultural income is also politically inexpedient. The Kelkar Committee is not the first to recommend taxation of agricultural income. As far back as 1972, the Committee on Taxation of Agricultural Wealth and Income

(Chairman: K.N. Raj) had also suggested direct taxation of agricultural income. More recently, the Tax Reforms Committee, 1991 (Chairman: Raja Chelliah) also favoured partial integration of agricultural income with non-agricultural income. However, these recommendations were never implemented.

The tax rental arrangement recommended by the Kelkar Committee is presumably based on the experience of the existing tax rental arrangement pertaining to additional excise duties on textiles, tobacco and sugar in lieu of sales tax. This arrangement was made way back in 1957 when the political climate of the country was far different from what it is presently. During the first two decades of Independence (1947-67), the Congress party ruled, with some exceptions, both at the Centre and in the States. This political homogeneity facilitated taxation agreements between the two tiers of the Government including the agreement reached in 1957. Since 1967, the politics of confrontation pursued by different political parties ruling at the Centre and in the States has hindered the rationalisation and harmonisation of India's tax system. Non-implementation of the recommendations of the Expert Committee on Replacement of Sales Tax by Additional Excise Duty, 1983 (Chairman: Kamlapati Tripathi) is a case in point. This Committee had recommended the replacement of sales tax by additional excise duty on *vanaspati*, drugs and medicines, cement, paper and paper board, and petroleum products.

Taxation of agricultural income is a State subject under the Constitution. Given the existing political equations, it is highly unlikely that the States would agree to surrender this right to the Centre.

To sum up, the near absence of direct taxation of the agricultural sector is partly due to the preponderance of big landlords and other vested interests in State legislatures. It shows how the rural rich have effectively resisted additional tax burden upon themselves. The absence or inadequacy of tax on agricultural incomes is an example of the insufficient use of taxation powers allotted to the States. Moreover, the exclusion of agricultural incomes from the income tax base provides opportunities for tax evasion by camouflaging taxable income and black money as gains from agriculture. It is not uncommon among the urban elite to own agricultural farms on the outskirts of metropolitan cities for the sole purpose of diverting their high non-agricultural incomes from a taxable zone to a tax haven. The unequal tax treatment of similar incomes, though from different sources, violates the principle of horizontal equity.

Endnotes

1. For a historical account of agricultural income tax in India, see Government of India, Ministry of Finance, *Report of the Taxation Enquiry Commission,* (Chairman: John Matthai), 1953-54, Vol. III, chapter 3.

2. Government of India, Ministry of Finance, R*eport of the Committee on Taxation of Agricultural Wealth and Income,* (Chairman: K.N. Raj), 1972.
3. Government of India, Planning Commission, *Sixth Five Year Plan*, p. 77.
4. Government of India, *Long-Term Fiscal Policy*, December 1985, p. 35.
5. Government of India, Ministry qf Finance, *Report of the Tax Reforms Committee,* (Chairman: Raja Chelliah), Part I, 1992, p. 26.
6. Government of India, Ministry of Finance and Company Affairs, *Report of the Task Force on Direct Taxes,* (Chairman: Vijay Kelkar), December 2002.

21

Sales Tax and State Level VAT

In India, sales tax in its modern form was levied for the first time by the Government of Central Provinces (now Madhya Pradesh) in 1938. [1] Since then, the levy has proved an outstanding development in the sphere of State finances. It has grown considerably in depth and coverage, and forms the mainstay of States' tax revenue. It is levied not only on consumer goods but also on raw materials and capital goods. In 1950-51, the relative share of sales tax was 26.1 percent: ₹ 58 crore out of a total collection of ₹ 222 crore from States' taxes. Recording a precipitous growth in relative revenue significance, sales tax was estimated to contribute 60.8 percent to States' own tax revenues in the 2013-14 budgets of the State Governments (Table 21.1). It is noteworthy that sales tax has now been replaced by State-VAT. VAT is simply sales tax with set-off provisions. Haryana was the first state to replace its sales tax by VAT on April 1, 2003. Other States have followed suit.

Table 21.1: Trends in the Relative Share of Sales Tax in States' Own Taxes: Selected Years

(₹ crore)

State taxes	1950-51	1960-61	1970-71	1980-81	1990-91	2000-01	2010-11	2013-14
A+B Revenue from States' own taxes	222 (100.0)	455 (100.0)	1,546 (100.0)	6,665 (100.0)	30,145 (100.0)	1,16,717 (100.0)	4,78,594 (100.0)	7,96,619 (100.0)
A. Direct Taxes	55 (24.7)	110 (24.2)	140 (9.1)	271 (4.1)	1,230 (4.1)	3,457 (2.9)	12,307 (2.6)	17,902 (2.2)
B. Indirect taxes of which	167 (75.3)	345 (75.8)	1,406 (90.9)	6,394 (95.9)	28,915 (95.9)	1,13,260 (97.1)	4,66,287 (97.4)	7,78,717 (97.8)
Sales tax	58 (26.1)	158 (34.7)	755 (48.8)	3,887 (58.3)	16,476 (54.6)	68,386 (58.6)	2,90,682 (60.7)	4,84,385 (60.8)

2013-14 Budget estimates

Figures in parentheses indicate corresponding percentages of the total revenue from States' own taxes.

Sources: Reserve Bank of India, *Report on Currency and Finance* (various years); and Government of India, Ministry of Finance, *Indian Public Finance Statistics, 2013-2014*, Tables 1.7 and 3.2.

21.1 Different Forms of Sales Tax

Sales tax is normally an *ad valorem* levy imposed on the seller with reference to the transaction of sale. On the basis of the stage of collection, sales tax is classified into: (a) multi-point sales tax, and (b) single-point sales tax.

21.1.1 Multi-point Sales Tax: As a multi-point levy, sales tax may be applied at two or more stages of production and distribution and becomes akin to a turnover tax applicable at each transaction of purchase and sale. Multi-stage sales tax is politically expedient. A given amount of revenue can be raised at a lower rate of taxation which also reduces the temptation for tax evasion.

The chief demerit of multi-point sales tax is its encouragement to vertical integration of production and distribution processes. Thus, it discriminates against non-integrated firms. Producers of finished products prefer to produce their own materials and components, and this tendency harms the interest of independent suppliers, particularly small ones. Furthermore, multi-point sales tax discriminates against those goods, and their consumers, which have to pass through numerous transactions. In view of these disadvantages, John Due has opined, "On administrative as well as economic and equity grounds the objections to the multi-stage form are so great as to suggest its complete rejection, regardless of circumstances". [2]

21.1.2 Single-point Sales Tax: A single-point sales tax applies to one stage, either at the manufacturing, or the wholesale, or the retail level. At the manufacturing level, sales tax applies to the sale by manufacturer of finished product and is similar to excise duty. At the wholesale level, the tax applies to the last wholesale transaction, i.e. purchase by retailer. The retail sales tax applies to the final sale which means sale to the consumer.

The main advantage of single-point sales tax is that it does not discriminate against non-integrated firms as does multi-point sales tax. It, thus, discourages vertical integration and promotes horizontal integration. As regards the stage of its imposition, the retail stage is considered the most satisfactory due to the following reasons.

1. Sales tax at the retail stage is collected when final sale to the consumer takes place. Thus, it avoids what economists call the cascading or pyramiding effect of a tax. The contention is that middlemen apply fixed percentage mark ups to purchase prices and if the purchase price include taxes (as is the case if sales tax is imposed at manufacturer's, or wholesaler's level), the mark ups will be applicable to the tax component of the purchase prices as well, a situation which must be avoided in the interest of the consumers.
2. A given revenue can be realised by applying a lower tax rate at the retail stage as compared to other stages because the margins of all middlemen are included at the final stage of sale, meaning thereby the enlargement of the tax base at the retail stage.

3. The desired change in the ratio of tax to consumer expenditure can be achieved more effectively in case of retail-stage sales tax. This will be difficult at 'other stages' because the margins of dealers on various goods, besides being applied to the tax component of the purchase prices, may differ significantly.
4. Sales tax at the retail stage can be shown separately from the price and thus made known to the purchaser, increasing tax consciousness among the taxpayers.
5. Expected changes in the rates of retail sales tax do not lead to changes in inventory position of the firms. Anticipated changes in the rates of sales tax at 'other stages' may influence inventory decisions of the firms causing dislocation in trade circles.

However, retail-stage sales tax has its own problems, the chief being the large number of taxpayers in the form of small shopkeepers and scattered retail outlets. In developing countries, the problem of tax administration is more acute in view of widespread illiteracy, lack of monetisation, and poor accounting practices. From administrative viewpoint, this form of taxation is costlier and cumbersome, offering ample scope for tax evasion and corruption.

Sales tax at manufacturing or wholesale stage is administratively preferable because the number of taxpayers is small and readily identifiable. However, the problem of 'cascading' will reappear. In fact, the farther we move from the retail level, the more serious the problem of 'cascading' becomes. In short, the problem boils down to a trade off between economic rationale and administrative efficiency. The relative weightage to competing objectives depends on political judgement and the economic circumstances under which the sales tax system has to operate.

21.2 Constitutional Provisions for the Regulation of Taxation of Inter-State Sales

The problems relating to taxation of inter-State sales were considered by the Drafting Committee of the Constituent Assembly. It proposed incorporation of provisions in the Constitution restricting the powers of the State Governments in respect of the levy of sales tax in the course of foreign trade, inter-State trade, and on essential commodities. In spite of opposition from some States, these provisions were finally incorporated in the Constitution as Article 286 (described below).

Under Entry 54 of List II (State List) in the Seventh Schedule of the Constitution, the States were given the power to levy "a tax on sales or purchases of goods other than newspapers". This provision was quite similar to Entry 48 of List II in the Seventh Schedule of the Government of India Act, 1935. However, under the Constitution, the States' power to levy sales tax was subject to a number of restrictions. These restrictions on the sale or purchase of goods as mentioned in Article 286 of the Constitution were the following.

1. No law of a State shall impose a tax on the sale or purchase of goods where such sale or purchase takes place: (a) outside the State, or (b) in the course of import of goods into, or export of goods out of, the territory of India.
2. Except in so far as the Parliament may by law otherwise provide, no law of a State shall impose a tax on the sale or purchase of any goods where such sale or purchase takes place in the course of inter-State trade or commerce.
3. No law made by the legislature of a State imposing a tax on the sale or purchase of any such goods as have been declared by Parliament by law to be essential for the life of the community, shall have effect unless it has been reserved for the consideration of the President and has received his assent.

In simple words, the States were prevented from taxing the following transactions: (a) Sales or purchases in the course of foreign trade; (b) Sales of goods delivered in another State for consumption purpose; and (c) Sales in the course of inter-State trade and commerce. Furthermore, the power of States to levy the tax on commodities declared to be 'essential' by the Parliament was made subject to the prior approval of the President.

21.2.1 Consequences of Constitutional Restrictions on Sales Tax: The first restriction resulted in considerable loss of revenue to States, which were levying sales tax on exports. The main losers in this category were Bombay, Bihar, Madhya Pradesh, Orissa, and Assam. Nevertheless, this was the least controversial provision of Article 286.

The second and third restrictions, the benefits of which applied equally to registered dealers, unregistered dealers, and consumers, led to large scale evasion and avoidance of tax and hence loss of revenue to the States in general. As the Taxation Enquiry Commission, 1953-54, observed, "Traders in one State started to sell direct to unregistered dealers and consumers in another. Similarly, consumers of valuable commodities tried to get these from dealers in another State rather than buy the articles from their local dealers. The practice grew for sales of goods within a State itself to be shown in the books of accounts as having been made to fictitious dealers outside the State and the goods having then been resold by those dealers to consumers within the State. For valuable commodities like motor vehicles, jewellery, watches, etc. this practice became very common. On transactions that could be shown to be in the course of inter-State trade, the 'exporting' State was prohibited under Article 286 from levying the sales tax; and if the goods delivered as a result of these transactions were shown to be received by individual consumers or unregistered dealers neither could any tax be levied on them by the 'importing' State. Thus, many of these transactions escaped sales tax altogether". [3]

The loss of revenue was more for States with single-point system as compared to States having multi-point sales taxation. This was so because the restriction was not applicable to sales in the State prior to the last point of sale for export to another State.

The constitutional restrictions led to uneconomic diversion of trade and production centres. The problems which the constitutional provisions sought to solve got further compounded *albeit* with a different nature. To quote, "The constitutional restrictions on sales taxation greatly increased the scope for evasion. While the problem before the Constitution had been multiple taxation (by different States) on the same act of inter-State sale, the problem after the Constitution was that inter-State sales frequently escaped taxation altogether". [4]

21.2.2 Essential Goods Act, 1952: As already noted, in addition to the above restrictions, Article 286 also prevented the States from levying tax on sales or purchases of goods declared by the Parliament to be essential for the life of the community, except with the previous assent of the President. For this purpose, the Parliament enacted the Essential Goods (Declaration and Regulation of Tax on Sale or Purchase) Act, 1952, and various commodities were declared as essential including cereals and pulses, fresh and dried fruits, fresh milk, meat, fish, salt, hides and skins, iron and steel, coal, fertilisers, petroleum products, and books.

As to the desirable purpose of the Act, the Taxation Enquiry Commission, 1953-54, noted, "It is obvious that the object of restricting the power of the states to levy a tax on the sale or purchase of 'essential goods' is to achieve some degree of uniformity in the tax burden on those goods, and not necessarily or in all cases to eliminate altogether the sales tax on such goods. When the Bombay Government sought the assent of the President to tax some of the 'essential goods' under their new multi-point tax system, the assent was given on condition that the tax burden on these goods should not in any event exceed the previous tax burden under the single-point system. This seems to indicate that the policy underlying the restriction is one of freezing the existing tax levied on these goods and of ensuring that new proposals to tax them are confined within reasonable limits". [5]

In spite of its desirable objectives, the enactment of the Essential Goods Act, 1952, led to various problems and criticism from some State Governments. Since the legislation was not retrospective, the States which had been levying sales tax on 'essential goods' prior to the passage of the Essential Goods Act, continued to levy the tax. However, those States which sought to levy the tax after the passage of the Act had to obtain the consent of the President. This evoked sharp resentment among the State Governments.

The resentment among the States was further fuelled by the fact that the

Central Government itself was levying relatively high rates of excise/customs duties on some of the so-called 'essential goods'.

21.3 Constitution (Sixth Amendment) Act, 1956

In view of the problems arising from constitutional restrictions on the taxation of inter-State sales, the Taxation Enquiry Commission, 1953-54, recommended as follows, "In essence, the sales tax must continue to be a State tax. However, power and responsibility of the State must end and that of the Union begin when the sales tax of one State impinges administratively and fiscally on the consumers of another State. Inter-State sales tax should be the concern of the Union". [6]

Consequently, the Constitution was amended by the Sixth Amendment Act of 1956. Under this Amendment, the Parliament was empowered to impose 'taxes on the sale or purchase of goods other than newspapers, where such sale or purchase takes place in the course of inter-State trade or commerce'. This new provision in the Constitution was made by inserting Entry 92A in List I (Union List) in the Seventh Schedule. Simultaneously, Entry 54 in List II (State List) was made subject to the provisions of the new Entry 92A of List I. Also, Article 269 of the Constitution was amended which added a new clause (1)(g) which permitted taxes on the sale or purchase of goods in the course of inter-State trade to be levied and collected by the Government of India but assigned to the States. [7] Again, clauses (2) and (3) of Article 286 of the unamended Constitution were substituted by new clauses to make it read as follows.

(1) No law of a State shall impose or authorise the imposition of a tax on the sale or purchase of goods where such sale or purchase takes place: (a) outside the State, or (b) in the course of import of goods into or export of goods out of the territory of India.

(2) Parliament may by law formulate principles for determining when a sale or purchase of goods takes place in any of the ways mentioned in clause (1).

(3) Any law of a State shall in so far as it imposes or authorises the imposition of a tax on the sale or purchase of goods declared by Parliament by law to be of special importance in inter-State trade or commerce, be subject to such restrictions and conditions in regard to the system of levy, rates and other incidents of the tax as Parliament may by law specify.

The new Article 286(2) gave Parliament the powers to define a sale outside a State. The new Article 286(3) is different from the old 286(3) in the following respect: In the old provision, Parliament had the authority to restrict State taxation of commodities declared by Parliament to be 'essential for the life of the community'. In the new provision, Parliament is empowered to restrict State taxation of goods declared to be of special importance in inter-State trade only. [8]

21.4 Central Sales Tax (CST) Act, 1956

Consequent upon the Constitution (Sixth Amendment) Act, 1956, the Central Sales Tax (CST) Act was passed in 1956. The following three main objectives of the CST Act were stated in the Preamble:

1. To formulate principles for determining when a sale or purchase of goods takes place in the course of inter-State trade or in the course of import into or export from India.
2. To provide for the levy, collection, and distribution of taxes on sale of goods in the course of inter-State trade or commerce.
3. To declare certain goods to be of special importance in inter-State trade and specify the restrictions to which State laws imposing taxes on the sale and purchase of such goods of special importance shall be subject.

21.4.1 Main Provisions of CST Act: The regulations contained in the CST Act provide, *inter alia*, for a degree of uniformity by prescribing a maximum rate of sales tax on certain goods considered important for the whole country. According to Section 3 of the CST Act, a sale or purchase of goods is deemed to take place in the course of inter-State trade if it: (a) occasions the movement of goods from one State to another, or (b) is effected by a transfer of documents of title to the goods during their movement from one State to another.

Section 14 of the Act declares certain goods to be of special importance in inter-State trade and commerce. These are: coal, cereals, cotton, cotton yarn, cotton fabrics, crude oil, hides and skins, iron and steel, jute, oilseeds, pulses, rayon and artificial silk fabrics, sugar, tobacco, woollen fabrics. The list of 'declared goods' originally covered by the Act in 1956 was expanded twice, once in 1957 to include textiles, sugar, and tobacco, and again in 1976 to include cereals (like wheat, paddy, rice etc.), crude oil, and pulses.

Section 15 of the Act lays down the rate structure. The rates are different depending upon the classes of goods and the status of the person to whom the goods are sold. Thus, goods are either 'declared goods' (goods of special importance) or 'non-declared goods' while a person may be a registered or a non-registered dealer. Based on these classifications, the rates of sales tax are prescribed by the Central Government though the tax is administered (i.e. assessed, collected and appropriated) by the State Governments by virtue of the powers delegated to them by the Central Government under Article 258(1) of Constitution.

The maximum prescribed rate of sales tax on 'declared goods' inside a State is 2 percent of the sale price and is not leviable at more than one stage. [9] Thus, although sales tax on intrastate sales is levied by the States, taxation of intrastate sales of 'declared goods' (goods of special importance) is subject to certain restrictions in terms of the nature of the levy (not to be levied at more than one stage) and the rate of tax (not more than 2 percent).

In the case of inter-State sale of such goods to registered dealers, the rate of tax is the same as applicable to the sale of such goods inside the exporting State. In respect of sale of 'declared goods' to non-registered dealers (including consumers) the CST is chargeable at twice the rate applicable to the same goods inside the State, i.e. 8 percent. Where 'non-declared' goods are sold in the course of inter-State trade to a registered dealer, the ceiling rate is 4 percent [10] or the rate applicable to internal sales of the concerned goods, whichever is lower. [11] However, on inter-State sale of non-declared goods to non-registered dealers, the rate of CST is 10 percent or the rate applicable to the sale of such goods inside the exporting State, whichever is higher. [12]

The Act further specifies that when a sales tax has been levied inside a State on any declared goods and such goods are sold in the course of inter-State trade, the tax so levied shall be refunded. Provision also exists that goods which are generally and unconditionally exempt from the sales tax within a State will also be exempt from CST in the course of inter-State trade.

21.4.2 Working of CST Act: It is clear as to why some kind of Central control is necessary on sales tax for larger national interest. Had Punjab, and Haryana been free to levy sales tax on foodgrains at will, the people of food deficit States would have suffered. Similarly, uncontrolled imposition of sales tax by West Bengal, and Bihar on iron and steel, and coal would have impeded the growth of engineering industry in Gujarat and Maharashtra.

CST Act authorises a State to tax residents of other States. Lest this power should be misused to export undue tax burden to the other States, the original scheme devised in 1956 kept the rate of CST low at 1 percent ensuring some reasonable revenue for the exporting States. However, over the years the rate of CST has been raised by stages to 4 percent. This trend has benefited industrially advanced States (like Maharashtra, Gujarat, Tamil Nadu, and West Bengal) at the cost of industrially backward States. Since manufactures are the main items of inter-State trade, the developed States are able to export a part of their taxation to other States. In effect, it amounts to transfer of financial resources from poorer States to well off States, much against the declared objective of regional balanced development and equitable distribution of resources among the States. Moreover, the high rate of CST hinders the free flow of trade and commerce within the country.

It may be suggested that the rate of CST should be reduced to the original level of 1 percent to safeguard the interests of poorer States. Furthermore, the Central Government should declare some more inputs as goods of special importance in inter-State trade to restrict the power of the States to tax such goods. However, these suggestions have met with stiff resistance from most State Governments. At the New Delhi Conference of Chief Ministers held on September 16-17, 1980, there was a unanimous opinion that the rate of CST should not be brought down from 4 percent to 1 percent. [13] However, it was agreed to constitute a panel of Chief Ministers to consider, *inter alia*, additions to the list of 'declared goods'. The Conference also expressed unanimity over the need for uniform sales tax laws in the country because various variants of the sales tax pose problems for the collecting authorities as well as for the taxpayers. The Chief Ministers' Conference decided to request the Law Commission to undertake, on a high priority basis, the drafting of a model sales tax law for consideration by the States.

21.5 Additional Duties of Excise (Goods of Special Importance) Act, 1957

Another landmark in the evolution of sales tax in India was the year 1956 when, following a voluntary agreement between the Centre and the States at a meeting of the National Development Council (NDC) held in December, 1956, it was decided to replace sales tax on textiles, tobacco, and sugar by additional duties of excise and to distribute revenues derived therefrom among the States. The agreement provided also that the share accruing to each State shall not in any case be less than the revenue realised from the levy of sales tax on these goods for the financial year 1956-57 in that State. The Council's decision was implemented through the Additional Duties of Excise (Goods of Special Importance) Act, 1957, the First Schedule of which prescribed the rates of additional duties of excise and the Second Schedule the scheme of distribution of the net proceeds among the States.

The Act does not debar States from the levy of sales tax on the specified commodities, but it does provide that if in any year any State levies and collects a tax on the sale or purchase of such commodities, no sum shall be paid to that State in that year by way of share out of the net proceeds of the additional duties of excise, unless the Central Government by special order decides otherwise. The commodities covered under the scheme (textiles, tobacco, and sugar) were declared goods of special importance in inter-State trade so that no State could find it worthwhile to opt out of the voluntary agreement not to impose sales tax on these goods. [14] The revenue derived from additional duties of excise, levied and collected by the Centre, is distributed among the States in accordance with the formula prescribed by the Finance Commission. The Fourth Finance Commission described it as a *tax rental arrangement.* [15]

21.5.1 Rationale of the Scheme: The scheme of additional duties of excise in lieu of sales tax has the following advantages:

1. It minimises tax evasion by levying the tax at first point and saving industry, trade, and consumers from administrative complexities involved in the collection and payment of sales tax.
2. It helps in maintaining uniformity in the prices of widely consumed goods throughout the country.
3. Such an arrangement contributes to the development of an integrated market by facilitating movement of goods across State borders.
4. Rationalisation of commodity taxation at the national level becomes easy.
5. Cost of collection is reduced.

21.5.2 Views of the State Governments: The scheme of additional duties of excise in lieu of sales tax has been in force for the last 40 years. While the business community has demanded extension of this scheme to other commodities, the States have generally remained disinclined in this regard. The distrust between the Centre and the States regarding the operation of this scheme by the Central Government is an irritant in Centre-State relations. States have argued that: (a) sales tax is the only elastic source of revenue available to them and in view of its regional applicability it is also the only effective instrument for shaping their economic policies, (b) replacement of it by Central levy will encroach on their constitutional rights leading to erosion of their financial autonomy, and (c) if taxes are levied and collected by a State itself then it is more conscious of its responsibilities towards the taxpayers. Subventions from the Centre may lead to reckless spending, causing fiscal indiscipline.

As regards the working of the existing scheme, the dissatisfaction of State Governments is borne out of their belief that revenue potential of additional duties of excise has not been fully exploited by the Centre. Their complaint is that the growth of revenue from additional excise duties on textiles, sugar, and tobacco lags behind the growth in revenue from basic excise duties on the same commodities. The States complain that once sales tax on the three commodities was replaced by additional excise duties, the Centre did not feel the need for consultation with the States for reviewing the working of the scheme. They claim that the growth rate of their sales tax revenue is much higher than the growth rate of the yield from additional excise duties.

21.5.3 Decisions of the National Development Council (NDC): Following complaints from the States, the whole issue was reconsidered by the NDC in its meeting held on December 28, 1970. The Council decided to continue the scheme with the following conditions: (a) that the incidence of additional duties would be stepped up to 10.8 percent of the value of clearances within a period of two or three years, (b) that a ratio of 2:1 between basic and additional excise duties would be achieved and maintained, (c) that specific duties would be converted into *ad valorem* duties except in regard to unmanufactured tobacco. It was also agreed that a Standing Review Committee consisting of representatives of the Central and State Governments with the Economic Adviser, Planning Commission, as convenor, would be set up and the same would meet at least once a year to review the working of the new arrangement and make such recommendations as may be necessary for its further improvement.

As a follow up action, specific duties were replaced by *ad valorem* rates and significant enhancements were made in additional excise duties in the Central budgets for the three consecutive years 1971-72 to 1973-74. The Standing Review Committee met for the first time in February 1981 and appointed a sub-committee which recommended that the incidence of 10.8 percent should be achieved in three stages: 8.5 percent by 1984-85; 9.75 percent by 1987-88; and 10.8 percent by 1989-90. The Ninth Finance Commission was informed by the Union Finance Ministry that the incidence achieved by the end of 1988-89 was 10.7 percent. The Commission hoped that the committed level of 10.8 percent would be actually achieved by the end of 1989-90. In a significant move, the Commission recommended that during its award period (1990-95), if in any year the incidence of additional excise duties falls short of the level of 10.8 percent of the value of clearances, the shortfall should be made good by the Centre by providing an equivalent amount by way of grants-in-aid to be distributed among the States in the same manner as recommended for sharing the proceeds of additional excise duties. [16] As regards the ratio between basic excises and additional excises, the Centre fulfilled its obligations by achieving the stipulated 2:1 ratio by 1981-82.

21.5.4 Expert Committee on Replacement of Sales Tax by Additional Excise Duty, 1983: As already noted, sales tax on textiles, tobacco, and sugar was replaced by additional duties of excise in 1957. The scheme of additional excise duties was proposed to be extended to some more commodities in 1980. At a conference of the Chief Ministers convened by the Centre on September 16-17 of that year, it was resolved to bring *vanaspati*, and life-saving drugs under additional excise duties in lieu of sales tax. It was also decided to constitute a committee of Chief Ministers to consider what other items could be added to the list for additional excise duties. However, the non-Congress (I) States viz. Kerala, Tamil Nadu, Tripura, and West Bengal did not agree with the resolution passed at the Chief Ministers Conference.

The matter was further examined at another conference of Chief Ministers held in February 1981, which recommended the appointment of an expert committee by the Central Government to look into this matter. The expert committee under the Chairmanship of Mr. Kamlapati Tripathi submitted its report

[17] in January 1983. It recommended the replacement of sales tax by additional excise duty on *vanaspati*, drugs and medicines, cement, paper and paper board, and petroleum products. The recommendations were considered in a conference of Chief Ministers held on November 2, 1983. However, the six Chief Ministers of the non-Congress (I) States, viz. Andhra Pradesh, Jammu and Kashmir, Karnataka, Tamil Nadu, Tripura, and West Bengal opposed the Centre's initiative to implement the recommendations. The recommendations of the Tripathi Committee were further discussed at a conference of Chief Ministers held in New Delhi on February 9-10, 1989. Unfortunately, no progress could be made in this regard and the matter is still hanging fire.

The opposition of non-Congress (I) States was based on the belief that implementation of the scheme would erode their revenue position. However, a close perusal of the recommendations of the Tripathi Committee suggests that it evolved elaborate formulae for protecting the financial interests of the States. In the case of three commodities, namely paper and paper board, *vanaspati*, and drugs and medicines, it suggested that the annual growth rate of the amount to be collected by way of additional excise duty in lieu of sales tax should be related to the future annual growth rate of sales tax revenue of all the States. For petroleum products and cement, which are substantially subject to administered prices, the Committee recommended and worked out linkages between the amount to be collected by way of additional excise duty from year to year and value of consumption on which normal sales tax would be leviable.

In spite of these safeguards, the apprehension of some States that their resource position would be adversely affected reflects their lack of confidence in the Centre in implementing the scheme sincerely. Thus, an important tax reform has become a casualty of the distrust between the Central and the State Governments. The scheme of additional excise duties in lieu of sales tax has merits of its own. In view of the safeguards provided by the Tripathi Committee and the Ninth Finance Commission, the scheme should not only be retained but extended to other commodities as well.

It is pertinent to mention here that during the first two decades of Independence (1947-67), the Congress party ruled, with some exceptions, both at the Centre and in the States. This political homogeneity facilitated taxation agreements between the two tiers of the Government, e.g. the agreement reached in 1957 regarding substitution of sales tax by excise duties on sugar, textiles, and tobacco. Since 1967, the politics of confrontation pursued by different political parties ruling at the Centre and in the States has hindered the process of rationalisation and harmonisation of commodity taxation. In fact, reform of commodity taxation is closely interwoven with the political process.

Unfortunately, the political response to economic logic so far has neither been adequate nor helpful.

21.6 Constitution (Forty-sixth Amendment) Act, 1982 and Consignment Tax

Consequent upon the Sixth Amendment of the Constitution, the Central Sales Tax (CST) Act was passed in 1956. Section 14 of the Act declares certain goods to be of special importance in inter-State trade while section 15 of the Act lays down the rate structure.

However, the CST Act left out of its ambit the consignments (or despatches or stock-transfers) from a company to its branch located in a different State. Since no sale is involved, it is called in-house transaction by a company. The loophole has come in handy for unscrupulous parties to evade sales tax by showing virtual sales as consignments from one State to another. By this method, the payment of CST is avoided. Only local sales tax becomes payable. Therefore, through the Constitution (Forty-sixth Amendment) Act, 1982, the Parliament was empowered to levy `taxes on the consignment of goods (whether the consignment is to the person making it or to any other person), where such consignment takes place in the course of inter-State trade or commerce.' This was done by inserting Entry 92B in List I of the Seventh Schedule and simultaneously amending Article 269 by inserting sub-clause 269(1)(h). Consignment tax is a levy on inter-State transfer of goods.

Ever since, the States have been pressing the Centre to levy the tax, the net proceeds of which are entirely assignable to States under Article 269. The proposed tax is intended to check avoidance of CST. The Commission on Centre-State Relations, 1988, also impressed upon the Government to "bring in suitable legislation in this regard without further loss of time". [18]

21.6.1 Issues Related to Consignment Tax: Though the necessary legislation is still to be enacted, industrial and commercial circles have expressed grave concern about the deleterious effects of the impending levy. Trade circles maintain that consignments become necessary in view of seasonal fluctuations in the demand for goods as well as frequent transport bottlenecks. Commercial practices like 'branch transfer' or 'transfer on consignment basis' also help manufacturer-supplier to reduce avoidable costs of holding high levels of inventory.

What will be the impact of consignment tax on prices? What should be the rate of tax? Who shall have the exemption powers? How will it affect the location of industries? How will the proceeds of this tax be shared among the States? These are some of the issues to be sorted out.

The impact of the consignment tax on prices will depend on the rate of the new levy and the commodities covered under its ambit. Since the new levy will be in addition to CST leviable at 4 percent, it is bound to push up prices. To minimise the inflationary potential, the rate of the new levy may preferably be fixed at a low level of 1 percent. It may be recalled that in 1956 when the CST Act was passed the rate was fixed at 1 percent. However, over the years the rate of CST has been raised by stages to the present level of 4 percent. Thus, the rate of proposed consignment tax should be low and pegged to that level through constitutional provisions to avoid frequent hikes as in the case of CST.

Furthermore, to lessen the adverse impact on prices, it is necessary to grant exemptions to items of mass consumption. To achieve this, it would be desirable that the power to grant exemptions from the proposed levy be concurrently enjoyed by the Centre and the States. The concurrent power of exemption would enable the Centre to ensure uniformity of taxation of goods of national importance, particularly those which are subject to the scheme of administered prices.

The levy of consignment tax may encourage lopsided industrial development of the country. Producers in States which are self-sufficient with respect to raw materials and the market for goods manufactured out of them will remain unaffected by the consignment tax. Conversely, the entrepreneurs in States which import raw materials from other States and also market their manufactures in other States will be doubly taxed, once on the raw materials and then on the manufactured goods. Under such circumstances, prospective entrepreneurs would be tempted to opt for self-sufficient States to enjoy price advantage on the final product, negating in the process the national policy of regional balanced development.

As regards the sharing of tax proceeds, it is apparent that producer-States like Maharashtra, and Gujarat would like the proceeds to accrue to the respective States in full. Contrarily, the backward States would prefer to see a higher proportion of the proceeds distributed among the States through the Finance Commission. At a conference of the Chief Ministers held in February 1989, it was agreed that 50 percent of the proceeds of the consignment tax would be retained by the collecting States and the remaining 50 percent would flow into a divisible pool from which the amount would be distributed among the States in accordance with the formula devised by the Finance Commission. At the same Conference, the Government announced its decision to introduce a Bill in this regard in the monsoon session of Parliament of that year. Since then nothing has been heard about this legislation.

Sales tax system has already played havoc with internal freedom of industry and trade. Enjoying their constitutional right, different State Governments levy sales tax on a wide range of commodities at different rates with different procedures and rules for its collection. In a scenario like this, the introduction of consignment tax will further confound the existing confusion about commodity taxation at the State level. The imposition of consignment tax would discourage free movement of goods from one State to another. Restricting movement of goods across State borders through tax practices runs counter to the needs of a growing and diversifying economy. Moreover, in view of the current experiment with MODVAT at the Central level to save industry of the cumulative effects of excise duty, the introduction of consignment tax would hinder the process of rationalisation of commodity taxation. Ideally, imposition of consignment tax should be avoided. In case it is unavoidable, a cautious approach is necessary keeping in view the national interest.

21.7 Present Nature of Sales Tax

Under the Constitution, the right to levy sales tax belongs to the State Governments. Each State is, therefore, empowered to collect tax on the sale of goods within its territory according to the rules framed by it. Thus, different State Governments levy sales tax on a wide range of commodities at different rates with diverse procedures and rules for its collection. The Central Government also enters the field in so far as it prescribes the ceiling rate of sales tax on goods in inter-State trade. In the case of three important commodities, viz. textiles, sugar, and tobacco, additional duties of excise are imposed in lieu of sales tax, the proceeds of which are distributed among the States.

Different States have adopted different variants of the sales tax due to a number of reasons including administrative convenience, ad hoc measures to increase tax revenues, and to attract enterprise in their respective areas. Sales tax in a State may take the form of a single point, double-point and/or multi-point levy. However, single-point is the main type of sales tax imposed on most commodities in all States. In most States a significant part of sales tax revenue originates from first-point levy, i.e. at the manufacturer's level. Some States also levy surcharges on sales tax as an ad hoc measures to augment their resources.

The rate structure of sales tax is further complicated in view of different lists of exemptions/concessions, numerous nominal rate categories, and different administrative procedures in each of the States. These variations have caused disparities in the effective rate of sales tax on similar commodities in different States. Agricultural commodities like cereals and pulses are either exempt or bear low rate of sales tax ranging from 2 to 3 percent. For most commodities, the rate of single-point levy varies between 4 to 8 percent. However, in the case of luxury items like motor cars, refrigerators, and VCRs, the rate may go up to even 15 percent in some States. The rate of multi-point levy hovers around 4 percent.

21.8 Problems Created by Sales Tax

Perhaps no other tax impinges on so large a number of interests as sales tax. Firstly, it hurts the consumers who ultimately bear its burden. Next, there are the dealers from whom it is collected, and in many cases the producers also come in its ambit in case it is levied at the manufacturer's level. Then there are the State Governments, always anxious to extend its scope and retain their hold on it. Furthermore, the Central Government decides the rate of sales tax on goods of special importance in inter-State trade. Consequently, the operation of sales tax creates a host of problems which may be summarised as follows.

1. Sales tax is a levy on commodities which, in most cases, are also subject to excise duties. As excise duty and sales tax are levied by different layers of Government, it becomes difficult to determine judiciously the impact of these levies on production, investment, and the consumers. No attempt to rationalise commodity tax system can succeed if the Centre and States act independently without co-ordination among themselves.
2. A closely related problem is the taxation of inputs and capital goods, by the Central and State Governments, through excise duties and sales tax respectively. Apart from generating cascading effect, sales taxation of inputs benefits the comparatively richer States at the cost of poorer States. To quote, "The (sales) taxation of inputs also means that its burden falls on consumers outside the State. While procedures exist for refund of excise duties on a product when it is exported outside the country, the sales tax paid on inputs is not rebated. In consequence, the more developed States which have attained high levels of agricultural or industrial production are able to derive additional resources, by taxing consumers in other States, while the resource mobilisation capacity of the less developed States, which have to depend on most of their needs being met by imports from other States, is weakened". [19] This reverse flow of funds is further strengthened by the frequent hikes in the rate of Central sales tax.

   Originally at 1 percent, the Central sales tax rate has steadily increased to 4 percent, thereby imposing undue burden on the importing States and defeating, in the process, the very objective of Central Sales Tax Act of 1956.

   To tackle the problem of cascading effect associated with the taxation of intermediate goods, recent reforms at the Central level provide instant credit of excise duty paid on inputs under the Modified Value Added Tax (MODVAT) scheme. Although State laws do provide relief through exemptions in regards to sales tax when inputs are sold to manufacturers, such concessions are limited and lack uniformity. This lacuna in the sales tax system has hindered reform of indirect tax system in India.

3. In order to attract trade and industry to their respective areas, some States have been indulging in a kind of *rate war* (competitive reductions in sales tax rates). It is true that some States lack infrastructural facilities and to compensate for that sales tax concessions come handy to attract industries, but this shortcut erodes the resource-base of the States, so vital for the development of infrastructure which alone guarantees their speedy development on permanent footing.

   Differential rates of sales tax on the same set of commodities in different States often lead to uneconomic diversion of trade as well as production centres. It is not uncommon for people of one State making purchases in other States to avoid or reduce sales tax liability. Apparently, purchases from lower tax States to those where rates are higher are beneficial so long as the cost of transporting goods is lower than the tax differential. Purchase of truck chassis in Daman (a Union Territory levying a low rate of 3 percent) by the residents of a far off State of Jammu and Kashmir is a popular case in point.

   Similarly, rate differentials may cause flight of capital and enterprise from high to low tax rate States thereby distorting natural selection of production centres based on geographical advantages, leading to unnecessary transportation of raw materials and finished goods and hence cost escalations. Such a misallocation of resources undermines economic efficiency and thereby retards developmental efforts.

4. Sales tax has another disadvantage in that it discourages horizontal integration and on the contrary encourages vertical integration in industries. Firms try to produce their own components in order to avoid sales tax. This tendency harms the growth of ancillary units which are mainly in the small-scale sector.

5. Different types of sales tax (multi-point, double-point, and single point) with varying procedures and rules in different States cause difficulties for the traders, particularly small ones, leading to harassment, corruption, and litigation.

21.9 Alternative Remedies

To deal with the foregoing weaknesses of the sales tax system, experts have put forward various suggestions.

21.9.1 Sales Tax as Central Levy: It is argued that through a constitutional amendment, the levy of sales tax can also be made a Central subject and thereafter a rationalised system of indirect taxation of domestic production and consumption can be administered by the Centre. This is a drastic suggestion which has not found favour with statesmen. The Taxation Enquiry Commission (TEC), 1953-54, was quite categorical in rejecting this suggestion. Emphasising the impracticability of centralisation of sales tax the Commission observed, "On account of its yield and flexibility, sales tax has come to occupy a large and indispensable place in the State financial systems. Centralisation of the tax must be ruled out. Difficulties which confront the tax administrations vary considerably in character and composition from State to State and taken together present a large and almost bewildering variety of problems". [20]

The views of the TEC appear to be still valid considering the present fiscal arrangements and political equations. Thus, a constitutional amendment to make sales tax a Central subject has to be ruled out.

21.9.2 Complete Substitution of Sales Tax by Excise Duty: It is suggested, particularly by the business community, that in place of sales tax corresponding enhancements should be made in Central excises the proceeds of which could be earmarked for distribution among the States. This will facilitate rationalisation of commodity taxation and also reduce the cost of collection apart from saving the business community from harassment from the differing sales tax practices of the various States.

Is a complete substitution of sales tax by excise duties possible? Unfortunately not. Like sales tax, excise duties cannot become universal in scope because of administrative reasons. For instance, the Centre has the legal power to impose excises on agricultural products but it has refrained from doing so. Similarly, small and tiny units of the industrial sector are left out because of administrative reasons.

However, what is small for excise duty may be large for the purpose of sales tax. The Indirect Taxation Enquiry Committee, 1977, estimated that nearly ₹ 500 crore of sales tax was being collected on goods not subject to excise duties such as agricultural products, articles of jewellery which for administrative or other reasons cannot be reached by excises. It concluded, "The consequence of a simple abolition of sales tax from the angle of resource mobilisation would be a substantial loss of revenue to compensate for which something like a 50 percent increase in excise duties on the average would be necessary, given the present base of excise taxation". [21]

Since excise duties are of all-India nature, they cannot take into account regional variations in the levels of income and patterns of consumption. However, different rates of sales tax in individual States permit consideration of regional factors. Moreover, if sales tax is levied at the retail stage, the value base of the tax is large and even low rates of tax can yield sufficient revenues. The cumulative effect is also absent.

21.9.3 Partial Substitution of Sales Tax by Excise Duty: The approach towards substitution of sales tax by excise duties has to be selective. Some arrangements already exist in this regard in the form of additional duties of excise in lieu of sales tax on three important commodities namely textiles, tobacco, and sugar. The extension of this arrangement to certain other commodities as recommended by Tripathi Committee has already been discussed in section 21.5 of this chapter.

21.10 Towards State Level VAT

21.10.1 Minimum Rate Agreement among States: As already noted, some States have been indulging in a sort of 'rate-war' to attract trade and industry to their respective regions. To avoid this unhealthy competition, the Chief Ministers agreed, at their conference in New Delhi on February 9-10, 1989, that all the States would adopt the minimum floor level rates as recommended by the Committee of Sales Tax Commissioners in its report of 1984 in respect of 29 identified items. The follow up action is yet to take place. Even at the regional level, the response is not encouraging. The Chief Secretaries of northern States (Punjab, Haryana, Himachal Pradesh, Rajasthan, Delhi, and Uttar Pradesh) had recommended in May 1994 that there should not only be a uniform rate of sales tax but the slabs of this tax be reduced in these States. The recommendation is still to be implemented. The lack of concern on the part of States to harmonise their sales tax systems is apparent.

21.10.2 Single-Point VAT: To deal with the cascading effects of a traditional turnover tax, some experts have suggested a single-point VAT at the Central level to replace both excise duties and sales taxes. Since sales tax is the most important source of tax revenue for the States, such a drastic suggestion, which will leave the States at the mercy of the Centre, is difficult to implement. Replacement of existing system of excises, sales taxation, and octroi by a comprehensive VAT would require amendment of the Constitution by a two-thirds majority in Parliament and its approval by more than half of the States. A comprehensive VAT at the national level has to be ruled out on economic as well as political considerations.

Switch over to VAT has to be an independent exercise by the Central Government and 25 State Governments. In this connection the Tax Reforms Committee, 1991, observed, "As regards sales tax, the Committee is of the view that this tax could be converted into a form of State VAT within the manufacturing sector. There may be no need for levying sales tax at more than two rates since the distributional and other non-revenue objectives could be left to be performed by the Central taxes which apply uniformly throughout the country". [22] Even this dual VAT system is difficult to achieve because it is highly unlikely that the 25 States will move in tandem to ensure smooth transition to a uniform system of VAT in place of their differing practices of sales tax. Thus, the problem of co-ordination is not only between the Centre and the States but also among the States themselves.

The introduction and extension of MODVAT scheme at the Central level is a step in the right direction to reform excise taxation. Unfortunately, similar reforms have not been introduced at the level of States. The State Finance Ministers' Conference held in New Delhi on May 27, 1994 failed to arrive at a consensus on the replacement of indirect taxes at the State level by a value added tax. The matter was deferred indefinitely by appointing a ten-member Committee of State Finance Ministers to go into this and related questions.

21.10.3 Switch Over to VAT: At a conference of Chief Ministers and Finance Ministers of the States in New Delhi on November 16, 1999, States and Union Territories decided to put an end to all sales tax-based incentives to industry and enforce floor rates of sales tax with effect from January 1, 2000. They also decided to move over to the simple, transparent and efficient regime of value added tax (VAT) with effect from April 1, 2001.

The agreement to impose a set of minimum rates (floor rates) of sales tax on all commodities will ensure sales tax uniformity throughout the country. Four general floor rates of zero percent, 4 percent, 8 percent and 12 percent and two special floor rates of 1 percent and 20 percent were agreed upon.

Essential commodities such as foodgrains, raw meat, eggs, milk and plain water will be subject to the zero rate. There will be a minimum sales tax rate of 4 percent on commodities such as edible oils, vanaspati, processed vegetables, kerosene, bicycles, chemicals and fertilisers. Products like electricals, tyres and tubes, butter and ghee, blades and razors, drugs and medicines, cooking gas, tea and coffee, biscuits and computers will attract a floor rate of 8 percent. Television sets, VCRs, air-conditioners, diesel, paints, telephone equipment and carpets will attract the highest floor rate of 12 percent.

The 1 percent special floor rate will apply to bullion, gold and silver while the 20 percent special floor rate will cover petrol, liquor, rectified spirit and narcotics.

It was also decided at the Conference that a standing committee of State Finance Ministers will be constituted to oversee the preparations for the switch over to VAT and to review the progress of the implementation of sales tax floor rates in the interim.

The decision to implement these sweeping tax reforms came about after the Union Finance Minister gave an assurance to make good any consequential revenue loss the States may suffer.

The prolonged tax war among the States had strained the finances of several States. The race among the States to lure industries by offering competitive concessions in sales tax is expected to come to an end. If implemented sincerely, these tax reforms at the level of States will go a long way in creating conducive climate for the growth of country's economy, industry and trade.

However, some fiscal experts feel that the floor rates of sales tax fixed are too high and hence unrealistic. Since the floor rates are already high, there is hardly any scope for individual States to determine effective rates above the floor level depending on expectations of growth of industry and trade in each state. Moreover, the high floor rates are contrary to the post-liberalisation policy of low tax rates to ensure better tax compliance. It is also being felt in some quarters that uniformity in tax rates is not necessarily a desirable objective to pursue. In many federations (e.g. USA), state governments compete with each other to attract industry and trade to their respective areas.

21.10.4 Empowered Committee of State Finance Ministers, 2001: At a Conference of Chief Ministers and Finance Ministers of various States held on July 5, 2001 in New Delhi, the report of the Empowered Committee of State Finance Ministers on VAT, headed by West Bengal Finance Minister Asim Kumar Dasgupta, was accepted and adopted for the introduction of VAT with effect from April 1, 2002. The VAT design recommended by the Committee had the following elements.

1. The VAT system will eliminate the cascading burden of taxation by setting off the tax paid on inputs against that on output.
2. It will reduce distortions in the economy caused by double taxation.
3. It will end market fragmentation with a uniform regime of taxation followed in all the States.
4. There will be one category of tax-exempted commodities for all the States.
5. There will be two VAT rates: a uniform 4 percent for all States on goods of basic necessities and a uniform floor rate of 10 percent for other commodities (except a few items such as bullion and liquor).
6. A uniform set of procedures for VAT assessment will also be followed by all the States, including the use of permanent account number (PAN) as a common business identifier.
7. The States which do not implement 100 percent uniform floor rates of sales tax by July-end 2001 should be penalised by discontinuing Central Government assistance.
8. The Centre has undertaken to make good any revenue loss to States on their switch over to VAT. A committee of State Finance Secretaries would evolve

clear and measurable criteria for judging revenue loss, if any, due to the introduction of VAT. It will also recommend the manner and quantum of compensation.

As many as 12 States agreed to implement VAT by April 1, 2002.

However, the road to the Indian common market seems to be dotted with hurdles. Many fear that VAT, as worked out by the Empowered Committee of the State Finance Ministers, would make the Indian market place chaotic and confusing. There are many issues which must be resolved to smoothen the transition to the modern and efficient system of VAT.

1. The uniform floor rate of 10 percent does not ensure that States would not charge various higher rates on the same commodity. There should be a cap rate of tax.
2. It is not sure whether the classification of goods into the zero rate VAT and the 4 percent VAT would be done on a scientific basis.
3. It is not clear what treatment would be given to inter-State trade. The biggest concern of industry and trade is the non-eligibility for set-off of CST paid on inputs sourced from across the State border.
4. The fate of exemptions/concessions being enjoyed by various industries under the sales tax system is uncertain when switch over to VAT takes place. By its very nature, VAT cannot be successfully implemented if there are too many exemptions and concessions.
5. A few States have not yet fully implemented even the uniform floor rates of sales tax.
6. From the Government side also, the promised amendment to the Central Sales Tax Act is still to be carried out. Moreover, it is not clear whether changes in CST would coincide with the transition to VAT or not. To reduce distortions, the business circles would like the CST (levied at 4 percent) to be abolished in one go rather than phased out.

The benefits of VAT at the State level can be achieved fully only when all the States comply with the recommendations of the Empowered Committee. If all the States move towards a uniform VAT system, it would be an example of cooperative federalism. The introduction of VAT in place of the existing sales tax system would make the common market dream a reality.

21.10.5 Agreement of January 23, 2002: At the Conference of State Finance Ministers held on January 23, 2002 a final decision was taken that all States and Union Territories would introduce VAT from April 2003. This position was reiterated by all States at the Conference of State Chief Ministers held on October 18, 2002. Empowered Committee of State Finance Ministers endorsed the suggestion that every State Legislation on VAT should have a minimum set of common features. Accordingly, a model VAT Bill was circulated to all the States. Introduction of VAT is expected to increase revenue buoyancy, as the coverage expands to value addition at all stages of production and distribution chain.

Again, at a meeting of the Finance Ministers of all States/Union Territories on January 17, 2003, States and Union Territories again reiterated their firm commitment to introduce VAT from April 1, 2003. It was decided that the VAT legislations of all States and UTs would have common provisions in respect of all important matters and that a simple VAT legislation with maximum convergence would be implemented. It was also agreed that along with the introduction of VAT, the origin based Central Sales Tax would be phased out. It was also agreed that the Additional Duties of Excise (Goods of Special Importance) Act would be suitably amended to empower States to levy sales tax/VAT on sugar, textiles and tobacco with a ceiling rate of 4 percent. This would be done without affecting the existing levy of Additional Duties of Excise on these items by the Union Government

In view of the apprehensions expressed by a large number of States about possible revenue losses in the initial years of introduction of VAT, an assurance was given to the States that the Government of India would compensate the States to the extent of 100 percent of revenue loss in the first year (2002-03), 75 percent of the loss in the second year (2003-04) and 50 percent of the loss in the third year (2005-06).

The Empowered Committee of State Finance Ministers agreed upon the following sequence of steps to ensure introduction of VAT in place of retail sales tax system in States.

1. Passing of VAT legislation and framing of rules and regulations.
2. Computerisation of dealers who will fall within the ambit of VAT.
3. Training of tax officials, traders and consumer associations.
4. Publicity for consumers.
5. Implementation of VAT, assigning VAT identification numbers to tax payers.
6. Implementing transitional measures for introduction of VAT.

21.10.6 Task Force on Indirect Taxes, 2002: The Task Force on Indirect Taxes (Chairman: Vijay Kelkar), unanimously acknowledged that VAT is a major reform in the indirect tax system of India. For a smooth and speedy implementation of VAT at the level of Centre and States, it made the following recommendations.

1. A publicity awareness programme should be started jointly by the Central and State Governments and the former should extend financial support for this, if required. Since State VAT is expected to be implemented from April 1, 2003 it is also necessary that the publicity awareness programme should be implemented at the earliest.

2. An attempt should be made towards uniformity of all State legislations, procedures and documentation relating to VAT.
3. The issue of compensation, if it arises, must be primarily tackled through mutually acceptable mechanism of additional resource mobilization through service tax and not through budgetary support.
4. With the introduction of VAT, all other local taxes be discontinued.
5. Whereas additional duty of excise may continue for textiles up to 2005, it may continue even thereafter for cigarettes which should not be subjected to VAT.
6. The VAT scheme should provide for grant of credit of duty by the importing State for the duty paid in the exporting State, in the course of inter-State movement of goods.

For the stability and continuity of VAT, the possibility of a VAT Council or a permanent suitable alternative, vested with adequate powers to take steps against discriminatory taxes and practices and eliminate barriers to free flow of trade and commerce across the country, should be explored.

21.10.7 Agreement of June 2004: At a meeting of the State Finance Ministers with the Union Finance Minister on June 18, 2004, it was decided that all States will introduce a uniform VAT from April 1, 2005. The proposed VAT will replace the taxes levied by different States like sales tax and octroi. Coinciding with the introduction of VAT, the Central Government will bring down the Central Sales Tax (CST) rate from 4 percent to 2 percent. The CST will be phased out in 2006-07. It was also decided that traders with an annual turnover up to ₹ 5 lakh will be exempt from VAT. This decision was aimed at ending traders' opposition to VAT. It may be recalled that States have missed at least five deadlines for the introduction of VAT, mainly due to resistance from trading community.

21.10.8 Salient Features of the State-level VAT Design: VAT is essentially a federal or central tax, while in India it is aimed at replacing State as well as Central sales taxes. Its effective implementation depends almost entirely on the co-operation of the State Governments. In an ideal situation, VAT is supposed to be a tax to end all taxes. Many countries that have adopted VAT do not levy excise duty, entry tax or luxury tax. However, State Governments in India are demanding the right to retain and, in fact, widen the tax net by levying a range of taxes, including entry tax. This would defeat the basic purpose of the imposition of VAT, namely unifying and harmonizing the complex commodity tax structure in the country.

A VAT regime is theoretically meant for a unified market in which the VAT levied can always be set off against taxes already paid, irrespective of the state-wise location of the manufacturing or trading entities. In India, these inter-state adjustments are proving to be difficult to implement in view of the existing constitutional provisions regarding distribution of taxation powers between the

Centre and the States. It needs, however, to be emphasised that the States must think in terms of economic development of the country as a whole and encourage the free flow of trade and commerce in the economy. A national approach is necessary to harmonise and rationalise the existing system of commodity taxation.

In view of the above constraints and also to provide some flexibility to the States, the Empowered Committee, through its deliberations over the years, finalised a design of VAT to be adopted by the States. The model design seeks to retain the essential features of VAT, while at the same time, providing a measure of flexibility to the States, to enable them to meet their local requirements. The main features of the VAT design finalised by the Empowered Committee are the following:

1. Rates of VAT on various commodities shall be uniform for all the States/UTs. There are 2 basic rates of 4 percent and 12.5 percent, besides an exempt category and a special rate of 1 percent for a few selected items. The items of basic necessities have been put in the zero-rate bracket or the exempted schedule. Gold, silver and precious stones have been put in the 1 percent schedule. There is also a category with 20 percent floor rate of tax, but the commodities listed in this schedule are not eligible for input tax rebate/set off. This category covers items like motor spirit (petrol), diesel, aviation turbine fuel, and liquor.
2. Model VAT design makes provision for eliminating the multiplicity of taxes. In fact, all the State taxes on purchase or sale of goods (excluding entry tax in lieu of octroi) are required to be subsumed in VAT.
3. Provision has been made for allowing input tax credit, which is the basic feature of VAT. However, since the VAT being implemented is intra-State VAT only and does not cover inter-State sale transactions, input tax credit will not be available on inter-State purchases.
4. There are provisions to make the system more business-friendly. For instance, there is provision for self-assessment by the dealers. Similarly, there is provision of a threshold limit for registration of dealers in terms of annual turnover of ₹ 5 lakh. Dealers with turnover lower than this threshold limit are not required to obtain registration under VAT and are exempt from payment of VAT. There is also provision for composition of tax liability up to annual turnover limit of ₹ 50 lakh.
5. Regarding the industrial incentives, the States have been allowed to continue with the existing incentives, without breaking the VAT chain. However, no fresh sales tax/VAT-based incentives are permitted.
6. Exports will be zero-rated, with credit given for all taxes on inputs/purchases related to such exports.

21.10.9 Progress of VAT Implementation: According to *Economic Survey,* 2006-07, "VAT has been introduced by 30 States/UTs so far. Tamil Nadu has implemented VAT from January 1, 2007. The union territory of Puducherry has communicated its decision to implement VAT from April 1, 2007. Uttar Pradesh has not yet taken any decision in this regard. Since Sales Tax/VAT is a State subject, the Central Government has played the role of a facilitator. A compensation formula has also been finalised in consultation with the States, for providing compensation, during 2005-06, 2006-07 and 2007-08, for any losses on account of introduction of VAT and compensation is being released according to this formula. Technical and financial support has also been provided to the States for VAT computerisation, publicity and awareness and other related aspects". [23]

Broadly speaking, the experience of implementing VAT has been quite encouraging. The new system has been received well by all the stakeholders, and the transition has been quite smooth with the Empowered Committee constantly reviewing the progress of implementation. The EC has advised the States to constantly interact with trade and industry to remove their apprehensions, if any, and to ensure that the benefits of VAT due to input tax credit and reduction in tax rates (wherever applicable) are passed on to the consumers. The EC is also persuading the remaining States/UTs to implement VAT at the earliest.

In short, India has adopted a dual system of VAT: Central VAT (CENVAT) at the Central level and State-VAT at the level of States.

Endnotes

1. For historical evolution of sales tax in India, see section 2.5 of chapter 2 of this book.
2. John F. Due, *The Problems of Tax Administration in Latin America,* (Baltimore: The John Hopkins Press, 1959), p. 417.
3. Government of India, Ministry of Finance, *Report of the Taxation Enquiry Commission, 1953-54* (Chairman: John Matthai), Vol. III, p. 26.
4. Walter Mahler, *Sales and Excise Taxation in India,* (New Delhi: Orient Longman Ltd., 1970), p. 154.
5. *Report of the Taxation Enquiry Commission,* 1953-54, Vol. III, op. cit., p. 30.
6. *Ibid.*, p. 519.
7. Under Article 258(1), the Union has the power to delegate to any State Government any of its executive functions (including the power to assess and collect sales tax on inter-State trade). Thus, the power to levy and collect sales tax on inter-State trade belongs to the Centre [Article 269(1)(g)] though it has delegated the power to collect it to the States.
8. Clause (3) of Article 286 was further amended by the Constitution (Forty-sixth Amendment) Act, 1982. In its present form it is as follows.
   Any law of a State shall in so far as it imposes, or authorises the imposition of:
   (a) a tax on the sale or purchase of goods declared by Parliament by law to be of special importance in inter-State trade or commerce; or
   (b) a tax on the sale or purchase of goods, being a tax of the nature referred to in sub-clause

(b), sub-clause (c) or sub-clause (d) of clause (29-A) of Article 366, be subject to such restrictions and conditions in regard to the system of levy, rates and other incidents of the tax as Parliament may by law specify.

9. In 1956, when the Central Sales Tax Act was passed the rate was fixed at 1 percent. Subsequently, it was raised to 2 percent, 3 percent, and 4 percent in 1958, 1966, and 1975 respectively. It was reduced to 3 percent and 2 percent in 2007 and 2008 respectively.
10. Originally, the rate was fixed at 1 percent in 1956. It was raised to 2 percent, 3 percent, and 4 percent in 1963, 1966, and 1975 respectively.
11. It means the States are free to fix the rate of sales tax on the internal sales of non-declared goods but there is a ceiling rate of 4 percent on the sale of such goods in inter-State trade. For example, if the rate of sales tax on internal sale is 6 percent, it will be 4 percent for inter-State trade, being lower of the two.
12. In other words, the rate of CST is a minimum of 10 percent. For example, if general sales tax is charged at the rate of 5 percent on the sale of colour television in a State, the rate of CST on the same will be 10 percent, being higher of the two rates. In 1956, the minimum rate was fixed at 7 percent but was raised to 10 percent by the Central Sales Tax (Amendment) Act, 1963.
13. To prepare for the implementation of national level Goods and Services Tax (GST), Central Government has also begun a phased reduction of Central Sales Tax (CST). The Central Government has brought down the level of CST over the last few years from 4 percent to 2 percent as a precursor to rolling out GST. This is because CST, which is an origin-based tax, is inconsistent with value added taxes, which are destination based—the two should not co-exist.
14. Internal as well as inter-State sales tax on goods of special importance is governed by the Central Sales Tax Act, 1956. The present rate of CST is 4 percent.
15. India's federal system of government creates a dual polity based on divided governmental functions and taxation powers. Taxation laws of the Central Government extend to the whole of the country while those of State Governments are applicable within their respective jurisdictions. A tax belonging to the States may be imposed with a varying base and/or rate in different States. Even the procedures and rules for its collection may differ from State to State. The lack of uniformity in the imposition of State tax laws can cause difficulties for traders and consumers and thus hinder inter-State trade. To overcome these problems, arrangements could be made to transfer from the States, the legal right to levy the tax, to the Centre with the proviso that revenue collected will be assigned to the States. This is known as 'tax rental arrangement'.
16. *Second Report of the Ninth Finance Commission,* December 1989, p. 34.
17. Government of India, Ministry of Finance, *Report of the Expert Committee on Replacement of Sales Tax by Additional Excise Duty,* (Chairman: Kamlapati Tripathi), January 1983.
18. Government of India, *Report of the Commission on Centre-State Relations,* (Chairman: Justice R.S. Sarkaria), 1988, Part I, p. 293.
19. Government of India, Ministry of Finance, *Report of the Indirect Taxation Enquiry Committee,* (Chairman: L.K. Jha), 1977, Part I, p. 50.
20. *Report of the Taxation Enquiry Commission,* 1953-54, Vol. III, op. cit., p. 519.
21. *Report of the Indirect Taxation Enquiry Committee,* 1977, Part I, op. cit., p. 49.
22. Government of India, Ministry of Finance, *Tax Reforms Committee-Final Report,* Part I, (Chairman: Raja Chelliah), August 1992, p. 174.
23. Government of India, *Economic Survey,* 2006-07, p. 46.

[17] in January 1983. It recommended the replacement of sales tax by additional excise duty on *vanaspati*, drugs and medicines, cement, paper and paper board, and petroleum products. These recommendations were considered in a conference of Chief Ministers held on November [illegible], 1983. However, the six Chief Ministers of the non-Congress (I) States, viz. Andhra Pradesh, Jammu and Kashmir, Karnataka, Tamil Nadu, Tripura and West Bengal opposed the Centre's initiative [illegible] recommendations. The recommendations of the Tripathi Committee were further discussed at a conference of Chief Ministers held in New Delhi [illegible]. Unfortunately, no progress could be made in this [illegible].

The opposition of the non-Congress (I) States was based on the belief that implementation of the [illegible] would erode their revenue position. However, a close perusal of the recommendations of the Tripathi Committee suggests that it evolved elaborate formulae for protecting the financial interests of the States. In the case of three commodities, namely paper and paper board, *vanaspati*, and drugs and medicines, it suggested that the annual growth rate of the amount to be collected by way of additional excise duty in lieu of sales tax should be related to the future annual growth rate of sales tax revenue of all the States. For petroleum products and cement, which are substantially subject to administered prices, the Committee recommended and worked out linkages between the amount to be collected by way of additional excise duty from year to year and value of consumption on which normal sales tax would be leviable.

In spite of these safeguards, the apprehension of some States that their resource position would be adversely [illegible] reflects their lack of confidence in the Centre in implementing the [illegible]. Thus, an important tax reform has become a casualty of the [illegible] between the Central and the State Governments. The scheme of additional excise duties in lieu of sales tax has [illegible]. In view of the safeguards provided by the Tripathi Committee and the [illegible] Finance Commission, the scheme should not only be retained but [illegible].

[illegible] here that during the first two decades of [illegible] Congress party ruled, with some exceptions, both at the Centre and in the States. This political homogeneity facilitated taxation [illegible] between the two tiers of the Government, e.g. the agreement reached [illegible] of sales tax by excise duties on sugar, textiles, and [illegible] the politics of confrontation pursued by different political [illegible] of the States has hindered the process of [illegible] of commodity taxation. In fact, reform of [illegible] intervowen with the political process.

Part VI: Federal Aspects of Indian Taxation

22

Centre-State Financial Relations

Constitutional provisions regarding taxation and borrowing powers of the Centre and the States, place the former in a commanding position. Not only the major sources of tax revenue belong to the Centre, its borrowing (internal and external) powers are also unlimited. Moreover, the Central Government enjoys the exclusive right to print currency. [1]

22.1 Inter-governmental Transfers

Though the Constitution creates a dual polity based on divided governmental powers and functions, this division is not watertight. As the Administrative Reforms Commission, 1968, observed, "Exact correspondence of resources and functions is not possible to secure in any federal situation but in India the balance is tilted rather heavily in favour of the Centre and the outstanding feature of the financial relationship between the Centre and the States consequently is that the former is always the giver and the latter the receivers. The favourable position given to the Centre in regard to financial resources reflects the strong-centre theme running through the Constitution and many feel that this has been an important factor in keeping the country united". [2]

Emergence of imbalances between functional responsibilities and financial resources of different tiers of government is a characteristic feature of all federations, particularly of those whose economies are more dynamic. Even in older federations (like the United States and Canada), financial conflicts between the national and sub-national governments persist and their once-for-all solution is difficult to find. The mismatch between functions and taxation powers occurs partly because of changing responsibilities of governments at different levels and partly because of the dominant position of federal government in regard to taxation powers, which is often by design. Therefore, vertical imbalances in terms of resources and expenditure responsibilities emerge between different levels of government calling for transfer of resources from the Centre to the States. This is the familiar problem of federal finance.

Thus, inter-governmental transfers are an inherent part of a multi-level fiscal system. Such transfers are justified on horizontal equity considerations.

22.2 Mechanism of Central Transfers to the States

Recognising the fact that the financial resources of the States may prove inadequate for undertaking welfare, maintenance, and development activities, the framers of India's Constitution did make elaborate, *albeit* complex, arrangements relating to flow of funds from the Centre to the States. The disequilibrium between proliferating functional responsibilities of the States and their own resources is corrected by Central transfers effected through three main channels.

1. Statutory transfers through the Finance Commission.
2. Plan transfers through the Planning Commission (now abolished).
3. Discretionary transfers for Centrally Sponsored Schemes, relief from natural calamities, and relief and rehabilitation of displaced persons.

Apart from these direct transfers, resources also flow to the States indirectly through the following channels.

1. Establishment/expansion of Central public sector enterprises.
2. Subsidised lending by banking and financial institutions.
3. Subsidised borrowing by the States from the Central Government and the banking system.

These may be called invisible transfers or sub-terranean transfers.

22.3 Transfer of Resources through the Finance Commission

Transfers routed through the Finance Commission pertain to sharing of certain Central taxes, and grants-in-aid of revenues of the States. In other words, although the taxation powers allocated to the Centre and the States are mutually exclusive yet all the taxes and duties levied by the Centre are not meant entirely for the Centre. In fact, revenues from certain taxes and duties leviable by the Centre are totally assigned to or shared with the States to supplement the revenues of the States in accordance with their needs.

The architects of the Constitution probably realised that even with a share in the proceeds of divisible taxes, some States might still need financial assistance. Accordingly, they made provision for annual grants-in-aid of revenues under Article 275(1) to such States as may be in need of assistance. Also, the Centre is required to give grants-in-aid to the States for the welfare of Scheduled Tribes and for raising the level of administration in Scheduled Areas and separately for Assam. These provisions which set apart a portion of Central revenues for the benefit of States indicate flexibility of India's Constitution in terms of distribution of financial resources between the Centre and the States.

22.3.1 Finance Commission: Although the Constitution provides for Central transfers, it neither indicates the share of the States in the divisible taxes nor prescribes any principles for the distribution of States' share among the States themselves. Framers of the Constitution consciously avoided permanent formulae in this regard in view of expected changes in the spheres of taxation and public expenditure. Thus, the precise manner of sharing taxes and the actual determination of grants is left to the deliberations of the Finance Commission which is appointed by the President (under Article 280) every quinquennium, or earlier if necessary. [3] The Finance Commission, consisting of a chairman and four members, recommends to the President, *inter alia,* the principles of distribution between the Union and the States of the proceeds of taxes and the allocation among the States of the shares of such proceeds. The recommendations of Finance Commissions are based on a detailed assessment of the financial position of the Central and State Governments. For this purpose, the Commissions visit the State Capitals and hold discussions with government leaders and officials. Discussions are also held with public finance experts and studies are commissioned on specific topics.

A. Powers and Procedures: Under sub-clause (2) and (4) of Article 280 of the Constitution, the qualifications which shall be requisite for appointment as Members of the Commission and the manner in which they shall be selected have to be determined by Parliament by law and the Commission shall have such powers in the performance of their functions as Parliament may by law confer on them.

The Constitution authorises the Commission to determine their procedure, while the Finance Commission (Miscellaneous Provisions) Act, 1951, has conferred on the Commission all the powers of a Civil Court under the Code of Civil Procedure, 1908. The Commission have also been empowered to require any person to furnish information on such points or matters as, in the opinion of the Commission, may be useful for, or relevant to, any matter under the consideration of the Commission. The powers conferred on the Commission are set out in detail in Section 8 of the Act mentioned earlier.

As the Sixth Finance Commission remarked, "The purpose of Finance Commission, as envisaged in the Constitution, is primarily to facilitate a periodical assessment of the fiscal needs of the States and the formulation on an objective basis of proposals for transfer of resources from the Centre to the States through devolution of taxes and grants-in-aid. But an incidental and by no means insignificant advantage of the appointment of a Finance Commission has generally been to rekindle interest in issues pertaining to financial relations between the Centre and the States and to promote an enlightened national debate on the several facets of our federal fiscal set up". [4]

Under Article 281 of the Constitution, the report of the Finance Commission, together with the Explanatory Memorandum on the action taken on the recommendations of the Commission, is laid on the Table of the House by the Government. Though the President is not bound to accept the recommendations of the Finance Commission, they are generally accepted in view of the quasi-judicial nature of the Commission. [5] By and large, the Finance Commissions have worked independently and some of them, particularly the recent ones, have been quite assertive. Award of a Finance Commission generates considerable interest in issues pertaining to financial relations between the Centre and the States. Thirteen Finance Commissions have reported since the commencement of the Constitution. The work of the Fourteenth Finance Commission is under way. The years of establishment, years of reporting, periods of award, and the names of Chairmen of various Finance Commissions are given in Table 22.1.

Finance Commission is a unique feature of the Indian Constitution having no parallel in the existing federal constitutions of the world. As the Commission on Centre-State Relations, 1988 observed, "Unlike the Commonwealth Grants Commission of Australia, the Indian Finance Commission is a Constitutional body and the objectivity in its role has been facilitated by keeping it outside the Union executive. Compared with its Australian counterpart, the Indian Finance Commission has a greater scope inasmuch as it recommends sharing of tax proceeds also, besides the grants-in-aid, and advises on other matters referred to it in the interest of sound finance. The absence of clear Constitutional provisions for revenue sharing created many problems in other federations and they had to evolve a variety of arrangements to overcome them. For example, in Canada, tax-rental arrangements were resorted to. In Australia, the Australian Commonwealth Grants Commission was set up to consider allocation of grants among the claimant States. Specific purpose grants, with strict enforcement conditions, came into existence in countries like USA". [6]

The Australian Commonwealth Grants Commission recommends special purpose grants to the claimant States, but the general grants are determined largely on the basis of negotiations at the political level. In India, the Finance Commission has replaced political bargaining by objective criteria in regard to devolution of resources, ensuring at the same time flexibility in revenue-sharing.

What is a Finance Commission expected to achieve? Its first task is to evolve a scheme of transfer of financial resources from the Centre to the States so as to ensure financial equilibrium at the two levels of Government during the period of its award. Secondly, it is to design formulae to allocate resources so transferred among the States.

The task of the Finance Commission consists of the following.

1. Forecasting resources and expenditure of the Central Government to determine the volume of resources to be transferred to the States during the ensuing five years.

2. Forecasting own current revenues of the States and non-Plan current expenditures.

Table 22.1: Chronology of Finance Commissions in India

Finance Commission	Year and Month of Establishment	Year and Month of Reporting	Period of Award	Name of the Chairman
First	November 1951	December 1952	1952-53 to 1956-57	K.C. Neogy
Second	June 1956	September 1957	1957-58 to 1961-62	K. Santhanam
Third	December 1960	December 1961	1962-63 to 1965-66	A.K. Chanda
Fourth	May 1964	August 1965	1966-67 to 1968-69	P.V. Rajamannar
Fifth	February 1968	July 1969	1969-70 to 1973-74	Mahavir Tyagi
Sixth	June 1972	October 1973	1974-75 to 1978-79	K. Brahmananda Reddy
Seventh	June 1977	October 1978	1979-80 to 1983-84	J.M. Shelat
Eighth	June 1982	April 1984	1984-85 to 1988-89	Y.B. Chavan
Ninth	June 1987	July 1988* and December 1989#	1989-90* and 1990-91 to 1994-95#	N.K. P. Salve
Tenth	June 1992	November 1994	1995-96 to 1999-00	K.C. Pant
Eleventh	July 1998	July 2000	2000-01 to 2004-05	A.M. Khusro
Twelfth	November 2002	November 2004	2005-06 to 2009-10	C. Rangarajan
Thirteenth	November 2007	December 2009	2010-11 to 2014-15	Vijay Kelkar
Fourteenth	January, 2013	December 2014	2015-16 to 2019-20	Y.V. Reddy

* First Report; #Second Report
Source: *Finance Commission Reports.*

3. Devising formula for distribution of States' share among the States themselves.

4. Filling the post-devolution projected gaps with grants between the non-Plan current expenditures and current revenues.

The task of a Finance Commission is by no means easy as it has to judge the conflicting claims, needs, and resources of the Centre and the States and evolve a scheme of transfers which would balance the needs and resources of the two layers of the Government.

Broadly speaking, the procedure adopted by the Finance Commission to fulfil its duties is as follows: On the basis of the trends in the finances of Central and State Governments, it prepares estimates of revenue and expenditure for the period of its award. It then decides the total amount of transfers from the Centre to the States so as to maintain the desired equilibrium in the finances of the two tiers of the Government. Thereafter, the total amount of transfers is broken down into devolution and grants-in-aid among the States. Transfer of resources from the Centre to the States is designed to correct vertical imbalances while the distribution of resources among the States (with wide differentials in fiscal capabilities and needs) aims at correcting horizontal imbalances.

Should Central transfers to the States through the Finance Commission be examined in their totality or item-wise? For a better understanding of the nature and role of these transfers, it is necessary to examine them from both angles. The total approach is significant to understand adjustments in vertical financial imbalances while item-wise approach reveals adjustments in horizontal financial imbalances. It is noteworthy that various items included in the aggregate transfers are not alike and therefore have different importance for different States.

Commenting upon the working of the Indian federal polity, the Sixth Finance Commission observed, "Among the various federal polities in the world today, the Indian federal fiscal system whether one views it as federal or quasi-federal, is undoubtedly among the few that have demonstrated remarkable resilience in coping satisfactorily with the new demands made on it from time to time. The provisions of the Constitution concerning financial relations between the Centre and the States seem to have been designed with great care and circumspection so as to forestall precisely the kind of difficulties that even the older federations do not appear to have overcome in securing closer correspondence between resources and functions of the different layers of Government. These observations should not be construed as implying that the present matrix of financial relations between the Centre and the States does not admit of improvement or simplifications. All that we would like to stress is that the financial provisions of our Constitution give enough room for reconciling such conflicts of interest as may arise from time to time between the Union and the constituent units. If despite these well conceived provisions of the Constitution, some signs of dissatisfaction are discernible in the actual conduct of financial affairs between the Centre and the States, the reasons are to be found partly in the stresses and strains which the national economy as a whole has had to face in recent years and also perhaps in the spirit in which the provisions of the Constitution have sometimes been worked". [7]

22.3.2 From Itemised Sharing to Global Sharing: The most important development in the field of Centre-State financial relations pertains to the new system of sharing Central taxes with the State Governments.

Prior to Constitution (Eightieth Amendment) Act, 2000, income tax and Union excise duties were the only taxes shared with the States, apart from the grants given in lieu of passenger tax, and the collections from additional excise duty in lieu of sales tax sugar, tobacco and textiles. Taxes on income and Union excise duties were shared with States under Articles 270 and 272 respectively. The aforesaid amendment altered the pattern of sharing of Central taxes between the Centre and the States significantly. It substituted a new Article for Article 270 and omitted the old Article 272. The new Article 270 provides for the sharing of the net proceeds of all Union taxes and duties with the States. However, the surcharge levied for purposes of the Union under Article 271 is excluded from the divisible pool.

Eleventh Finance Commission was the first to make recommendations in accordance with the new provisions of the Constitution.

22.4 Fourteenth Finance Commission (FFC)

The Finance Commission is a Constitutional body formulated under Article 280 of the Indian Constitution. It is constituted every five years by the President of India to review the state of finances of the Union and the States and suggest measures for maintaining a stable and sustainable fiscal environment. It also makes recommendations regarding the devolution of taxes between the Center and the States from the divisible pool which includes all Central taxes (excluding surcharges and cesses) which the Centre is constitutionally mandated to share with the states.

Fourteenth Finance Commission (FFC) was appointed on January 2, 2013 under the chairmanship of Y.V. Reddy, former Governor of Reserve Bank of India (RBI). Other members of the commission included Abhijit Sen, Sushma Nath, M. Govinda Rao and Sudipto Mundle.

In addition to the primary objectives mentioned above, the terms of reference for the commission sought suggestions regarding the principles which would govern the quantum and distribution of grants-in-aid (non-plan grants to states), the measures, if needed, to augment State government finances to supplement the resources of local government and to review the state of the finances, deficit and debt conditions at different levels of government.

22.4.1 Main Recommendations of FFC: FFC submitted its recommendations for the period 2015-16 to 2019-20. They are likely to have major implications for Center-State relations, for budgeting by, and the fiscal situation of, the Centre and the States. Some of the major recommendations of FFC are as follows:

FFC radically enhanced the share of the states in the central divisible pool from the existing 32 percent to 42 percent which was the biggest ever increase in vertical tax devolution. The previous two Finance Commissions, viz. Twelfth Finance Commission (period 2005-06 to 2009-10) and Thirteenth Finance Commission (period 2010-11 to 2014-15) had recommended a share for states share of 30.5 percent (increase of 1 percent) and 32 percent (increase of 1.5 percent), respectively in the central divisible pool.

FFC formulated a new horizontal formula (Table 22.2) for the distribution of the states' share in divisible pool among the states. There are changes both in the variables included/excluded as well as the weights assigned to them. Relative to the Thirteenth Finance Commission, FFC incorporated two new variables: 2011 population and forest cover; and excluded the fiscal discipline variable.

Several other types of transfers were proposed including grants to rural and urban local bodies, a performance grant along with grants for disaster relief and revenue deficit. These transfers totaled to approximately ₹ 5.3 lakh crore for the period 2015-16 to 2019-20.

FFC did not make any recommendation concerning sector specific-grants unlike the Thirteenth Finance Commission.

Table 22.2: Horizontal Devolution Formulas of the Thirteenth and Fourteenth Finance Commissions

Variable	Weights Accorded	
	Thirteenth Finance Commission	Fourteenth Finance Commission
Population (1971)	25	17.5
Population (2011)	0	10
Fiscal capacity/income distance	47.5	50
Area	10	15
Forest cover	0	7.5
Fiscal discipline	17.5	0
Total	100	100

Sources: Thirteenth and Fourteenth Finance Commissions.

All states stand to gain from FFC transfers in absolute terms. The biggest gainers in absolute terms under General Category States were Uttar Pradesh, West Bengal and Madhya Pradesh while for Special Category States they were Jammu & Kashmir, Himachal Pradesh and Assam. A better measure of impact is benefit per capita. The major gainers in per capita terms were Kerala, Chhattisgarh and Madhya Pradesh for GCS and Arunachal Pradesh, Mizoram and Sikkim for SCS.

FFC recommendations are expected to add substantial spending capacity to budgets of states. FFC transfers have more favorable impact on the states (only among the GCS) which are relatively less developed which is an indication that the FFC transfers are progressive, i.e. states with lower per capita net state domestic product (NSDP) receive on average much larger transfers per capita. This indicates that the FFC recommendations do go in the direction of equalizing the income and fiscal disparities between the major states.

A final interesting finding relates to the decomposition of the resource transfers through tax devolution due to the increase in the divisible pool per se and due to the change in the horizontal devolution formula itself. The significant impact due to increase in the divisible pool is on states like Uttar Pradesh, Bihar, Madhya Pradesh, West Bengal and Andhra Pradesh (United) while states like Arunachal Pradesh, Chhattisgarh, Madhya Pradesh, Karnataka and Jharkhand are the major gainers due to a change in the horizontal devolution formula which now gives greater weight to a state's forest cover.

The spirit behind the FFC recommendations is to increase the automatic transfers to the states to give them more fiscal autonomy and this is ensured by increasing the share of states from 32 to 42 percent of divisible pool. However, there is concern that fiscal space or fiscal consolidation path of the Centre would be adversely affected. To ensure that the Centre's fiscal space is secured, the suggestion is that there will be commensurate reductions in the Central Assistance to States (CAS) known as *plan transfers.*

FFC has made far-reaching changes in tax devolution that will move the country toward greater fiscal federalism, conferring more fiscal autonomy on the states. This will be enhanced by the FFC-induced imperative of having to reduce the scale of other central transfers to the states. In other words, states will now have greater autonomy on the revenue and expenditure fronts.

In sum, the far-reaching recommendations of the FFC will further the Government's vision of cooperative and competitive federalism.

Endnotes

1. For historical evolution of Centre-State financial relations in India, see section 2.7 of chapter

2 of this book.

2. Administrative Reforms Commission, *Report of the Study Team on Centre-State Relationships*, Vol. I, 1968, p. 15.
3. Since the President is guided in all his decisions by the advice of the Central Council of Ministers (Article 74), the appointment of the Finance Commission and the determination of its terms of reference becomes the prerogative of the Central Government for all practical purposes. This prerogative of the Centre is often criticised because the Centre itself is a party to the *dispute* between the Centre and the States regarding sharing of financial resources, and the role of the Finance Commission is that of an arbiter.
4. *Report of the Sixth Finance Commission*, 1973, p. 5.
5. Article 280(3) requires the Finance Commission to make recommendations to the President who is to lay the same under Article 281 before each House of Parliament. It is nowhere laid down in the Constitution that recommendations of the Commission shall be binding upon the Government of India. They are, therefore, non-justiciable. However, to safeguard the interests of the States in the Union taxes which are divisible, the Constitution provides (Article 274) that no bill or amendment which: (i) varies the rate of tax in which the States are interested; (ii) affects the principles on which moneys are distributable; or (iii) imposes any surcharge on any such tax for the purpose of the Union, shall be introduced or moved in the Parliament except on the recommendation of the President. The Centre has generally accepted the major recommendations of the Finance Commissions though there are some instances of partial acceptance of such recommendations. For example, the Centre did not accept the entire set of recommendations of the Eighth Finance Commission relating to the first year (1984-85) of the five year period covered by it. The Centre held the view that by the time the report was submitted (April 30, 1984), the Central and the State budgets had been passed and it was late to reopen the estimates. However, it was widely felt that this decision of the Government was in violation of the spirit of Article 280 of the Constitution.
6. *Report of the Commission on Centre-State Relations*, Part I, 1988, op. cit., p. 254.
7. *Report of the Sixth Finance Commission*, 1973, p. 5.

23

State-Local Financial Relations in India

This chapter describes the functional responsibilities and sources of revenue of local bodies, explains the present constitutional arrangements relating to State-Local fiscal relations in India, and examines the role of various statutory bodies in this regard.

Rapid urbanisation has increased the functional responsibilities of municipalities in India. To meet the scale and challenge of urbanisation, municipal governments are always looking for additional funds from various sources. Since a significant part of national income originates in urban areas, efforts must be made to maintain and enhance urban productivity which, in turn, depends on the level and quality of urban infrastructure. The demand for urban infrastructure services has increased, and is likely to accelerate further, due to rising personal incomes, rapid growth of population, and general increase in economic activities. Inability of municipal governments to meet the rising demand would adversely affect growth prospects of the economy.

23.1 Functions of Local Bodies

Functional responsibilities of local bodies vary from country to country and within a country. Still some common patterns are discernible. Broadly speaking, the functions of a local body (e.g. a municipality) can be divided into the following three categories.

23.1.1 Essential Civic Functions: The main function of a municipality is to provide and maintain core (or essential) civic services. These include: refuse collection, street lighting, water supply, sewage disposal, fire protection, abattoirs, and primary health services. These are services for which decision-making rests with the municipalities.

23.1.2 Regulatory Functions: These functions pertain to regulation of industry, trade and construction activities. Municipalities issue licences, permits and levy fees of various kinds, and also impose fines for violation of rules and regulations. Charges for regulatory functions should be so fixed as to cover at least the cost of administration and surveillance. If these services are subsidised it would put strain on resources.

23.1.3 Agency Functions: These are functions (e.g. protection of environment) which are funded out of State revenues by specific transfers.

23.2 Financing of Local Bodies

In the public finance literature, the following general rules are mentioned as regards the financing of local bodies.

1. Where the benefits of a local public service are measurable and accrue to readily identifiable individuals/households within a jurisdiction, user charges are the most appropriate method of financing the service.
2. Local public services which are services to general public in the sense that identification of beneficiaries and measurement of benefits to individuals/ households is difficult, should be financed by taxes on local residents. Such services include traffic control, street lighting, security, and general administration.
3. Services the benefits of which spill over to neighbouring jurisdictions should be financed by intergovernmental transfers. These services include health, education, anti-pollution measures, and other social welfare activities.
4. Long-term borrowings are the appropriate source to finance capital projects with long-term gains.

Higher level governments generally assign certain taxes to local bodies to augment their resources. Tax literature suggests the following principles regarding assignment of taxes to local bodies.

1. Municipal governments should be assigned those taxes that are leviable on bases which are 'immobile' or 'location-specific' and those whose burden cannot be exported outside the municipal jurisdiction. Property tax is a case in point.
2. Local tax base should be easily identifiable and its incidence transparent.
3. Tax yield should be stable, predictable, and buoyant.
4. Rate schedule of the tax should possess a reasonable degree of progressivity.
5. The tax should be easy to administer.

Based on the foregoing considerations, the following taxes are generally assigned to local bodies: (a) property tax, (b) entertainment tax, (c) tax on professions, (d) tax on advertisements, and (e) octroi/tolls.

23.3 Constitutional Provisions

Entry 5 of List II (State List) of the Seventh Schedule to the Constitution of India refers to local bodies as institutions created by State Governments. Furthermore, the Directive Principles of the Constitution (Article 40) requires the strengthening of the units of local self-government in the States, particularly *panchayati raj* institutions. However, little was done in this regard during the first three decades of Independence. As a result, these institutions could not function effectively because of: (a) inadequate devolution of functions and financial powers, (b) failure to hold regular elections and prolonged supersession, and (c) lack of participation from weaker sections of society. Consequently, local bodies in many States had become weak and ineffective as units of self-government in our democratic set up. It was only in 1991 that Bills were introduced in the Parliament to amend the Constitution for providing constitutional status to the *panchayats* and municipalities.

23.4 Decentralisation Initiative, 1992

The Seventy-third and Seventy-fourth Amendment Bills relating to *panchayats* and municipalities respectively were introduced in the Parliament in September 1991 to provide constitutional remedy for the inadequacies plaguing these bodies which were unable to perform effectively as vibrant democratic units of self-government. The Bills were referred to two joint bodies of Parliament and after necessary revision were reintroduced in July 1992, and passed by Parliament in December 1992. Both the Bills were ratified by the required number of States [Article 368(ii)] and the President gave his assent in April 1993. The Seventy-third Amendment Act relating to *panchayats* came into force from April 24, 1993. The Seventy-fourth Amendment Act relating to municipalities came into force from June 1, 1993. The changes made by the Seventy-third and Seventy-fourth Amendment Acts to the Constitution were of historical importance and are summarised in Table 23.1.

The passage of the Constitution (Seventy-third Amendment) Act, 1992 marked a watershed in the history of modern India. With this amendment, a uniform structure of *panchayats* emerged throughout the country.

Article 243G read with Eleventh Schedule of the Constitution explicitly requires the States to devolve powers and authority on *panchayats* which may be necessary to enable them to function as institutions of self-government. The Eleventh Schedule of the Constitution is reproduced in Table 23.2.

Similarly, the passage of the Constitution (Seventy-fourth Amendment) Act, 1992 was a landmark in the history of municipal administration in India. Article 243W read with Twelfth Schedule of the Constitution provides the illustrative list for the devolution of functions to the municipalities. The Twelfth Schedule of the Constitution is reproduced in Table 23.3. Many States have amended their municipal laws to ensure conformity with the new constitutional provisions.

In short, *panchayats* and municipalities are now constitutional bodies forming third tier to the federal polity of India. India's decentralisation initiative in the form of Seventy-third and Seventy-fourth Amendments poses challenges and offers opportunities.

Table 23.1: Seventy-third and Seventy-fourth Constitutional Amendment Acts

Act	Date on which came into force	Amendments made
Constitution (Seventy-third Amendment) Act 1992	24.4.1993	A new Part IX relating to Panchayats was inserted. In clause (3) of Article 280, sub-clause (bb) was inserted which provides for measures to supplement the resources of the Panchayats. Eleventh Schedule added to the Constitution which provides an illustrative list for the devolution of functions to Panchayats.
Constitution (Seventy-fourth Amendment) Act, 1992	1.6.1993	A new Part IXA relating to Municipalities was inserted. In clause (3) of Article 280, sub-clause (c) was re-lettered as sub-clause (d) and before sub-clause (d) as so re-lettered, sub-clause (c) was inserted which provides for measures to supplement the resources of the Municipalities. Twelfth Schedule added to the Constitution which provides an illustrative list for the devolution of functions to Municipalities.

Source: Government of India, Ministry of Law, Justice and Company Affairs, *The Constitution of India (Supplement to the Third Edition)*, 1994.

23.5 Constitution (Seventy-fourth Amendment) Act, 1992

Through this amendment a new Part IX-A relating to municipalities was incorporated in the Constitution to provide for, *inter alia,* the constitution of three types of municipalities, viz. *Nagar Panchayat* for a transitional area, i.e. an area in transition from a rural to urban area [1]; Municipal Council for smaller urban area, and Municipal Corporation for larger urban area (Article 243Q).

The Constitution (Seventy-fourth Amendment) Act, 1992 conferred constitutional status to the structure and mandate of municipalities so as to enable them to function as vibrant democratic and self-governing institutions at the grassroots level.

The objectives of the Seventy-fourth Amendment included decentralisation of power and popular participation in the planning, management, and delivery of civic services. The salient features of the Seventy-fourth Amendment were the following.

Table 23.2: Eleventh Schedule of the Constitution (Article 243G)

1.	Agriculture, including agricultural extension.
2.	Land improvement, implementation of land reforms, land consolidation and soil conservation.
3.	Minor irrigation, water management and watershed development.
4.	Animal husbandry, dairying and poultry.
5.	Fisheries.
6.	Social forestry and farm forestry.
7.	Minor forest produce.
8.	Small-scale industries, including food processing industries.
9.	Khadi, village and cottage industries.
10.	Rural housing.
11.	Drinking water
12.	Fuel and fodder.
13.	Roads, culverts, bridges, ferries, waterways and other means of communication.
14.	Rural electrification, including distribution of electricity.
15.	Non-conventional energy sources.
16.	Poverty alleviation programmes.
17.	Education, including primary and secondary schools.
18.	Technical training and vocational education.
19.	Adult and non-formal education.
20.	Libraries.
21.	Cultural activities.
22.	Markets and fairs.
23.	Health and sanitation, including hospitals, primary health centres and dispensaries.
24.	Family welfare.
25.	Women and child development.
26.	Social welfare, including welfare of the handicapped and mentally retarded.
27.	Welfare of the weaker sections, and in particular, of the Scheduled Castes and the Scheduled Tribes.
28.	Public distribution system.
29.	Maintenance of community assets.

Table 23.3: Twelfth Schedule of the Constitution (Article 243W)

1.	Urban planning including town planning.
2.	Regulation of land-use and construction of buildings.
3.	Planning for economic and social development.
4.	Roads and bridges.
5.	Water supply for domestic, industrial and commercial purposes.
6.	Public health, sanitation conservancy and solid waste management.
7.	Fire services.
8.	Urban forestry, protection of the environment and promotion of ecological aspects.
9.	Safeguarding the interests of weaker sections of society, including the handicapped and mentally retarded.
10.	Slum improvement and upgradation.
11.	Urban poverty alleviation.
12.	Provision of urban amenities and facilities such as parks, gardens, play-grounds.
13.	Promotion of cultural, educational and aesthetic aspects.
14.	Burials and burial grounds; cremations, cremation grounds and electric crematoriums.
15.	Cattle ponds; prevention of cruelty to animals.
16.	Vital statistics including registration of births and deaths.
17.	Public amenities including street lighting, parking lots, bus stops and public conveniences.
18.	Regulation of slaughter houses and tanneries.

23.5.1 Salient Features:

1. It provides a framework for the assignment of appropriate governmental functions to municipalities through the Twelfth Schedule of the Constitution read with Article 243W. The Twelfth Schedule defines the functional domain of municipalities. Many of the functions included in this Schedule have distributional and developmental attributes.
   The Twelfth Schedule generally contains traditional functions of municipalities. However, some non-traditional functions are also discernible from the list. These are: (a) protection of the environment and promotion of ecological aspects, (b) safeguarding the interests of weaker sections of society including the handicapped and mentally retarded, (c) urban poverty alleviation, and (d) promotion of cultural and aesthetic aspects.
2. States are statutorily required to constitute a finance commission (Article 243-I and 243-Y), once in every five years, to recommend to their legislatures

measures to improve municipal finances including: (i) assignment of taxes, duties, tolls, and fees, (ii) sharing of state taxes, and (iii) provision of grants-in-aid.

3. The Finance Commission constituted by the Government of India is obligated to recommend measures to augment the Consolidated Fund of State Governments to supplement the resources of the municipalities on the basis of the recommendations made by the State Finance Commissions [Article 280(3)(c)].
4. It is mandatory to constitute in every State at the district level a District Planning Committee to consolidate and prepare development plan for the district as a whole (Article 243ZD). Similarly, it is mandatory to constitute in every metropolitan area a Metropolitan Planning Committee to prepare a development plan for the metropolitan area as a whole (Article 243ZE).
5. It mandates that a municipality if dissolved by a State Government, must be reconstituted within six months [Article 243U(3)]. This is meant to ensure the continuity of civic affairs by 'elected' representatives of the people.
6. It ensures reservation of seats for women and other disadvantaged categories (Article 243T).

The situation existing before and after the Seventy-fourth amendment is summarised in Table 23.4.

23.5.2 New Status of Municipalities: The Seventy-fourth amendment was made with the intention to make municipalities self-governing units. Are they so?

In the federal polity of India, local bodies are institutions created by the State Governments (entry 5 of List II of the Seventh Schedule). They enjoy only those powers and responsibilities which are assigned to them. Twelfth schedule of the Constitution lists the functions and responsibilities that may be transferred to municipalities. The permissive nature of Seventy-fourth Amendment is clear and the State Governments enjoy full discretion as regards the transfer of functions to municipalities.

No doubt, municipalities have acquired constitutional status after the said Amendment, they are completely dependent on respective State Governments in terms of self-governance.

23.5.3 Desirability and Feasibility of Uniformity in Municipal Functions: A careful reading of the Twelfth Schedule shows that many of the functions listed in it found place in the Municipal Acts of various States even before the enactment of the conformity legislations by them. Hence, the Twelfth Schedule has been generally accepted as a guiding list of municipal functions.

Should there be all-India uniformity in delegating functions and financial powers to local bodies? There is a weak case for all-India uniformity as regards functional domain of local bodies. State Governments and their local bodies have diverse economic and social conditions. It is by no means rational to expect uniformity in the functions and powers of the Greater Bombay Municipal Corporation and the municipality of a small township of a backward State. Similarly, it is debatable if local bodies should have uniform taxation powers.

Table 23.4: Status of Municipalities in India

Before the 74th Amendment	After the 74th Amendment
No all-India framework for devolution of functions	12th Schedule read with Article 243W of the Constitution provides guide points for assignment of functions to municipalities.
High degree of arbitrariness in the system of fiscal transfers from the State Governments to municipalities. No periodic assessment of financial needs of municipalities	State Finance Commission (SFC) to be constituted statutorily in every State every Fifth year (Article 243-I and 243-Y) to review the financial position of municipalities and suggest measures to improve the same.
No role for the National Finance Commission as regards the finances of urban local bodies.	National Finance Commission is required to augment the Consolidated Fund of State Governments to supplement the resources of the municipalities on the basis of the recommendations made by the SFCs [Article 280(3)(c)].
Absence of constitutional bodies to prepare development plans for local areas.	Mandatory constitution of District Planning Committees (Article 243ZD) and Metropolitan Planning Committees (Article 243ZE) for consolidation and preparation of development plans.
Failure to hold regular elections and prolonged supersessions.	A municipality if dissolved by a State Government must be reconstituted within six months [Article 243U(3)].
Lack of participation from weaker sections of society	Reservation of seats for women and other disadvantaged categories (Article 243T).

Though it will be useful to prepare a reference list regarding functions (Eleventh and Twelfth Schedules), assigned taxes, shareable taxes, user charges, fees etc., all-India uniformity in these matters would be too much to expect.

Feasibility of all-India uniformity as regards the functional jurisdiction of municipalities is poor in view of the permissive nature of Seventy-fourth Amendment. It is highly unlikely that all the States of India would make uniform transfer of functions and financial powers to their respective municipalities. All-India uniformity in the functions of municipalities has to be ruled out in view of inter-State disparities.

Even at the level of a State, uniformity is not desirable in view of diverse city conditions and intra-State disparities. This fact has been recognised by the Constitution while providing for the constitution of three types of municipal bodies: *Nagar Panchayats*, municipal councils, and municipal corporations (Article 243Q). However, it does not distinguish between the functional domains of the three types of municipal bodies. The determination of the functions of municipalities of different sizes is left to the wisdom of the State Governments.

However, there exists a case for uniformity of functions among similar municipalities in a State. If a State chooses to allocate dissimilar functions and powers to similar municipalities (say municipal councils), there can be genuine resentment among the municipalities discriminated against. It is here, that objective criteria based on population size, geographical area, or constitutional categorisation (Article 243Q) is needed to prevent misuse of political authority.

The Constitution should provide, at least, a list of minimum functions to be transferred to municipalities of various types by the State Governments.

23.5.4 Role of State Finance Commissions: The State Finance Commission is set up under Article 243-I read with Article 243-Y of the Constitution. It is required to review the financial position of the municipalities and make recommendations as to:

(a) the principles which should govern–

i. the distribution between the State and the Municipalities of the net proceeds of taxes, duties, tolls and fees leviable by the State, which may be divided between them, and the allocations between the Municipalities of their respective shares of such proceeds.

ii. the determination of the taxes, duties, tolls and fees which may be assigned to, or appropriated by the municipalities.

iii. the grants-in-aid to municipalities from the Consolidated Fund of the State.

(b) the measures needed to improve the financial position of the municipalities.

(c) any other matter referred to the Finance Commission in the interest of sound finance of the municipalities.

As required under the Constitution, all State Governments have set up finance commissions. These State Finance Commissions (SFCs) are expected to strengthen local bodies so that they may function as democratic units for the socio-economic development of urban and rural areas of our country.

The task of the First Finance Commission of a State was difficult and arduous in the absence of precedence and it was expected to make suo moto all such studies in areas which never existed before. Nevertheless, the work of the First Finance Commission was crucial because it paved the way for subsequent commissions. The following observations may be made in this regard.

1. The new Constitutional arrangement (Seventy-fourth Amendment) implies that the whole range of a State's tax revenue is open to sharing with municipalities. SFCs are expected to evolve principles of tax assignment, tax sharing, and grants to municipalities with a view to mitigate their weak financial position. They are also required to evolve criteria with regard to adequacy and objectivity of grants.
2. Sharing of State tax revenue with municipalities depends wholly on the discretion of State Government.
3. In determining devolution of funds, the SFCs would do well to keep in mind, *inter alia*, the following factors.

(a) Resource position of the State.

(b) Normative deficits of municipalities. Any system which underestimates the gap between revenue and expenditure should be discouraged.

(c) The degree of dependence of municipalities for funds on the State Government.

(d) Capacity of a municipality to utilise devolved resources.

(e) A State Finance Commission may consider introduction of a system of incentives and disincentives into the entire governmental grants on objective lines. Municipalities which are able to raise resources through levy of user charges and benefit taxes should be considered for incentive grants from the State Government.

A. Determination and Filling of Budgetary Gaps: A State Finance Commission has to determine the budgetary gaps of municipalities for the period of its award. Thereafter, it has to devise formulae for filling the gaps so determined.

(a) Determination of the Budgetary Gaps: Two approaches may be followed for this purpose: (a) trend growth rate, and (b) normative approach.

Under the first approach, average annual growth rate in a variable during a reference period (say 1994-95 through 2003-04) is worked out and the same is projected for a future period (say 2004-05 through 2008-2009). It is assumed that past behaviour of the variable will be repeated in future. Thus, 'actuals' or 'accounts' of revenue and expenditure of a government may be used to compute the average annual growth rate of the two aggregates over a stated period. Applying the computed average to a future period, one can work out estimated revenue, expenditure and budgetary gap for any future year.

Under the second method, revenue of a government is assessed normatively and certain norms are applied to assess expenditure. In other words, 'needs' and 'capacities' of different governments are assessed normatively and such normative assessments are used to meet budgetary gaps of the governments. More specifically, fiscal performance of a government is judged on the basis of *what ought to be* rather than *what it actually is*.

In the context of the work of a State Finance Commission, normative approach should apply to both the State Government and municipalities and that the assessment of revenue and expenditure should be done in a manner so as to maintain incentives for greater revenue efforts and economy in spending.

(b) Filling the Gap: Once budgetary gaps of municipalities are determined, the next task of a State Finance Commission is to devise formulae for filling these gaps. For this purpose, it has to work out a judicious mix of tax devolution and grants.

It is noteworthy that the term 'gap-filling' in the context of State-municipal fiscal relations has a different connotation than at the national level.

At the national level, even after the transfer to the States of a share of divisible taxes, the resources of some of the States may remain inadequate to meet their needs. Thus, a Finance Commission determines the grants equal to deficit of each State so that the non-Plan revenue accounts of the States are balanced or left with a surplus every year. In other words, deficits of non-Plan revenue account which remain after tax devolution are covered through grants. This is called the gap-filling approach (or more appropriately net gap-filling approach).

It is possible that even before tax devolution from the Centre, some high-income States have surplus in their non-Plan revenue account. Thus, while a State cannot be denied a part of a shared Central tax even if it has no demonstrated financial need, grants are given upon genuine financial needs of the States.

However, the working of a State Finance Commission is different. Like the National Finance Commission, it is not bound by any constitutional restrictions regarding the type of taxes to be shared with municipalities. In fact, the whole field of State taxation is open to it for determining tax devolution. In other words, tax devolution and grants are to be used simultaneously to cover the budgetary gaps of municipalities. In this case, gap-filling means how to cover the projected budgetary gaps of municipalities through a judicious mix of tax devolution and grants with due regard to the underlying principles of the two methods to effect transfers from a higher to a lower level government.

23.6 Municipal Commercial Borrowings

Plan allocations of Central and State Governments are the chief source of financing capital projects of municipal governments. Other sources of finance include: (a) internal resources of municipalities, (b) institutional resources (HUDCO etc.), and (c) multilateral agencies.

The scope for additional funds from Central and State Governments is limited in view of the pressing need to reduce fiscal deficit. Similarly, institutional finances at low cost are unlikely to be available in the wake of financial sector reforms. Under such circumstances, municipal authorities should be permitted access to the capital market to mobilise additional resources. Recent expansion and modernisation of capital market in India suggests that inflow of capital into equity and debt market is quite high if attractive rate of return is offered.

23.6.1 Rationale for Municipal Commercial Borrowings: It is both fair and efficient that projects with long-term benefits are financed through long-term borrowings. If long-term capital projects are financed out of current revenues and/or short-term borrowings, the future generations would enjoy free-riding. Since the benefits of a capital project are reaped over a long period of time, i.e. by more than one generation of tax payers, the financing of such projects should place the repayment burden on the present as well as future generations.

30.6.2 Limitations: Municipal access to capital market, though desirable, is hindered by a variety of factors which may be classified into two categories: (a) restrictions imposed by the higher level government, and (b) other constraints.

The Constitution of India imposes various types of restrictions on the borrowing powers of the State Governments which, in turn, impose restrictions on the borrowing powers of the municipalities under them. Since borrowings by the lower level government are guaranteed, in most cases, by the higher level government, the latter has a right to impose such restrictions. These restrictions apply to: (a) type of debt, (b) amount of debt, (c) term of the debt, and (d) use of debt funds. Approval of the higher level government, which is often cumbersome, is needed before the debt is floated.

Thus, no municipal authority can borrow without an explicit sanction of its State Government. When the loan amount exceeds ₹ 25 lakh or the repayment period is over 30 years, local borrowings need Central approval under the provisions of the Local Authorities Loan Act, 1914 (a Central Legislation).

Among the 'other constraints', the more important are the following: Low credit worthiness of municipalities, their poor tract record as borrowers, and lack of trustworthy financial intermediaries.

Despite the foregoing hurdles, some municipalities in India have successfully tapped the bond market.

23.6.3 Factors Determining Success of Municipal Bonds: To attract a share of capital market for municipalities, the following conditions need to be satisfied.

1. Urban infrastructure projects should be commercially viable.
2. Municipal bonds are rated by some recognised credit rating institution. This will help build confidence of investors in the bond issue as well as help in its subsequent trading on the secondary market.
3. Such bonds should carry tax concessions.
4. Revenues accruing to the municipal entity are sufficiently elastic.
5. Security behind the debt taken by the municipal entity is sound.
6. Municipal entity makes provision for the creation of debt-servicing funds and the legal procedures for seeking recourse in the event of default.
7. Municipal entity is competent to pledge revenues for debt-servicing and extend collateral in terms of commercial property, plant and machinery and other assets.

23.7 Privatisation of Municipal Services

The scope for privatisation of some municipal services in order to reduce costs is a moot question.

Municipalities alone cannot handle huge infrastructural projects like water supply, sewage disposal, and urban transport. Involvement of central, state, and private sector is required to meet the scale of investment needed in these areas. Similarly, greater participation of private sector is desirable in the provision of civic services, particularly those the consumption of which can be attributed to individuals/households. There are many types of arrangement in respect of public-private partnership depending on situation. However, care should be taken not to dilute current social commitments while embarking on public-private partnership.

The historical and ideological resistance to private sector participation persists in most places. Consequently, few local bodies have tried out private sector participation in civic services on any significant scale. Wherever it has happened, the experiment has remained limited to disposal of solid wastes, and maintenance of parks.

The disenchantment with utility enterprises of municipalities is not conceptual but borne out of their inefficient and sometimes corrupt management. The merits of privatisation are seen in terms of improvement in efficiency and reduction in the budgetary burden of state-owned enterprises.

Though the need for private sector participation is widely felt, it is not openly expressed. Very rarely political parties have spoken publicly against the public sector. Contrarily, there is a stiff opposition by political parties to any move to undermine the importance of public sector. The strong unions of public sector enterprises come in handy for politicians to prevent the erosion of state and municipal activities.

To sum up, rural local self-governance is critical to rural transformation. The 73rd Amendment to the Constitution seeks to endow the Panchayats with such power and authority as may be required to enable them to function as genuine institutions of self-governance. Inherent in this devolution is the expectation that it would lead to social justice with economic development and effective local governance with emphasis on the following:

1. Social and political empowerment of village communities, particularly of the hitherto marginalized segments.
2. Accountability of local government functionaries to be elected as local representatives.
3. Greater control of village communities over natural resources.

As Panchayati Raj is included in the State list of the Seventh Schedule of the Constitution, the States are responsible for devolution of powers to the Panchayats and thus need to take steps for effective devolution of powers and authority as envisaged under Article 243G read with the Eleventh Schedule of the Constitution.

Endnote

1. Here, 'a transitional area', 'a smaller urban area', or 'a larger urban area' means such area as the Governor may specify by public notification having regard to the population of the area, the density of the population, the revenue generated for local administration, the percentage of employment in non-agricultural activities and such other factors.

Part VII: International Aspects of Indian Taxation

24

International Double Taxation

Business and investment operations of individuals and companies are becoming increasingly international in scope in the wake of current wave of globalisation and openness sweeping across the countries of the world. Tax systems of different countries differ in terms of types of taxes, definition of income and expenses, exemptions and concessions, rates and collection procedures. Varying tax practices of different countries complicate decision-making by multinational enterprises as to what is most profitable on an international basis. The study of international taxation becomes relevant in this context.

24.1 What is Double Taxation?

Double taxation (or tax duplication) occurs when the same base (e.g. income) is assessed twice, either by the same tax jurisdiction or by two competing tax jurisdictions, either at different levels of government in a country or at the same level of government in different countries. All the three versions of double taxation are described below.

24.1.1 Double Taxation by the Same Tax Jurisdiction: A common example of this kind of double taxation is the taxation of corporate earnings, first in the form of corporate income tax, and then in the form of personal income tax on dividends distributed to shareholders. Tax laws usually contain provisions which mitigate or even eliminate tax duplication of this kind. Under one method, a shareholder is granted credit against his tax liability on overall income for the tax paid by the company on distributed profits. The credit may be granted on full or partial basis (say 50 percent) on account of company tax on distributed profits.

24.1.2 Double Taxation by Competing Tax Jurisdictions at Different Levels of Government in a Country: Double taxation of this type arises when different levels of government impose taxes on the same base, e.g. taxation of income by Federal and State Governments in USA, and Canada. This kind of double taxation arises due to joint occupancy of tax fields. [1]

24.1.3 Double Taxation by Competing Tax Jurisdictions at Same Level of Government in Different Countries: This kind of double taxation is also called *international double taxation* or *territorial multiple taxation.* In this case, two sovereign countries claim jurisdiction in taxing the same base, usually income.

24.2 International Double Taxation

International double taxation occurs when a taxpayer is resident in one country but has a source of income situated in another country so that tax is imposed by both the countries on the same income. Thus, international double taxation arises due to overlapping of two tax claims of two or more countries. OECD has defined international double taxation as "the imposition of comparable taxes in two (or more) states on the same taxpayer in respect of the same subject matter for identical periods". [2]

In most cases, individuals work in countries where they live and companies invest in countries in which they are resident. However, world economies are becoming increasingly international and flow of labour and capital from one country to another is common. Multinationals operate in a number of countries, and individual investors possess internationally diversified investment portfolios. Thus, companies and individuals receive foreign income in the form of profits, dividends and royalties. When a person undertakes cross-border activities or maintains connections in two or more countries, he is likely to encounter the tax laws of another country. That encounter influences the way in which the person is taxed in his home country. This is how the tax systems of different countries get linked with each other.

Like international law, there is no such thing as international taxation. Taxes are not international because they are not levied at an international level by any supranational authority. Taxes are levied by central, state and local governments. International taxation (or more appropriately international tax law) includes all those rules which affect the taxation of a person and which are different from the rules that would apply if all his activities and connections were in a single country. These rules include the laws, regulations, juridical pronouncements and practices of different countries. They are meant to minimise/eliminate international tax duplication so that international flow of labour and capital is not unduly obstructed.

24.3 Assignment Rules of Foreign Income

Two fundamental assignment rules govern the right of nations to impose taxes on foreign income: (a) the source rule or the territoriality rule, and (b) the residence or domicile rule.

24.3.1 Source Rule: The source rule holds that income ought to be taxed in the country in which it originates irrespective of whether the income accrues to a resident or a non-resident assessee. The claim for tax jurisdiction is made on the ground that source country allows non-residents to use its infrastructure and other inputs for production purposes and therefore it can legitimately take a bite into their earnings.

24.3.2 Residence Rule: According to the residence rule, the power to tax foreign income should belong to the country in which the taxpayer resides. The claim of the residence (or home) country rests on the ground that the source (or host) country utilises and benefits from manpower and other resources trained and perfected by the home country. The tests of residence including nationality of individual assessees are complex and vary from country to country. Similarly, different countries follow different rules to define a domestic/foreign company.

24.4 Methods to Alleviate International Double Taxation

The problem of international tax duplication can be avoided if all the countries follow either the source or the residence rule. In practice, most countries exercise source and residence rules concurrently. If a country observes only the residence rule, then it surrenders tax claim on incomes which originate within its political jurisdiction and accrue to non-residents. A country would normally not go for this option which favours the foreigners vis-à-vis its own citizens. In most cases, countries tax their residents on their world income, and the non-residents on their incomes originating within their borders. International tax duplication arises when the country of residence extends the tax net to the world income of a taxpayer and the host country follows the source rule. Double taxation of this kind discourages international movement of factors of production.

Various methods may be followed by concerned countries to reduce or even eliminate double taxation of foreign-source income of their residents.

24.4.1 Exemption Method: A country may voluntarily and unilaterally sacrifice its tax claim on the foreign income of its residents. In other words, foreign income of residents is exempt from taxation in the home country. For example, there is no further tax on repatriated profits in countries such as France, and Germany.

24.4.2 Foreign Tax Credit: The home country permits deduction of taxes paid by the residents in the host country (on dividends, royalties etc.) from the tax on world-wide income due in the home country. The foreign tax credit is a mechanism provided unilaterally by a number of countries to alleviate the effect of double taxation. The object is to reduce tax on foreign-source income to the extent that income has already been taxed in the foreign jurisdiction. Under the tax credit system, the taxpayer pays the higher of the two taxes. If the foreign tax is the same or higher than the domestic tax, then the tax credit reduces the domestic tax liability on the foreign income to nil.

A foreign tax credit system was introduced in Australia on July 1, 1987. Under this system, the foreign-source income of residents is taxed at normal rates in Australia, with a credit granted for the foreign taxes paid. Other important countries which operate a tax credit mechanism as a means of eliminating double taxation are USA, UK, Canada, and Japan.

A. Tax Sparing Credit: Developing countries often give tax incentives, e.g. tax holiday to encourage foreign investments. Many developed countries provide, in their double tax treaties with developing countries, for a tax sparing credit. Under tax sparing, the investor is deemed to have paid the tax foregone in the country of source (say, India) so that the investor's country of residence (say, USA) grants a tax credit for the tax not charged by the source country. In other words, the residence country treats the income remitted as if it had been fully taxed and had not benefited from the tax incentives (of the host country). This ensures that the full benefit of the tax incentive goes to the investor and is not simply transferred to the residence country's treasury.

24.4.3 Bilateral Tax Treaties: International double taxation is also avoided through bilateral tax treaties (or double tax treaties). A double tax treaty is a convention or an agreement among countries for the avoidance of double taxation of income and capital and bringing uniformity in the allocation of taxation rights in cross-border situations. It is essentially a bargain between two treaty countries as regards the division of tax revenue between them in respect of income falling to be taxed in both jurisdictions. Since treaty negotiations involve bargaining, each side seeks concessions from the other and it is not necessary that strict *quid pro quo* is achieved in the end.

Apart from relieving double taxation, a double tax treaty aids commercial relations between treaty partners. It creates an environment of fiscal certainty which encourages trade and investment between countries. It provides rules for resolving problems of dual residence or dual source of income, defines the different forms of taxable income, and determines the taxing rights of the two treaty countries. An important provision of all double tax treaties is the machinery for administrative co-operation between the tax authorities of treaty partners.

The advantages and disadvantages of a double tax treaty depend on the flow of trade and investment between treaty partners. If these flows are in balance, which is a rarity, the benefits and costs would be truly reciprocal. Where the flows of trade and investment are unbalanced, the advantages of the treaty may be weighed more in favour of one treaty partner than the other, though the provisions of the treaty may be expressed in reciprocal terms. This is generally the case regarding tax treaties between developed and underdeveloped countries where flows of trade and investment are one-sided.

Most tax treaties are bilateral. Some international organisations have done commendable work in the development and harmonisation of bilateral double tax conventions. Model tax treaties drawn up by these organisations have helped to harmonise national approaches to double tax relief. They have facilitated the negotiation of tax treaties by eliminating the need for elaborate analysis and protracted discussion of every issue involved in each treaty.

In 1963, OECD published a Draft Double Taxation Convention. In 1977, it issued a Model Double Taxation Convention based on the experience of OECD member states since 1963. The OECD Model gives the primary right of taxation to the state of residence. It operates largely in favour of the developed capital exporting countries, and to the consequent detriment of underdeveloped countries which are net importers of foreign investment.

In 1966, OECD issued a draft convention on estates and inheritances. In 1982, it published a revised version of the same which included gifts also. The OECD conventions have been widely accepted among OECD member states and other developed countries.

The United Nations adopted a resolution in 1967 to constitute a group of experts on tax treaties between developed and developing countries. Special problems arise where a double tax treaty is concluded between developed and developing countries. Based on the report of the group of experts, the United Nations issued in 1979 a Manual for tax treaty negotiators. In 1980, it issued its Model Double Taxation Convention between Developed and Developing Countries.

The basic difference between the United Nations model and the OECD model is that the former predominantly gives the source country the right to tax income while the latter grants the country of residence the right to tax income. The United Nations model is generally used when one of the countries is a developing one. This is so because normally investments flow from a developed country to a developing country which *ipso facto* means that incomes flow from developing to developed countries, i.e. developing countries are the source of income.

24.4.4 Multilateral Tax Treaties: Multilateral double tax treaties, though considered at different times in various contexts, have not gained acceptance for being complex. It is difficult to understand and apply a multilateral treaty than a bilateral one. Moreover, a multilateral convention is less flexible in terms of amendment, revision, or termination.

Though multilateral approach is not generally followed, there are, at least, three notable multilateral double income tax agreements.

1. **Andean Pact:** This agreement among the member states of Andean Group (Bolivia, Chile, Columbia, Ecuador, Peru, and Venezuela) is based on the principle of giving the state of source the exclusive right of taxation.
2. **Comecon Conventions:** There are two multilateral agreements for the avoidance

of double taxation among 8 of the 10 member states of Comecon (Bulgaria, Czechoslovakia, erstwhile GDR, Hungary, Mongolia, Poland, Romania, erstwhile USSR, Cuba, and Vietnam). The last two are not signatories to the multilateral agreements.

3. **Nordic Countries:** A multilateral treaty covering tax on income and capital exists among Nordic countries (Denmark, Finland, Iceland, Norway, and Sweden).

24.5 International Tax Evasion and Tax Avoidance

See section 10.2 of chapter 10 of this book.

Endnotes

1. It relates to concurrent taxation powers enjoyed by different tiers of government in a federal polity. Concurrent taxation powers are a characteristic feature of fiscal federalism in USA, Canada, and Australia. Most tax fields in these countries are jointly occupied by the federal and provincial governments. Thus, personal income tax, corporation tax, general sales tax, and consumption tax (excise duty) are levied by the Federal as well as Provincial Governments in Canada. The only notable exception is the customs duties which belong exclusively to the Federal Government.
   The overlapping taxation powers often cause friction not only between the federal and provincial governments but also among the provinces *inter se* as regards the sharing of a tax base. The problem is solved through tax rental and tax sharing negotiations and agreements.
   In India, the Central and the State Governments have no concurrent powers of taxation. Taxes with inter-state base and those in the case of which all-India uniformity in rates is needed to facilitate industry and trade are vested in the Central Government. Taxes which are location-specific and relate to subjects of local consumption are with the States. The absence of joint occupancy of tax fields has successfully minimised double taxation, duplicate tax administration, and tax rivalry between the Centre and the States, and among the States themselves.
2. OECD, *Model Double Taxation Convention of Income and Capital*, 1977, p. 7.

25

Indian Law on Double Tax Relief

25.1 Provisions of Income Tax Act, 1961 on Double Tax Relief

As in most other countries, India gives unilateral as well as treaty relief in respect of foreign taxes suffered by Indian residents on their foreign income. Sections 90 and 91 of the Act deal with relief from international double taxation. Section 90 is for taxpayers who have paid the tax to a country with which India has signed a DTAA, while section 91 provides relief to taxpayers who have paid tax to a country with which India has not signed a DTAA.

Section 90 of the Act gives relief bilaterally through tax treaties. It provides, *inter alia*, that a treaty may be entered into: (a) for grant of relief in respect of income which is taxed in both the countries, (b) for the avoidance of double taxation on income, (c) for exchange of information for the prevention of evasion or avoidance of income tax, and (d) for the recovery of income tax.

Broadly speaking, India's tax treaties contain two alternatives: (a) Income which arises in the territory of one of the contracting States is not taxed by the other contracting State (exclusion method). (b) Income is taxed in both the countries in accordance with their respective tax laws but the country of the residence of the taxpayer allows him a credit against the tax charged thereon in the country of the source of such income (tax credit method). Where any such agreement for avoidance of double taxation exists, the provisions of the Act apply to the extent they are more beneficial to the assessee.

Section 91 grants unilateral relief from double taxation to the residents in respect of foreign tax paid abroad. It is noteworthy that Section 91 comes into force only when relief is not available under Section 90. Following are the requirements of Section 91: (a) the assessee should be a resident of India in the previous year, (b) such income should not be deemed to accrue in India under the provisions of the Act, (c) the income should be taxed in both the countries and there is no double tax treaty with that country, and (d) the assessee should have in fact paid the tax in such foreign country either by deduction or otherwise.

Thus, if an Indian resident proves that tax has been paid in respect of his income which accrued or arose to him in the countries with which India has no agreement for double taxation relief, he is entitled to a deduction from the Indian income tax payable by him.

25.2 Main Features of a Typical Tax Treaty between India and another Country

India has entered into tax treaties with 88 countries. This means that there are agreed rates of tax and jurisdictions on specified types of income arising in a country to a tax resident of another country.

25.2.1 Scope of the Treaty: A typical tax treaty between India and another country covers only residents of India and the other contracting country who have entered into the agreement with India. Such agreement generally provides that the laws of the two contracting states will govern the taxation of income in respective states except when express provision to the contrary is made in the agreement.

Chapter I (Articles 1 and 2) of a typical tax treaty contain the personal scope of the tax treaty and the taxes covered under the treaty. Chapter II (Articles 3 and 4) deal with general definitions. For instance, Article 3 generally deals with definitions of the terms like State, tax, person, company, enterprise, international traffic, nationals, competent authority etc. Article 4 defines the term "resident" for the purpose of a given tax treaty. Normally, the term "resident of one of the States" means any person who, under the laws of that State, is liable to tax therein by reason of his domicile, residence, place of management or any other criterion of a similar nature.

A situation may arise when originally the tax provision in the other contracting state gave concessional treatment compared to India at a particular time but Indian laws were subsequently amended to bring incidence of tax to a level lower than the tax rate existing in the other contracting state. Since the tax treaties are meant to be beneficial and not intended to put taxpayers of a contracting state to a disadvantage, Section 90 of the Income Tax Act, 1961 specifies that where the Government of India has entered into a Double Taxation Avoidance Agreement with other countries, then the provision of the relevant DTAA or the Income Tax Act, 1961 whichever is more beneficial to the assessee, shall be applicable.

25.2.2 Permanent Establishment: Article 5 of the tax treaties entered into by India with different countries defines the term "permanent establishment" as fixed place of business through which the business of an enterprise is wholly or partly carried on. More specifically, the term "permanent establishment" includes: (a) a place of management, (b) a branch, (c) an office, (d) a factory, (e) a workshop, (f) a mine, an oil or gas well, a quarry or any other place of extraction of natural resources, (g) a warehouse, in relation to a person providing storage facilities for others, (h) a farm, plantation or other place where agriculture, forestry, plantation or related activities are carried on, (i) a store or premises used as a sales outlet, (j) an installation or structure used for the exploration or exploitation of natural resources, and (k) a building site or construction, installation or assembly project or supervisory activities in connection therewith.

A comparative study of articles on permanent establishment in respect of certain selected tax treaties reveals that there is no uniformity or consistency in defining the existence of a permanent establishment based on the minimum threshold period of existence.

25.2.3 Provisions for Taxation under the Tax Treaties: Chapter III of India's tax treaties deals with taxation of income including income from immovable property, business profits, dividends, interest, royalty, technical fees and the like.

A. Income from Immovable Property (Article 6): Article 6 provides that income derived by a resident of one of the States from immovable property situated in the other State may be taxed in that other State.

B. Business Profits (Article 7): Imposition of tax on a foreign enterprise is done only if it has a permanent establishment in the contracting state. Tax is computed by treating the permanent establishment as a distinct and independent enterprise.

In determining the profits of a permanent establishment, most tax treaties allow as deduction, expenses which are incurred for the purposes of the business of the permanent establishment, including executive and general administrative expenses.

The UN Model Convention (generally followed by India), inter alia, states that in the determination of profits of a permanent establishment, no deduction shall be allowed for amounts paid (otherwise than towards reimbursement of actual expenses) by the permanent establishment to the head office of the enterprise or any of its other offices, by way of royalties, fees or other similar payments in return for the use of patents or other rights, or by way of commission, for specific services performed. In this respect, it is interesting to note that except in respect of tax treaties with a few countries, the above provision of UN Model Convention has not been considered in many of the treaties. This implies that in respect of most of the tax treaties, expenditure incurred by the permanent establishment towards royalties, fees for technical services etc. would become an allowable expenditure, thereby reducing the taxable income leading to loss of revenue.

Further, most tax treaties provide that no profits shall be attributed to a permanent establishment by reason of the mere purchase by that permanent establishment of goods or merchandise for the enterprise. The profits to be attributed to the permanent establishment shall be determined by the same method year by year unless there is good and sufficient reason to the contrary.

C. Income from Air and Shipping Transport (Articles 8 and 8A): Income derived from the operation of air transport in international traffic by an enterprise of one contracting state will not be taxed in the other contracting state. In respect of an enterprise of one contracting state, income earned in the other contracting state from the operation of ships in international traffic, will be taxed in that contracting state wherein the place of effective management of enterprise is situated. However some treaties contain provisions to tax the income in the other contracting state also, although at reduced rate. These provisions do not apply to coastal traffic.

D. Associated Enterprises (Article 9): In order to plug loop holes for tax evasion, Article 9 in tax treaties provides for taxing the notional income in case of associated enterprises. Where an enterprise of a Contracting State participates directly or indirectly in the management, control or capital of an enterprise of the other Contracting State and conditions are made or imposed between the two enterprises in their commercial or financial relations which differ from those which would be made between independent enterprises, then any profits which would, but for those conditions, have accrued to one of the enterprises, but, by the reason of those conditions, have not so accrued, may be included in the profits of that enterprise and taxed accordingly.

E. Dividends (Article 10): India generally follows the UN Model for taxation of various sources of income like dividends, interest, royalty and technical fees. Rates of tax, which may be withheld from dividends, interest, royalty are to be negotiated bilaterally, unlike the OECD Model which specifies thee maximum rate. However, where a tax treaty provides for a particular mode of computation of income, the same shall be followed irrespective of the provisions of the Income Tax Act.

Dividends paid by a Company which is a resident of a Contracting State to a resident of the other Contracting State will be taxed in both the States. Where a company which is a resident of a Contracting State derives profits or income from the other Contracting State, that other State may not impose any tax on dividends paid by the company, except insofar as such dividends are paid to be a resident of that other State or insofar as the holding in respect of which the dividends are paid is effectively connected with a permanent establishment or a fixed base situated in that other State.

F. Interest (Article 11): Interest paid in a Contracting State to resident of the other Contracting State is chargeable to tax in both the States. This, however, shall not apply if the beneficial owner of the interest, being a resident of a Contracting State, carries on business in the other Contracting State in which the interest arises, through a permanent establishment situated therein, or performs in that other Contracting State independent personal services from a fixed base situated therein, and the debt-claim in respect of which the interest is paid is effectively connected with such permanent establishment or fixed base. In such case the provisions of Article 7 or Article 14~~, as the case~~ may be, shall apply.

G. Royalties, Fees for Technical Services (Article 12): Generally, royalties, fees for technical services and payments for the use of equipment arising in one of the States and paid to a resident of the other State is taxed in both the States. The term "royalties" is normally defined as payments of any kind received as a consideration for the use of, or the right to use, any copyright of literary, artistic or scientific work, including cinematograph films, or films or tapes used for radio or television broadcasting, any patent, trade mark, design or model, plan, secret formula or process, or for the use of, or the right to use, industrial, commercial, or scientific equipment, or for information concerning industrial, commercial or scientific experience but does not include any payments in respect of the operation of mineral deposits, sources and other natural resources. The term "fees for technical services" is usually defined as payments of any kind to any person, other than payments to an employee of the person making the payments and to any individual for independent personal services, in consideration for services of a managerial, technical or consultative nature. Those tax treaties which have provisions for taxation of "payments for the use of equipment" define it as payments of any kind received as a consideration for the use of, or the right to use industrial, commercial or scientific equipment.

It is noteworthy that while some tax treaties have provisions for taxation of royalties, fees for technical services and payments for use of equipment, some others only have provisions for royalties.

Some double taxation avoidance agreements provide that income by way of interest, royalty or fee for technical services is charged to tax on net basis. This may result in tax deducted at source from sums paid to non-residents which may be more than the final tax liability. The assessing officer has therefore been empowered under Section 195 to determine the appropriate proportion of the amount from which tax is to be deducted at source. There are instances where as per the Income Tax Act, tax is required to be deducted at a rate prescribed in tax treaty. However this may require foreign companies to apply for refund. To obviate such difficulties Section 2(37A) provides that tax may be deducted at source at the rate applicable in a particular case as per Section 195 on the sums payable to non-residents or in accordance with the rates specified in DTAAs.

Section 195 specifies the withholding tax rates for various categories of income. Tax is deductible at source under Section 195 at these specified rates or rates specified in Double Taxation Avoidance Agreements entered into by the Central Government under Section 90, whichever is lower.

H. Capital Gains: Capital gains will be taxed in the state where the capital asset is situated at the time of sale. More specifically, gains derived by a resident of a Contracting State from the alienation of immovable property situated in the other Contracting State may be taxed in that other State. Similarly, gains from the alienation of movable property forming part of the business property of a permanent establishment which an enterprise of a Contracting State has in the other Contracting State may be taxed in that other State. Gains from the alienation of any property other than those mentioned above shall normally be taxable only in the Contracting State of which the alienator is a resident.

I. Independent Personal Services: Income derived by an individual who is a resident of a Contracting State from the performance of professional services or other independent activities of a similar character shall be taxable only in that State. However, if he has a fixed base regularly available to him in the other Contracting State for the purpose of performing his activities, the income may be taxed in the other Contracting State but only so much of it as is attributable to that fixed base. (The term professional services include especially independent scientific, literary, artistic, educational or teaching activities as well as the independent activities of physicians, surgeons, lawyers, engineers, architects, dentists and accountants).

J. Dependent Personal Services: Salaries, wages and other similar remuneration derived by a resident of a Contracting State in respect of an employment shall be taxable only in that State unless the employment is exercised, in the other Contracting State. If the employment is so exercised, such remuneration as is derived therefrom may be taxed in that other State. Most of the tax treaties provide that where the recipient is present in the source country for a period not exceeding 183 days in the concerned year and remuneration is paid by an employer who is not a resident of the source country, then remuneration so received shall be taxable only in the country of residence of the recipient.

K. Directors' Fees: Directors' fees and similar payments derived by a resident of one of the Contracting States as a member of the Board of Directors of a company which is a resident of the other Contracting State may be taxed in that other State.

L. Entertainers: Income derived by residents of one of the Contracting States as entertainers, such as theatre, motion picture, radio or television artists, musicians and athletes, from their personal activities as such exercised in the other Contracting State, may be taxed in that other State.

M. Pensions and Annuities: Pensions and annuities paid to a resident of one of the Contracting States shall be taxable only in that State.

N. Government Service: Remuneration, other than a pension or annuity, paid by one of the Contracting States or political sub-division or local authority of that State to any individual in respect of services rendered in the discharge of governmental functions shall be taxable only in that State. However, such remuneration shall be taxable only in the other Contracting State if the services are rendered in that other State and the recipient is a resident of that other State.

O. Professors and Teachers: Where a professor or teacher who is a resident of one of the Contracting States visits the other Contracting State for a period not exceeding two years for the purpose of teaching or carrying out advanced study or research at a university, college, school or other educational institution, any remuneration that person receives for such teaching, advanced study or research shall be exempt from tax in that other State to the extent to which such remuneration is subject to tax in the first-mentioned State.

P. Students and Trainees: Where a student or trainee, who is a resident of one of the Contracting States or who was a resident of that State immediately before visiting the other Contracting State and who is temporarily present in that other State solely for the purpose of his education or training, receives payments from sources outside that other State for the purpose of the his maintenance, education or training, those payments shall be exempt from tax in that other State.

25.2.4 Provisions Regarding Elimination of Double Taxation: In order to avoid double taxation it is provided that if a resident of India becomes liable to pay tax either directly or by deduction in the other country in respect of income from any source, he shall be allowed credit against the Indian tax payable in respect of such income to an amount not exceeding the tax borne by him in the other country on that portion of the income which is taxed in the said other country. The same benefit is available to the resident of the other Country, on income taxed in India.

In respect of incomes on which taxes are either exempted or reduced, the country of residence will not take the exempted income into account while determining the tax to be imposed on the rest of the income.

A. Non-discrimination Clause: Most of the bilateral tax treaties have a non-discrimination clause which provides that the nationals of a Contracting State shall not be subjected in the other Contracting State to any taxation or any requirement connected therewith which is more burdensome than the taxation and connected requirements to which nationals of that other State in the same circumstances and under the same conditions are or may be subjected. The same holds for taxation on permanent establishment which an enterprise of a Contracting State has in the other Contracting State.

B. Mutual Agreement Procedure: Tax treaties lay down a mutual agreement procedure (MAP) for resolving disputes arising out of their application. The taxpayer may approach the competent authority of the contracting state of which he is a resident where he feels that the assessment to be made or order passed is not in accordance with the terms of the treaty. The competent authority shall endeavour to resolve the dispute by mutual agreement with the competent authority of the other Contracting State, with a view to the avoidance of taxation which is not in accordance with the Agreement. (The case is normally required to be presented within two years from the first notification of the action which gives rise to taxation not in accordance with the Agreement).

The Central Board of Direct Taxes vide instruction of November 2002, has laid down the following procedure for giving effect to the resolution of dispute under MAP:

- Applicant shall be required to give an acceptance to the decision arrived at under MAP and that he will forego any right to appeal on the same issue.
- Where the issue is under appeal, the assessing officer shall also obtain an undertaking from the assessee regarding withdrawal of appeal on the issue.

C. Exchange of Information: Bilateral tax treaties provide that competent authorities of contracting states shall exchange such information as is necessary for applying the provisions of the treaty or of domestic laws of the contracting states concerning taxes covered by the treaty. This clause is included with a view to prevent fraud or evasion of taxes. It is further provided that any information received by a Contracting State shall be treated as secret and shall be disclosed only to persons or authorities (including courts and administrative bodies) involved in the assessment or collection of, the enforcement or prosecution in respect of, or the determination of appeals in relation to the taxes which are the subject of the Convention. Such persons or authorities shall use the information only for such purposes but may disclose the information in public court proceedings or in judicial decisions.

The competent authorities shall, through consultation, develop appropriate conditions, methods and techniques concerning the matters in respect of which such exchanges of information shall be made, including, where appropriate, exchanges of information regarding tax avoidance.

25.3 Double Taxation Relief Where No Tax Treaty Exists

Section 91 grants unilateral relief from double taxation to the residents in respect of foreign tax paid abroad. It is noteworthy that Section 91 comes into force only when relief is not available under Section 90. Following are the requirements of Section 91: (a) the assessee should be a resident of India in the previous year, (b) such income should not be deemed to accrue in India under the provisions of the Act, (c) the income should be taxed in both the countries and there is no double tax treaty with that country, and (d) the assessee should have in fact paid the tax in such foreign country either by deduction or otherwise.

Thus, if an Indian resident proves that tax has been paid in respect of his income which accrued or arose to him in the countries with which India has no agreement for double taxation relief, he is entitled to a deduction from the Indian income tax payable by him.

25.4 Issues Relating to Indo-Mauritius Tax Treaty

As tax treaties (or DTAAs) are country-specific, the contours of taxation and concessions granted vary based on the comparative advantage that India enjoys with them. In this context, Indo-Mauritius tax treaty has been of considerable concern. The trends indicate Mauritius as the top investing country in India. The fact that a small economy like Mauritius is the largest foreign investor in a huge economy like India surpassing developed nations like USA, Japan and UK, calls for further investigation.

A study of the articles dealing with residency and taxation of capital gains reveals that special consideration was given to business entities of Mauritius (perhaps in view of the fact that Mauritius was a less developed country than India). The tax treaty with Mauritius was signed in August 1982. The treaty specified that capital gains made on the sale of shares of Indian companies by investors resident in Mauritius would be taxed only in Mauritius and not in India. For almost 10 years, the treaty existed only on paper since foreign institutional investors (FIIs) were not allowed to invest in Indian stock markets. This changed in 1992 when FIIs were allowed into India.

Coinciding with this liberalization of the Indian economy, the Government of Mauritius promulgated the Mauritius Offshore Business Activities Act, 1992 to regulate the offshore business in that country. This Act allowed foreign companies to register in Mauritius for investing abroad. A body corporate registered under the laws in Mauritius would be a resident in Mauritius and thus 'subject to taxation' as a resident. Income Tax Act of Mauritius provided that offshore companies were liable to pay 'zero percent' tax. Thus, by bringing an offshore company within the definition of resident, not only was the benefit of offshore company extended to it but also the benefits of residency allowable under the DTAA bestowed on it. This led to establishment of conduit companies in Mauritius through which investors of third countries routed their investment to India. By doing so, they avoided paying capital gains tax altogether and also enjoyed low rates of dividend and income taxes in Mauritius (Mauritius does not have a capital gains tax).

The above position has led to concern among tax authorities in India about the loss of rightful revenue. A Report of the Central Board of Direct Taxes observed, “In effect, the whole exercise of avoidance of double taxation turned out to be avoidance of taxation altogether”. Two questions have been challenging the basis of the Indo-Mauritius tax treaty.

- Is India giving away much more in tax exemptions than it is getting in investments?
- Will investments come to India even if the lucrative routes through Mauritius don’t exist?

The Joint Parliamentary Committee (that presented its ‘Report on Stock Market Scam’ to the Parliament on December 21, 2003) in its observation on the Indo-Mauritius tax treaty noted that “there could be substantial revenue loss due to the ‘residency clause’ in the Indo-Mauritius DTAA”. It, therefore, recommended that companies investing in India through Mauritius should be required to file a declaration of ownership with RBI, to the effect that all the directors and effective management was in Mauritius.

25.4.1 Supreme Court on Indo-Mauritius DTAA: The tax authorities in India, recognizing the need to curtail the ‘abuse’ of the Indo-Mauritius treaty denied the benefit of the treaty (March 2000) to some offshore business companies (OBCs) registered in Mauritius that had claimed exemption from tax under the Income Tax Act, by rejecting the certificate of residence furnished by them. Such OBCs were claiming exemption of capital gains from stock market operations, which gave the right of taxation of such capital gains to Mauritius.

At around the same time, there were fluctuations in the stock markets and general perception that the action of the department denying the benefit of Mauritius residency to some Mauritius based FIIs was the root cause for such fluctuations. It was projected that this would have or had resulted in huge outflows of foreign investment from India. To clear the doubts, as also clarify the intent of the Indo-Mauritius DTAA, the Central Board of Direct Taxes issued Circular 789 dated April 13, 2000 requiring, *inter alia*, the assessing officer to accept the certificate of residence granted under the local legislation of Mauritius to OBCs operating from third countries including India.

Considering a public interest litigation (PIL), Delhi High Court quashed the above circular as bad in law on the grounds that the income tax officer was entitled to lift the corporate veil in order to ascertain whether a company was actually resident of Mauritius or not in exercise of his quasi-judicial powers and any attempt by the Board to interfere with this would be contrary to the intendment of the Act. In the aftermath of the Delhi High Court judgment foreign direct investment as well as portfolio flows nosedived. Very likely fund managers chose other investment destinations that continued to offer attractive tax concessions. What was needed in India was to plug the loopholes and not invalidate the beneficial provisions of the tax treaty.

The Supreme Court then upheld the sanctity of rules framed under bilateral tax treaties. The honourable Supreme Court in its judgment in the case of *Azadi Bachao Andolan* on October 7, 2003 upholding the issue of circular by the Board as also the Indo-Mauritius DTAA, held that:

- Indo-Mauritius DTAC (1983) is not *ultra vires* of the powers of the Central Government under Section 90, on account of its susceptibility to "treaty shopping".
- Circular 789 of April 2000 issued by the Board falls within the parameters of the powers exercisable by the Board under Section 119. The circular does not in any way crib, cabin or confine the powers of the assessing officer with regard to any assessment. It merely formulates guidelines to be applied in the matters of assessment of assessees covered by the provisions of Indo-Mauritius DTAA.
- Merely because, at a given time there may be an exemption from income tax in respect of particular head of income, it is not correct to say that the taxable entity is not liable to taxation.

The Supreme Court took note of the fact that, "In recent years, India has been the beneficiary of significant foreign funds through the Mauritius Conduit. Although economic reforms in India since 1991 permitted such capital transfers, the amount would have been much lower without the India-Mauritius tax treaty". The Supreme Court's action in upholding the validity of the Circular had a number of positive implications for currency inflows into the country. Through the circular, the Central Board of Direct Taxes (CBDT) allowed investors incorporated in Mauritius to claim tax exemptions on their investments routed through that country.

During the pendency of the proceedings before the Supreme Court, the Board issued a circular on February 10, 2003 clarifying that where an assessing officer finds and is satisfied that an entity is resident of both India and Mauritius, he would be free to proceed to determine the residential status under the DTAA by invoking what is otherwise also known as the 'tie-breaker' clause. It further stated that where it was found that the company had its place of effective management in India, then, notwithstanding it being incorporated in Mauritius, *it would be taxed under the DTAA in India.*

In the context of the tax treaty, Finance Minister P. Chidambaram stated,

"The government has no intention of introducing long-term capital gains tax or to carry out a one-sided review of the India-Mauritius tax avoidance treaty. The India-Mauritius treaty has been debated threadbare. Due to a host of economic, political and diplomatic reasons, we are not proposing any unilateral revision of the treaty".

The provisions of the Indo-Mauritius tax treaty continue to be a subject of debate. Despite the Supreme Court judgement quoted above and the assurance from the Finance Minister, there is still a section of legislators and bureaucrats who feel that India is giving away much more in tax exemptions than it is receiving in investments and that these tax concessions are uncalled for. In view of the above, it becomes imperative for the Government to constantly review the trends in foreign institutional investments and take adequate precautions to avoid investments by conduit companies formed with the primary purpose of taking advantage of the treaty.

25.5 Transfer Pricing Regulations in India

Taxing provisions for transfer pricing have become imperative, in the context of increasing participation of multinational groups in economic activities in India. However, transfer pricing solutions need to be flexible enough to adapt to the growing business of a multinational group, taking into account the organisation's perception of the risks of adverse tax assessments. Prior to April 2001, there were no detailed provisions in India relating to transfer pricing and determination of arm's length price. Foreign banks in India, for instance, are known to have shown profits after about one-third or even half of the actual profits were siphoned off under various global allocations, including head office costs. Even seemingly innocuous costs like research and development costs overseas, are often transfer pricing irregularities because of the price at which these transactions take place.

With globalisation of the Indian economy, a need was felt for a detailed and separate regulation for administering transfer pricing. Absence of such regulations not only results in litigation but loss of revenue to the exchequer as well. The Finance Minister, in his Budget speech (2000-01) stated, "The presence of multinational enterprises in India and their ability to allocate profits in different jurisdictions by controlling prices in intra-group transactions has made the issue of transfer pricing a matter of serious concern". In the same Budget, the Finance Minister announced that necessary legislative changes for transfer pricing will be made in the Finance Bill based on the recommendations of an Expert Group set up in November 1999.

The Finance Act, 2001 introduced detailed Transfer Pricing Regulations in India with effect from April 1, 2001 corresponding to the assessment year 2002-

2003. The rules for transfer pricing were notified on August 21, 2001.

The sections and rules under the Income Tax Act dealing with transfer pricing regulations include Sections 92 to 92F, 271(1)(c), 271AA, 271BA , 271G and Rules 10A to 10E.

25.6 Taxation of Non-residents in India

Income which is subject to charge of tax varies according to the residential status of a taxpayer. In the case of a person *resident* in India, all income derived from whatever source is within the scope of taxation. However, in the case of a *non-resident,* the tax liability extends only to income which: (a) is received or is deemed to be received in India by or on behalf of the non-resident, and (b) accrues or arises, or is deemed to accrue or arise, to the non-resident in India. It is evident that income which accrues or arises outside India (i.e. foreign income) is beyond the scope of tax liability in India in the case of a non-resident.

Since the scope of income chargeable to tax in India is dependent upon the residential status of the taxpayer, it is important to understand the terms resident and non-resident which have a technical meaning under the law.

25.6.1 Rules to Determine Residential Status: Section 6 of the Act lays down the test of residence for different taxable entities. Here, the residential status of the two major taxable entities, viz. individuals and companies is discussed.

The residential status of an assessee may not remain the same in each income year. An assessee who is resident during one year may be a non-resident in the next year. Moreover, the residence of an assessee has nothing to do with his domicile or nationality. Also, residential status of an assessee is the same for all sources of income.

A. Residents in India:

(a) Individuals: An individual is said to be resident in India in any previous year if he satisfies any of the following two *basic conditions*: (i) He was in India in the previous year for a period of 182 days or more; or (ii) he was in India for a period of 365 days or more during the four years preceding the previous year and 60 days or more during the previous year (182 days or more in the case of an Indian citizen or a person of Indian origin coming on a visit to India or in case of an Indian citizen going abroad as a member of the crew of an Indian ship or for employment). [1] Although these conditions require the personal presence of the assessee in India, his stay in India for a particular number of days in different cases need not be continuous in a previous year.

(b) Company: An Indian company (i.e. a company registered under the Companies Act, 1956) is always resident in India. A foreign company is treated as resident in India only if control and management [2] of its affairs is situated wholly in India during the previous year. A foreign company is non-resident if control and management of its affairs is either wholly or partly situated out of India during the previous year. A company is simply either a resident or a non-resident.

B. Non-residents: An individual is non-resident in India if he satisfies neither of the two basic conditions mentioned above for an individual to be resident in India.

C. Not Ordinarily Resident: An individual who: (a) has been a non-resident in India in 9 out of the 10 previous years preceding the relevant previous year, or (b) has been in India for an aggregate period of 729 days or less during the 7 previous years preceding that year, would be regarded as person not ordinarily resident in India.

25.6.2 Relationship between Residential Status and Tax Incidence: Incidence of tax on an assessee depends on his residential status. Under Section 5 of the Act, the tax liability of different classes of assessees on the basis of their residence is as follows.

A. Resident: An assessee who is resident and ordinarily resident in India is assessed to tax in respect of income: (i) received or deemed to be received in India in the previous year by him or on his behalf, (ii) which accrues or arises or is deemed to accrue or arise to him in India during such year, and (iii) which accrues or arises to him outside India during such year.

B. Non-resident: Non-resident assessee is chargeable to tax in respect of income: (i) received or is deemed to be received in India during the previous year by or on behalf of such person, and (ii) which accrues or arises or is deemed to accrue or arise to him in India during such year.

C. Not Ordinarily Resident: An assessee who is a resident but not ordinarily a resident is assessed to tax in respect of income: (i) received or deemed to be received in India in the previous year by him or on his behalf, (ii) which accrues or arises or is deemed to accrue or arise to him in India during such year, and (iii) which accrues or arises to him outside India during such year and is derived from a business controlled in or a profession set up in India. It means income accrued outside India from a business controlled from outside India or a profession set up outside India is not chargeable to tax in the case of resident but not ordinarily resident class of assessees. For a resident and ordinarily resident assessee, income accruing in any part of the world is chargeable to tax.

The incidence of income tax on various categories of assessees according to their residential status is summarised in Table 25.1. It is evident that income received or deemed to be received in India or income accruing or deemed to accrue in India are taxable in the case of all assessees, irrespective of their residential status.

The aforesaid provisions of the Act point out that tax incidence is the highest in the case of a resident and ordinarily resident taxpayer. It is lower for resident but not ordinarily resident assessees, and lowest in the case of non-residents.

Table 25.1: Tax Liability of Different Types of Income on the Basis of Residential Status in India

Type of Income	Residential Status of the Assessee		
	Resident and ordinarily resident	Resident but not ordinarily resident	Non-resident
1. Income received or deemed to be Received in India	Taxable	Taxable	Taxable
2. Income accruing or arising or Deemed to accrue or arise in India	Taxable	Taxable	Taxable
3. Income earned and received outside India from a business controlled in or A profession set up in India	Taxable	Taxable	Non-taxable
4. Income earned and received outside India from a business controlled from outside India or a profession set up outside India	Taxable	Non-taxable	Non-taxable

25.7 Tax Incentives for Non-resident Indians

Over the last few decades, a good number of Indians have found career opportunities in the developed West and oil exporting Arab countries. Most of them have adopted foreign countries as their permanent homes. Although settled abroad, many of them continue to have their roots in India so that they may return to their homeland should the circumstances so demand.

Considering the number of Indians abroad, their relative sound financial status and their desire to make investments in their country of origin, attractive interest rates are offered on their deposits in India. Similarly, the income tax law contains special incentives to attract non-resident investments into India. The purpose of these incentives/concessions is to establish useful and strong links between Indians abroad and their homeland. In fact, the inflow of funds from non-residents has emerged, in recent years, as a strategic tool of development policy with the following objectives in view: (a) to augment foreign exchange resources for strengthening economic base of the country, (b) to tide over the chronic deficits in the balance of payments, (c) to raise the overall level of investments in the economy, (d) to induct modern technology into India, and (e) to provide an emotional shot to non-residents to plan and maintain their financial links with the home country.

The Act provides, under various sub-sections of Section 10, a large number of tax concessions to non-residents, the important ones being the following.

1. Exemption from tax of any income from interest on such securities as the Central Government may specify.
2. Exemption from tax of interest on money in non-resident (external) account.
3. Income from interest on specified savings certificates, received by a non-resident, being a citizen of India or a person of Indian origin, is exempt from income tax provided such certificates are subscribed to in convertible foreign exchange remitted from outside India.
4. Income of a consultant under a technical assistance grant agreement is exempt from tax.
5. Income in connection with any technical assistance programme is exempt from tax.
6. Interest on non-resident (non-repatriable) Rupee Deposit Scheme is exempt from tax.
7. Interest payable by a scheduled bank on deposits in foreign currency is exempt from tax.
8. Interest on bonds for non-resident Indians is exempt from tax.
9. Income in respect of foreigners such as passage money, remuneration to officials of embassies is exempt from tax.

25.8 Assessment and Collection of Tax from Non-residents in India

Notwithstanding the various concessions/exemptions given to non-residents under the income tax law, a stringent and pervasive system of assessment and collection of tax is followed. For example, the conditions laid down for the test of residence are not diluted and no relief is granted even if the stay of an assessee in India exceeds or falls short of the prescribed limits just by one day.

The income of a non-resident assessee is assessed for tax purposes either directly or indirectly (i.e. through his agent). The agent can either be a duly constituted agent or a person who can be treated as an agent. If there is no duly constituted agent, the tax authorities are empowered to treat any of the following class of persons as the agent of a non-resident.

1. A person employed by or on behalf of the non-resident.
2. A person having a business connection with the non-resident.
3. A person from whom the non-resident is in receipt of any income either

directly or indirectly.

4. A person who is trustee of the non-resident.
5. A person who has acquired any capital asset from a non-resident if that asset is situated in India.

It is noteworthy that any of the persons mentioned above and treated as agent should be in India at the time of assessment, though he need not necessarily be a resident in India. In other words, even a non-resident may be an agent for a non-resident assessee.

Still further, an agent may be a person who does not belong to any of the above-mentioned five categories. In short, any person may be treated as an agent of a non-resident if he has some connection with the income sought to be assessed. Under the law there are elaborate guidelines concerning the appointment and liabilities of a duly constituted agent.

1. The agent is chargeable as a representative assessee of the non-resident for the incomes which are received or deemed to be received and accrue or are deemed to accrue in India.
2. The agent should have some connection with the income sought to be assessed in his hands even though the income belongs to the non-resident.
3. The agent is assessable for such incomes only as may belong to the non-residents and not to the residents.
4. The agent is assessed in the same manner and to the same extent as the non-resident himself would have been.
5. No one would be treated as an agent unless there is a liability to income tax on the non-resident.
6. The liability of the agent is personal and not conditional upon his having in hand any funds of the profit of the non-resident.

A person who is treated as an agent of a non-resident is given an opportunity of being heard before he is treated as such. And if he is treated as the agent of a non-resident, he enjoys the right to deduct from the payments to the non-resident an amount equal to the tax estimated to be paid on the profits made by the non-resident in India.

The problem of tax recovery from the non-resident becomes more serious where there is no agent who can be made liable by the tax authorities for the purpose. To deal with such situations, the income tax law has devised the following two methods:

1. Deduction of tax at source.
2. Recovery of tax from assets.

Under the law, any income from salaries, interest on securities and dividends is subject to deduction of tax at source. The person responsible for paying such incomes is required to deduct income tax at source at the prescribed rates and deposit the same with the Government within the prescribed time limit. Deduction of tax at source is made on all such sums payable to a non-resident which are chargeable to income tax. Such sums may also include payments other than salaries, interest on securities and dividends [Section 195].

In case where there is no agent from whom the tax, payable by a non-resident, may be recovered or if it has not been deducted at source, the tax authorities are empowered to recover the tax from any assets of the non-resident which are in India or which may come to India any time later. Under the law there is no time limit for the recovery of a tax through this method.

The income tax law deals specifically with the assessment and collection of tax: (i) on profits of non-residents from shipping business, and (ii) on persons leaving India for good.

Cases may arise where non-residents are engaged in shipping business in India as the owners or charterers of ships without employing an agent from whom the tax on profits of such business can be recovered. To meet such cases the law provides that where a ship carries passengers or other items, 7.5 percent of the amount paid or payable in this respect to the owner or the charterer shall be deemed to be his income accruing in India for such carriage [Section 44B]. It is immaterial whether such an amount is paid or is payable in or out of India. Before leaving any port in India, the master of the ship has to prepare and furnish to the tax authorities a return of the full amount paid or payable to the owner or charterer of the ship in respect of the carriage of passengers or other items at that port since the last arrival of the ship there. This means the master of the ship is required to furnish a full account of carriage charges of the passengers etc. booked at the Indian port. On receipt of the return, the income tax officer has to assess the income and determine the amount of tax payable at the rates applicable to non-resident assessees.

The master of the ship may be exempted from furnishing such a return if the income tax officer is satisfied that the former has made satisfactory arrangement of furnishing the return and payment of tax through some other person acting on his behalf. As a cross-checking, port clearance is not granted to the ship until the collector of customs is satisfied that the tax assessable has been duly paid or that satisfactory arrangement for its payment has been made. Thus, cross-checking through inter-departmental co-operation is an important device to collect taxes from non-residents.

Another interesting provision of the income tax law pertains to the assessment and collection of tax from a person, resident or non-resident, who in the opinion of tax authorities, may leave India during the current assessment year for good [Section

230]. In such a case the total income of that individual for the period from the expiry of the previous year up to the probable date of his departure from India is chargeable to tax in the same assessment year. [3] Where the income of such an individual cannot be determined properly, the income tax officer is authorised to estimate the same as per his own judgement without prejudice to the assessee. Individuals falling under this provision of the income tax law are required to obtain a tax clearance certificate from the foreign section of income tax office before leaving India.

Endnotes

1. The term non-resident Indians refers to individuals, being citizens of India or persons of Indian origin, who are not residents in India. A person is said to be of Indian origin if he, or either of his parents, or any of his grandparents, was born in undivided India.
2. The expression *control and management* means the direction, management and control and the directing power of its affairs are situated at a place where the directors' meetings are held and not at a place where shareholders' meetings are held.
3. Understandably, this is a departure from the general practice that the income of the previous year is to be assessed in the assessment year immediately following.

Part VIII: Time Series Tax Statistics of India: 1950-51 to 2013-14 / 2015-16

Table 1: Combined Tax Revenue, Breakdown between Direct and Indirect Taxes with Percentage Shares, and Tax-GDP Ratios: 1950-51 to 2013-14

(₹ crore)

Year	Combined tax revenue* (3+4)	Direct taxes	Indirect taxes	Col. 3 as % of Col. 2	Col. 4 as % of Col. 2	Col. 2 as % of GDP	Col. 3 as % of GDP	Col. 4 as % of GDP
1	2	3	4	5	6	7	8	9
1950-51	627	231	396	36.8	63.2	6.03	2.22	3.81
1951-52	739	244	495	33.0	67.0	6.69	2.21	4.48
1952-53	678	252	426	37.2	62.8	6.25	2.32	3.93
1953-54	672	242	430	36.0	64.0	5.69	2.05	3.64
1954-55	720	240	480	33.3	66.7	6.45	2.15	4.30
1955-56	768	259	509	33.7	66.3	6.75	2.28	4.48
1956-57	890	288	602	32.4	67.6	6.57	2.13	4.44
1957-58	1,045	327	718	31.3	68.7	7.49	2.34	5.15
1958-59	1,089	344	745	31.6	68.4	7.00	2.21	4.79
1959-60	1,216	378	838	31.1	68.9	7.42	2.31	5.11
1960-61	1,350	402	948	29.8	70.2	7.52	2.24	5.28
1961-62	1,543	449	1,094	29.1	70.9	8.12	2.36	5.75
1962-63	1,865	560	1,305	30.0	70.0	9.13	2.74	6.39
1963-64	2,325	693	1,632	29.8	70.2	9.91	2.95	6.96
1964-65	2,599	743	1,856	28.6	71.4	9.50	2.71	6.78
1965-66	2,922	734	2,188	25.1	74.9	10.13	2.54	7.58
1966-67	3,261	767	2,494	23.5	76.5	9.98	2.35	7.63
1967-68	3,456	780	2,676	22.6	77.4	9.03	2.04	6.99
1968-69	3,759	840	2,919	22.3	77.7	9.28	2.07	7.21
1969-70	4,200	963	3,237	22.9	77.1	9.42	2.16	7.26
1970-71	4,752	1,009	3,743	21.2	78.8	9.98	2.12	7.86
1971-72	5,575	1,171	4,404	21.0	79.0	10.93	2.30	8.64
1972-73	6,436	1,346	5,090	20.9	79.1	11.45	2.39	9.05
1973-74	7,389	1,552	5,837	21.0	79.0	10.80	2.27	8.53
1974-75	9,223	1,834	7,389	19.9	80.1	11.42	2.27	9.15
1975-76	11,182	2,493	8,689	22.3	77.7	12.90	2.88	10.02
1976-77	12,332	2,585	9,747	21.0	79.0	13.20	2.77	10.43
1977-78	13,237	2,680	10,557	20.2	79.8	12.51	2.53	9.97
1978-79	15,528	2,851	12,677	18.4	81.6	13.54	2.49	11.06
1979-80	17,683	3,096	14,587	17.5	82.5	14.06	2.46	11.60
1980-81	19,844	3,268	16,576	16.5	83.5	13.26	2.18	11.08
1981-82	24,142	4,133	20,009	17.1	82.9	13.73	2.35	11.38
1982-83	27,242	4,492	22,750	16.5	83.5	13.85	2.28	11.57
1983-84	31,525	4,907	26,618	15.6	84.4	13.77	2.14	11.62
1984-85	35,814	5,330	30,484	14.9	85.1	13.96	2.08	11.88
1985-86	43,267	6,252	37,015	14.4	85.6	14.94	2.16	12.78
1986-87	49,538	6,889	42,650	13.9	86.1	15.29	2.13	13.17
1987-88	56,977	7,483	49,493	13.1	86.9	15.47	2.03	13.44
1988-89	66,925	9,757	57,168	14.6	85.4	15.32	2.23	13.09
1989-90	77,693	11,165	66,528	14.4	85.6	15.48	2.22	13.25

Contd...

Year	Combined tax revenue* (3+4)	Direct taxes	Indirect taxes	Col. 3 as % of Col. 2	Col. 4 as % of Col. 2	Col. 2 as % of GDP	Col. 3 as % of GDP	Col. 4 as % of GDP
1	2	3	4	5	6	7	8	9
1990-91	87,722	12,260	75,462	14.0	86.0	14.96	2.09	12.87
1991-92	1,03,198	16,657	86,541	16.1	83.9	15.31	2.47	12.84
1992-93	1,14,166	19,387	94,779	17.0	83.0	14.74	2.50	12.24
1993-94	1,21,961	21,713	1,00,248	17.8	82.2	13.68	2.44	11.25
1994-95	1,47,849	28,878	1,18,971	19.5	80.5	14.14	2.76	11.38
1995-96	1,75,259	35,777	1,39,482	20.4	79.6	14.29	2.92	11.37
1996-97	2,01,056	41,061	1,59,995	20.4	79.6	14.17	2.89	11.27
1997-98	2,20,659	50,538	1,70,121	22.9	77.1	14.03	3.21	10.82
1998-99	2,33,017	49,119	1,83,898	21.1	78.9	12.92	2.72	10.20
1999-00	2,74,583	60,864	2,13,719	21.4	78.6	13.65	3.02	10.62
2000-01	3,05,320	71,762	2,33,558	23.5	76.5	14.08	3.31	10.77
2001-02	3,14,535	73,108	2,41,427	23.2	76.8	13.39	3.11	10.28
2002-03	3,56,277	87,365	2,68,912	24.5	75.5	14.08	3.45	10.63
2003-04	4,14,084	1,09,546	3,04,538	26.5	73.5	14.59	3.86	10.73
2004-05	4,94,370	1,37,093	3,57,277	27.7	72.3	15.25	4.23	11.02
2005-06	5,87,688	1,67,635	4,20,053	28.5	71.5	15.91	4.54	11.37
2006-07	7,36,708	2,31,376	5,05,331	31.4	68.6	17.15	5.39	11.77
2007-08	8,70,329	3,18,839	5,51,490	36.6	63.4	17.45	6.39	11.06
2008-09	9,15,450	3,27,981	5,87,469	35.8	64.2	16.26	5.83	10.43
2009-10	10,00,844	3,76,995	6,23,849	37.7	62.3	15.45	5.82	9.63
2010-11	12,71,666	4,50,822	8,20,843	35.6	64.4	16.31	5.78	10.53
2011-12	14,67,891	5,01,395	9,66,496	34.2	65.8	16.29	5.57	10.73
2012-13	17,26,549	5,74,681	11,51,868	33.3	66.7	17.22	5.73	11.49
2013-14	20,32,489	6,79,298	13,53,192	33.4	66.6	17.87	5.97	11.90

* Total tax revenue of the Central and State Governments.

2012-13 = Revised estimates; 2013-14 = Budget estimates.

Note: The ratios to GDP at market prices are based on CSO's National Accounts 2004-05 series.

Source: Rearranged data from Government of India, Ministry of Finance, *Indian Public Finance Statistics, 2013-2014*, Tables 1.7 and 1.8. Columns 5 and 6 calculations own.

Table 2: Gross Central Taxes, Breakdown between Direct and Indirect Taxes with Percentage Shares, and Tax-GDP Ratios: 1950-51 to 2013-14

(₹ crore)

Year	Gross Central taxes*(3+4)	Direct taxes	Indirect taxes	Col. 3 as % of Col. 2	Col. 4 as % of Col. 2	Col. 2 as % of GDP	Col. 3 as % of GDP	Col. 4 as % of GDP
1	2	3	4	5	6	7	8	9
1950-51	405	176	229	43.4	56.6	3.89	1.69	2.20
1951-52	512	190	322	37.1	62.9	4.63	1.72	2.91
1952-53	445	186	259	41.8	58.2	4.10	1.71	2.39
1953-54	420	166	254	39.5	60.5	3.56	1.41	2.15
1954-55	455	161	294	35.4	64.6	4.07	1.44	2.63
1955-56	485	171	314	35.2	64.8	4.27	1.50	2.76
1956-57	570	194	376	34.0	66.0	4.21	1.43	2.78
1957-58	692	230	462	33.2	66.8	4.96	1.65	3.31
1958-59	701	238	463	34.0	66.0	4.51	1.53	2.98
1959-60	794	269	525	33.9	66.1	4.85	1.64	3.20
1960-61	895	292	603	32.6	67.4	4.99	1.63	3.36
1961-62	1,054	337	717	32.0	68.0	5.54	1.77	3.77
1962-63	1,285	423	862	32.9	67.1	6.29	2.07	4.22
1963-64	1,634	550	1,084	33.7	66.3	6.96	2.34	4.62
1964-65	1,821	600	1,221	32.9	67.1	6.65	2.19	4.46
1965-66	2,061	598	1,463	29.0	71.0	7.14	2.07	5.07
1966-67	2,307	657	1,650	28.5	71.5	7.06	2.01	5.05
1967-68	2,353	655	1,698	27.8	72.2	6.15	1.71	4.44
1968-69	2,510	698	1,812	27.8	72.2	6.20	1.72	4.47
1969-70	2,822	826	1,996	29.3	70.7	6.33	1.85	4.47
1970-71	3,206	869	2,337	27.1	72.9	6.73	1.82	4.91
1971-72	3,873	1,047	2,826	27.0	73.0	7.59	2.05	5.54
1972-73	4,505	1,233	3,272	27.4	72.6	8.01	2.19	5.82
1973-74	5,070	1,375	3,695	27.1	72.9	7.41	2.01	5.40
1974-75	6,322	1,650	4,672	26.1	73.9	7.83	2.04	5.78
1975-76	7,609	2,205	5,404	29.0	71.0	8.78	2.54	6.23
1976-77	8,271	2,328	5,943	28.1	71.9	8.85	2.49	6.36
1977-78	8,858	2,405	6,453	27.1	72.9	8.37	2.27	6.10
1978-79	10,525	2,528	7,997	24.0	76.0	9.18	2.21	6.98
1979-80	11,974	2,818	9,156	23.5	76.5	9.52	2.24	7.28
1980-81	13,179	2,997	10,182	22.7	77.3	8.81	2.00	6.80
1981-82	15,847	3,786	12,061	23.9	76.1	9.01	2.15	6.86
1982-83	17,696	4,139	13,557	23.4	76.6	9.00	2.10	6.89
1983-84	20,721	4,498	16,223	21.7	78.3	9.05	1.96	7.08
1984-85	23,471	4,798	18,673	20.4	79,6	9.15	1.87	7.28
1985-86	28,670	5,620	23,050	19.6	80.4	9.90	1.94	7.96
1986-87	32,838	6,236	26,602	19.0	81.0	10.14	1.92	8.21
1987-88	37,665	6,752	30,913	17.9	82.1	10.23	1.83	8.40
1988-89	44,474	8,830	35,644	19.9	80.1	10.18	2.02	8.16
1989-90	51,636	10,003	41,633	19.4	80.6	10.29	1.99	8.29

Contd...

Year	Gross Central taxes*(3+4)	Direct taxes	Indirect taxes	Col. 3 as % of Col. 2	Col. 4 as % of Col. 2	Col. 2 as % of GDP	Col. 3 as % of GDP	Col. 4 as % of GDP
1	2	3	4	5	6	7	8	9
1990-91	57,577	11,030	46,547	19.2	80.8	9.82	1.88	7.94
1991-92	67,361	15,353	52,008	22.8	77.2	10.00	2.28	7.72
1992-93	74,636	18,140	56,496	24.3	75.7	9.64	2.34	7.29
1993-94	75,742	20,299	55,443	26.8	73.2	8.50	2.28	6.22
1994-95	92,297	26,973	65,324	29.2	70.8	8.83	2.58	6.25
1995-96	1,11,224	33,564	77,660	30.2	69.8	9.07	2.74	6.33
1996-97	1,29,762	38,898	90,864	30.0	70.0	9.14	2.74	6.40
1997-98	1,39,220	48,282	90,938	34.7	65.3	8.85	3.07	5.78
1998-99	1,43,797	46,601	97,196	32.4	67.6	7.97	2.58	5.39
1999-00	1,71,752	57,960	1,13,792	33.7	66.3	8.54	2.88	5.66
2000-01	1,88,603	68,305	1,20,298	36.2	63.8	8.70	3.15	5.55
2001-02	1,87,060	69,197	1,17,863	37.0	63.0	7.97	2.95	5.02
2002-03	2,15,905	83,363	1,32,542	38.6	61.4	8.53	3.29	5.24
2003-04	2,54,348	1,05,091	1,49,257	41.3	58.9	8.96	3.70	5.26
2004-05	3,04,957	1,32,183	1,72,774	43.3	56.6	9.41	4.08	5.33
2005-06	3,66,151	1,62,337	2,03,814	44.3	55.7	9.91	4.40	5.52
2006-07	4,73,513	2,25,045	2,48,467	47.5	52.5	11.03	5.24	5.79
2007-08	5,93,147	3,12,220	2,80,927	52.6	47.4	11.89	6.26	5.63
2008-09	6,05,298	3,19,892	2,85,406	52.8	47.2	10.75	5.68	5.07
2009-10	6,24,527	3,67,595	2,56,932	58.9	41.1	9.64	5.67	3.97
2010-11	7,93,072	4,38,515	3,54,556	55.7	44.3	10.17	5.63	4.55
2011-12	8,88,898	4,88,160	4,00,738	54.9	45.1	9.87	5.42	4.55
2012-13	10,38,037	5,59,677	4,78,360	53.9	46.1	10.35	5.58	4.77
2013-14	12,35,870	6,61,396	5,74,474	53.5	46.5	10.87	5.82	5.05

* Before transferring States' share in Central taxes.

2012-13 = Revised estimates; 2013-14 = Budget estimates.

Note: The ratios to GDP at market prices are based on CSO's National Accounts 2004-05 series.

Source: Rearranged data from Government of India, Ministry of Finance, *Indian Public Finance Statistics, 2013-2014*, Tables 1.7 and 1.8. Columns 5 and 6 calculations own.

Table 3: Share of States in Central Taxes, Breakdown between Direct and Indirect Taxes with Percentage Shares, and Tax-GDP Ratios: 1950-51 to 2013-14

(₹ crore)

Year	States' share in Central taxes (3+4)	Direct taxes	Indirect taxes	Col. 3 as % of Col. 2	Col. 4 as % of Col. 2	Col. 2 as % of GDP	Col. 3 as % of GDP	Col. 4 as % of GDP
1	2	3	4	5	6	7	8	9
1950-51	48	48	--	100.0	0.0	0.46	0.46	---
1951-52	53	53	--	100.0	0.0	0.48	0.48	---
1952-53	73	56	17	76.7	23.3	0.67	0.52	0.16
1953-54	73	58	15	79.5	20.5	0.62	0.49	0.13
1954-55	71	57	14	80.3	19.7	0.64	0.51	0.13
1955-56	74	57	17	77.0	23.0	0.65	0.50	0.15
1956-57	78	51	27	65.4	34.6	0.58	0.38	0.20
1957-58	116	76	40	65.5	34.5	0.83	0.54	0.29
1958-59	148	75	73	50.7	49.3	0.95	0.48	0.47
1959-60	152	79	73	52.0	48.0	0.93	0.48	0.45
1960-61	165	90	75	54.5	45.5	0.92	0.50	0.42
1961-62	179	98	81	54.7	45.3	0.94	0.52	0.43
1962-63	224	99	125	44.2	55.8	1.10	0.48	0.61
1963-64	260	124	136	47.7	52.3	1.11	0.53	0.58
1964-65	258	131	127	50.8	49.2	0.94	0.48	0.46
1965-66	276	130	146	47.1	52.9	0.96	0.45	0.51
1966-67	373	142	231	38.1	61.9	1.14	0.43	0.71
1967-68	416	181	235	43.5	56.5	1.09	0.47	0.61
1968-69	491	200	291	40.7	59.3	1.21	0.49	0.72
1969-70	621	300	321	48.3	51.7	1.39	0.67	0.72
1970-71	755	365	390	48.3	51.7	1.58	0.77	0.82
1971-72	945	470	475	49.7	50.3	1.85	0.92	0.93
1972-73	1,062	495	567	46.6	53.4	1.89	0.88	1.01
1973-74	1,170	539	631	46.1	53.9	1.71	0.79	0.92
1974-75	1,225	522	703	42.6	57.4	1.52	0.65	0.87
1975-76	1,599	742	857	46.4	53.6	1.84	0.86	0.99
1976-77	1,690	662	1,028	39.2	60.8	1.81	0.71	1.10
1977-78	1,798	685	1,113	38.1	61.9	1.70	0.65	1.05
1978-79	1,957	717	1,240	36.6	63.4	1.71	0.63	1.08
1979-80	3,406	876	2,530	25.7	74.3	2.71	0.70	2.01
1980-81	3,791	1,014	2,777	26.7	73.3	2.53	0.68	1.86
1981-82	4,274	1,034	3,240	24.2	75.8	2.43	0.59	1.84
1982-83	4,640	1,148	3,492	24.7	75.3	2.36	0.58	1.78
1983-84	5,245	1,188	4,057	22.7	77.3	2.29	0.52	1.77
1984-85	5,777	1,252	4,525	21.7	78.3	2.25	0.49	1.76
1985-86	7,490	1,865	5,625	24.9	75.1	2.59	0.64	1.94
1986-87	8,476	2,170	6,306	25.6	74.4	2.62	0.67	1.95
1987-88	9,597	2,595	7,002	27.0	73.0	2.61	0.70	1.90
1988-89	10,669	2,750	7,919	25.8	74.2	2.44	0.63	1.81

Contd...

Year	States' share in Central taxes (3+4)	Direct taxes	Indirect taxes	Col. 3 as % of Col. 2	Col. 4 as % of Col. 2	Col. 2 as % of GDP	Col. 3 as % of GDP	Col. 4 as % of GDP
1	2	3	4	5	6	7	8	9
1989-90	13,232	3,922	9,310	29.6	70.4	2.64	0.78	1.85
1990-91	14,535	4,121	10,414	28.4	71.6	2.48	0.70	1.78
1991-92	17,197	5,104	12,093	29.7	70.3	2.55	0.76	1.79
1992-93	20,522	6,057	14,465	29.5	70.5	2.65	0.78	1.87
1993-94	22,240	7,767	14,473	34.9	65.1	2.50	0.87	1.62
1994-95	24,843	8,560	16,283	34.5	65.5	2.38	0.82	1.56
1995-96	29,285	11,274	18,011	38.5	61.5	2.39	0.92	1.47
1996-97	35,061	13,516	21,545	38.5	61.5	2.47	0.95	1.52
1997-98	43,548	21,102	22,446	48.5	51.5	2.77	1.34	1.43
1998-99	39,145	14,480	24,665	37.0	63.0	2.17	0.80	1.37
1999-00	43,481	16,523	26,958	38.0	62.0	2.16	0.82	1.34
2000-01	51,945	18,655	33,290	35.9	64.1	2.40	0.86	1.54
2001-02	53,398	21,492	31,906	40.2	59.8	2.27	0.92	1.36
2002-03	56,122	21,473	34,649	38.3	61.7	2.22	0.85	1.37
2003-04	67,366	28,492	38,874	42.3	57.7	2.37	1.00	1.37
2004-05	80,159	36,828	43,331	45.9	54.1	2.47	1.14	1.34
2005-06	95,887	44,511	51,376	46.4	53.6	2.60	1.21	1.39
2006-07	1,22,331	60,454	61,876	49.4	50.6	2.85	1.41	1.44
2007-08	1,53,600	80,650	72,950	52.5	47.5	3.08	1.62	1.46
2008-09	1,61,979	85,674	76,305	52.9	47.1	2.88	1.52	1.36
2009-10	1,67,992	1,05,911	62,181	63.0	37.0	2.59	1.63	0.96
2010-11	2,23,203	1,31,394	91,809	58.9	41.1	2.86	1.69	1.18
2011-12	2,59,412	1,52,270	1,07,142	58.7	41.3	2.88	1.69	1.19
2012-13	2,95,922	1,69,935	1,25,987	57.4	42.6	2.95	1.69	1.26
2013-14	3,51,792	1,95,248	1,56,544	55.5	44.5	3.09	1.72	1.38

2012-13 = Revised estimates; 2013-14 = Budget estimates.

Note: The ratios to GDP at market prices are based on CSO's National Accounts 2004-05 series.

Source: Rearranged data from Government of India, Ministry of Finance, *Indian Public Finance Statistics, 2013-2014*, Tables 1.7 and 1.8. Columns 5 and 6 calculations own.

Table 4: Net Central Taxes, Breakdown between Direct and Indirect Taxes with Percentage Shares, and Tax-GDP Ratios: 1950-51 to 2013-14

(₹ crore)

Year	Net Central taxes* (3+4)	Direct taxes	Indirect taxes	Col. 3 as % of Col. 2	Col. 4 as % of Col. 2	Col. 2 as % of GDP	Col. 3 as % of GDP	Col. 4 as % of GDP
1	2	3	4	5	6	7	8	9
1950-51	357	128	229	35.8	64.2	3.43	1.23	2.20
1951-52	459	137	322	29.8	70.2	4.15	1.24	2.91
1952-53	372	130	242	34.9	65.1	3.43	1.20	2.23
1953-54	347	108	239	31.1	68.9	2.94	0.91	2.02
1954-55	384	104	280	27.1	72.9	3.44	0.93	2.51
1955-56	411	114	297	27.7	72.3	3.61	1.00	2.61
1956-57	492	143	349	29.1	70.9	3.63	1.06	2.58
1957-58	576	154	422	26.7	73.3	4.13	1.10	3.02
1958-59	553	163	390	29.5	70.5	3.56	1.05	2.51
1959-60	642	190	452	29.6	70.4	3.92	1.16	2.76
1960-61	730	202	528	27.7	72.3	4.07	1.13	2.94
1961-62	875	239	636	27.3	72.7	4.60	1.26	3.35
1962-63	1,061	324	737	30.5	69.5	5.19	1.59	3.61
1963-64	1,374	426	948	31.0	69.0	5.86	1.82	4.04
1964-65	1,563	469	1,094	30.0	70.0	5.71	1.71	4.00
1965-66	1,785	468	1,317	26.2	73.8	6.19	1.62	4.56
1966-67	1,934	515	1,419	26.6	73.4	5.92	1.58	4.34
1967-68	1,937	474	1,463	24.5	75.5	5.06	1.24	3.82
1968-69	2,019	498	1,521	24.7	75.3	4.98	1.23	3.75
1969-70	2,201	526	1,675	23.9	76.1	4.93	1.18	3.76
1970-71	2,451	504	1,947	20.6	79.4	5.15	1.06	4.09
1971-72	2,928	577	2,351	19.7	80.3	5.74	1.13	4.61
1972-73	3,443	738	2,705	21.4	78.6	6.12	1.31	4.81
1973-74	3,900	836	3,064	21.4	78.6	5.70	1.22	4.48
1974-75	5,097	1,128	3,969	22.1	77.9	6.31	1.40	4.49
1975-76	6,010	1,463	4,547	24.3	75.7	6.93	1.69	5.24
1976-77	6,581	1,666	4,915	25.3	74.7	7.04	1.78	5.26
1977-78	7,060	1,720	5,340	24.4	75.6	6.67	1.62	5.04
1978-79	8,568	1,811	6,757	21.4	78.9	7.47	1.58	5.89
1979-80	8,568	1,942	6,626	22.7	77.3	6.81	1.54	5.27
1980-81	9,388	1,983	7,405	21.1	78.9	6.27	1.33	4.95
1981-82	11,573	2,752	8,821	23.8	76.2	6.58	1.57	5.02
1982-83	13,056	2,991	10,065	22.9	77.1	6.64	1.52	5.12
1983-84	15,476	3,310	12,166	21.4	78.6	6.76	1.45	5.31
1984-85	17,694	3,546	14,148	20.0	80.0	6.90	1.38	5.51
1985-86	21,180	3,755	17,425	17.7	82.3	7.32	1.30	6.02
1986-87	24,362	4,066	20,296	16.7	83.3	7.52	1.26	5.27
1987-88	28,068	4,157	23,911	14.8	85.2	7.62	1.13	6.49
1988-89	33,805	6,080	27,725	18.0	82.0	7.74	1.39	6.35
1989-90	38,404	6,081	32,323	15.8	84.2	7.65	1.21	6.44

Contd...

Year	Net Central taxes* (3+4)	Direct taxes	Indirect taxes	Col. 3 as % of Col. 2	Col. 4 as % of Col. 2	Col. 2 as % of GDP	Col. 3 as % of GDP	Col. 4 as % of GDP
1	2	3	4	5	6	7	8	9
1990-91	43,042	6,909	36,133	16.1	83.9	7.34	1.18	6.16
1991-92	50,164	10,249	39,915	20.4	79.6	7.44	1.25	5.92
1992-93	54,114	12,083	42,031	22.3	77.7	6.99	1.56	5.43
1993-94	53,502	12,532	40,970	23.4	76.6	6.00	1.41	4.60
1994-95	67,454	18,413	49,041	27.3	72.7	6.45	1.76	4.69
1995-96	81,939	22,290	59,649	27.2	72.8	6.68	1.82	4.86
1996-97	94,701	25,382	69,319	26.8	73.2	6.67	1.79	4.88
1997-98	95,672	27,180	68,492	28.4	71.6	6.08	1.73	4.36
1998-99	1,04,652	32,121	72,531	30.7	69.3	5.80	1.78	4.02
1999-00	1,28,271	41,437	86,834	32.3	67.7	6.37	2.06	4.32
2000-01	1,36,658	49,650	87,008	36.3	63.7	6.30	2.29	4.01
2001-02	1,33,662	47,705	85,957	35.7	64.3	5.69	2.03	3.66
2002-03	1,59,783	61,890	97,893	38.7	61.3	6.31	2.45	3.87
2003-04	1,86,982	76,599	1,10,382	41.0	59.0	6.59	2.70	3.89
2004-05	2,24,798	95,355	1,29,443	42.4	57.6	6.93	2.94	3.99
2005-06	2,70,264	1,17,826	1,52,438	43.6	56.4	7.32	3.19	4.13
2006-07	3,51,182	1,64,591	1,86,591	46.9	53.1	8.18	3.83	4.34
2007-08	4,39,547	2,31,570	2,07,977	52.7	47.3	8.81	4.64	4.17
2008-09	4,43,319	2,34,218	2,09,101	52.8	47.2	7.87	4.16	3.71
2009-10	4,56,536	2,61,684	1,94,851	57.3	42.7	7.05	4.04	3.01
2010-11	5,69,869	3,07,121	2,62,747	53.9	46.1	7.31	3.94	3.37
2011-12	6,29,486	3,35,890	2,93,596	53.4	46.6	6.99	3.73	3.26
2012-13	7,42,115	3,89,742	3,52,373	52.5	47.5	7.40	3.89	3.51
2013-14	8,84,078	4,66,148	4,17,930	52.7	47.3	7.77	4.10	3.68

* After transferring States' share in Central taxes.

2012-13 = Revised estimates; 2013-14 = Budget estimates.

Note: The ratios to GDP at market prices are based on CSO's National Accounts 2004-05 series.

Source: Rearranged data from Government of India, Ministry of Finance, *Indian Public Finance Statistics, 2013-2014*, Tables 1.7 and 1.8. Columns 5 and 6 calculations own.

Table 5: States' Own Taxes, Breakdown between Direct and Indirect Taxes with Percentage Shares, and Tax-GDP Ratios: 1950-51 to 2013-14

(₹ crore)

Year	States' own taxes (3+4)	Direct taxes	Indirect taxes	Col. 3 as % of Col. 2	Col. 4 as % of Col. 2	Col. 2 as % of GDP	Col. 3 as % of GDP	Col. 4 as % of GDP
1	2	3	4	5	6	7	8	9
1950-51	222	55	167	24.7	75.3	2.13	0.53	1.61
1951-52	227	54	173	23.8	76.2	2.05	0.49	1.57
1952-53	233	66	167	28.3	71.7	2.15	0.61	1.54
1953-54	252	76	176	30.2	69.8	2.13	0.64	1.49
1954-55	265	79	186	29.8	70.2	2.37	0.71	1.67
1955-56	283	88	195	31.1	68.9	2.49	0.77	1.71
1956-57	320	94	226	29.4	70.6	2.36	0.69	1.67
1957-58	353	97	256	27.5	72.5	2.53	0.70	1.83
1958-59	388	106	282	27.3	72.7	2.50	0.68	1.81
1959-60	422	109	313	25.8	74.2	2.58	0.67	1.91
1960-61	455	110	345	24.2	75.8	2.54	0.61	1.92
1961-62	489	112	377	22.9	77.1	2.57	0.59	1.98
1962-63	580	137	443	23.6	76.4	2.84	0.67	2.17
1963-64	691	143	548	20.7	79.3	2.95	0.61	2.34
1964-65	778	143	635	18.4	81.6	2.84	0.52	2.32
1965-66	861	136	725	15.8	84.2	2.98	0.47	2.51
1966-67	954	110	844	11.5	88.5	2.92	0.34	2.58
1967-68	1,103	125	978	11.3	88.7	2.88	0.33	2.56
1968-69	1,249	142	1,107	11.4	88.6	3.08	0.35	2.73
1969-70	1,378	137	1,241	9.9	90.1	3.09	0.31	2.78
1970-71	1,546	140	1,406	9.1	90.9	3.25	0.29	2.95
1971-72	1,702	124	1,578	7.3	92.7	3.34	0.24	3.09
1972-73	1,931	113	1,818	5.8	94.2	3.44	0.20	3.23
1973-74	2,319	177	2,142	7.6	92.4	3.39	0.26	3.13
1974-75	2,901	184	2,717	6.3	93.7	3.59	0.23	3.36
1975-76	3,573	288	3,285	8.1	91.9	4.12	0.33	3.79
1976-77	4,061	257	3,804	6.3	93.7	4.35	0.28	4.07
1977-78	4,379	275	4,104	6.3	93.7	4.14	0.26	3.88
1978-79	5,003	323	4,680	6.5	93.5	4.36	0.28	4.08
1979-80	5,709	278	5,431	4.9	95.1	4.54	0.22	4.32
1980-81	6,665	271	6,394	4.1	95.9	4.45	0.18	4.27
1981-82	8,295	347	7,948	4.2	95.8	4.72	0.20	4.52
1982-83	9,546	353	9,193	3.7	96.3	4.85	0.18	4.67
1983-84	10,804	409	10,395	3.8	96.2	4.72	0.18	4.54
1984-85	12,343	532	11,811	4.3	95.7	4.81	0.21	4.60
1985-86	14,597	632	13,965	4.3	95.7	5.04	0.22	4.82
1986-87	16,701	653	16,048	3.9	96.1	5.16	0.20	4.95
1987-88	19,311	731	18,580	3.8	96.2	5.24	0.20	5.05
1988-89	22,452	928	21,524	4.1	95.9	5.14	0.21	4.93
1989-90	26,057	1,162	24,895	4.5	95.5	5.19	0.23	4.96
1990-91	30,145	1,230	28,915	4.1	95.9	5.14	0.21	4.93

Contd...

1991-92	35,837	1,304	34,533	3.6	96.4	5.32	0.19	5.12
1992-93	39,530	1,247	38,283	3.2	96.8	5.10	0.16	4.94
1993-94	46,219	1,414	44,805	3.1	96.9	5.19	0.16	5.03
1994-95	55,552	1,905	53,647	3.4	96.6	5.31	0.18	5.13
1995-96	64,034	2,213	61,822	3.5	96.5	5.22	0.18	5.04
1996-97	71,294	2,163	69,131	3.0	97.0	5.02	0.15	4.87
1997-98	81,439	2,256	79,183	2.8	97.2	5.18	0.14	5.04
1998-99	89,220	2,518	86,702	2.8	97.2	4.95	0.14	4.81
1999-00	1,02,831	2,904	99,927	2.8	97.2	5.11	0.14	4.97
2000-01	1,16,717	3,457	1,13,260	2.9	97.1	5.38	0.16	5.22
2001-02	1,27,475	3,911	1,23,564	3.1	96.9	5.43	0.17	5.26
2002-03	1,40,372	4,002	1,36,370	2.8	97.2	5.55	0.16	5.39
2003-04	1,59,736	4,455	1,55,281	2.8	97.2	5.63	0.16	5.47
2004-05	1,89,413	4,910	1,84,503	2.6	97.4	5.84	0.15	5.69
2005-06	2,21,537	5,298	2,16,239	2.4	97.6	6.00	0.14	5.85
2006-07	2,63,195	6,331	2,56,864	2.4	97.6	6.13	0.15	5.98
2007-08	2,77,182	6,619	2,70,563	2.4	97.6	5.56	0.13	5.43
2008-09	3,10,152	8,089	3,02,063	2.6	97.4	5.51	0.14	5.37
2009-10	3,76,316	9,400	3,66,917	2.5	97.5	5.81	0.15	5.66
2010-11	4,78,594	12,307	4,66,287	2.4	97.6	6.14	0.16	5.98
2011-12	5,78,993	13,235	5,65,758	2.3	97.7	6.43	0.15	6.28
2012-13	6,88,512	15,004	6,73,508	2.2	97.8	6.87	0.15	6.72
2013-14	7,96,619	17,902	7,78,717	2.2	97.8	7.01	0.16	6.85

2012-13 = Revised estimates; 2013-14 = Budget estimates.

Note: The ratios to GDP at market prices are based on CSO's National Accounts 2004-05 series.

Source: Rearranged data from Government of India, Ministry of Finance, *Indian Public Finance Statistics, 2013-2014*, Tables 1.7 and 1.8. Columns 5 and 6 calculations own.

Table 6: States' Total Tax Revenue, Breakdown between Direct and Indirect Taxes with Percentage Shares, and Tax-GDP Ratios: 1950-51 to 2013-14

(₹ crore)

Year	States' total tax revenue* (3+4)	Direct taxes	Indirect taxes	Col. 3 as % of Col. 2	Col. 4 as % of Col. 2	Col. 2 as % of GDP	Col. 3 as % of GDP	Col. 4 as % of GDP
1	2	3	4	5	6	7	8	9
1950-51	270	103	167	38.1	61.9	2.60	0.99	1.61
1951-52	280	107	173	38.2	61.8	2.53	0.97	1.57
1952-53	306	122	184	39.9	60.1	2.82	1.12	1.70
1953-54	325	134	191	41.2	58.8	2.75	1.13	1.62
1954-55	336	136	200	40.5	59.5	3.01	1.22	1.79
1955-56	357	145	212	40.6	59.4	3.14	1.28	1.86
1956-57	398	145	253	36.4	63.6	2.94	1.07	1.87
1957-58	469	173	296	36.9	63.1	3.36	1.24	2.12
1958-59	536	181	355	33.8	66.2	3.45	1.16	2.28
1959-60	574	188	386	32.7	67.3	3.50	1.15	2.36
1960-61	620	200	420	32.3	67.7	3.46	1.11	2.34
1961-62	668	210	458	31.4	68.6	3.51	1.10	2.41
1962-63	804	236	568	29.4	70.6	3.94	1.16	2.78
1963-64	951	267	684	28.1	71.9	4.05	1.14	2.92
1964-65	1,036	274	762	26.4	73.6	3.79	1.00	2.78
1965-66	1,137	266	871	23.4	76.6	3.94	0.92	3.02
1966-67	1,327	252	1,075	19.0	81.0	4.06	0.77	3.29
1967-68	1,519	306	1,213	20.1	79.9	3.97	0.80	3.17
1968-69	1,740	342	1,398	19.7	80.3	4.30	0.84	3.45
1969-70	1,999	437	1,562	21.9	78.1	4.48	0.98	3.50
1970-71	2,301	505	1,796	21.9	78.1	4.83	1.06	3.77
1971-72	2,647	594	2,053	22.4	77.6	5.19	1.16	4.03
1972-73	2,993	608	2,385	20.3	79.7	5.32	1.08	4.24
1973-74	3,489	716	2,773	20.5	79.5	5.10	1.05	4.05
1974-75	4,126	706	3,420	17.1	82.9	5.11	0.87	4.23
1975-76	5,172	1,030	4,142	19.9	80.1	5.96	1.19	4.78
1976-77	5,751	919	4,832	16.0	84.0	6.16	0.98	5.17
1977-78	6,177	960	5,217	15.5	84.5	5.84	0.91	4.93
1978-79	6,960	1,040	5,920	14.9	85.1	6.07	0.91	5.16
1979-80	9,115	1,154	7,961	12.7	87.3	7.25	0.92	6.33
1980-81	10,456	1,285	9,171	12.3	87.7	6.99	0.86	6.13
1981-82	12,569	1,381	11,188	11.0	89.0	7.15	0.79	6.36
1982-83	14,186	1,501	12,685	10.6	89.4	7.21	0.76	6.45
1983-84	16,049	1,597	14,452	10.0	90.0	7.01	0.70	6.31
1984-85	18,120	1,784	16,336	9.9	90.1	7.06	0.70	6.37
1985-86	22,087	2,497	19,590	11.3	88.7	7.63	0.86	6.77
1986-87	25,177	2,823	22,354	11.2	88.8	7.77	0.87	6.90
1987-88	28,908	3,326	25,582	11.5	88.5	7.85	0.90	6.95
1988-89	33,121	3,678	29,443	11.1	88.9	7.58	0.84	6.74
1989-90	39,289	5,084	34,205	12.9	87.1	7.83	1.01	6.81

Contd...

1990-91	44,680	5,351	39,329	12.0	88.0	7.62	0.91	6.71
1991-92	53,034	6,408	46,626	12.1	87.9	7.87	0.95	6.92
1992-93	60,052	7,304	52,748	12.2	87.8	7.75	0.94	6.81
1993-94	68,459	9,181	59,278	13.4	86.6	7.68	1.03	6.65
1994-95	80,395	10,465	69,930	13.0	87.0	7.69	1.00	6.69
1995-96	93,320	13,487	79,833	14.4	85.6	7.61	1.10	6.51
1996-97	1,06,355	15,679	90,676	14.7	85.3	7.49	1.10	6.39
1997-98	1,24,987	23,358	1,01,629	18.7	81.3	7.95	1.49	6.46
1998-99	1,28,365	16,998	1,11,367	13.2	86.8	7.12	0.94	6.18
1999-00	1,46,312	19,427	1,26,885	13.3	86.7	7.27	0.97	6.31
2000-01	1,68,662	22,112	1,46,550	13.1	86.9	7.78	1.02	6.76
2001-02	1,80,873	25,403	1,55,470	14.0	86.0	7070	1.08	6.62
2002-03	1,96,494	25,475	1,71,019	13.0	87.0	7076	1.01	6.76
2003-04	2,27,102	32,947	1,94,155	14.5	85.5	8.00	1.16	6.84
2004-05	2,69,572	41,740	2,27,834	15.5	84.5	8.31	1.29	7.03
2005-06	3,17,424	49,809	2,67,615	15.7	84.3	8.59	1.35	7.25
2006-07	3,85,526	66,785	3,18,740	17.3	82.7	8.98	1.56	7.42
2007-08	4,30,782	87,269	3,43,513	20.3	79.7	8.64	1.75	6.89
2008-09	4,72,131	93,763	3,78,368	19.9	80.1	8.39	1.67	6.72
2009-10	5,44,308	1,15,311	4,28,997	21.2	78.8	8.40	1.78	6.62
2010-11	7,01,797	1,43,701	5,58,096	20.5	79.5	9.00	1.84	7.16
2011-12	8,38,405	1,65,505	6,72,899	19.8	80.2	9.31	1.84	7.47
2012-13	9,84,434	1,84,939	7,99,495	18.8	81.2	9.82	1.84	7.97
2013-14	11,48,411	2,13,150	9,35,261	18.6	81.4	10.10	1.87	8.22

* States' share in Central taxes plus States' own taxes.
2012-13 = Revised estimates; 2013-14 = Budget estimates.
Note: The ratios to GDP at market prices are based on CSO's National Accounts 2004-05 series.
Source: Rearranged data from Government of India, Ministry of Finance, *Indian Public Finance Statistics, 2013-2014*, Tables 1.7 and 1.8. Columns 5 and 6 calculations own.

Table 7: Income Tax (Including Corporation Tax) Collections*: 1950-51 to 2015-16

(₹ crore)

Year	Gross Central Taxes	Income Tax	Col. 3 as % of Col. 2
1	2	3	4
1950-51	405	172	42.5
1951-52	415	185	36.1
1952-53	445	182	40.9
1953-54	420	161	38.3
1954-55	455	156	34.3
1955-56	485	165	34.0
1956-57	570	199	34.9
1957-58	692	215	31.1
1958-59	701	221	31.5
1959-60	794	250	31.5
1960-61	895	277	31.9
1961-62	1,054	316	30.0
1962-63	1,285	407	31.7
1963-64	1,634	533	32.6
1964-65	1,821	580	31.9
1965-66	2,061	576	27.9
1966-67	2,307	637	27.6
1967-68	2,353	636	27.0
1968-69	2,510	678	27.0
1969-70	2,822	801	28.4
1970-71	3,206	843	26.3
1971-72	3,873	1,009	26.1
1972-73	4,505	1,187	26.3
1973-74	5,070	1,328	26.2
1974-75	6,322	1,583	25.0
1975-76	7,609	2,076	27.3
1976-77	8,263	2,178	26.4
1977-78	8,858	2,223	25.1
1978-79	10,525	2,428	23.1
1979-80	11,974	2,731	22.8
1980-81	13,179	2,816	21.4
1981-82	15,847	3,446	21.7
1982-83	17,696	3,755	21.2
1983-84	20,721	4,192	20.2
1984-85	23,471	4,484	19.1

Contd...

1985-86	28,671	5,374	18.7
1986-87	32,837	6,038	18.4
1987-88	37,666	6,620	17.6
1988-89	44,474	8,648	19.4
1989-90	51,636	9,739	18.7
1990-91	57,577	10,606	18.4
1991-92	67,361	14,584	21.6
1992-93	74,636	16,787	22.5
1993-94	75,742	19,183	25.3
1994-95	92,297	25,847	28.0
1995-96	1,10,354	32,090	29.1
1996-97	1,28,762	36,798	28.6
1997-98	1,39,221	37,113	26.7
1998-99	1,43,797	44,764	31.1
1999-00	1,71,752	56,339	32.8
2000-01	1,88,603	67,460	35.8
2001-02	1,87,060	68,613	36.7
2002-03	2,16,266	82,038	37.9
2003-04	2,54,348	1,04,949	41.3
2004-05	3,04,958	1,31,948	43.3
2005-06	3,66,152	1,64,906	45.0
2006-07	4,73,512	2,19,411	46.3
2007-08	5,85,410	3,04,445	52.0
2008-09	6,27,949	3,44,600	54.9
2009-10	6,24,537	3,77,040	60.4
2010-11	7,93,072	4,45,275	56.4
2011-12	8,89,176	4,93,159	55.5
2012-13	10,36,235	5,57,813	53.8
2013-14	11,38,734	6,37,535	56.0
2014-15	12,51,391	7,04,678	56.3
2015-16	14,49,490	7,97,995	55.1

*Before transferring States' share.

2014-15 = Revised estimates; 2015-16 = Budget estimates.

Sources: Government of India, Ministry of Finance: 1. *Explanatory Memorandum on the Budget of the Central Government* (various years); 2. *Receipts Budget* (various years); 3. *Budget at a Glance*, 2015-16; Column 4 calculations own.

Table 8: Wealth Tax Revenue: 1957-58 to 2015-16

(₹ crore)

Year	Yield	Year	Yield
1957-58	7	1987-88	101
1958-59	10	1988-89	122
1959-60	12	1989-90	179
1960-61	8	1990-91	231
1961-62	8	1991-92	307
1962-63	10	1992-93	468
1963-64	11	1993-94	154
1964-65	11	1994-95	105
1965-66	12	1995-96	74
1966-67	11	1996-97	78
1967-68	11	1997-98	113
1968-69	11	1998-99	162
1969-70	16	1999-00	133
1970-71	15	2000-01	132
1971-72	25	2001-02	135
1972-73	36	2002-03	154
1973-74	36	2003-04	136
1974-75	39	2004-05	145
1975-76	54	2005-06	250
1976-77	60	2006-07	240
1977-78	48	2007-08	315
1978-79	55	2008-09	400
1979-80	64	2009-10	506
1980-81	67	2010-11	687
1981-82	78	2011-12	788
1982-83	90	2012-13	846
1983-84	93	2013-14	1,008
1984-85	107	2014-15	950
1985-86	153	2015-16	... (Abolished)
1986-87	174		

An annual tax on net wealth was introduced in India with the enactment of the Wealth Tax Act, 1957 which came into force from April 1 of that year.

2014-15 = Revised estimates; 2015-16 = Budget estimates.

Sources: Government of India, Ministry of Finance: 1. *Explanatory Memorandum on the Budget of the Central Government* (various years); 2. *Receipts Budget* (various years); 3. *Budget at a Glance*, 2015-16.

Table 9: Central Excise Collections*: 1950-51 to 2015-16

(₹ crore)

Year	Gross Central Taxes	Excise Revenue	Col. 3 as % of Col. 2
1	2	3	4
1950-51	405	68	16.8
1951-52	512	79	15.4
1952-53	445	79	17.7
1953-54	420	92	21.9
1954-55	455	105	23.1
1955-56	485	142	29.3
1956-57	570	185	32.5
1957-58	692	268	38.7
1958-59	701	307	43.8
1959-60	794	354	44.6
1960-61	895	414	46.3
1961-62	1,054	482	45.7
1962-63	1,285	599	46.6
1963-64	1,634	730	44.7
1964-65	1,821	801	44.0
1965-66	2,061	898	43.6
1966-67	2,307	1,034	44.8
1967-68	2,353	1,148	48.8
1968-69	2,510	1,321	52.6
1969-70	2,822	1,524	54.0
1970-71	3,206	1,758	54.8
1971-72	3,873	2,061	53.2
1972-73	4,505	2,324	51.6
1973-74	5,070	2,602	51.3
1974-75	6,322	3,230	51.1
1975-76	7,609	3,845	50.5
1976-77	8,263	4,221	51.1
1977-78	8,858	4,448	50.2
1978-79	10,525	5,367	51.0
1979-80	11,974	6,011	50.2
1980-81	13,179	6,500	49.3
1981-82	15,847	7,421	46.8
1982-83	17,696	8,059	45.5
1983-84	20,721	10,222	49.3
1984-85	23,471	11,151	47.5
1985-86	28,671	12,956	45.2

Contd...

1986-87	32,837	14,470	44.1
1987-88	37,666	16,426	43.6
1988-89	44,474	18,841	42.4
1989-90	51,636	22,406	43.4
1990-91	57,577	24,514	42.6
1991-92	67,361	28,110	41.7
1992-93	74,636	30,832	41.3
1993-94	75,742	31,697	41.8
1994-95	92,297	37,347	40.5
1995-96	1,10,354	40,187	36.4
1996-97	1,28,762	45,008	34.9
1997-98	1,39,221	47,962	34.4
1998-99	1,43,797	53,246	37.0
1999-00	1,71,752	61,902	36.1
2000-01	1,88,603	68,526	36.3
2001-02	1,87,060	72,555	38.8
2002-03	2,16,266	82,310	38.1
2003-04	2,54,348	90,774	35.7
2004-05	3,04,958	99,125	32.5
2005-06	3,66,152	1,11,226	30.4
2006-07	4,73,512	1,17,613	24.8
2007-08	5,85,410	1,27,947	21.9
2008-09	6,27,949	1,08,359	17.3
2009-10	6,24,527	1,03,621	16.6
2010-11	7,93,072	1,38,299	17.4
2011-12	8,89,176	1,45,608	16.4
2012-13	10,36,235	1,76,535	17.0
2013-14	11,38,734	1,70,198	14.9
2014-15	12,51,391	1,85,480	14.8
2015-16	14,49,490	2,29,808	15.8

*Before transferring States' Share.

2014-15 = Revised estimates; 2015-16 = Budget estimates.

Sources: Government of India, Ministry of Finance: 1. *Explanatory Memorandum on the Budget of the Central Government* (various years); 2. *Receipts Budget* (various years); 3. *Budget at a Glance*, 2015-16; Column 4 calculations own.

Table 10: Revenue from Customs Duties: 1950-51 to 2015-16

(₹ crore)

Year	Gross Central Taxes	Customs Revenue	Col. 3 as % of Col. 2
1		3	4
1950-51	405	157	38.8
1951-52	512	230	44.9
1952-53	445	172	38.7
1953-54	420	156	37.1
1954-55	455	182	40.0
1955-56	485	163	33.6
1956-57	570	170	29.8
1957-58	692	177	25.6
1958-59	701	135	19.3
1959-60	794	152	19.1
1960-61	895	170	19.0
1961-62	1,054	209	19.8
1962-63	1,285	246	19.1
1963-64	1,634	335	20.5
1964-65	1,821	397	21.8
1965-66	2,061	339	16.4
1966-67	2,307	585	25.4
1967-68	2,353	513	21.8
1968-69	2,510	446	17.8
1969-70	2,822	423	15.0
1970-71	3,206	524	16.3
1971-72	3,873	695	17.9
1972-73	4,505	857	19.0
1973-74	5,070	996	19.6
1974-75	6,322	1,332	21.1
1975-76	7,609	1,419	18.6
1976-77	8,263	1,554	18.8
1977-78	8,858	1,824	20.6
1978-79	10,525	2,423	23.0
1979-80	11,974	2,924	24.4
1980-81	13,179	3,409	25.9
1981-82	15,847	4,300	27.1
1982-83	17,696	5,119	28.9
1983-84	20,721	5,583	26.9
1984-85	23,471	7,041	30.0
1985-86	28,671	9,526	33.2

Contd...

1986-87	32,837	11,475	34.9
1987-88	37,666	13,702	36.4
1988-89	44,474	15,805	35.5
1989-90	51,636	18,036	34.9
1990-91	57,577	20,644	35.9
1991-92	67,361	22,257	33.0
1992-93	74,636	23,776	31.9
1993-94	75,742	22,193	29.3
1994-95	92,297	26,789	29.0
1995-96	1,10,354	35,757	32.4
1996-97	1,28,762	42,851	33.3
1997-98	1,39,221	40,193	28.9
1998-99	1,43,797	40,668	28.3
1999-00	1,71,752	48,419	28.2
2000-01	1,88,603	47,542	25.2
2001-02	1,87,060	40,268	21.5
2002-03	2,16,266	44,852	20.7
2003-04	2,54,348	48,629	19.1
2004-05	3,04,958	57,661	18.9
2005-06	3,66,152	65,067	17.8
2006-07	4,73,512	86,327	18.2
2007-08	5,85,410	1,00,766	17.2
2008-09	6,27,949	1,08,000	17.2
2009-10	6,24,527	83,324	13.4
2010-11	7,93,072	1,35,813	17.1
2011-12	8,89,176	1,49,328	16.8
2012-13	10,36,235	1,65,346	15.9
2013-14	11,38,734	1,72,085	15.1
2014-15	12,51,391	1,88,713	15.0
2015-16	14,49,490	2,08,336	14.2

2014-15 = Revised estimates; 2015-16 = Budget estimates.

Sources: Government of India, Ministry of Finance: 1. *Explanatory Memorandum on the Budget of the Central Government* (various years); 2. *Receipts Budget* (various years); 3. *Budget at a Glance*, 2015-16; Column 4 calculations own.

Table 11: Key Deficit Indicators of the Central Government: 1970-71 to 2015-16

(₹ crore)

Year	Fiscal Deficit	Primary Deficit	Revenue Deficit
1970-71	1,408	803	(-) 163
1971-72	1,727	1,057	100
1972-73	2,179	1,403	15
1973-74	1,733	851	(-) 237
1974-75	2,302	1,301	(-) 765
1975-76	3,029	1,802	(-) 886
1976-77	3,802	2,314	(-) 298
1977-78	3,680	2,034	(-) 430
1978-79	5,710	3,726	(-) 292
1979-80	6,392	4,100	694
1980-81	8,299	5,695	2,037
1981-82	8,666	5,471	392
1982-83	10,627	6,689	1,308
1983-84	13,030	8,235	2,540
1984-85	17,416	11,442	4,225
1985-86	21,858	14,346	5,889
1986-87	26,342	17,096	7,777
1987-88	27,044	15,793	9,137
1988-89	30,923	16,645	10,515
1989-90	35,632	17,875	11,914
1990-91	44,632	23,134	18,562
1991-92	36,325	9,728	16,261
1992-93	40,173	9,098	18,574
1993-94	60,257	23,516	32,716
1994-95	57,703	13,644	31,029
1995-96	60,243	10,198	29,731
1996-97	66,733	7,255	32,654
1997-98	88,937	23,300	46,449
1998-99	1,13,349	35,466	66,976
1999-00	1,04,717	14,467	67,596
2000-01	1,18,816	19,502	85,234
2001-02	1,40,955	33,495	1,00,162
2002-03	1,45,072	27,268	1,07,879
2003-04	1,23,272	(-) 816	98,262
2004-05	1,25,202	(-) 1,732	78,338
2005-06	1,46,435	13,805	92,299

Contd...

2006-07	1,42,573	(-) 7,699	80,222
2007-08	1,26,912	44,118	52,569
2008-09	3,26,515	1,33,821	2,41,273
2009-10	4,18,482	2,05,389	3,38,998
2010-11	3,73,591	1,39,569	2,52,252
2011-12	5,15,990	2,42,840	3,94,348
2012-13	4,90,190	1,77,020	3,64,282
2013-14	5,02,858	1,28,604	3,57,048
2014-15	5,12,628	1,01,274	3,62,486
2015-16	5,55,649	99,504	3,94,472

2014-15 = Revised estimates; 2015-16 = Budget estimates.

Sources: 1. Reserve Bank of India, *Handbook of Statistics on Indian Economy*, 2004-05, p. 169, Table 103; 2. Government of India, *Economic Survey*, 2006-07, p. 21, Table 2.2; 3. Government of India, Ministry of Finance, Budget Papers, *Budget at a Glance*, 2015-16.

Table 12: Revenue from Agricultural Income Tax Levied by State Governments: 1950-51 to 2013-14

(₹ crore)

Year	Yield	Year	Yield
1950-51	3	1982-83	30
1951-52	4	1983-84	44
1952-53	4	1984-85	84
1953-54	4	1985-86	127
1954-55	5	1986-87	104
1955-56	8	1987-88	63
1956-57	8	1988-89	64
1957-58	8	1989-90	93
1958-59	8	1990-91	169
1959-60	9	1991-92	202
1960-61	10	1992-93	111
1961-62	9	1993-94	107
1962-63	10	1994-95	98
1963-64	9	1995-96	154
1964-65	11	1996-97	103
1965-66	10	1997-98	182
1966-67	11	1998-99	241
1967-68	12	1999-00	150
1968-69	10	2000-01	76
1969-70	14	2001-02	23
1970-71	11	2002-03	14
1971-72	13	2003-04	15
1972-73	12	2004-05	28
1973-74	12	2005-06	17
1974-75	14	2006-07	15
1975-76	29	2007-08	26
1976-77	35	2008-09	1,604
1977-78	62	2009-10	124
1978-79	80	2010-11	173
1979-80	58	2011-12	152
1980-81	46	2012-13	128
1981-82	38	2013-14	135

2012-13 = Revised estimates; 2013-14 = Budget estimates.

Sources: 1. Reserve Bank of India: (a) *Report on Currency and Finance* and (b) *Supplement to Finances of State Governments* (various years); 2. Government of India, Ministry of Finance, *Indian Public Finance Statistics, 2013-2014*, Table 3.2 (excerpted).

Table 13: Land Revenue Collections of State Governments: 1950-51 to 2013-14

(₹ crore)

Year	Yield	Year	Yield
1950-51	49	1982-83	189
1951-52	48	1983-84	213
1952-53	57	1984-85	282
1953-54	71	1985-86	353
1954-55	73	1986-87	382
1955-56	78	1987-88	447
1956-57	83	1988-89	594
1957-58	88	1989-90	690
1958-59	92	1990-91	607
1959-60	95	1991-92	636
1960-61	97	1992-93	617
1961-62	95	1993-94	732
1962-63	120	1994-95	1,141
1963-64	123	1995-96	1,326
1964-65	120	1996-97	1,074
1965-66	112	1997-98	1,090
1966-67	90	1998-99	1,031
1967-68	96	1999-00	1,070
1968-69	114	2000-01	1,377
1969-70	103	2001-02	1,717
1970-71	113	2002-03	1,722
1971-72	101	2003-04	2,156
1972-73	93	2004-05	2,531
1973-74	157	2005-06	2,704
1974-75	161	2006-07	3,069
1975-76	230	2007-08	3,287
1976-77	183	2008-09	4,338
1977-78	166	2009-10	5,131
1978-79	188	2010-11	7,537
1979-80	152	2011-12	7,077
1980-81	146	2012-13	9,112
1981-82	205	2013-14	11,740

2012-13 = Revised estimates; 2013-14 = Budget estimates.

Sources: 1. Reserve Bank of India: (a) *Report on Currency and Finance* and (b) *Supplement to Finances of State Governments* (various years); 2. Government of India, Ministry of Finance, *Indian Public Finance Statistics, 2013-2014*, Table 3.2 (excerpted).

Table 14: Revenue from Sales Tax Levied by State Governments: 1950-51 to 2013-14

(₹ crore)

Year	States' Own Tax Revenue	Sales Tax	Col. 3 as % of Col.2
1	2	3	4
1950-51	222	58	26.1
1951-52	227	59	26.0
1952-53	233	57	24.5
1953-54	252	66	26.2
1954-55	265	74	27.9
1955-56	283	82	29.0
1956-57	320	98	30.6
1957-58	353	117	33.1
1958-59	388	124	32.0
1959-60	422	137	32.5
1960-61	455	159	34.9
1961-62	489	181	37.0
1962-63	580	208	35.9
1963-64	691	268	38.8
1964-65	778	318	40.9
1965-66	861	368	42.7
1966-67	954	442	46.3
1967-68	1,103	508	46.1
1968-69	1,249	572	45.8
1969-70	1,378	657	47.7
1970-71	1,546	755	48.8
1971-72	1,702	826	48.5
1972-73	1,931	976	50.5
1973-74	2,319	1,143	49.3
1974-75	2,901	1,550	53.4
1975-76	3,573	1,944	54.4
1976-77	4,061	2,270	55.9
1977-78	4,379	2,414	55.1
1978-79	5,003	2,773	55.4
1979-80	5,709	3,211	56.2
1980-81	6,665	3,888	58.3
1981-82	8,295	4,893	59.0
1982-83	9,546	5,496	57.6
1983-84	10,804	5,706	52.8
1984-85	12,343	7,060	57.2

Contd...

1985-86	14,597	8,429	57.7
1986-87	16,701	9,640	57.7
1987-88	19,311	11,183	57.9
1988-89	22,452	13,120	58.4
1989-90	26,057	15,060	57.8
1990-91	30,145	17,667	58.6
1991-92	35,837	21,064	58.8
1992-93	39,530	23,349	59.1
1993-94	46,219	27,638	59.8
1994-95	55,552	33,154	59.7
1995-96	63,865	35,477	55.5
1996-97	71,294	41,896	58.8
1997-98	81,439	45,351	55.7
1998-99	89,220	49,250	55.2
1999-00	1,02,831	57,592	56.0
2000-01	1,16,717	68,386	58.6
2001-02	1,27,475	71,379	56.0
2002-03	1,40,372	79,425	56.6
2003-04	1,59,736	89,658	56.1
2004-05	1,89,413	1,10,597	58.4
2005-06	2,21,537	1,32,845	60.0
2006-07	2,63,195	1,60,137	60.8
2007-08	2,77,182	1,65,750	59.8
2008-09	3,10,152	1,89,753	61.2
2009-10	3,76,316	2,29,786	61.1
2010-11	4,78,594	2,90,682	60.7
2011-12	5,78,993	3,58,055	61.8
2012-13	6,88,512	4,12,486	59.9
2013-14	7,96,619	4,84,385	60.8

2012-13 = Revised estimates; 2013-14 = Budget estimates.

Sources: 1. Reserve Bank of India (a) *Report on Currency and Finance* and (b) *Supplement to Finances of State Governments* (various years); 2. Government of India, Ministry of Finance, *Indian Public Finance Statistics, 2013-2014*, Table 3.2; Column 4 calculations own.

Table 15: Revenue from State Excise Duty: 1950-51 to 2013-14

(₹ crore)

Year	Yield	Year	Yield
1950-51	48	1982-83	1,343
1951-52	49	1983-84	1,384
1952-53	46	1984-85	1,839
1953-54	45	1985-86	2,052
1954-55	45	1986-87	2,421
1955-56	45	1987-88	2,864
1956-57	46	1988-89	3,081
1957-58	46	1989-90	3,864
1958-59	47	1990-91	4,795
1959-60	50	1991-92	5,439
1960-61	53	1992-93	6,365
1961-62	59	1993-94	7,106
1962-63	63	1994-95	7,747
1963-64	73	1995-96	8,516
1964-65	84	1996-97	8,848
1965-66	96	1997-98	11,383
1966-67	109	1998-99	13,438
1967-68	131	1999-00	15,092
1968-69	159	2000-01	15,825
1969-70	174	2001-02	17,150
1970-71	194	2002-03	18,833
1971-72	234	2003-04	19,548
1972-73	279	2004-05	22,061
1973-74	354	2005-06	26,192
1974-75	387	2006-07	30,592
1975-76	435	2007-08	35,551
1976-77	505	2008-09	42,478
1977-78	570	2009-10	50,169
1978-79	583	2010-11	61,407
1979-80	698	2011-12	74,762
1980-81	824	2012-13	88,559
1981-82	1,115	2013-14	98,368

2012-13 = Revised estimates; 2013-14 = Budget estimates.

Sources: 1. Reserve Bank of India: (a) *Report on Currency and Finance* and (b) *Supplement to Finances of State Governments* (various years); 2. Government of India, Ministry of Finance, *Indian Public Finance Statistics, 2013-2014*, Table 3.2.

Table 16: Revenue from Entertainment Tax Levied by State Governments: 1950-51 to 2013-14

(₹ crore)

Year	Yield	Year	Yield
1950-51	---	1982-83	299
1951-52	6	1983-84	370
1952-53	6	1984-85	412
1953-54	6	1985-86	308
1954-55	6	1986-87	427
1955-56	7	1987-88	382
1956-57	9	1988-89	423
1957-58	9	1989-90	342
1958-59	11	1990-91	412
1959-60	11	1991-92	349
1960-61	13	1992-93	464
1961-62	15	1993-94	426
1962-63	18	1994-95	447
1963-64	23	1995-96	440
1964-65	25	1996-97	796
1965-66	29	1997-98	1,035
1966-67	35	1998-99	926
1967-68	26	1999-00	907
1968-69	43	2000-01	1,203
1969-70	50	2001-02	827
1970-71	58	2002-03	816
1971-72	63	2003-04	755
1972-73	77	2004-05	3,107
1973-74	100	2005-06	695
1974-75	125	2006-07	768
1975-76	150	2007-08	865
1976-77	175	2008-09	1,086
1977-78	181	2009-10	1,160
1978-79	205	2010-11	1,244
1979-80	231	2011-12	1,920
1980-81	255	2012-13	1,800
1981-82	304	2013-14	2,030

2012-13 = Revised estimates; 2013-14 = Budget estimates.

Sources: 1. Reserve Bank of India: (a) *Report on Currency and Finance* and (b) *Supplement to Finances of State Governments* (various years); 2. Government of India, Ministry of Finance, *Indian Public Finance Statistics, 2013-2014*, Table 3.2.

Select Bibliography

Select Bibliography

A.R. Prest, *Public Finance in Theory and Practice,* London: Weidenfeld and Nicolson, 1970.

Administrative Reforms Commission, *Report of the Study Team on Centre-State Relationships*, Volume I, 1968.

Alan Peacock and Francesco Forte (eds.), *The Political Economy of Taxation,* Basil Blackwell, Oxford, 1981.

Alan Tait, Wilfrid Gratz and Barry Eichengreen, "International Comparisons of Taxation for Selected Developing Countries, 1972-76", *IMF Staff Papers*, Volume 26, March 1979.

Alberto Alesina and R. Perotti, "The Political Economy of Budget Deficits", *IMF Staff Papers*, 1995.

Alejandro Foxley, Eduardo Aninat, and J.P. Arellano, *Redistributive Effects of Government Programmes: The Chilean Case,* Pergamon Press, 1979.

C.T. Sandford and others, *Costs and Benefits of VAT,* London: Heinemann Educational Books, 1981.

C.V. Brown and P.M. Jackson, *Public Sector Economics,* Oxford: Martin Robertson and Co. Ltd., 1983.

C.Y. Mansfield, "Elasticity and Buoyancy of a Tax System: A Method Applied to Paraguay", *IMF Staff Paper*, Volume 19, No. 2, July 1972.

Durga Das Basu, *Introduction to the Constitution of India,* New Delhi: Prentice-Hall of India Private Ltd., 1987.

G.S. Sahota, *Indian Tax Structure and Economic Development*, Asia Publishing House, Bombay, 1961.

Government of India, *Report of the Indian Taxation Enquiry Committee*, 1924-25, Volume I (President: Charles Todhunter).

—*Report of the Income Tax Investigation Commission,* (Chairman: Srinivasa Varadachariar), 1948.

—*Report of the Taxation Enquiry Commission,* (Chairman: John Matthai), 1953-54, Volumes I, II and III.

—*Report of the Customs Reorganisation Committee,* (Chairman: F.C. Budhwar), 1957-58.

—*Report of the Direct Taxes Administration Enquiry Committee,* (Chairman: Mahavir Tyagi), 1958-59.

—Central Excise Reorganisation Committee, (Chairman: A.K. Chanda), 1963.

—*Report of the Committee on Sales Tax,* (Chairman: R.G. Saraiya), 1964.

—*Final Report on Rationalisation and Simplification of Tax Structure,* (Chairman: S. Bhoothalingam), 1968.

—*Final Report of Direct Taxes Enquiry Committee,* (Chairman: K.N. Wanchoo),

December 1971.
——Ministry of Finance, *Report of the Committee on Taxation of Agricultural Wealth and Income,* (Chairman: K.N. Raj), 1972.
——*Report of the Central Excise (Self-Removal Procedure) Review Committee,* (Chairman: B. Venkatappiah), 1973.
——*Report of the Indirect Taxation Enquiry Committee,* (Chairman: L.K. Jha), 1977, Part I.
——*Report of the Indirect Taxation Enquiry Committee,* (Chairman: L.K. Jha), Part II, January 1978.
——*Final Report of Direct Tax Laws Committee,* (Chairman: C.C. Chokshi), 1978.
——*Report of the Expert Committee on Tax Measures to Promote Employment,* (Chairman: V.M. Dandekar), 1980.
——Economic Administrative Reforms Commission, *Report on Tax Administrations,* 1981-83.
——*Report of the Expert Committee on Replacement of Sales Tax by Additional Excise Duty,* (Chairman: Kamlapati Tripathi), January 1983.
——Central Board of Excise and Customs, *Guide to MODVAT.*
——*Aspects of the Black Economy in India,* March 1985.
——*Long Term Fiscal Policy,* December, 1985.
——*Report of the Technical Study Group on Central Excise Tariff,* (Chairman: J. Datta), Part I, 1985.
——*Study Group on Taxation of Expenditure,* Final Report, 1987.
——*Report of the Commission on Centre-State Relations,* (Chairman: R.S. Sarkaria), 1988, Part I.
——*Interim Report of the Tax Reforms Committee,* (Chairman: Raja Chelliah), December 1991.
——*Final Report of the Tax Reforms Committee,* (Chairman: Raja Chelliah), Part I, 1992.
——*Advisory Group on Tax Policy and Tax Administration for the Tenth Plan,* (Chairman: Parthasarathi Shome), 2001.
——*Report of the Task Force on Direct Taxes,* (Chairman: Vijay Kelkar), December 2002.
——*Report of the Task Force on Indirect Taxes,* (Chairman: Vijay Kelkar), December 2002.
——*White Paper on State-Level Value Added Tax,* (Chairman: Asim Kumar Dasgupta), 2005.
——*Rationalisation of Customs and Excise Duties on Edible Oils and Oilseeds,* (Chairman: Ashok Lahiri), 2006.
——Ministry of Finance, *White Paper on Black Money,* May 2012.
——Planning Commission, *Five Year Plans.*
——Ministry of Finance, *Budget Papers* (various years).
——Ministry of Finance, *Economic Survey* (various issues).

——*Reports of Finance Commissions*.
——Ministry of Finance, *Indian Public Finance Statistics,* (various issues).
——Ministry of Law and Justice, *Constitution of India.*

Gyan Chand, *The Essentials of Federal Finance: A Contribution to the Problem of Financial Re-adjustment in India,* Humphrey Milford, Oxford University Press, 1930.

Institute of Fiscal Studies, *The Structure and Reform of Direct Taxation,* Report of a Committee Chaired by Professor J.E. Meade, London: George Allen and Unwin, 1978.

J.A. Kay and M.A. King, *The British Tax System,* Oxford University Press, 1978.

J.F.J. Toye (ed.), *Taxation and Economic Development,* London: Frank Cass and Company.

James Cutt, *Taxation and Economic Development in India,* New Delhi: Vikas Publications, 1969.

James Danziger, *Making Budgets,* London: Sage Publications, 1978.

Jesse Burkhead, *Government Budgeting,* New York: John Wiley and Sons, 1956.

John Wojthley and William Ludwin, *Zero-Base Budgeting in State and Local Government,* New York: Praeger Publishers, 1979.

Lok Sabha Secretariat, New Delhi, *Abstracts on Parliamentary Procedures, 1986.*

M.M. Sury, Sales Tax in India Since 1938, *Journal of the Indian School of Political Economy*, Volume 7, No. 1, January-March 1996.

——Customs Duties in India Since 1859, *Journal of the Indian School of Political Economy*, Volume 7, No. 1, January-March 1995.

——Excise Duties in India: 1894-1994, *Journal of the Indian School of Political Economy*, Volume 6, No. 1, January-March 1994.

——Income Tax in India Since 1860, *Journal of the Indian School of Political Economy*, Volume 5, No. 1, January-March 1993.

——Centre-State Financial Relations in India: 1870-1990, *Journal of the Indian School of Political Economy*, Volume 4, No. 1, January-March 1992.

——South Asia: Trends in Taxation, *Bulletin for International Fiscal Documentation* (Amsterdam), Volume 46, No. 4, April 1992.

——Tax Structure Developments in India: 1950-90, *Journal of the Indian School of Political Economy*, Volume 3, No. 1, January-March 1991.

——India: Structure and Evaluation of the Income Tax System, *Asian-Pacific Tax and Investment Bulletin* (Singapore), Volume 8, Nos. 2 and 3, 1990.

——India: Theoretical and Practical Aspects of Capital Gains Tax, *Bulletin for International Fiscal Documentation* (Amsterdam), Volume 44, June 1990.

——India: Structure and Reform of Indirect Taxes, *Bulletin for International Fiscal Documentation*, (Amsterdam), Volume 42, October 1988.

——Excise Concessions to Small Scale Industries in India: Some Issues, *Small Industry Bulletin for Asia and the Pacific* (United Nations, ESCAP, Bangkok), No. 22, 1987.

—India: Decline of Direct Taxes, *Bulletin for International Fiscal Documentation* (Amsterdam), Volume 41, June 1987.

—Buoyancy and Elasticity of Union Excise Revenue in India: 1950-51 to 1080-81, *Margin*, Volume 18, No. 1, October 1985.

—Elasticity of Tax Revenue: Some Measurement Problems, *Indian Economic Journal*, Volume 26, Part I, 1978.

Mark Krasnick, *Fiscal Federalism,* Toronto: University of Toronto Press, 1986.

Naomi Caiden and Aaron Wildavsky, *Planning and Budgeting in Poor Countries,* New York: John Wiley and Sons, 1974.

Nicholas Kaldor, *Indian Tax Reform: Report of a Survey,* Government of India, Ministry of Finance, 1956.

—*An Expenditure Tax,* London: George Allen and Unwin Ltd., 1955.

P.M. Bakshi, *The Constitution of India,* Delhi: Universal Law Publishing Co. Pvt. Ltd.

R.W. Bahl, *Tax Revenue Forecasting in Developing Countries: A Conceptual Analysis,* IMF, DM/72/83.

Raja J. Chelliah, "Trends in Taxation in Developing Countries", *IMF Staff Papers,* Volume 18, July 1971.

Raja J. Chelliah, Hessel Bass and Margaret Kelly, "Tax Ratios and Effort in Developing Countries, 1969-71", *IMF Staff Papers*, Volume 22, March, 1975.

Reserve Bank of India, *Report on Currency and Finance* (various years).

—*Handbook of Statistics on Indian Economy* (various years).

—*Bulletins.*

—*Occasional Papers.*

—*Supplement on Finances of State Governments.*

—*Report of the Committee on Financial System,* (Chairman: M. Narasimham), 1991.

—*Report of the Committee on Banking Sector Reforms,* (Chairman: M. Narasimham), 1998.

—*Report of the Advisory Group on Transparency in Monetary and Financial Policies,* (Chairman: M. Narasimham), 2000.

Richard Aronson, *Public Finance,* New York: McGraw-Hill Book Company, 1985.

Richard M. Bird, *Taxation and Development,* Harvard University, 1970.

Richard M. Bird and Oliver Oldman (ed.), *Readings on Taxation in Developing Countries,* The Johns Hopkins Press, Baltimore, 1967.

Richard Musgrave and Peggy Musgrave, *Public Finance in Theory and Practice,* New York: McGraw-Hill Book Company, 1989.

Robert Lee and Ronald Johnson, *Public Budgeting Systems,* Baltimore: University Park Press, 1977.

Roy T. Gobin, "An Analysis of the System of Sales Taxation in Caribbean Market", *Public Finance*, Volume XXXV, No. 2, 1980, pp. 272-273.

S.L. Shakdher, *The Budget and the Parliament,* New Delhi: National Publishing House, 1979.

S.S. Tarapore, *Domestic Debt Management Policy and Monetary Control*, 18th SEANZA Central Banking Course Lectures, Reserve Bank of India, Mumbai, 1990.

—Monetary Policy, Internal Debt and Autonomy of the Central Bank, *Macroeconomics and Monetary Policy: Issues for a Reforming Economy* (eds.) Montek S. Ahluwalia, Y.V. Reddy and S.S. Tarapore, 2002.

Simon James and Christopher Nobes, *The Economics of Taxation,* Oxford: Philip Allan, 1978.

U. Thorat, "Developing Bond Markets to Diversify Long-Term Development Finance: Country Study of India", *Asia-Pacific Development Journal*, June 2002.

United Nations, Department of Economic Affairs, *A Manual for Economic and Functional Classification of Government Transactions,* New York, 1958.

V.G. Rao, *The Responsiveness of Tax System in India*, New Delhi: Allied Publishers Pvt. Ltd., 1979.

Walter Mahler, *Sales and Excise Taxation in India,* New Delhi: Orient Longman Ltd., 1970, p. 154.

Index

Index